ASIAN POPULAR CULTURE

This book examines different aspects of Asian popular culture, including films, TV, music, comedy, folklore, cultural icons, the Internet and theme parks. It raises important questions such as: What are the implications of popularity of Asian popular culture for globalization? Do regional forces impede the globalizing of cultures? Does the Asian popular culture flow act as a catalyst or conveying channel for cultural globalization? Does the globalization of culture pose a threat to local culture? It addresses two seemingly contradictory and yet parallel processes in the circulation of Asian popular culture: the interconnectedness between Asian popular culture and western culture in an era of cultural globalization that turns subjects such as Pokémon, hip-hop or cosmopolitan into truly global phenomena, and the local derivatives and versions of global culture that are necessarily disconnected from their origins in order to cater for the local market. It thereby presents a collective argument that, whilst local social formations, patterns of consumption and participation in Asia are still very much dependent on global cultural developments and the phenomena of modernity, such dependence is often concretized, reshaped and distorted by the local media to cater for the local market.

Anthony Y.H. Fung is Director and Professor in the School of Journalism and Communication at the Chinese University of Hong Kong. He is the co-author of the book *New Television Globalisation and the East Asian Cultural Imagination*, and author of *Global Capital, Local Culture: Localization of Transnational Media Corporations in China*.

Media, Culture and Social Change in Asia

Series Editor: Stephanie Hemelryk Donald
University of New South Wales

Editorial board:

Devleena Ghosh, *University of Technology, Sydney*
Peter Horsfield, *RMIT University, Melbourne*
Chris Hudson, *RMIT University, Melbourne*
K.P. Jayasankar, *Unit for Media and Communications, Tata Institute of Social Sciences, Bombay*
Michael Keane, *Queensland University of Technology*
Tania Lewis, *RMIT University, Melbourne*
Vera Mackie, *University of Melbourne*
Kama Maclean, *University of New South Wales*
Anjali Monteiro, *Unit for Media and Communications, Tata Institute of Social Sciences, Bombay*
Laikwan Pang, *Chinese University of Hong Kong*
Ursula Rao, *University of New South Wales*
Gary Rawnsley, *University of Leeds*
Ming-yeh Rawnsley, *University of Leeds*
Jo Tacchi, *RMIT University, Melbourne*
Adrian Vickers, *University of Sydney*
Jing Wang, *MIT*
Ying Zhu, *City University of New York*

The aim of this series is to publish original, high-quality work by both new and established scholars in the West and the East, on all aspects of media, culture and social change in Asia.

1 Television Across Asia
Television industries, programme formats and globalisation
Edited by Albert Moran and Michael Keane

2 Journalism and Democracy in Asia
Edited by Angela Romano and Michael Bromley

3 Cultural Control and Globalization in Asia
Copyright, piracy and cinema
Laikwan Pang

4 Conflict, Terrorism and the Media in Asia
Edited by Benjamin Cole

5 Media and the Chinese Diaspora
Community, communications and commerce
Edited by Wanning Sun

6 Hong Kong Film, Hollywood and the New Global Cinema
No film is an island
Edited by Gina Marchetti and Tan See Kam

7 Media in Hong Kong
Press freedom and political change
1967–2005
Carol P. Lai

8 Chinese Documentaries
From dogma to polyphony
Yingchi Chu

9 Japanese Popular Music
Culture, authenticity and power
Carolyn S. Stevens

10 The Origins of the Modern Chinese Press
The influence of the Protestant missionary press in late Qing China
Xiantao Zhang

11 Created in China
The great new leap forward
Michael Keane

12 Political Regimes and the Media in Asia
Edited by Krishna Sen and Terence Lee

13 Television in Post-Reform China
Serial dramas, Confucian leadership and the global television market
Ying Zhu

14 Tamil Cinema
The cultural politics of India's other film industry
Edited by Selvaraj Velayutham

15 Popular Culture in Indonesia
Fluid identities in post-authoritarian politics
Edited by Ariel Heryanto

16 Television in India
Satellites, politics and cultural change
Edited by Nalin Mehta

17 Media and Cultural Transformation in China
Haiqing Yu

18 Global Chinese Cinema
The culture and politics of hero
Edited by Gary D. Rawnsley and Ming-Yeh T. Rawnsley

19 Youth, Society and Mobile Media in Asia
Edited by Stephanie Hemelryk Donald, Theresa Dirndorfer Anderson and Damien Spry

20 The Media, Cultural Control and Government in Singapore
Terence Lee

21 Politics and the Media in Twenty-First Century Indonesia
Edited by Krishna Sen and David T. Hill

22 Media, Social Mobilization and Mass Protests in Post-Colonial Hong Kong
The power of a critical event
Francis L.F. Lee and Joseph M. Chan

23 HIV/AIDS, Health and the Media in China
Imagined immunity through racialized disease
Johanna Hood

24 Islam and Popular Culture in Indonesia and Malaysia
Edited by Andrew N. Weintraub

25 Online Society in China
Creating, celebrating, and instrumentalising the online carnival
Edited by David Kurt Herold and Peter Marolt

26 Rethinking Transnational Chinese Cinemas
The Amoy-dialect film industry in Cold War Asia
Jeremy E. Taylor

27 Film in Contemporary Southeast Asia
Cultural interpretation and social intervention
Edited by David C.L. Lim and Hiroyuki Yamamoto

28 China's New Creative Clusters
Governance, human capital, and investment
Michael Keane

29 Media and Democratic Transition in South Korea
Ki-Sung Kwak

30 The Asian Cinema Experience
Styles, spaces, theory
Stephen Teo

31 Asian Popular Culture
The global (dis)continuity
Edited by Anthony Y.H. Fung

ASIAN POPULAR CULTURE

The global (dis)continuity

Edited by Anthony Y.H. Fung

LONDON AND NEW YORK

First published 2013
by Routledge
2 Park Square, Milton Park, Abingdon, Oxon OX14 4RN

Simultaneously published in the USA and Canada
by Routledge
711 Third Avenue, New York, NY 10017

Routledge is an imprint of the Taylor & Francis Group, an informa business

© 2013 selection and editorial material, Anthony Y.H. Fung; individual chapters, the contributors

The right of the editor to be identified as author of the editorial material, and of the authors for their individual chapters, has been asserted in accordance with sections 77 and 78 of the Copyright, Designs and Patents Act 1988.

All rights reserved. No part of this book may be reprinted or reproduced or utilised in any form or by any electronic, mechanical, or other means, now known or hereafter invented, including photocopying and recording, or in any information storage or retrieval system, without permission in writing from the publishers.

Trademark notice: Product or corporate names may be trademarks or registered trademarks, and are used only for identification and explanation without intent to infringe.

British Library Cataloguing in Publication Data
A catalogue record for this book is available from the British Library

Library of Congress Cataloging in Publication Data
Library of Congress Cataloging-in-Publication Data
Asian popular culture / edited by Anthony Y.H. Fung.
p. cm. -- (Media, culture and social change in Asia ; 31)
Includes bibliographical references and index.
1. Popular culture--Asia. 2. Culture and globalization--Asia. 3. Mass media and culture--Asia. 4. Asia--Civilization--21st century. 5. East and West. I. Fung, Anthony Y. H. II. Series: Media, culture, and social change in Asia series ; 31.
DS12.A7356 2013
306.095--dc23
2012043372

ISBN: 978-0-415-55716-0 (hbk)
ISBN: 978-0-415-55717-7 (pbk)
ISBN: 978-0-203-58127-8 (ebk)

Typeset in Bembo
by GreenGate Publishing Services, Tonbridge, Kent

CONTENTS

Contributors	x
Acknowledgements	xiv

1 Introduction
Asian popular culture: the global (dis)continuity   1
Anthony Y.H. Fung

PART I

The dominance of global continuity: cultural localization and adaptation   **19**

2 When Chinese youth meet Harry Potter: translating
consumption and middle–class identification   21
John Nguyet Erni

3 One region, two modernities: Disneyland in Tokyo
and Hong Kong   42
Micky Lee and Anthony Y.H. Fung

4 Comic travels: Disney publishing in the People's
Republic of China   59
Jennifer E. Altehenger

5 Saving face for magazine covers: new forms of
transborder visuality in urban China   76
Eric Kit-wai Ma

viii Contents

6 Cultural consumption and masculinity: a case study of
GQ magazine covers in Taiwan   94
Hong-Chi Shiau

PART II
Global discontinuity: the local absorption of global culture   111

7 An unlocalized and unglobalized subculture: English
language independent music in Singapore   113
Kai Khiun Liew and Shzr Ee Tan

8 "Only mix, never been cut": the localized production
of Jamaican music in Thailand   139
Viriya Sawangchot

9 Popular online games in the Taiwanese market: an
examination of the relationships of media globalization
and local media consumption   154
Lai Chi Chen

10 The rise of the Korean cinema in inbound and
outbound globalization   172
Shin Dong Kim

PART III
Cultural domestication: a new form of global continuity   195

11 Pocket capitalism and virtual intimacy: Pokémon as a
symptom of post–industrial youth culture   197
Anne Allison

12 Playing the global game: Japan brand and globalization   213
Kukhee Choo

Contents **ix**

PART IV
China as a rising market: cultural antagonism and globalization

231

13 China's new creative strategy: the utilization of cultural soft power and new markets 233
Michael Keane and Bonnie Rui Liu

14 Renationalizing Hong Kong cinema: the gathering force of the mainland market 250
Michael Curtin

Index 267

CONTRIBUTORS

Jennifer E. Altehenger is Lecturer for Contemporary Chinese History at King's College London. She has published articles on the history of Chinese cartoon production and satire. She is completing a monograph on the history of law propaganda, cultural production and mass campaigns in the early PRC and after.

Anne Allison is a cultural anthropologist who researches the intersection between political economy, everyday life and the imagination in the context of late capitalist, post-industrial Japan. Her work spans the subjects of sexuality, pornography and maternal labour to the globalization of Japanese youth products and the precarity of irregular workers. She is the author of *Nightwork: Sexuality, Pleasure, and Corporate Masculinity in a Tokyo Hostess Club* (University of Chicago Press, 1994), *Permitted and Prohibited Desires: Mothers, Comics, and Censorship in Japan* (University of California Press, 2000), *Millennial Monsters: Japanese Toys and the Global Imagination* (University of California Press, 2006) and *Precarious Japan* (forthcoming from Duke University Press).

Lai Chi Chen is Associate Professor in the School of Communication and Journalism at Shantou University in China. She received her PhD degree from the University of Westminster and worked at National Chou Tong University as a post-doctoral researcher in Taiwan. She is particularly interested in Asian popular culture, including the Asian online gaming industries and South Korean trendy dramas, which focus on the process of content production, consumption and reproduction in the intra-Asian markets. Her research interests also include new media, international communication and media globalization.

Kukhee Choo received her PhD degree from the University of Tokyo and teaches in the Department of Communication at Tulane University. Her research focuses on globalization and cultural policies, Trans-Asian media flow, and gender and body in popular culture. Choo has written for journals such as *Postscript* and *Women*, and has also contributed to various anthologies. Choo is currently working on her book that examines the Japanese government's global promotion of popular culture such as anime, manga and video games.

Michael Curtin is Mellichamp Professor of global studies in the Department of Film and Media Studies at the University of California, Santa Barbara. His books include *The American Television Industry* (with J. Shattuc, Palgrave Macmillan, 2009); *Reorienting Global Communication: Indian and Chinese Media Beyond Borders* (with H. Shah, University of Illinois Press, 2010) and *Playing to the World's Biggest Audience: The Globalization of Chinese Film and TV* (University of California Press, 2007). He is currently working on *Media Capital: The Cultural Geography of Globalization*. With Paul McDonald, he is co-editor of the International Screen Industries book series for the British Film Institute and, with Louis Leung, is co-editor of the *Chinese Journal of Communication*.

John Nguyet Erni is Professor and Chair of the Department of Cultural Studies, Lingnan University, Hong Kong. He has published widely on critical public health, Chinese consumption of transnational culture, queer media and youth popular consumption in Hong Kong and Asia. His books include *Understanding South Asian Minorities in Hong Kong: A Critical Multicultural Approach* (with Lisa Leung, Hong Kong University Press, 2013), *Cultural Studies of Rights: Critical Articulations* (Routledge, 2011), *Internationalizing Cultural Studies: An Anthology* (with A. Abbas, Blackwell, 2005), *Asian Media Studies: The Politics of Subjectivities* (with S.K. Chua, Blackwell, 2005) and *Unstable Frontiers: Technomedicine and the Cultural Politics of "Curing" AIDS* (Minnesota, 1994). He is currently completing a book project on the legal modernity of rights.

Anthony Y.H. Fung is Director and Professor in the School of Journalism and Communication at the Chinese University of Hong Kong. His research interests and teaching focus on popular culture and cultural studies, gender and youth identity, cultural industries and policy, political economy of communication and new media studies. He has authored and edited more than ten Chinese and English books, including *New Television Globalization and East Asian Cultural Imaginations* (with M. Keane and A. Moran, Hong Kong University Press, 2007), *Global Capital, Local Culture: Transnational Media Corporations in China* (Peter Lang, 2008), *Embedding into our lives: New Opportunities and Challenges of the Internet* (with L. Leung and P. Lee, The Chinese University Press, 2008) and *Development of the Hong Kong Film Industry* (with J. Chan and C.H. Ng, The Chinese University Press, 2009).

Michael Keane is Centre Fellow at the Queensland University of Technology, Brisbane. He works at the Australian Research Council Centre of Excellence for

xii Contributors

Creative Industries and Innovation. Michael is author or editor of more than a dozen books on China's media and creative industries.

Shin Dong Kim is Professor of Communication at Hallym University, Korea, and is the Founding Director of the Institute for Communication Arts and Technology (iCat) based at the same University. His research and teaching areas stretch from political economy of media and communication, to communication and mobility, global media culture and industry. He served visiting appointments at Dartmouth College, Peking University, Sciences Po Paris and City University of Hong Kong, among others. He studied media/communication and sociology at Indiana University, University of Chicago and Korea University.

Micky Lee is Associate Professor of Media Studies at Suffolk University, Boston. She received her PhD from University of Oregon. She has published more than a dozen journal articles on feminist political economy, telecommunications, new information and communication technologies, and information, media and finance.

Kai Khiun Liew received his BA(Hons) and MA from the National University of Singapore and his PhD from University College London. Prior to his current position as Assistant Professor at the Wee Kim Wee School of Communication and Information at the Nanyang Technological University, Kai Khiun did his Postdoctoral Fellowship at the Asia Research Institute at the National University of Singapore. With topics ranging from transnational Chinese-based music from Hong Kong and Taiwan to Southeast Asia as well as hip-hop and heavy metal subcultures, and more recently, on the Korean Wave, Kai Khiun has published journals articles and book chapters on popular music in East and Southeast Asia.

Bonnie Rui Liu is currently working in the Creative Industries Faculty at the Queensland University of Technology. She received her PhD from Queensland University of Technology in 2011. She was Lecturer at the Communication University of China. Her research areas include journalism, media and communication, and her PhD research focused on the independent television production industry in China.

Eric Kit-wai Ma teaches communication at the Chinese University of Hong Kong. His books include *Desiring Hong Kong, Consuming South China* (Hong Kong University Press, 2011), *Hong Kong, China: Learning to Belong to a Nation* (with G. Mathews and T. Lui, Routledge, 2008) and *Culture, Politics and Television in Hong Kong* (Routledge, 1999). His articles appear in journals such as *Visual Anthropology, Cultural Studies, International Journal of Cultural Studies, Social Text, Positions* and *Inter-Asia Cultural Studies*. He has written and edited more than 20 books in Chinese; the most recent ones include *Trends Factory: A Visual Ethnography* (Fudan University Press, 2011) and *Mediated Modernity: A Dialogue between Communication and Social*

Theories (with X. Zhang, Fudan University Press, 2012). He writes columns for a Hong Kong newspaper, *Ming Pao Daily* and Beijing's *International Herald Leader*.

Viriya Sawangchot teaches popular culture and cultural studies at Research Institute for Languages and Cultures of Asia, Mahidol University, Thailand. He is also a co-founder of Watthanasala Centre for Cultural Studies. He has published widely in the area of Thai popular music and popular culture both in Thai entertainment magazine and academic journal. His most recent research is Thai Cultural Industries Policy.

Hong-Chi Shiau is Professor of Communications Management and Gender Studies at Shih-Hsin University in Taiwan. He is particularly interested in the intersection of gender, race, class and cultural identity as it is negotiated in an increasingly global environment. His previous research focuses on music, cinema and fashion industries. He received his PhD in media studies from Temple University.

Shzr Ee Tan is Lecturer at Royal Holloway, University of London, currently researching musical activities on new media platforms in overseas Chinese communities. Her research touches on phenomena ranging from viral videos to politico-musical activism on the Internet. Shzr Ee completed her PhD at the School of Oriental and African Studies, studying Amis aboriginal folksong of Taiwan in interacting contexts of the village, the cultural troupe, the popular music industry and Christian missionisation. Her other interests include music and gender, music and politics, urban ethnomusicology and connections between music and food cultures. She has published on music, media and politics in Singapore and in the Chinese diaspora, as well as on aboriginal song in Taiwan. Her recent book, *Beyond 'Innocence': Amis aboriginal song in Taiwan as an Ecosystem* was published with Ashgate in 2012.

ACKNOWLEDGEMENTS

I am indebted to the series editor, Professor Stephanie Donald, who is very encouraging and supportive all the way to publication of this edited book. I am most grateful to all the contributors of the volume. I really valued the intellectual process in which I interacted and worked with these friends in the past two years. Finally I would like to thank Daniel Reeves, Brian Yeung and Yvonne Lau for their hard work and help in editing and proof-reading.

1

INTRODUCTION
Asian popular culture:
the global (dis)continuity

Anthony Y.H. Fung

What is Asian popular culture? The chimera of Asian pop culture is perhaps perceived as something cute, something eerie, something fancy, and something exotic as opposed to the complex and well-established symbols and icons of western popular imaginaries such as Batman, Snoopy, E.T., the psychedelic pop music of the Beatles, and Hollywood. We as academics understand that this stereotypic understanding of Asian popular culture is not intellectually true, and therefore we tend to rebuff it and vilipend it *ad rem*. Yet, this attitude, at the same time, may compel us to easily brush off any debate on the core nature of Asian popular culture. In other words, despite imprecision and apocrypha, arguably we could use such characterizations, stereotypes, and even misrepresentations as a departure to help us understand the current phenomena and trajectories in Asian pop culture developments. In reality, it is evident that we do witness the lopsided flow of Hollywood cultures (such as Disney) to Asia. Very few made-in-Asia commercial imaginaries are sold and distributed in Europe or North America as they are believed to be unable to satisfy the appetites of those audiences, at least in the eyes of many distributors and producers. In this globalizing age in which transnational media industries predominantly control the flow of most pop culture imaginaries, the importation of pop culture from the "other global worlds" to Asia is the unpenetrable commercial strategy, while the reverse is always regarded as exceptional and something against the commercial, and perhaps cultural, norm. The formation of popular culture in Asia, therefore, has more or less been evolving in response to the globalizing culture that is imposed upon them (e.g. Allen and Sakamoto's analysis of the Japanese pop culture, 2006). That active global continuity used to largely define what Asian pop culture is, but what is emphasized in this volume, is that this phenomenon is changing.

What we find in Asia today are numerous and diverse forms of popular culture; those mainly connected to global production, a few culturally indigenous forms

2 Anthony Y.H. Fung

that consciously disconnect and distinguish themselves from the West and stand out in the global market, many hybrid forms that lie in between the continuum of global–local production and circulation networks, and even some elaborate cultural forms and products that can be converted to something global for certain situations. This book does not present a definition of Asian pop culture—which may practically be unfeasible owing to the diversity of Asian cultural products— but presents the readers cases of highly popular Asian pop imaginaries that can be connected to the discourse of globalization under the current theme of global (dis)continuity of the political economy.

In this volume, global (dis)continuity specifically refers to the degree of continuity of the modes and structures of operation of transnational cultural corporations, which conventionally dominate in the transplant of cultural products from the West to Asia in which local adaptations and modifications arise. In this changing political economic milieu, such political and social hierarchies, however, have experienced an about-face. We now see new forms and structures of operation that we have never seen before in processes of cultural globalization, including production, circulation, and consumption. What is occurring is not only changes in the cultural logic of globalization and localization of popular cultural forms, but also changes in concrete strategies, with large corporations now building up production capacity and distribution networks to generate a reserve global flow from Asia to the rest of the world. Some locales in Asia, including China and Japan, have become stable hubs or the nexus of global media, and are subsequently able to market culture to regional areas, as well as in their own market. It is by and through these global transnational corporations that Asia is being connected and reconnected to the rest of the world and within its own region.

With such a framework set, this anthology explicates the structure of the production, distribution, circulation, and consumption of Asian pop culture, and bases all the analyses from different Asian cities (including China, Hong Kong, Taiwan, Japan, Korea, Singapore, and Thailand) on real historical contexts with the common thread of theoretical inquiry on cultural and media globalization. Thus, many chapters begin with a macro semi-political economic analysis of the context in which these Asian popular cultures are grounded and, then, depending upon the disciplinary approaches of the authors, are followed with structural analysis, cultural studies of text, or studies on audiences and consumption. All these cases converge on the central theme of global (dis)continuity, thereby adding to and encouraging academic discussion on the subject matters concerned. There are case discussions that should be familiar to global consumers, ranging from the discussion of pop music (e.g. hip-hop and reggae), fashion magazines (e.g. *GQ*, *Esquire*, and *Cosmopolitan*), Hollywood movies (e.g. Harry Potter), to cultural brands such as Disneyland and its related commodities—the production, reproduction, or circulation of which have spanned across Asia and the other global worlds. They might or might not be Asian origins, but these culture imaginaries are disseminated and circulated from and to Asia. They not only have strong cultural implications to the local Asian societies they are disseminated in, but they are also vivid examples that characterize the phenomenon of global continuity of the geopolitical, political, and economic models. Strong evidence of cultural discontinuity is also documented and discussed, with comics and animations from Asia, such as Pokémon, serving as an example of how cultural products can be stripped of their Asian identity and marketed to the Americas and Europe. Select cases of Asian popular culture in this study can therefore be seen as a cultural interface between the impetus of cultural globalization, in terms of production and circulation, and the markets and audiences that receive the global products. Global continuity or discontinuity can result in the possibility of cultural connection or the elusion of it, and also reconnection or disconnection between Asia and the rest of the world on various levels.

On the production side, the studies in this book illustrate the concrete mechanism of the global flows, or the import and export of such cultural products and commodities, which in turn elucidate the cultural logic of such perceived needs for a global connection in Asia. Evidently, the entire structure of the continuity of globalization is unnatural, and is manipulated and driven commercially by transnational, regional, and local cultural corporations and/or politically controlled by governments or semi-official bodies who control their local media and access to it. On a macro level, with the worsening global economy, it seems that the political–economic forces coming from the major cultural power centers of the world also are pushing for a boundary-free and seemingly more oracular version of globalization in the hope of reaping more profit from global markets. A decade earlier, cultural globalization perhaps was merely an extension of soft power, asides from economic interests. However, with the recent financial crisis in the USA, globalization is now, more often than not, seen as an economic panacea for its national economy. Thus, the world will see more of the pushing forces of globalization than ever before, and this global structure has been perpetuated and continuously strengthened. These trends have also been occurring in Asian nation states that are attempting to globalize their cultural products, including Korea, Japan, and China.

While there is global cultural continuity, discontinuity of conventional practices can be seen as another economic means steered by transnational cultural corporations; these practices are viewed as the set up of an alternate route for cultural flows to flow from Asia to the West, the origins of these transnational corporations. As illustrated by Anne Allison in Chapter 11, Japan serves as the nexus for this new trend. Allison's analysis of the cultural product Pokémon illustrates that it is not just about Japan's national capabilities of reversing the flow of globalization by conquering the western markets, but the entirely new cultural flow is in fact a conscious effort of the global cultural corporations to invent and prescribe a new structure of cultural business. Such discontinuity of their conventional business models does, however, create new forms of cultural connection between Asia and non-Asian countries, but merely in different forms.

In this book, there is a specific type of cultural discontinuity that is taking shape. Michael Curtin suggests (Chapter 14) that within Asia, China is often seen as a rising global power that has accumulated a vast amount of media capital, such new business models, despite being under the influence of global capital, do not necessarily yield

4 Anthony Y.H. Fung

greater cultural connections between Asia and the rest of the world. China is more of a regional media exporter, or an exporter of media to other Asian nations. These regional flows (which have yet to be seen) would be a contestation between regional forces and global forces, controlled by China and global capitals respectively. Will local musicians in Singapore abandon the production of hip-hop and instead choose to go back to their ethnic roots by incorporating Chinese musical elements into their local productions of music? Will Korea continue to be shaped by Hollywood aesthetics or will it adopt a more distinctly regional taste in the future? In the long run, the new regionally/globally involved production structure may destabilize the cultural absorption of western popular culture in Asia.

The framework of global (dis)continuity is also applicable to the study of cultural consumption and aesthetics. Global cultural artifacts, icons, images, and brands have strong and long-term appeal to the Asian consumers who aspire to 'catch up' to global trends and modernity. To better target and serve local Asian markets, global cultural corporations have localized their global cultural forms, ideas, and products. In practice, the decentered locale of production and circulation enables fashion magazine producers, film distributors, game developers, music composers, and theme park managers to undertake a post-Fordist and neo-institutionalist logic in which they can select, modify, and distort global cultures for local Asian audiences. The extent to which the local consumption aligns with or disconnects from the global taste and aesthetic shows the tensions, ambivalence, and conflicts between the global and the local. Therefore, it is necessary to undertake a concrete analysis of how market forces interrupt the continuity of the operating structures of global corporations. On a micro level, what should then be examined is how these cultural products are localized and adapted to cater to local needs.

These illustrations of cultural connection, reconnection, or disconnection caused by changes in global structures of production in response to market and consumer needs goes beyond simple patterns of consumer reception and interpretation. The increasing hybridization of popular culture in terms of the differential cultural expressions and rituals of youth under different contexts begets various values such as modernity, cosmopolitanism, and homogenization (Wise, 2008). While some may be uncritical of globalization and perceive it to be a celebration of the uniqueness of different social, political, and cultural formations, there undeniably has also been growing resistance and criticism against this (perhaps disguised) form of capitalist expansion, transnational universalism, and even political dominance (Hopper, 2007). However, contrary to such anti-globalization arguments, global popular culture in Asia (such as the Disneyland theme park in Hong Kong) limits while also enables the preservation of cultural or regional autonomy under special circumstances (Rethman et al., 2010). With similar colonial and imperial legacies, the widely circulated global popular cultures have become the resources for youth in disparate Asian communities to articulate and express their identities in regards to social formation, including gender, class, generational, and cultural identities; at times, these expressions can become quite independent of the commodifying nature of global capital (Rodriques and Smaill, 2008).

With this set of phenomena as its core emphasis, two different versions of cultural circulation and consumption of Asian pop culture are observed: first, the interconnectedness between Asian popular culture and global (mainly western) cultures in an era of cultural globalization and, second, the local derivatives of global cultures that are purposely disconnected from their origins in order to cater to local/regional markets. Different situations therefore form into a collective argument; whilst local social formations, patterns of consumption, and participation in Asia are still very much dependent on global cultural developments and the phenomena of modernity (a discourse of cultural continuity), such dependence is often reshaped and distorted by the decentered local media for the local market or to create local hype among unsettled fans. This is a practical and economic concern that tends to result in cultural (dis)connections in varying degrees between the global culture and the consumer. However, some authors emphasize the "rising Asia thesis." These authors believe that Asia is also capable of creating a popular culture of its own which is a disjuncture of the global discourse, and is sometimes even able to reverse the traditional globalization flows by exporting to other nations, regionally and globally.

The proposed framework then can be used to engage in discussion with current globalization literature, in particular, with studies that emphasize hybrid formations. Authors such as Berger and Huntington (2003) describe the globalization phenomenon as "many globalizations," a term that unerringly captures the different levels, variations, and versions of globalization—partial, hybrid, or reverse globalization as they exist today in Asia. This culture of hybridization, or global mélange as Jan Nederveen Pieterse (2009) puts it, produces new regional and/or international cultural interactions, permutations, differences, and even hierarchies, as well as discord and frictions within the region and local audiences. It is perhaps undeniable that the sources of these globalized cultures are mainly of American origin, but the processes and consequences of globalization–localization is far from Americanization or cultural imperialism (Berger and Huntington, 2003). The different cultural forms produced pertaining to the process of globalization could be better described by how much the global cultural corporations, the local market, and/or regional forces have collectively connected or disconnected themselves. By indexing the degree of connection between the global and the local along a continuum, a framework of cultural (dis)continuity could be established and explicate why and how this phenomena of popular culture in Asia exists and thrives.

The book then divides the discussion of such cultural dis(continuity) into four different modes under which global culture is being disconnected, connected, or reconnected to Asian popular culture, either unwittingly or willfully. Of course, these four modes are just quick ways to conceptualize these diverse permutations; admittedly, there are many other variations. What has been emphasized here is the fact that there are multiple possibilities in which these hybrid cultural forms exist.

6 Anthony Y.H. Fung

The dominance of global continuity: cultural localization and adaptation

Part I of the book deals with the dominant paradigm of global-Asian interconnectedness in the context of the structures and operations of global cultural business practices already in place. It describes and prescribes how global popular culture is being transplanted in Asia; it is perhaps perceived as Americanization or western modernization. The popular culture being transplanted generally retains its original nature and global content; the cultural permutations mainly occur on a level of adaptation, meaning there are different interpretations and appropriations of the culture. While the forces of localization can be attributed to economic and/or political interest, the processes of cultural adaptation and glocalization is active and dynamic. In some cases, the nature of the original global products ends up being compromised. This cultural adaptation demonstrates a negotiated outcome between the forces of globalization and market needs.

The part begins with John Nguyet Erni's study of Harry Potter consumers (Chapter 2). In Erni's empirical study there is an examination of the "Pottermania" craze by middle-class Chinese youth in a Chinese society and economy that has developed exponentially in recent decades. What Erni discovers is that the Pottermania trend is more than just a phase in Chinese popular culture; it demonstrates that these Chinese youth are subject to an identity in progress of aspiring to become global, resisting ideas of previous generations, and becoming middle class. Through the examination of the Chinese youth's consumption and translation of the Harry Potter series, it is evident that the youth counterproject the Harry Potter characters through two planes. First, the youth frequently compare their own character qualities to those of the Harry Potter characters and, second, they relate the magical world of Harry Potter as something akin to the West, while the "muggle" world is related back to Chinese society.

New consumption patterns have cropped up in Chinese society—consumption has become like an ideology that represents a new, liberal generation against the social and economic restrictions of the previous Maoist generation. The rise of a middle-class culture and material consumption in China, therefore, inevitably leads to the formation of an ambivalent cultural positivity that alternates between embracing elitist, middle-class culture to criticizing the idealization of a "well-off society." Ironically, Chinese authorities have shown their implicit approval of using western cultural imports such as Harry Potter to encourage idealizing well-off societies, middle-class culture, and material consumption. Harry Potter in China is ultimately viewed as a symbol of power, liberation, creativity, and, above all, a world of fantasy that provides the Chinese an escape from their own stifling social environment. This temporarily resolves the social contradictions that the Chinese authorities may be unable to permanently solve at the moment.

The side effect of the consumption of and identification with the Harry Potter series by Chinese youth is the youth's connection to global culture, and the development of the belief that "becoming global" is something inevitable to their personal development and to the national development of China. Ultimately, the Harry Potter series in China is a perpetuation of globalization; it is a case of the west entering an Asian market, as well as a fundamental sign that China is striving to modernize and westernize.

In Chapter 2, Lee and Fung use the term modernity as a synonym to describe the urge of Chinese society to become global. In their study of the Disneyland theme parks in Tokyo and Hong Kong, they explore how locals in each city view and utilize the parks. The Asian visitors of these theme parks fundamentally view the west as an imaginary concept that they strive to become more like. Locals of Tokyo and Hong Kong view the construction of a Disneyland in their cities as an affirmation of modernity and becoming global. By experiencing and consuming the images and products of Disneyland, Asian visitors believe that they are building a modern and western identity.

Furthermore, Lee and Fung connect the business operations of Disney (which is a kind of global continuity of cultural structures) with the notion of modernity in Hong Kong and Tokyo. Modernity in Hong Kong is argued to have been designed by the British colonial state, leading to reinforced differences between the Hong Kong Chinese and mainland Chinese. Additionally, the mainland Chinese are unfamiliar with Disney characters and "values," and are therefore unable to enjoy Disneyland the "proper way." Disneyland is, instead, a site for them to experience modernity and the West on Chinese soil. Modernization in Tokyo began in the aftermath of World War II; Japanese popular culture is therefore familiar with global products and has appropriated western ideas and images into something uniquely Japanese. Thus, visitors of Tokyo Disneyland are receptive consumers of Disney, experiencing Disneyland as it should be. Ultimately, Lee and Fung's study demonstrates that Disney, a global cultural corporation, is bringing western modes of modernity to Asian locals, while Asia's desires to modernize (in order to become like the West) is becoming more and more evident. Asia has become more connected to western/global cultures through the continual branching out of Disneyland in Asian cities, though it may lead to consequences such as the erosion of local culture (or the "Disneyfication of society"), a weakened state (as Disney controls management of the theme parks), and idealization of the west (the notion that to become modern is to become like the West).

In Chapter 4, Jennifer E. Altehenger continues the discussion on Disney's globalization by examining the travels of Disney comics in the People's Republic of China (PRC). The accelerated development and growth of China's economy in the last decades of the twentieth century has undoubtedly contributed to various global corporations extending their reach into the PRC. Altehenger's article takes us along China's "Disneyfication" journey that first began in the 1930s. Altehenger's specific focus on the distribution of the Walt Disney Company's print publications into China is indicative of the importance of a dynamic and global nature (transnational production, dissemination, and production) in extending their scope of business.

8 Anthony Y.H. Fung

Previously, the Disney corporation was seen as an important player in the Cold War's ideological battles, as a corporation that diffused American ambitions and capitalist ideologies into foreign nations. However, Altehenger argues that Disney today, along with other similar transnational actors, plays an integral role in catering to the demands of Asian middle-class consumers (a group that is increasingly and significantly growing); a similar argument is made in Erni's study of Harry Potter in Chapter 2. Much of this is due to Disney's transnational travels; Disney has fundamentally furthered global consumerism and is inherently a part of the global youth culture.

Through the case studies of two Disney comics, *Ultimate Fans of Mickey Mouse* and *W.i.t.c.h.*, Altehenger demonstrates modern China's willingness and ability to initiate and implement cultural openness, even if it is seemingly motivated by national economic ambitions. Disneyfication is no longer regarded as a form of cultural imperialism because ordinary citizens and consumers of China have localized, internalized, and integrated Disney into their own culture, and this is the ultimate contributing factor of Disney's success in China. Disney is a classic case of demonstrating the dominance of global continuity.

An emerging trend of global continuity can be seen in the global magazine businesses' operations in Asia. Globalization of such media demonstrates how capitalist economies rely on the visual to generate consumption in a post-Fordist economy. Ma and his research team (Chapter 5), over the course of four months, observed and analyzed the management and operations of Trends Group, the company that publishes the major lifestyle magazines in China, including *Men's Health*, *Esquire*, *Cosmopolitan*, and *FHM*. Ma's study attempts to grasp the workings and consequences of transborder visuality in a society that has undergone rapid changes and development in recent decades. The sheer growth in numbers of affluent middle-class Chinese has led to a yearning for a modernity that is connected to the West and the rest of the world.

The Trends Tower is used by Ma as a theoretical metaphor—it is a "factory" where visual cultures (international, regional, or local) are reproduced and repurposed into an identity for Chinese middle-class consumers. Ma's study advances our understanding of cultural globalization by showing that the growing Chinese consumer market has allowed China to dictate which aspects of modernity they desire, and subsequently allow into the country. There are patterns of progression evident on the front covers of *Trends* magazines. The local editors of *Trends* first focused on exploiting the global, then shifted to focusing on collaboration between the global and local, and, finally, to a marketing emphasis on Chinese and Asian aspects. Ma's study fundamentally demonstrates that the Chinese state and Chinese businesses have been profiting from being connected to global cultures; they are able to utilize global and modern resources. This includes utilizing global images and technology to build up national markets and transform them into an appealing identity product for those local Chinese that aspire to become part of the global, modern, middle-class world. Basically, this transborder visuality illustrates not only the perpetuation of globalization of China through lifestyle magazines, but also the power of the Chinese state and market to harness the global for their own purposes.

Taiwan's *GQ* magazine is another example that shows the increasing bargaining power of local consumption power; it demonstrates that local as well as global agents play an equally significant role in Taiwanese culture in shaping notions of gender roles in society. Internationally, *GQ*, originally an American magazine, predominantly featured foreigners (mainly caucasians) on their front covers in order to brand itself as an American magazine. However, in Hongchi Shiau's content analysis of the front covers of *GQ Taiwan* in the years 1998 to 2009, a discovery is made that local models have increasingly become featured on front covers (Chapter 6). This is due to two factors: first, local readers are able to personally relate more to local models and, second, because of the localization project of international luxury brands. Deviating from the traditional business standard, *GQ* also began to switch from only featuring males on front covers to featuring females, thereby appeasing their target readership and distancing themselves from the gay readership. Though the western notion of "new man culture" is prevalent in non-Asian societies, *GQ Taiwan* has undoubtedly been shying away from this culture. Instead, *GQ Taiwan* has become increasingly influenced by notions of metrosexuality and embraced localized "consumption masculinities."

Global discontinuity: the local absorption of global culture

Part II of the book features how the creation of local pop culture in emerging Asian cosmopolitans (such as Thailand, Taiwan, Singapore, and Korea), though desegregated from global business structures, has produced pop culture that absorbs heavily and readily global cultures in its trajectories of development. In these cosmopolitan locales, it is either the local audiences that are recalcitrant to global cultures or the transnational corporations that are reluctant to extend their reach because of perceived market risks (due to political restrictions and/or low profits). Thus, it is somewhat up to local producers to use their creativity to create their own business models and adapt to or create consumer tastes in their production of pop culture. There have been previous cases of failures as the authors in this session will briefly discuss but, today, these emerging cosmopolitan areas have found new potentialities primarily through connecting their indigenous culture and contextual specialties to global cultures, aesthetics, technologies, and more. Though these local producers are independent, they fundamentally are still catering to local audiences with a taste for the global; the cultural formations in these areas have absorbed and mimicked global forms, consciously inserting them into their local cultural values. The case studies documented in this volume illustrate the process of how creative producers internalize cultural logic into their own cultural production, and also how they have achieved huge success within their countries and regionally across Asia.

In Chapter 7, Kai Khiun Liew and Shzr Ee Tan demonstrate how local music can appropriate global musical forms; they show that the Singaporean indie music scene is undoubtedly culturally connected to the West. The indie music scene in Singapore has been influenced by western indie, both musically and linguistically, and has successfully penetrated global music markets. Liew and Tan's study highlights the connection of Singaporean indie music to the global—Singaporean indie music is not a localized brand of indie that caters to local markets, but one that is evidently rooted in western origins. Through this entire process, the development of Singaporean indie is not driven by commercial global forces from the outside, but is driven by authorities from within Singaporean society. The Singaporean state is able to take advantage of such locally produced music to promote a positive international image of Singapore as a nation that is modern and cosmopolitan. Singaporean indie music can therefore be regarded as a conscious effort of Singapore's post colonial state to integrate itself into the global political economy and to steer the nation toward westernization and modernization.

However, Liew and Tan also point out that such indie music in Singapore has created a unique social dialect in that there is a difficulty for locals in identifying, authenticating, and locating their own cultural formations in this particular genre of music. Furthermore, there is a consistent and definite disconnection between local indie music and the local consumers due to questions of authenticity, legitimacy, and notions of inferiority. At the same time, this nationally driven English language music would not satisfy western notions of "world music." This active cultural absorption may be perceived as a global connection in the eyes of the Singaporean state, but it ultimately suffocates the possibility for Singapore's multi-ethnic society to forge its own identity using their own cultural resources.

Pop music is one of the common domains in Asia that demonstrates this local cultural absorption of global culture. In Chapter 8, Viriya Sawangchot illustrates that Thailand has locally produced its own Jamaican style reggae and ska since the 1980s, influenced both internally and externally. Such production has brought new musical styles to the local Thai music scene which, in turn, shapes and influences the former. Through the study of three Thai reggae artists, Viriya illustrates how reggae of all forms (including rasta reggae, Jamaican reggae, and international reggae) has penetrated the Thai music scene. The creation of new musical styles in Thailand and the subsequent flourishing of local studio albums has allowed local artists to establish their own unique musical styles that draws inspiration from the global as well the local. Even though Thailand's brand of reggae and their motivations to create music is different from the rest of the world, the reggae that is produced in Thailand ultimately blends together local and global elements that satisfies the local market, giving rise to resistance against conventional music. Theoretically, the multiple processes of the local absorbing global cultures signifies the connection as well as disconnection of the local to the global.

Asides from pop music, the online gaming industry is another dominant form of worldwide entertainment; its success depends largely on global distribution processes. Taiwan's online game industry and market that Lai Chi Chen introduces in Chapter 9 is one that perpetuates the notion of interconnection between Asian popular culture and western popular culture. An example of this interconnection

Introduction **11**

can be found in the huge popularity of massive multi-player online role-playing games (MMORPG) of American origin, most notably, *World of Warcraft*. With the introduction of so-called "cute" games from Korea and Japan, there are also hints that regional flows of culture within Asia are on the rise. More importantly, as a Chinese-speaking society, Taiwan has become an Asian production hub of "wuxia" MMORPG online games; these games are generally shaped by the local cultures of Taiwan as well as global cultures.

In his study, Lai-Chi explores theories of globalization, regionalization, and modernity in relation to the Taiwanese game market; he analyzes the reception, consumption, and localization of online games in Taiwan. Through his analysis, it becomes evident that the expansion and success of online games in Taiwan can be attributed to the rise of modern technologies (introduced mainly from the West), and also to the fact that online gaming has become successfully implanted into local communities as a localized popular culture. Though the games that make up the Taiwanese market are localized to suit the preferences of Taiwanese gamers, these games use resources and elements from all over the globe.

Evidently, the Taiwanese case is different from the Singaporean case—in Singapore, the absorption of global music elements thwarts local creativity, but in Taiwan, the acceptance and acceleration of global modernity in East Asia has allowed them to develop their own game cultures and other popular cultures. Lai-Chi's analysis of the Taiwanese game market and its Asian expansion also highlights a new cultural trend—that global continuity (in terms of the transnational cultural companies' distribution and production network of pop culture) is no longer the single force at work in Asia. The cultural absorption of game cultures in Taiwan (that aim to satisfy domestic consumer demands above all else) has undeniably become a rising regional market force of culture within East Asia. A similar concept is developed in Shin Dong Kim's study of modern South Korean cinema in Chapter 10.

Kim uses the term "inbound globalization" to describe how globalization has been conducive to the recent transformative success of the South Korean film industry, the term "outbound globalization" to describe how it has been made possible for South Korea to export its movies regionally and internationally. Referencing Appadurai's classic description of global "scapes," Kim notes that the inbound globalization of Korean cinema had been in place for many decades through the finanscapes, ideoscapes, and mediascapes of the West and/or Hollywood. After years of glocalization through consumption, without depending on established and structured global networks, South Korean cinema has gradually learned and acquired the film aesthetics, genres, and techniques from Hollywood. Today, new Korean filmmakers are able to hybridize foreign filmmaking know-how with local sentiments and cultures—they internalize and nationalize cultures from the outside in order to produce their modern Korean films. Previously, Korean cinema was inundated with conservative policies such as limiting the number of imports of foreign films. Nevertheless, these policies progressed to opening up the Korean film market along with a relaxation of the screen quota system; this demonstrates

12 Anthony Y.H. Fung

that Korea's new system of film production fosters corporate investment, packaged cinema, blockbuster films, and large exports of domestic films.

Kim analyzes how the dichotomy of the Chungmuro system and Korean views of western films versus local films—the perception that western films were culturally superior whereas domestic films were of low quality—were ultimately abolished and erased. Kim attributes this to factors such as political democratization, new state policies, and a new generation of film producers and viewers that ultimately led to the quickening of processes of globalization. First, Kim delves into the current state of Korean cinema and explicates how going to the theaters has become a popular cultural activity and how the development of national cinema has progressed and exceeded expectations in recent decades. Subsequently, Kim attributes the recent success of the film industry to the new generation of directors (the so-called "386 generation" that is well educated and free from traditional pressures, allowing their creativity to bloom) and of viewers (whose film literacy has greatly improved) who created the conditions for the national film industry to succeed.

Kim's study on the silent revolution of South Korean cinema posits that globalization or the absorption of global culture can lead to positive change and success for local production and commercial cultural industries, as is similar to the case of the Taiwanese online game industry. With the influence of the Korean wave of popular culture in other regions, the final outcome for Korea of such globalization processes indirectly nourishes a new sense of modernity within the Asian region, demonstrating that not just the foreign can become global, modern, and popular. Perhaps this is, for Asia, a unique, distinct, and alternate route for Asian nation states to boost national competitiveness to compete with other global capitals.

Cultural domestication: a new form of global continuity

Part III narrates a new form of cultural connectedness to Asia; it is one that is culturally dissimilar from conventional ways of marketing western products to Asia. It can be deemed as a sort of "reverse globalization" in which the Asian popular culture is specifically assembled and packaged to target the western market. In the past, Asian cultural exports to the West were thought of as a non-viable business strategy but, today, it is the transnational cultural corporations that pioneer the new cultural flows. Thus, reverse globalization is by no means a global discontinuity. On the contrary, global continuity has been enlarged in that the decentering and commercially perspicacious globalizing agents now take a more active role with their interest not just in the western markets. Asian producers and distributors do play a role; however, in the previous process described, transnational global corporations undoubtedly carry more weight in rediscovering Asian culture, "de-Asianizing," and globalizing these cultures, and finally domesticating these cultures in places where the global capital comes from. In today's globalized age, cultural agents in the form of transnational cultural companies are as dynamic, fluid, and progressive as the audiences—they search, acquire, and distill Asian cultures and sequester it for their own commercial use. This process is perceived as a type of cultural domestication by and through the global economy and its machines. Furthermore, this process is strong proof that global agents are beginning to stray away from their origins, are discontinuing with the traditional practices of global-to-Asia cultural flows, and are playing a vital role in connecting the western market to the resourceful Asian market. Examined in this category are mainly Japanese cultural products. We might find these Japanese cultural products more domestic to the American market than the Japanese market after such a process of cultural adaption.

Among the various Asian cultural products that are well known to the West, Pokémon is the classic one. Since the late 1990s, the explosive popularity of Pokémon (originally a Nintendo video game that has since branched off into movies, television, comic books, and trading cards) has prevailed in American and European markets. Though Pokémon was originally designed to target young Japanese boys, its double nature of intimacies and cooperation along with its goal of continual accumulation and acquisition (which somewhat parallel the western capitalistic ethos) has allowed it to dominate both Asian and western global culture. This has undeniably created a platform for Japanese cultural products to penetrate the global youth market. Pokémon products possess the flexibility that allows a relation to youth who reside in postindustrial, capitalist, consumerist societies to be established. Fundamentally, Pokémon has become popular among the youth of the "millennial era" (those who live in the era of millennial capitalism and postindustrial conditions), as it was designed to relieve the stress of youth who are accustomed to consumption, but ultimately yearn for human connectedness. Pokémon's rich playworld, a new sort of play and social phenomenon, promotes communication, interactivity, and accumulation. These processes are also repeated in the real-life marketplace and players become personally invested into Pokémon's fantasy world; arguably, Pokémon players become compulsive and addictive virtual and material consumers.

Through her case study on Pokémon in Chapter 11, Allison demonstrates that the global youth market is receptive to Japanese cultural exports and actually strengthened the Japanese connection to the global world through the enhancement of their soft, cultural power; Japan's ability to influence real and virtual worlds is undeniable. Nevertheless, the popularity of Pokémon cannot yet be classified as a typical case of perpetuation of globalization where an Asian culture has conquered the western market. Pokémon models how (by means of an integrated transnational network) an Asian region can equally create a cultural export that is appealing to western consumers and able to compete in global markets.

In Chapter 12, Kukhee Choo continues the discussion on the global influence of Japanese popular culture by tracing its global dissemination back to the 1960s and by exploring the Japanese Content industry. Choo's study traces the historical and, in particular, political/governmental processes in the culturalization of popular Japanese commodities. Early globalization of Japanese culture was firmly based on a strategic disconnection between the product and consumer, meaning that western audiences were fundamentally unaware of and disconnected from the

14 Anthony Y.H. Fung

products' Japanese origins. Simply put, western consumers were unaware of the fact that they were consuming "made in Japan" cultural products. The success of Japanese cultural exports in the beginning can be attributed to the *mukokuseki*, or "nation-less," aspect of Japanese products.

As aforementioned, Japan's early entertainment exports fared well in the global market. Subsequently, American markets took advantage of this and domesticated Japanese cultural forms and values. This domestication of culture as a consequence of globalization has gradually built up the preferences of western audiences for Asian products; it has also led to the internalization of Japanese export products as their own. Historically, it was not until the last decades of the twentieth century that Japanese culture would become reconnected to global export markets when the Japanese government began to recreate Japan's image and identity through their popular culture exports. This explains why and how Japan is able to maintain a prominent position in the global market in today's contemporary era.

Today, Japanese policymakers aspire to brand, market, and sell Japanese culture on the basis of its distinct Japanese nature. In Choo's study, there is an exploration in the ways in which the Japanese government has recently attempted to support their national content industries. Through promoting national policies in support of these industries and their dissemination abroad, the national government has elevated the status of the content industries to be a part of traditional Japanese "high arts culture." These state policies are founded on two main motivations: first, the quest to build soft power through economic means and, second, their desire to create a widespread, distinct Japanese identity and image that can be easily marketed throughout the world. Through supporting and marketing Japanese culture, Japan has further connected to and integrated into global markets. Therefore, in this case, Japan has not been weakened by globalization but has, instead, been able to strengthen their position in global markets. Seemingly, Japan has recently devised and adopted more systematic policies to continue the process of cultural domestication in western markets, but the continual viability of Japanese cultural products in non-Asian markets is another topic of discussion in itself.

China as a rising market: cultural antagonism and globalization

Part IV of this book deals with the heated debate on China's exercise of soft power through media and cultural industries. The authors in this part attempt to explicate what it means for the world if China is on the rise culturally. In Chapter 13, Michael Keane and Bonnie Rui Liu believe that the new creative strategy of China, in regards to television and film production culture, is the process and outcome of negotiations between China and the transnational companies attempting to penetrate the Chinese market. On the other hand, in Chapter 14, Michael Curtin argues the opposite; he suggests that China has been unable to translate its national power into soft, cultural power, thereby remaining impotent in regards to participating in global business flows.

Despite different viewpoints, both studies relay that China views globalization as a menace to their national sovereignty; China has resorted to various tactics to impede foreign popular culture in effectively operating in China.

When global capitals and the PRC are at odds, the continuity of cultural globalization is interrupted and delayed. Global corporations in China, in fact, fall into business traps rarely encountered in other western and Asian regions where nation states generally enact (whether voluntarily or involuntarily) open policies to welcome these transnational corporations. The resulting consequence is a situation of cultural antagonism in which the global cultural corporations, attempting to maintain the continuity of global networks, structures, and hierarchies in China, ultimately are forced to confront China, negotiate with Chinese authorities, and enter the Chinese market with great risks. Paradoxically, for the sake of global continuity, the structure itself forgets its own calculated logic of capitalist profit and revenue. Thus, even though few of the commercial projects started out by these transnational cultural corporations (ranging from music corporations to television and film companies) are lucrative, we are still seeing new ventures of these transnational corporations in China (Fung, 2008).

Keane and Liu's article directly tells readers of how China has utilized soft, cultural power in reaching their national mission. They document evidence about how the Chinese state has actively attempted to reverse China's cultural trade deficit by stimulating creativity and innovation of media industries in order to enhance China's soft power, cultural influence, and security. However, despite the trend toward commercialization, the structural reforms to China's production culture operate within the rigid limits of China's political framework. Film and television productions have little incentive to be creative when their top priority is balancing the state's vested interests and the profitability of their production.

Globalization is evidently at work in China. One way to quicken innovation is to rely on international corporations to professionalize an industry. The authors in Chapter 13 highlight the processes in which China is restructuring and modernizing their creative industries in film and television through openness and collaboration with the global. However, cultural insecurities, along with national insecurities, are accompanied by the spread of western values inherently embedded in cultural imports; the Chinese authorities fear losing ideological control, weakening traditional culture, and reinforcing a western consumer ethos. In response to the perceived risks, the Chinese state has chosen to reinforce restrictions on foreign corporations and foreign imports in China which effectively terminate, break down, and discontinue the global structure within the nation. Even though Chinese policymakers understand the need to fix the internal, structural problems of national media and cultural sectors through new industry policies, creative strategies, and higher quality of content, the market consideration seems to be secondary.

Michael Curtin also addresses the same issue—in the wake of globalization, China has devised different levels of national political action to contest cultural domination, while the West takes advantage of the interim openness to enter the

Chinese market. There are, however, a couple of questions that remain: is Beijing strong enough economically and politically to reduce the impact of globalization? Will Beijing become strong enough to replace the West and become the new centre for cultural activity in Asia? In his article, Curtin uses Hong Kong cinema as an example to illustrate how China has seen success in exerting its influence through tactical manipulation over foreign competitors, including Hong Kong film companies. In general, the logic of control to defy globalization is simple—the state grants support to those who are aligned with the state and sanction those who threaten the mainland industry and, above all, the ideology of the state.

Through tracing the recent history of the Hong Kong film industry, Curtin elaborates that the downfall of the industry was due to Hong Kong's deliberate attempt to kowtow to the Chinese market; this process, however, was not a direct political force from China. Rather, Hong Kong film producers had developed anxiety about being back under Chinese control and the result was Hong Kong film production that alienated local movie audiences. The interplay of political controls and profit factors have caused the Hong Kong film industry to undergo what Curtin terms "resinicization." Curtin demonstrates that the resinicization of the Hong Kong film industry is furthering the disintegration of Hong Kong as a media capital. In light of these realizations, the future of Hong Kong cinema can be summed up easily. Through resinicization, the Hong Kong industry may fare well in local and regional markets. Nevertheless, though the industry is modernized, it will ultimately remain globally disconnected and be unable to again attain media capital status if it is to stay under the control of mainland rhetoric. Nowadays, the Hong Kong film industry is no longer a flourishing hub of creativity, but an industry that has acclimatized to Chinese policies and censors. In this case, China is seen as a powder keg that discontinues the global hierarchy of cultural flows and the cultural connection in Asia.

We are living in an era that is overseeing the redistribution of global national, economic, and cultural power. Apart from China, I believe that there will be more cases that disrupt the globalization processes that have been prevalent in Asia for decades. Many nations could be ignited by cultural antagonism in their region but, in other countries, there may be nations ignited by the existing global structure and capitalist ideology that has preserved the dominant global system. Asides from the dominant processes of cultural adaptation, cultural absorption, and cultural domestication, many other processes that have not been discussed in this book will flourish and bourgeon. Cultural regionalism led by China and other rising East Asian regions, in addition to cultural globalism, will remake the cultures of Asia. Cultural connection, reconnection, and disconnection are the constant processes that make Asia an intellectually exciting field for empirical academic enquiry.

Bibliography

Allen, M. and Sakamoto, R. (2006) *Popular Culture, Globalization and Japan*. New York: Routledge.

Berger, P. and Huntington, S. (2003) (eds) *Many Globalizations: Cultural Diversity in the Contemporary World*. New York: Oxford University Press.

Fung, A. (2008) *Global Capital, Local Culture: Transnational Media in China*. New York: Peter Lang.

Hopper, P. (2007) *Understanding Cultural Globalization*. Cambridge: Polity Press.

Pieterse, J.N. (2009) (2nd edition) *Globalization and Culture: Global Mélange*. Lanham, MD: Rowman & Littlefield Publishers.

Rethman, P., Szeman, I., and Coleman, W. (2010) *Cultural Autonomy: Frictions and Connections*. Vancouver: University of British Columbia Press.

Rodriques, U. and Smaill, B. (2008) *Youth, Media and Culture in the Asia Pacific Region*. Cambridge: Cambridge Scholars Publishing.

Wise, J.M. (2008) *Cultural Globalization: A User's Guide*. Malden, MA: Wiley-Blackwell.

PART I

The dominance of global continuity

Cultural localization and adaptation

2

WHEN CHINESE YOUTH MEET HARRY POTTER

Translating consumption and middle-class identification[1]

John Nguyet Erni

Introduction

In the year 1999, the already famous book series Harry Potter arrived in China; during this time a steady influx of foreign popular culture was visibly beginning to transform Chinese society into an increasingly robust and globalized consumer culture. Scholars and critics have debated how this consumerist turn in Chinese society exposes the processes of global dialectics, stretching everyday life and social agency between commodity enchantment and exploitative commodification (Davis 2005; Poon 2003; Wang 2005). This study will not only analyze the aforementioned debate, but will instead look at the contextual forces as well as the self-reflections made by young Chinese readers as the explanatory framework for addressing the effect of Harry Potter on the cultural imagination of materialism, inter-generational differences, and middle class life in China today.

Observers of China would undoubtedly mark China's accession to the World Trade Organization (WTO) in 2001 as a watershed moment that complemented China's change in status to a rising "post-socialist" society that has become a formidable player in the global market. Before China's WTO accession, foreign capital could enter the children's publishing market of China only through the buying and selling of publication rights. Nevertheless, by 2003, foreign interests and investment through cooperation with domestic publishers and/or bookshops had begun to penetrate the Chinese market; foreign products such as those created by the Walt Disney Company, AOL Time Warner Incorporated, Bertelsmann AG, McGraw-Hill, and the Pearson Group saturated the domestic market. Data released by the General Administration of Press and Publication in China highlight that in the year 2003, out of the 7,588 children's titles published in China, 2,942 (close to 40 percent) were titles that had been translated or adapted. Furthermore, around 1.5 million USD worth of children's titles were imported into China in the

22 John Nguyet Erni

same year (Hai 2006). Notably, this dollar figure does not include other imported children's products associated with foreign titles, such as toys, clothes, DVDs, games, music, stationary, and more.[2]

Since 1999, the crazed consumption of Harry Potter products in urban China, also known as "Pottermania," has exceeded in both volume and sales as compared to all other foreign children's books available in the nation's history. In fact, "Harry Potter, or "Ha-li-Bo-te" as he is known in Chinese, could be the biggest thing since Chairman Mao's little red book, and shake up the staid, preachy world of Chinese children's books" (Hutzler 2000). The publishing of the Harry Potter box set in 2002 by the state-owned People's Literature Publishing House, printing 600,000 copies the first time, was a major literary event in China. As the average print-run for children's books in China was around 20,000 in the early 2000s, the output of Harry Potter by People's Literature was an astonishing figure. The distribution chief of People's Literature even used his own 11-year-old son to help promote the books; his son appeared in an interview and stated: "While reading the first book, I was already anticipating the second" (Hutzler 2000). The intermittent waves of Harry Potter promotions in China persisted, as the cinematic release of *Harry Potter and the Deathly Hallows* (the second part of the final volume of the series) in August 2011, garnered critical success (there were reports of it earning over 40 million USD its first three weeks of showing).

The focus of this study is to explore the reception of the Harry Potter franchise, namely the books and films, by Chinese youth in Shanghai, and to examine the larger contextual forces that underwrite such consumption. The theoretical contemplation undertaken here is of the relation between the local reading of a transnational text (assumed to be accompanied by acquisition of new cultural capital) by Shanghainese youth, and the formation of an active yet problematic discourse regarding the rise of the urban Chinese middle class. In this study, this is viewed as a theoretical contemplation on the relation between two kinds of cultural agency: an active agency formed through direct engagement and a constructed agency shaped by the state and popular sources. Though I have explored this constructed agency in previous studies (Erni 2008), I will revisit and elaborate upon this concept later on in this chapter. Little, however, has been researched about the active agency; an exploration of this cultural agency would shed light on how Chinese readers of Harry Potter live their lives in reality, and how their engagement with Harry's world leads them to rethink their own lives.

The empirical fieldwork for this study was undertaken in Shanghai in 2006 and 2007; during this time a series of individual and focus group interviews were conducted, and a research company was hired and consulted with to assist in data sampling and analysis. The qualitative part of this project focused on the narratives and peer discussion among 30 Shanghai youths—14 females and 16 males ranging in ages from 13 to 27. Among these youth, five were primary school students, seven were secondary school students, eight were university students, while the remaining ten were in the work force.[3] Their self-reported household incomes ranged from around 6,000 RMB to about 10,000 RMB, with a few over

30,000 RMB. According to Davis' study of consumer life in Shanghai in 2003, the average annual per capita urban income for the middle 20 percent of the population was 7,753 RMB, while that of the next 20 percent of the population was 10,463 RMB (Davis 2005). Therefore, our subjects of study fall squarely into the middle-class to upper-middle-class strata; this conforms to our research design that solely focuses on middle-class youth consumption of Harry Potter. What is also interesting to note from Davis' study is that the average expenditures of the middle 20 percent of Shanghai's population was 5,848 RMB, and that of the next 20 percent was 7,547 RMB. Perhaps the spending of 70 percent of one's income is another sign of middle-class consumer life.

The interviews I conducted first revolved around conversations of each respondent's common, everyday leisure consumption; these interviews were conducted with the individual participants who were occasionally joined by family members, schoolmates, and/or peers. Second, the conversations turned to perception and self-perception of the term "middle class." The respondents were asked to reflect upon this question through simple concepts such as level wealth accumulation, property/car possession, the nature of one's job, educational attainment, consumption habits, favorite places to frequent, and network of friends, by using a more complex but open-ended discussion of subjective feelings, experience, and reflection. The idea behind these conversations was to pinpoint the youths' views on their values—the value of money, of class-derived power, and of social equality. Our interview process was framed with the belief that these two contextual questions regarding consumption life and the discourse about middle-class culture would be crucial in placing their reception of Harry Potter. We hoped for this particular flow to produce a space for them to explore the relational field of discourse into which they could orient their reaction to Harry Potter. This was to explicitly avoid a simple textual reading; the flow, we hoped, would facilitate a more dynamic reading of the social text.

Apart from the individual and focus groups interviews, eight of our participants were asked to write a diary for a one-month period set before and around the time of the release of a new Harry Potter book in 2006. For the most part, the diary was an open exercise. However, the participants were given a few guidelines; they were instructed to focus on, first, their personal feelings, vocabulary, and thoughts on Harry Potter (including the characters, plot, role of magic, and thoughts about the author, J.K. Rowling) and, second, their reflection on the consumption of Harry Potter in relation to their other popular culture consumption (both Chinese and foreign imported popular culture).[4]

Subsequent data coding, categorization, and analysis has produced an interesting theory that during the Chinese youths' encounters with Harry Potter, they express an alternating embrace and critique of "middle classness," but this ambivalence does not necessarily lead to a critical attitude toward the commodified world, which they interestingly correlate with the world of magic and wizardry. On one hand, this suggests that middle-class culture (which the participants are aware they are a part of) offers the comfort, creativity, freedom, and seduction of consumption as associated with Harry's magical adventures and the structure of Hogwarts as an institution for kids. On the other hand, middle classness, to them, also signifies excess, arrogance, and an unrealistic gaze regarding the future. Nonetheless, this latter sentiment is not necessarily linked to the consumption of Harry Potter; rather, it seems to stem from the traditional, family-based value of self-restraint analogous to a modest outlook concerning the rapidly changing economy and world. When analyzing the youths' views on consumption and middle-class culture, we found that they often draw on their home life/families and school life/peers, taking from the value systems of these immediate environments as discursive points of reference. Some specific examples are associating spending money with family teachings about frugality, contrasting personal freedom with the rigidities of school life, and resistance of outdated expectations from parents, schools, and even the state, through creativity. The tendency to turn to family and school systems as systems of value essentially signifies a resistance to traditionalism, as outlined by our participants through their evidential generation gap with their parents and institutional obsolescence. In all, the youths' strong fascination with the power of magic (an in-text allusion) is coupled with a fervent consciousness of the changing times and economy boom (an extra-textual reference), bringing forth a cautiously enchanting tale about middle-class personhood. It is a cautious tale because of the realization of the fantasy (therefore false) nature of consumption, bliss, and middle-class freedom, yet enchanting because the fantastical serves to be momentary escape from the drudgeries of family, school, and work life. To put it simply, these youth clearly understand that wizardry can only be found in a fantasy world, but who wants to be a mere Muggle?[5]

What do these findings tell us about globalization? Evidently, the Chinese youth view Harry Potter as the locus of cultural superiority. The western tale of magic and heroism fascinates the youth in a definitive manner—it presents to them the practice of creativity that they see lacking in their immediate environments. The foreign, when signified as something creative, suggests a successful linkage with the global. Furthermore, the interface with the global through Harry Potter allows the Chinese youth to express their frustration toward their stifling social environment. Though one may believe that this one-sided celebration of the West denotes naïveté, it is quite the contrary. The fragments of Chinese wisdom, as attained from family and school teachings, manage to pull the youth away from unfettered individualism that they still seem to associate with the West. Nevertheless, this is a weak ambivalence; most of the youth we spoke to believe that "becoming global"(and its associated liberal values of freedom, individuality, creativity, etc.) is an inevitable part of their personal development, if not part of the development of China as a whole. Before analyzing these claims, it is pertinent to first review the popularity of Harry Potter in China and its impact on local imagination regarding children and children's literature.

Pottermania in China: popular and intellectual construction

Since the release of the first book, the success of Harry Potter has always been seen as a fan-driven miracle. The enormous success of Harry Potter was not a result anticipated by marketers; in fact, J.K. Rowling had a hard time finding a publisher in England, many of whom found her manuscripts to be too long and too slow. Even when Bloombury Press agreed to publish Rowling's book in 1996, it offered her a meager contract and warned her not to expect to get rich from writing children's books. In China, middle-class "fandom" is also what drives Pottermania.

Only after Harry Potter became a blockbuster hit in the West, and when considerable traffic began to emerge on the internet surrounding the Potter buzz, the Chinese publishing world took notice. Despite the aforementioned record-breaking publication of Harry Potter box sets by the People's Literature Publishing House, book sales had a slow start in China. It was not until the theatrical release of the first Harry Potter movie in China that book sales began to take a favorable turn (Wei 2008). In major cities such as Shanghai, Beijing, and Guangzhou, long lines of middle-class and well-educated Chinese children began to appear in cinemas and bookstores, anxious to watch and read Harry Potter. Furthermore, Harry Potter even became a part of school life; school teachers formed reading clubs for Potter fans and English classes in schools began to adopt the books in their lessons. While searching for cultural resonance, translators of the Harry Potter books drew on traditional Chinese legends of ghost stories and martial arts stories; for example, the magical spells of Harry Potter were alluded to incantations recited by legendary kung-fu masters prior to fighting (Hutzler 2000).

In China, the popularity and success of Harry Potter has opened up two major cultural debates: first, whether or not China should heed the allure of the West or strengthen the appeal of traditional Chinese children's literature and, second, whether or not China should embrace commercialism or rethink literary and aesthetic values in the children's literary culture. Regarding the first debate, there is a general lament in Chinese society over their youths' unfamiliarity with traditional mythical characters of Chinese legends, namely the Monkey King, Najah, and Fa Mulan. What is even more distressing, perhaps, is the fact that some Chinese children are aware of these mythical Chinese characters, but have low levels of interest toward them in comparison to their spellbound fascination of the characters portrayed in Harry Potter. There have been many recent articles published with headlines such as "Universal Potter" (Jing 2007) and "Harry Potter vs. Local Heroes" (Tang 2005); the *Beijing Review* affirms that the popularity of Harry Potter signifies that China's youth is increasingly embracing western/global popular culture and that it even serves as a criticism of the paucity of imagination in Chinese children's literature. Wei pointedly remarks: "Although there are over 10,000 children's books produced annually in China, few books leave readers with the deep impression created by the Harry Potter world of spells, sorcery, and galloping centaurs" (Wei 2008).

26 John Nguyet Erni

As for the second debate prompted by the Harry Potter phenomenon, there has been a tendency to reiterate the traditional distinction between high culture and low culture. On one side, Chinese magazines and popular literary journals celebrate Harry Potter as a commercial success and link it to the increasingly open policy environment of the current Hu-Wen government. Since 2004, China's specialist children's publishing houses have increased from two to 30, the staff employed in children's publishing has gone from 200 to more than 3,000. Writers and illustrators of children's literature have also increased from about 200 to more than 3,000. Nowadays, 523 of the 569 publishers in China are competing to publish children's literature (Hai 2006).

The intensely competitive market for children's publishing has resulted in forcing publishing companies to obtain exclusive intellectual property rights. In 2001, *China Online* reported that the success of Shanghai-based East Hope Group attaining the Harry Potter trademark was part of a long line of successful intellectual property rights obtained by the company. To date, East Hope Group now owns the rights to the words "hope," "*qiangda*" (which means powerful), and "*shouhuo*" (which means harvest). In this regard, Harry Potter is not merely a character associated with the children's book industry, but a name synonymous with capitalist-style blockbuster-ism armed with advanced commercial operations. In hailing the commercial success of Harry Potter in China, these magazines and journals are seemingly encouraging Chinese children's literature to restructure and update its style, its focus on children's creativity and imagination, and its ideological function.

On the other side, the defense of aesthetic values in children's literature in China is linked to its domestic liberalization in the public sphere. Tang Rui, a critic of children's literature and the assistant editor-in-chief of the China Fine Arts Publishing Group, discusses the "Harry Potter effect" in Chinese literary circles by placing its success in context of the recent ideological liberalization of literary production in China. Tang suggests that the success of Potter was only made possible by a literary renaissance experienced since the Cultural Revolution:

> The generation of younger writers who grew up during the Cultural Revolution ... now became the leading children's writers, and they had a very different valuation of life and literary conception from the pre-Cultural Revolution generation. Debate raged at this time about whether children's literature should educate children or reflect human reality; whether the essence of children's literature is instructional or aesthetic; whether children's literature should go along with childish superficiality or pursue artistic profundity; whether children's literature should disclose the seamy side of life, and so on. In this period, the subjects of children's literature expanded into many fields of real life, its themes dug deep into humanity and writing styles were diverse. The old restrictions were broken up and new exploration and experiment emerged. This was a prosperous period for children's literature.
>
> *Tang 2006*

Tang goes on to suggest that, interestingly, in China, the Harry Potter effect has literally produced two opposing tendencies, one aesthetically and ideologically conservative and the other pop-commercial. Without disparaging the pop-commercial tendency, Tang nonetheless suggests that this commercialism will be short lived, due to the fact that young commercial writers of children's literature have minimal regard for the idea of literary creativity and individuality, and literature is much more dictated by marketing. Tang believes that these young commercial writers "came in for more and more criticism for their slapdash writing and lack of individuality" (Tang 2006). Throughout Tang's discussion, she demonstrates a strong preference toward the works of Chinese literary greats in the field of children's literature, such as Wenxuan Cao, Zhilu Zhang, Xin Gang Chang, and Jin Bo. The writers' insistence on using and promoting the classic Chinese aesthetic style in children's literature has won great appreciation from both the public and government. Their work echoes state sentiments, stated in a 2004 government document:

> Newspapers, magazines, and other children's publications should take it as their responsibility to provide better spiritual nourishment for young people, and try to be good teachers or friends to help them broaden their horizon and improve themselves, and try to be a spiritual garden in which the young can mould their characters and enjoy themselves.
>
> *Hai 2006*

Tang concludes her position by stating: "As a result of chasing big sellers in the short term, more and more books for children have been published in China, but few of them have been outstanding" (Tang 2006). This attenuation of commercially measured success in children's literature is representative of the pervasive view that even though Harry Potter can create a healthy competitive market structure for literary production, the series, aesthetically speaking, is lower quality and thus should remain a small part of the China's children's literary culture.

Undoubtedly, the advancement of the Harry Potter phenomenon in China cannot be deemed as hostile to western or global commercial culture. Rather, many commentaries were enthusiastic in embracing the benefits of international exposure of Chinese youths through Harry Potter and other similar phenomena. Yet the stronger interest of the discourse seems to lie in tempering the commercialism of Harry Potter in favor of seeing it as a tool for reviving patriotic aesthetics through the children's publishing industry. But how do Chinese youth feel about Harry Potter, its commercialism and aesthetic values? The following section will delve into a discussion of the data found and what it suggests about the Chinese youths' own sense of agency with respect to their reading pleasure, their placement of Harry Potter in their consumption lifestyle, and their self-reflection on the question of middle class. We turn first to our informants' textual engagement with the book series.

28 John Nguyet Erni

Counter projection through the characters of Harry Potter

"Because I want to grow up to be a powerful person, I pay a lot of attention to powerful people ... I am fascinated by them," says Xi, a 15-year-old male.[6] The most frequent characterization that our young participants attribute to the central figures of Harry Potter is the notion of power. However, by this, they are not speaking of Harry's magical powers; the students in the book are, in fact, characterized as innocent students of a large school whose curriculum touches on mysterious teachings. Lin, a 27-year-old female, points out that "though Harry is a student at Hogwarts, a magic school, his sorcery powers are not very strong, but in fact very weak. He is just a brave boy who takes on many challenges."[7] Miao, a 13-year-old male, echoes his sentiments, stating that Hermione "has strong will power. Her ability to overcome obstacles in her life is very much like Harry's." The youth interviewed for this study perceive the books' emphasis to be not on magical power but, ultimately, on the personal qualities of the fictional characters; the characters' ability to perform wizardry only serves as an acquired skill that complements their already admirable characteristics. The youth attribute the following adjectives to describe the characters of Harry Potter: virtuous, independent, pure, brave, and rational; they also appreciate the characters' ability to solve problems in critical moments and stand for justice. One 14-year-old female, Liu, praises Hermione for her bravery and compares Hermione with her own character:

> Hermione is not only a pretty face—she is very smart, especially during critical moments like in the secret chamber. If it was not for Hermione in the chamber, poor Harry would not have even known what was going to hurt him! I, too, take care of my friends a lot. Though I may not be as smart as Hermione, I am a strong decision maker, just like her.

Yet, Liu's own correlation to a fictional character is an exception among our youth participants. For most of our participants, the admirable qualities and virtues found in the Harry Potter characters were not something to be found in themselves, but something that was missing among their own characters and in the characters of youth like themselves. Zhou, a 20-year-old female, states:

> Harry is very brave. He does not rely on others' powers to accomplish a task, which also makes him very independent. I, on the other hand, am chronically deficient in terms of independence. I am perpetually lazy and nothing like him. Harry's ability to solve his own problems is the basis upon which he is able to extend help to others.

Lin, a 27-year-old female, reflects and elaborates:

> I feel that the Harry Potter books and films send readers and viewers a message of solidarity and friendship; these are values that westerners care about.

Also, Harry Potter tells us the importance of being independent; Harry, when he was still young [at the beginning of the series], went to Hogwarts all by himself ... he is very self-reliant. In China, Chinese parents indulge and spoil their children, but in the West, children learn to be independent. Every week, I go home and bring back my dirty laundry for my mother to wash—I am totally dependent on her. I remember one incident where my friend asked her school if she could bring her mother along ... I felt ashamed of her. This shows Chinese parents' excessive love for their children.

Contrasting their own characters to the books' characters extends into an intercultural comparison; evidently, their fondness for the books' characters leads to admission of their own weaknesses. This counter projection extends from a personal scale to a cultural scale.

It is apparent that the Chinese youths' reading of the Harry Potter books and their counter projection through the books' characters takes place on two interlocking planes. First, it appears on a conventional plane of relating to something fictional and, second, it appears on what can be called a generic plane of relating to a fantasy space inherent to children's literature. In this way, the personal qualities they attribute to the characters of the book (independent, courageous, virtuous) and the qualities they, in return, attribute to themselves, are mediated by two planes. In regards to the conventional plane of relating to fictional characters, Chinese youth readers consider the personal qualities of Harry, Hermione, Ron, and others in the novels, and relate these characteristics back to their own. Nevertheless, the comparisons they determine, whether positive or negative, do not affect their conclusion that life is always more adventurous in a fiction story! Yet, in regards to the second plane governed by the genre of children's literature, in which fantasy is a vital component, the Chinese youths' counterprojection takes on a different meaning. In Harry Potter, fantasy is constituted primarily through the division between the wizarding world and the so-called Muggle world. Harry's heroism begins only with the marking of, and transformation from, his original Muggle heritage; ultimately, he is different from other wizards because he transgresses the border between the two realms. In this second plane of reading space, the young readers' recognition of their own personal weaknesses therefore seems to point to a double identification. Such recognition could be understood as the readers' identification with ordinary Muggles, against which the exciting and impressive adventures of Harry and his friends would direct them to spotting their own inadequacies. It could even be said that the characterization of their own parents (as the cause of their failure to mature) in fact arises from identifying with Dudley, Harry's cousin, who develops a bullying attitude due to his Muggle parents who spoil him with an excess of food and toys. In the world of Harry Potter, entry into the wizarding world (which would be parallel to entry into a school in real life), creates opportunities for personal growth, improvement, and freedom; the readers' recognition of their own weaknesses may be what prompts them in identifying with Harry. Ultimately, Harry's transcendence may be translated by young readers as hope for escape. As Cui, a 16-year-old female admits: "I envy those who have superpowers—they can do what others cannot." Yie, a 22-year-old male, concurs:

> When reality proves to be uncomfortable and unlucky over here, you can immerse yourself in another world. When this fantasy world proves to be too much, you can return to the real world and make some improvements in your real life. I think it is good to have this second imaginary world as everybody needs an escape from reality sometimes.

The double identification by the young readers, with Muggles on one side and with Harry and the wizarding world on the other, is a generic feature of the books. However, it should be noted that this double identification can be simultaneously read as a feature of intercultural encounters; this is possible since these youth participants frequently expand their comparisons from an individual level to an intercultural plane. These youths' contrasting views between Chinese and western societies must not be seen as a simple dichotomy or hierarchy but, in fact, as an ambiguity. In paralleling the Muggle world with the Chinese world, the indulgence of children is ironically a symbol of neglect; however, we still live in the real world, the immediate and visceral environment felt by our readers. In paralleling Harry's magical world to the West, the progression and growth into youth is a symbol of liberation, yet it is liberation produced by fantasy. The Chinese youths' contrasting views between Chinese and western societies should thus be seen as an alternation, as a pendulum that swings both ways, with each movement occupying an empty space (the tail end point) and an acquired space (the front end point), and with another swing reversing those spaces. This concept of alternation is preferred because viewing these participants' beliefs as wholeheartedly "pro-West" is too simplistic and does not conform to our data. This idea of alternation suggests an ambiguous attitude, which seems to be in accordance with their true beliefs. This study will consider and undertake the discourse of the double space of reading in order to return our emphasis to the fantasy nature of children's literature. However, this discourse is also undertaken due to the theme of alternation, and its appearance as a recurring and structuring idea in the participants' views regarding consumption and middle class identity as filtered through their reading of Harry Potter.

A new consumption lifestyle

There exists today significant scholarship concerning China's consumer revolution marked by the rise of a middle-class culture (Buckley 1999; Davis 2000; Glassman 1991; Goodman 1999; McElroy 2002; Wang 2005). Empirical proof of China's so-called "new rich" has been confirmed by researchers, whose focus has been on elements such as private home acquisition and home improvement (Davis 2005; Li 1998), the purchasing of investment and insurance (Mseka 2001), and the purchase of luxury automobiles (Eckholm 2001). Furthermore, researchers such as

Farrer and Gillette have found further evidence of the new consumer lifestyles of China's new rich; various social activities such as dance-hall culture (Farrer 2000) and bridal fashion culture (Gillette 2000) have proved popular and showed up in China's urban centers. Part of the explanatory framework concerning the middle-class cultural boom concerns the link between China's new rich and the country's unprecedented openness to transnational trade of cultural commodities. Since the 1990s, there has been a multitude of research regarding China's globalization, including Buckley (1999), Ching (2001), Goodman (1996), Khan and Riskin (2001), Lee (2003), Moore (2000), Ross (2006), and Yan (2002).

However, it is the studies of consumption for and by children and youth in China's new consumer society that are most relevant to this chapter. The past three decades in China have overseen the implementation of the controversial one child policy along with the country's market liberalization, leading to increased consideration of and attention toward children's achievement and material satisfaction (Davis and Sensenbrenner 2000; Li 1998; Wang 2005). Chinese parents who experienced economic depravity during the Mao years, who are now raising a single child, have turned to consumption as a means to provide a better life for their only child. Many children in China today, due to being the only child of the family in addition to the relative affluence of their families, are receiving a good education, participating in well-planned learning activities beyond normal schooling, and are exposed to many consumer goods. In China, just like it has occurred in the West, spending on children's leisure and enrichment activities has created the emergence of class distinctions (albeit vague), if not also class inequality (Davis and Sensenbrenner 2000; Seiter 1993; Steinberg and Kincheloe 1998). Tracing the processes of social class reproduction in China, however, can be done through examining variations in the consumer experiences of youth and children such as music consumption, sports, and fast food culture (Brownell 2001; Efird 2001; de Kloet 2010; Yan 2000).

Sociologist Deborah Davis has noted that China's popular press talks about the rise of consumerism using the banal rhetoric of marketers and that of party officials who endorse private entrepreneurship and neo-liberal economics. She continues: "When, however, one listens to consumers themselves reflect on purchases as part of a larger conversation about their leisure time or expectations for the future, the sociological terrain becomes a complex performance space with observable degrees of freedom" (Davis 2005). Moreover, "approached through the processes of narration and dialogue, consumer cultures are more likely to be as polyvalent and multi-leveled as the social positions and the temporal framing of the participants" (Davis 2005).

One of the most striking statements made during a group interview was by Xi, a 21-year-old male. Xi exclaimed: "Eat it all and spend it all—this will make you happy and healthy!" Cui, a 16-year-old female, added: "I feel that it is better to be wealthy—we should all aim for the good life!" Zhang, a 27-year-old female, also added her thoughts:

I like going out to bars and nightclubs; there are all kinds of different people to look at. We only go to those places after a hard day of work because we are stressed, and we want to sit around and relax. We do not pull all-nighters there.

The young participants in our study also spoke of other favored leisure activities such as karaoke, and the consumer goods they preferred to purchase, such as luxury brand perfume, shoes, handbags, and cars. Those participants who were financially less well-off than the others would perhaps mention a wealthy relative's possessions or a friend's outstanding qualities. Miao, a 13-year-old-male, says:

My uncle lives a pretty good life. The position he holds at his company is even higher up than the manager's, therefore, he is given a private car. Whenever we go to visit our grandma, my uncle always picks us up in his private car. He and his family live in Qang Qiao, and they have not one, but two computers in their home!

Xu, a 15-year-old male, adds:

My friend, he is different from others. He is different not because he comes from a wealthy family, but because he previously attended a private school. The private school put a lot of attention on the self-worth and overall quality of their students. In our current class, I feel as though my friend's self-confidence is like a smell he carries with him and spreads around; I really feel as though he is extremely confident, in his words and actions.

In China, attendance in a private school symbolizes being a part of the middle class. Thus, from Xu's comments and his evident transposition of class identity into an admirable trait, he accords an almost mythical effervescence to China's new rich (for example, the "smell" his friend carries with him and spreads around).

While some of the youth interviewed for this study outlined and adhered to the classic consumerist disposition of "work hard, play hard," other interviewees referred to their spending habits as being part of the "new world." A number of these youth even felt the need to defend their self-proclaimed extravagance. For instance, Yie spoke of his mother's request for him to mark down his daily and monthly expenditures:

In my opinion, keeping a record of your expenditures is old fashioned and unnecessary, but my mom has always urged me to do it. But to me, it is ridiculous—the money you have spent is already spent, what is the point in remembering how much you spent? To prove to yourself that you spent your money correctly? Or to remind yourself how you spent your money in an incorrect manner?

Lin adds:

> People from the older generations always worry about the future. However, I believe that you have to spend money in order to make money—you cannot make money by just leaving your money idle. You have to spend more money in order to motivate yourself to earn more money. For example, if you think that $1,000 is already a lot of money, you are too easily satisfied and will not be motivated to make more money.

This cross-generational comparison is often unprompted, which signals the discomfort of Chinese youth with Mao's era of frugality. The motto, "eat it all, spend it all," encompasses not only light-hearted attitudes characteristic of times when the economy is doing well, it also seems to incorporate a serious underlying critique of the social and economic restrictions of the older era.

Notably, our participants' discourse about cross-generational differences further reveals a sense of pressure they receive from their parents and the perceived outdated conventional ideas of their parents. The pressures these Shanghainese youth speak of goes even beyond the problem of spending. Miao, a 13-year-old male, admits: "My mother puts a tight grip on me. If I get bad exam results, that will surely mean a scolding from my parents!" Zhou, a 20-year-old female, simply states: "I do not always want my parents to always look over my shoulders. I do not enjoy always being under their control!" Cui, an outspoken teenage girl, voiced her strong opinion:

> I feel tremendous pressure to do well in school. Getting an education is really for my parents; they put so much emphasis on my performance in school. When in class, the bad behavior of other children is usually tolerated ... as for me, however, I carry the label of "enthusiastic party member," and I cannot slip at all. It feels like I am acting in a drama! The stress starts at every morning at 8am and does not end until school is out.

Yie, a 25-year-old female who worked as a sales manager, moved out of her home a year prior to our interview with her, and told us:

> If I were to continue living at home, I am sure the divide between my parents and I would grow. My habit of going out early and going home late would affect my parents, so they even agreed that it was a good idea for me to move out. Though my parents wanted me to take over the family business, I am hesitant to say yes, as I want to create my own life journey.

In the eyes of the Chinese youth interviewed, consumption leads to a simple black-and-white dichotomy they construct between China's modern youth versus their Mao-era parents. The idea of "spending as liberation" is a notion that is significant to them in a particular way; it is an ideology that is meant to topple

34 John Nguyet Erni

over a restrictive social structure symbolized by parental control. In order to fully understand this view of "consumption as resistance" as unique to a generation of Chinese youth born into an era of materialism, we must consider what they say in conjunction with their own construction of what they deem to be middle class. The youths' resistance toward their parents and the socially restrictive world they associate with their parents does not necessarily stem from consumption, but from a whole "taste culture" which the youth place at a hierarchically higher position than the cultural world of their parents. Specifically, it is a taste culture mediated first, through the value of independence and, second, through an awareness of class cultivated through education and familiarity with western culture. By placing this taste culture at a position higher than the culture experienced by their parents, our interviewees ultimately imply that the "old world" of their parents is not only restrictive, but also shows a lack of class, taste, and education.

Middle class culture: a partial identification

In my previous studies I contended that the Chinese youth who craze about Harry Potter are those who give off a visible impression of a growing middle-class society capable of enjoying and performing the complex task of "translating" cultures; in other words, these youth are positioned as the cultural intermediaries of globalization. Meanwhile, the same impression also commands an internal reach, toward the urban Chinese population aspiring to become middle class (Erni 2008). One of the most common responses given by the youth participants when asked to define middle-class culture is their association of it with aspiration toward autonomous personhood, or personal independence. Fung, female, and 16 years old, explains: "[Middle class people] must have their own perspective and value system, which guides their life's goals. They also must have their own strong character, and again, their own point of view." Xen, a 20-year-old female, concurs: "[The middle class] have a free way of living ... they do not have many restrictions, or anybody controlling them." Here, a problem seems to present itself: are such beliefs and remarks formed by a middle-class experience, or do they signify an aspirational construct about a changing (and therefore partial) state of affairs? When we interviewed our participants it became clear that their own subjectivity was founded upon the contentions of "partial middle classness"; meaning that their own experiences of improved affluence and their aspirations and desires for "becoming affluent" are two states of identity that coexist. In this context, a partial middle-class subjectivity is thus a contentious subjectivity. Such partiality is a matter of overlapping agencies derived from active experiences (the notion that one feels they are middle class) as well as constructed experiences (the notion that one is middle class because the world says so). After all, these Shanghainese youth grew up in a society widely perceived as a society that is economically well-off.

In his 2002 report presented to the 16th plenary session of the Chinese Communist Party National Congress, former President Jiang Zemin announced that China had "generally accomplished [its] aim of [creating] a well-off society"

(Qiu 2005). Since his remarks, the idea of being well-off or middle class has produced many colloquial expressions in Chinese, such as *xiaoji*, *xiaokang*, *xinrenlei*, and *gaojihue*. Back in 1991, the National Bureau of Statistics (NBS), along with 11 ministerial level departments, defined 16 criteria needed in order for living standards to be considered "well-off"; these included GDP per capita, Engel's coefficient (the share of food expenses in daily total expenditure), the average income for urban residents, the average net income for rural residents, and more. According to the NBS, China had fulfilled 13 of these criteria by the end of 2000, with the exceptions of the average net income of rural residents, protein consumption per capita, and basic medical care for the rural populace. The NBS further claimed that China had achieved 96 percent of the "well-off" criteria for 2000, compared to only 48 percent in 1990 (Qiu 2005).

Meanwhile, Chinese media and business corporations joined forces to create the appearance of a vibrant and well-off society. Jingyu Li of the Chinese Academy of Social Sciences, nonetheless, expresses skepticism toward what he perceives to be a hyperbolic fanning of a trendy idea. He states in his essay, entitled *Are you middle Class yet? The middle class bubble in China*:

> In China, whenever there is a term that appears in the public domain to depict people's desired living condition, a lot of people will become its followers overnight. For instance, the notorious "petty bourgeoisie" was once a popular term. Today, it is the term "suddenly middle-class" … The middle-class market seems to have become a big piece of cake that mainland businesses are aggressively fighting for. Tailor-made houses, cars, insurance plans, and travel packages for the middle class blossomed in just two to three years. There are experts who even invented terms like "upper middle class," "lower middle class," "blue collar middle class," and "white collar middle class," etc. They are finding evidence and suppositions for the idea of the middle class, while fanning the flames for the middle-class market.
>
> *Li 2004*

Li continues his argument by stating that "as the term middle class has so little intrinsic meaning, we have to admit that it can hardly be recognized as a class … the best it can be is to be regarded as an elite culture" (Li 2004). In concurrence with Li's assessment, I suggest that it is only through the discourse of elitism (which refers to an attitude and a subjective conceit) that we are able to grasp the Chinese youths' own sense of "partial middle-class" identification.

Most of the Shanghainese youth we interviewed replied affirmatively when we asked them whether or not they had heard of the term "well-off society." The youth also went on to define a well-off society by associating it with a particular level of education and exposure to western and/or Japanese cultures; these factors together constitute a "classy" existence in the youths' minds. Lin elaborates:

I believe what it means to be middle class is to be well-off and carefree. The middle class have high salaries and enjoy buying trendy items. To be middle class means a monthly salary of around 10,000 RMB, working for a foreign-owned corporation, and being a homeowner. Also, middle-class people often frequent trendy locations around town like famous clubs, and regularly go to concert halls to attend live shows.

Yang, a 17-year-old male, however, points to what he calls the "level of culture." He contrasts what he deems as the "true" middle-class people with the middle class who only became affluent suddenly; Yang claims the latter "only know where to buy luxury items, but do not know how to properly use them. They only want to possess the best material items, but have little idea how to enjoy those items." Xen, a 20-year-old female, agrees with Yang, but adds that this so-called "cultural level"must be linked to a familiarity with foreign cultures; she states:

They especially like to buy limited edition items, especially those that are imported from foreign countries. These middle-class people travel frequently and purchase material goods while they are abroad ... they are not particularly interested in purchasing Chinese-made goods.

As aforementioned, there has been a focus on the participants' aspirational discourse. However, what we found through the interviews was that many of the youth alternate between admiration and criticism of the "well-off society." For example, Lin, a 27-year-old female, believes that "middle-class people will never befriend white collar workers. The middle class do not want to be in the same social circle as the white collar workers; they only associate with those in their own social circles." She continues:

At the top of the class pyramid, the middle class despise the white collar and blue collar workers; others that are not part of the middle class feel this attitude emanating from them. When the middle class speak, it is hard for others [not part of the middle class] to follow ... for example, when they speak of golf, the different golfing techniques, and different types of golf clubs. If you are one of the unprivileged and have never had the opportunity to play golf in your life, the middle class would laugh at you.

Zhang, a 27-year-old female, summarizes the elitism of the middle class:

The lower classes have no chance of rising to the upper class ... very few Cinderella stories happen in reality. Also, communication between different classes is very rare—the privileged associate with others that are like them, and the underprivileged do the same.

Interestingly enough, although many of the participants criticized class polarization, they do not seem to be aware of the generational polarization they themselves make. To these youths, to escape from the older set of values espoused by their parents' generation means marking one's identity as firmly belonging to the new era; yet, in this well-off society and environment, the youths discover class polarization, if not antagonism. Herein lies the youths' state of "partial middle classness," an intermediate kind of elitist subjectivity in abeyance.

Conclusion

Mapping the partial "identity in progress" as suggested above, along with the progress that the People's Republic has made in the last 30 years due to economic reform, we can say that the ideology of a well-off society has produced a compelling but mystifying Chinese elite class. This elite class, in turn, has been renamed middle class; this demonstrates that the history of reform has resulted in a culture of self-enchantment mediated by half beliefs, or partial identification. However, it is important to distinguish this self-enchantment from processes of self-deceit; the kind of Chinese middle-class modernity that is examined in this study has little to do with false consciousness in the Marxist sense. Rather, we believe that the participants in our study articulate a genuine ambivalence. Their access to the world of Harry Potter and the entire symbolic set of cultural capital that comes with it, seems to bring forth what I deem to be "ambivalent cultural positivity" (Erni 2008). This ambivalent but positive cultural attitude expresses itself through an alternation; on one hand, they happily embrace the idea of middle class, which offers them a sense of the new, delight, self-empowerment, and autonomy from restrictive social structures. On the other hand, though, they criticize the discourse about the well-off society in an attempt to demystify it as a state and media-led construction (Wang 2005).

At the beginning of this chapter, I framed this essay as a theoretical contemplation on the relation between two kinds of cultural agency (regarding Chinese youth and their encounters with Harry Potter and other similar global culture): an active agency formed through direct engagement and a constructed agency delivered by state and popular sources. The points made about partial identification speak to this sense of a double cultural agency. In this light, the alternating praise and critique of middle-class culture through engagement with Harry Potter means that the dialectics of enchantment and disenchantment remain central to the cultural space of modern childhood and youth in urban China today. Pottermania in China is a vivid representation of a global interface, which, at its center, finds a generation of kids growing up in a rapidly globalizing world. In this study, the cultural imaginary of the urban Chinese youth is in a state of "becoming global," symbolically articulated through generational change and resistance, as well in a state of "becoming middle class," rendered through an ambivalent and self-questioning elitist subjectivity.

38 John Nguyet Erni

Notes

1 The work described in this study was fully supported by a grant from the Research Grant Council of the Hong Kong Special Administrative Region (Project no.: 9040854 (CityU 1282/03H)). The author would like to thank Anthony Fung, who was the co-investigator of this project. He is also grateful to Tang Le (Melody) and Michael Chan for their research assistance.

2 While books may be imported to China, magazines and journals have a different fate. The number of journals has certainly increased since the mid-1970s (blossoming to 7,000 by the mid-1980s) but China's literary magazines and art and culture journals tend to mirror the national standard bearers. The party-state remains a significant publisher and producer of culture. The main outlets for writers remain the party's stable of literary magazines and its publishing houses (see Goodman 2001).

3 **Table 1** Interviewee profiles

	Pseudonym	Sex	Age	Education/occupation		Pseudonym	Sex	Age	Education/Occupation
1	Peng	F	20	Univ. sophomore	15	Yang	M	17	High school
2	Wang	F	18	Univ. freshman	16	Wu	F	18	High school
3	Yie	M	22	Clerk in French Embassy	17	Yuan	M	21	Univ. junior
4	Hwang	F	25	Customer service	18	Gao	M	20	Univ. freshman
5	Jiang	M	16	High school	19	Cui	F	17	Univ. sophomore
6	Zhu	M	26	Graphic designer	20	Lo	M	13	Middle school
7	Xia	M	21	Univ. junior	21	Xiu	M	13	Middle school
8	Yau	F	12	Middle school	22	Miao	M	13	Middle school
9	Liu	F	14	Middle school	23	Xu	M	15	High school
10	Fung	F	16	High school	24	Xen	F	20	Clerk in trading firm
11	Zhao	F	24	Clerk in telecomm. co.	25	Zhang	F	27	Clerk in business firm
12	Lu	M	23	Univ. freshman	26	Zhou	F	13	Univ. sophomore
13	Mo	F	22	Med. student	27	Lin	F	27	Clerk in real estate firm
14	Xi	M	21	Clerk	28	Yin	M	18	High school

4 The template we suggested to our informants for writing their diaries was as follows:
1   Relationship with HP
1.1   Personal feelings and thoughts about HP
1.11 Thoughts and feelings toward characters
1.12 Fantasy
1.13 Comments about different volumes
1.14 Reflections after reading/viewing
1.15 Differences between the watching the films and reading the books
1.2   Visiting HP websites
1.3   Reading news about HP
1.4   Consumption of HP-related products
1.5   Discussion of HP with others
1.6   J.K. Rowling
1.7   Usage of HP
1.8   Other issues in relation to HP
1.9   Comparison with other literature/movies (e.g. *Lord of the Rings*; *Monkey King*)
2   Relationship with popular culture
2.1   Contact with western culture
2.2   Idol-worshipping
2.3   Consumption (popular culture products)
2.31 Clothing
2.32 Entertainment
2.33 Personal care
2.34 Idol-related products
2.4   Consumption (entertainment/leisure/hobbies/services)
2.41 Games
2.42 Entertainment
2.43 Mass media
2.44 Food
2.5   Other issues in relation to popular culture.
5 Interestingly, the word "Muggle" is translated into Chinese as "maagua," which connotes something or someone as dumb, dull, or slow.
6 All names are pseudonyms.
7 All direct quotes are translated by the author. He thanks his Research Assistant Michael Chan for his help.

Bibliography

Brownell, S. (2001) "Making Dream Bodies in Beijing: Athletes, Fashion Models, and Urban Mystique in China," in N.N. Chen, C.D. Clark, S.Z. Gottschang, and L. Jeffrey (eds) *China Urban: Ethnographies of Contemporary Culture*, Durham, NC: Duke University Press.

Buckley, C. (1999) "How a Revolution Becomes a Dinner Party: Stratification, Mobility and the New Rich in Urban China," in M. Pinches (ed.) *Culture and Privilege in Capitalist Asia*, London and New York: Routledge.

Ching, L. (2001) "Globalizing the Regional, Regionalizing the Global: Mass Culture and Asianism in the Age of Late Capital," in A. Appadurai (ed.) *Globalization*, Durham, NC: Duke University Press.

Davis, D. (2005) "Urban consumer culture," *China Quarterly*, 183: 692–709.

Davis, D.S. (2000) *The Consumer Revolution in Urban China*, Berkeley: University of California Press.

Davis, D.S. and Sensenbrenner, J.S. (2000) "Commercializing Childhood: Parental Purchases for Shanghai's Only Child," in D.S. Davis (ed.) *The Consumer Revolution in Urban China*, Berkeley: University of California Press.

de Kloet, J. (2010) *China with a Cut: Globalization, Urban Youth, and Popular Culture*, Amsterdam: Amsterdam University Press.

Eckholm, E. (2001) "Emerging Middle Class Hits the Road in China," *New York Times*, October 6, A27.

Efird, R.(2001) "Rock in a Hard Place: Music and the Market in Nineties Beijing," in N.N. Chen, C.D. Clark, S.Z. Gottschang, and L. Jeffrey (eds) *China Urban: Ethnographies of Contemporary Culture*, Durham, NC: Duke University Press.

Erni, J.N. (2008) "Enchanted: Harry Potter and Magical Capitalism in Urban China," *Chinese Journal of Communication*, 1: 138–155.

Farrer, J. (2000) "Dancing Through the Market Transition: Disco and Dance Hall Sociability in Shanghai," in D.S. Davis (ed.) *The Consumer Revolution in Urban China*, Berkeley: University of California Press.

Gillette, M. (2000) "What's in a Dress? Brides in the Hui Quarter of Xi'an," in D.S. Davis (ed.) *The Consumer Revolution in Urban China*, Berkeley: University of California Press.

Glassman, R.M. (1991) *China in Transition: Communism, Capitalism, and Democracy*, New York: Praeger.

Goodman, D.S.G. (1996) "The People's Republic of China: The Party-State, Capitalist Revolution and New Entrepreneurs," in R. Robison and D.S.G. Goodman (eds) *The New Rich in Asia*, New York and London: Routledge.

Goodman, D.S.G. (1999) "The New Middle Class," in M. Goldman and R. MacFarquhar (eds) *The Paradox of China's Post-Mao Reforms*, Cambridge, MA: Harvard University Press.

Goodman, D.S.G. (2001) "Contending the Popular: Party-State and Culture," *Positions*, 9: 245–252.

Hai, F. (2006) "Paving a Road to the Azure Sky: The Present and Future of Chinese Children's Publishing," *Bookbird*, 44: 79–85.

Hutzler, C. (2000) "Harry Potter China Campaign Begins," *Associated Press*. Online. Available at: http://www.cesnur.org/recens/potter_059.htm.

Jing, X. (2007) "Universal Potter," *Beijing Review*, 50: 22.

Khan, A.R. and Riskin, C. (2001) *Inequality and Poverty in China in the Age of Globalization*, Oxford and New York: Oxford University Press.

Lee, C.C. (2003) "The Global and the National of the Chinese Media," in C.C. Lee (ed.) *Chinese Media, Global Contexts*, New York: Routledge.

Li, C. (1998) *China: The Consumer Revolution*, Singapore: John Wiley & Sons.

Li, J. (2004) "Are You Middle Class Yet? The Middle Class Bubble in China," *Xinwen Zhoukan*.

McElroy, D. (2002) "China Faces a Middle-Class Mutiny," *The Daily Telegraph*, 13 April.

Moore, T.G. (2000) "China and Globalization," in S.S. Kim (ed.) *East Asia and Globalization*, Maryland: Rowman & Littlefield.

Mseka, A. (2001) "China to Become World's Largest Insurance Market," *Advisor Today*, 96: 34–35.

Poon, N. (2003) "Subsumption or Consumption?" *Cultural Anthropology*, 18: 469–492.

Qiu, X. (2005) "No Well-off Farmers, No Well-off China," *Asia Times Online*. Online. Available at: http://www.atimes.com/atimes/China/GD29Ad03.html.

Ross, A. (2006) *Fast Boat to China*, New York: Pantheon Books.

Seiter, E. (1993) *Sold Separately: Parents and Children in Consumer Culture*, New Jersey: Rutgers University Press.

Steinberg, S.R. and Kincheloe, J.L. (1998) *Kinderculture: The Corporate Construction of Childhood*, Colorado: Westview Press.

Tang, R. (2006) "Chinese Children's Literature in the 21st Century," *Bookbird*, 44: 21–29.

Tang, Y. (2005) "Harry Potter versus Local Heroes," *Beijing Review*, September 8.

Wang, J. (2005) "Bourgeois Bohemians in China? Neo-tribes and the Urban Imaginary," *China Quarterly*, 532–548.

Wei, M. (2008) "Harry Potter Weaves his Magic in China," *China Today*, January.

Yan, Y. (2000) "Of Hamburger and Social Space: Consuming McDonald's in Beijing," in D.S. Davis (ed.) *The Consumer Revolution in Urban China*, Berkeley: University of California Press.

Yan, Y. (2002) "Managed Globalization: State Power and Cultural Transition in China," in P.L. Berger and S.P. Huntington (eds) *Many Globalizations: Cultural Diversity in the Contemporary World*, Oxford and New York: Oxford University Press.

3

ONE REGION, TWO MODERNITIES

Disneyland in Tokyo and Hong Kong

Micky Lee and Anthony Y.H. Fung

Asia, as a vast geographical region, can hardly be considered a homogeneous entity in economic terms. At the start of the twenty-first century, the region consisted of developed economies, most notably Japan, fast-growing economies such as China and India, as well as economies that were hardly integrated into the global economy, such as Sri Lanka and Nepal. Since the countries of Asia are at different stages of economic development, we can assume that these populations have unequal access to communication technologies and transnational media cultures. Despite the region's drastic divergences of economic development, political and business leaders in Asia and elsewhere certainly believe that Asia will catch up to, if not surpass, North American and European economies sometime in the twenty-first century. What emerges from this assumption is that Asia will fundamentally be more like the West—economically, politically, and socially. Scholars of globalization studies have long been fascinated by the question of cultural homogenization—some lament at the ubiquity of McDonald's, Starbucks, and Disney in major cities in the world, while others argue that the locals in these cities use and understand global cultures differently.

This chapter will aim to continue the study of cultural homogenization by looking at the Disneyland theme parks in Tokyo and Hong Kong through the assessment how the locals in these two cities make sense of the park. From our ethnographic observations, there is strong evidence that in a global site such as Disneyland, the locals do not attempt to emulate western behavior; yet, global sites train the local populations to be global consumers. Furthermore, global sites would not transform Asia into a region like the West, instead they provide symbols for Asians to experience the West as an imaginary concept. The desire to experience the West probes the locals to consume signs and symbols that represent the West, which consequently complete the modernity project.

What is modernity? What does it entail? Gidden described in his book *The Consequences of Modernity* that modernity is the "modes of social life or organization which emerged in Europe from about the seventeenth century onwards and which subsequently became more or less worldwide in their influence" (Giddens 1990). He also describes the consequences of modernity, two of which are the separation of time and space and the disembedding of social systems.

In pre-modern societies, one's experience of time is space bound, and one's experience of space is time bound. For example, human beings in pre-modern societies planned their actions and activities based on the time of day and based on the season of the year. Without electricity and modern transportation, pre-modern human beings were more likely to work on production (such as farming) in places close to their place of residence. In fact, there may not be a strong sense of the separation of the work place from the residence. Modern luxuries and transportations such as trains and motor vehicles enable modern beings to work on production away from home. Additionally, the invention of electricity allowed workers to extend their working day into nightfall. Arguably, the concept of leisure time emerged when these workers realized the desire to partake in non-work activities during their free time; shopping, traveling, and various forms of entertainment.

Arguably, human relations in pre-modern societies were relatively fixed; familial ties (such as the ties between parents and children) and societal roles and relations (such as between a landlord and farmer) define both production and reproduction. The fixed relations dictate who is to work, and who is to stay at home. In those days, working-class parents would require their children to work in order to make ends meet. In modern societies, however, human relations are more flexible. Production and reproduction activities are determined by more than just familial and societal roles and relations. Today, in most societies, working-class children attend school and are legally forbidden to work. During school holidays, Disneyland is a popular vacation destination visited by families of all social classes. Inside the theme park, all visitors, regardless of class, are promised to be treated equally. For example, some visitors may earn less than Disneyland employees, but will be treated with common courtesy. Similarly, in the park, children from affluent families and working-class families generally do not relate to each other based on their parents' professions and income. In the service industry, customers are those who can pay, regardless of their class background.

Giddens believes that modernity is inherently a western project, which has a universal impact on other societies (Giddens 1990). If Giddens is correct, then to be modern is to be more like the West; in fact, the West evaluates the modernity of other societies according to its own standard of modernity. Historically, Asian societies learned of modernity under western colonization and foreign occupation. Therefore, modernity in Asia has always been linked to and related to the West. The building of Disneyland in Asia should, therefore, be considered as a part of the modernity project. Not only has the Disney Corporation been keen on introducing the park to Asia, but various Asian states have also been willing to oblige in opening

44 Micky Lee and Anthony Y.H. Fung

their doors to a foreign company in order to illustrate and bring western modes of modernity to their locals.

The political economy of communication

While investigating the building of Disneyland in various Asian cities, this study employs a political economic perspective. According to Mosco, political economy is "the study of the social relations, particularly power relations, that mutually constitute the production, distribution, and consumption of resources" (Mosco 2005). This perspective pays attention to the media institutions and corporations that produce commodities in the media and cultural markets. Media corporations decide what to produce and how these goods are distributed and consumed in both domestic and international markets. The political economic approach also takes into account the relation between the state and the market. State policies such as taxation, media regulations, and press freedom may at times impede or facilitate market activities. Historically, political economists have done extensive studies on media industries in North America and Europe, but they have done relatively few studies in the Asian region. In discussing the influence of the political economic perspective in the developing world, Mosco affirms that most studies and discourses took place in Latin America, while there has been little that has taken place in Asia (Mosco 2009). As aforementioned, many political and business leaders have their sights set on Asia as the next world-leading economy—the Asian market is seen as an oil well because of its huge populations. Therefore, the political economic approach is undeniably valuable for us to understand how transnational corporations work with Asian states to open up the Asian media market.

Wasko is one researcher who has carried out extensive political economic analysis on Disney (Wasko 2001; Wasko *et al.* 2001); instead of looking at the content of Disney media (such as the images from Disney movies and the aesthetic images of Disneyland) and how the audience understands Disney, Wasko looks at the business operations of the Disney Corporation. Disneyland is a means for the company to maximize its profits; the theme park is, in fact, the division of the corporation that makes the most profit. According to Davis, two-thirds of Disney's operating costs came from theme parks during the late 1980s and early 1990s (Davis 1996). The following strategies are utilized by Disneyland to ensure maximum profit. First, Disneyland employs synergy. In order to promote Disney films, Disney characters are integrated into the parks as part of rides and games. An example is the *Toy Story* ride in Tomorrowland. In turn, the theme park can also be promoted on Disney television network. Second, Disneyland employs the strategies of commodification and consumption. The theme parks have gift shops and restaurants for visitors to shop and spend money. It is common for visitors to exit a game through the gift shop. It is Disney's intention for visitors to take a commercialized experience home, in the form of a stuffed toy, for example. Third, Disneyland takes great care to determine their entrance fee. Though the ticket price to enter the theme park is not unaffordable, the total cost for a family of four can be expensive. Moreover, visitors often have to pay for lodging inside the park. A trip to Disneyland can be a major expense for a family of moderate means. Nevertheless, Disneyland is a common trip destination for most American families. An informal survey in our classes revealed that most American college students have been to one, if not two, Disneylands. Some would go to Disneyland with friends and family every year. Fourth, Disneyland "recycles old materials" by blending classic Disney characters with modern Disney characters. Classic characters such as Snow White and the Seven Dwarves and Cinderella, along with modern characters such as Buzz Lightyear, both have a prominent presence in the theme parks. Though younger generations may more readily recognize characters such as Lilo and Stitch and Nemo, rather than Snow White and Goofy, classic Disney characters help to attract an older generation. Fifth, another prominent strategy that the Disney Corporation employs is global expansion. A theme park is an extremely effective take-off point for the penetration of multinational entertainment media (Davis 1996). Outside of the USA, Disneyland was built in populous, global cities such as Paris, Tokyo, and Hong Kong; Disney also recently decided to open a fourth international park in Shanghai which will open its doors in 2015. The international parks do not differ dramatically from the American ones as the company is not keen on investing in creating new concepts. The company believes that the attraction of Disneyland is its faithfulness to the original Disneyland in California. As the following analysis will show, Disney wants tourists to feel as though they were visiting the original park in Anaheim.

In the next two sections, we contextualize the features of Tokyo Disneyland and Hong Kong Disneyland and explicate how both locations have been constructing such modernity since the mid-twentieth century.

Modernity in Hong Kong

Hong Kong Disneyland opened its doors in December 2006, making it the third Disneyland to be built and operated outside of the United States. Despite its small scale, Hong Kong Disneyland had ambitious plans to attract five million visitors annually. As of early 2009, attendance figures have been astonishingly disappointing. In order to attract more visitors and to compete with the new Disneyland in Shanghai, the Disney Corporation decided to open three more themed areas in 2011. Arguably, the Disney Corporation has been introducing the Disney brand to mainland Chinese who visit Hong Kong. Nevertheless, evidence from attendance figures and ethnographic observations show that mainland Chinese tourists do not enjoy the theme park in the way that the company intends it to be. Even though mainland Chinese tourists are unfamiliar with Disney characters, it has not stopped them from visiting Hong Kong Disneyland. In one of our earlier studies, we asked why Hong Kong Disneyland did not localize Disneyland to accommodate the taste of mainland Chinese visitors (Fung and Lee 2009). In this study, we revisit this question by applying Giddens' concept of modernity to understand the different economic and cultural conditions under which Disneyland was introduced to Japan and to Hong Kong. First, we discuss how modernity was designed for the Hong Kong locals.

Turner and Ngan argue that modernity was designed by the British government for the Hong Kong population in order to suppress social unrest in the 1960s (Turner and Ngan 1995). Annexed to Britain after two opium wars, Hong Kong served as an important entrepôt during the 150 years of British colonization. Similar to other colonization experiences, the British colonial government was not interested in initiating and supporting unity among the Chinese living in Hong Kong. The open border between Hong Kong and mainland China allowed the Chinese to move freely. When the Chinese Communist Party formally took control of China in 1949, many Chinese, particularly those with money and private property, migrated to Hong Kong in fear of seizure of their personal assets and capital. As the population of Hong Kong exploded in the 1950s, it became clear that Hong Kong was not a temporary shelter for most Chinese but a permanent residence for many. The colonial government turned a blind eye to the desires of Hong Kong Chinese that yearned for a sense of belonging, that yearned for a national home.

The Star Ferry Riot of 1966 sparked social unrest among local Hong Kong residents. Dissatisfied with the fare hike of the cross harbor ferry, local residents initiated a high-profile demonstration against the ferry company as well as the colonial government. In turn, the colonial government decided to deploy police to suppress local unrest; this was based on the fear that the Chinese Communist Party was behind the local demonstrators. At the same time, the colonial government realized that local residents needed a common identity and a sense of belonging to the colony. Turner and Ngan suggest that the Hong Kong identity was designed and constructed to create a difference between the Chinese in Hong Kong and the Chinese in mainland China (Turner and Ngan 1995).

The success of a united Hong Kong Chinese identity also depended upon the growing economic power of the populace, and the prevalence of popular culture in Hong Kong. As an entrepôt, Hong Kong not only served as a trading center between east and west during the 1960s, but also as a manufacturing center for exported goods. The British colonial government explained the miraculous economic development of Hong Kong by the hard-working nature of the Hong Kong Chinese; however, low labor cost, and low taxes and tariffs all attracted foreign investment. Undeniably, the influx of foreign capital contributed to Hong Kong's economic development as well.

As Lee wrote in 2009, the so-called "Factory Girl" was hailed as the modern woman in the discourse of Hong Kong popular culture in 1960 (Lee 2009). The state and media often have used and continue to use women to represent modernity (Young 2003). The Factory Girl epitomizes two significant characteristics of modernity: the separation of time and space, and the disembedding of social systems. Factory work creates standardized work hours and leisure hours for the workers. The Factory Girl was laborer during the day and a consumer during her leisure time after work. The Factory Girl was hailed as a modern woman because she worked outside of the household for a living; the salary she earned allowed her to be economically independent. Hong Kong popular culture in the 1960s also promoted the

Factory Girl as a modern ideal, evident through many events. First, the state-sponsored trade shows in which a Miss Trade Show pageant was held, demonstrates this. The Factory Girl was not only a productive worker, but she was also an aesthetic object to look at. Second, Cantonese films starring Po Chun Chan and Fong Fong Siu narrate the romantic trials and tribulations of ordinary, modern women. Popular songs hailed the "million years to come" for the Factory Girl. What is remarkable about the Factory Girl identity is that it is a predominately consumer identity. Although the Factory Girl is defined by her job, it was ultimately the beauty, the freedom, and the independence that was emphasized. The Factory Girl shared very few common interests with women living under Mao's China in the 1960s, where women were seen as asexual proletarians.

From the 1960s up until the handover in 1997, the Hong Kong Chinese identity has undergone several major changes. The Factory Girl became something of the past when factories moved north across the border, and when women began to occupy more white collar and professional jobs. Furthermore, the state redesigned the Hong Kong Chinese identity at the juncture of every political crisis, such as the Sino-British Declaration promulgated in 1984, and the subsequent waves of emigration to Canada, Australia, and the USA. The design and development of the Hong Kong Chinese identity has been a successful campaign. The difference between the Hong Kong Chinese and the mainland Chinese is so ingrained among the locals that they have come to view the mainland Chinese as the inferior other. The Hong Kong Chinese is believed to be modern, western, street smart, and money minded, while the mainland Chinese is viewed as culturally backward and poor. In order to ensure Hong Kong Disneyland is attractive to the mainland Chinese, the park has to ensure that the difference between Hong Kong and mainland Chinese be emphasized, not eliminated. The local media of Hong Kong are always keen on pointing out the "uncivilized" behavior of the mainland Chinese in the park; behaviors such as smoking, jumping queues, and children urinating in public are among the many actions that are looked down upon. Perhaps these actions are not as common as the media claim, but local Hong Kong media uses the case of Disneyland to maintain and reinforce the difference between mainland Chinese and Hong Kong Chinese.

Hong Kong Disneyland

The Hong Kong Disneyland was a joint investment between the Hong Kong government and the Disney Company; both parties negotiated behind closed doors before the agreement was announced to the Hong Kong public. There was a major outcry, however, due to the unequal nature of the partnership—the Hong Kong government was responsible for 90 percent of construction costs, while holding only 57 percent of the shares of the joint venture. In addition, the Hong Kong government leased the land for free, and built necessary infrastructure (such as railways and highways) and supporting facilities (such as the police and fire stations). Meanwhile, Disney assumed full control of the management and retained the profits from merchandise sales. Why would the Hong Kong government agree to such an unfair deal?

Lee argues that Hong Kong Disneyland wanted, post-1997, to achieve their aspiration in becoming "Asia's world city" (Lee 2009). The chief secretary at the time, Anson Chan, made it known to the public that Hong Kong and Disneyland are two well-known global brands. To position Hong Kong successfully in the post-colonial era, the government itself promotes Hong Kong as Asia's world city; curiously, Hong Kong locals do not identify Hong Kong as China's world city. The distancing and emptying of Hong Kong from China once again reinforces the differences between Hong Kong Chinese and mainland Chinese.

Does the Disney Corporation share the same goals as the Hong Kong government? Fundamentally, what interests the Disney Corporation is the strategic location of Hong Kong. Still fettered by draconian Chinese government regulations, foreign media companies cannot expand to China without forming a joint venture with local companies. Foreign media companies also have to face arbitrary media regulations by the Chinese government. For example, the American magazine *Rolling Stone* was forced to shut down after its debut issue; this shows that the Chinese government has strict control over all media content in the country. In order to pave their way to China, Disney decided that a theme park in Hong Kong would be an important first step to expand to the Chinese market. Before the Chinese watch the Disney Channel and Disney movies, they are encouraged to be familiarized with the world of Disney and to adapt to the Disney lifestyle; a theme park serves these purposes well.

Occupying only 100 acres, Hong Kong Disneyland is much smaller than the two American Disneylands as well as their Japanese and European counterparts; it is a miniature of the original Anaheim theme park. As aforementioned, the second phase of Hong Kong Disneyland was suspended due to disappointing attendance figures. The Disney Corporation did not plan for the Hong Kong theme park to be a full-scale Disneyland. The corporation hoped that a sampling of the Hong Kong park would entice the mainland Chinese to visit the authentic and original park (Orwall 1999). There are four main destinations in the Hong Kong theme park: Main Street USA, Tomorrowland, Adventureland, and Fantasyland. Additionally, the two hotels (Hong Kong Disneyland Hotel and Disney's Hollywood Hotel) located outside the park are modeled after their counterparts in the USA.

The journey to Disneyland does not begin at the entrance, but at the Hong Kong train stop, Sunny Bay. A Disney railway line was built specially for the park; the train that takes passengers to Disneyland is intended to be a part of the magic kingdom. The windows of the train are in the shape of Mickey Mouse's head, while sculptures of Disney characters are displayed in the compartments. Additionally, the Disneyland stop is unlike other train stations on the Hong Kong railway line; the Disney stop is reminiscent of the Victorian era. Arguably, the train station heightens the anticipation of the passengers, which may trigger more consumption in the park as visitors would have already been acclimated to Disney. Additionally, the train station serves as a teaser for future patronage to those who cannot afford to visit the theme park.

During their negotiations with Disney, the Hong Kong government suggested that Chinese elements could be integrated into the park. The Disney Company rejected the suggestion, noting that the park should provide an authentic experience for visitors (Slater 1999). However, Disney changed its mind when mainland Chinese visitors did not seem excited to pose for pictures with Mickey Mouse (Fowler 2008). Though the theme park aims to provide an authentic Disney experience for visitors, the languages they choose to utilize, the restaurant menus, and the inventory of the gift shops reflects efforts of localization.

Hong Kong Disneyland caters to three main target groups—local residents, mainland Chinese, and visitors from Asia and around the world. Most of the signs in the park are written in both English and traditional Chinese characters. Furthermore, Disneyland employees are required to be fluent in conversational English, Cantonese, and Mandarin. However, as we stated in an earlier study, only two games in the Hong Kong Disneyland provide services in three languages. *Stitch Encounter*, an interactive game, allows visitors to choose between attending a Mandarin, Cantonese, or English show (Fung and Lee 2009). *Jungle River Cruise* provides Cantonese, Mandarin, or English tour guides aboard the boats. Other attractions only provide Cantonese and English services. For example, the *Lion King* music festival is narrated in English, but is accompanied by occasional story synopses in Cantonese. The ride, *The Many Adventures of Winnie the Pooh*, has English audio only. The live show *Golden Mickeys* is narrated in Cantonese while the songs are sung in English; the screens next to the stage provide visitors with English and Chinese subtitles. The language barrier may not be an obstacle to visitors who are familiar with Disney characters and products. Because children are Disney's main target group, the language barrier may not be an obstacle at all. Arguably, amusement such as fireworks and parades would catch a child's attention as much as a ride would.

Hong Kong Disneyland takes into account the culinary and shopping tastes of Chinese consumers. Food stalls and restaurants sell familiar Chinese delicacies such as dumplings, noodle soup, barbecue meat with rice, barbecue pork buns, and dim sum. These Chinese delicacies are sold alongside traditional western street food such as hotdogs and corn on the cob. Another area that the park accommodates Chinese consumers is the gift shops. For example, a shop in Main Street USA sells Disney jewelry in 24 carat gold; gold is a precious metal that is a perennial favorite of the Chinese. Furthermore, the gift shops also sell Mickey Mouse stuffed dolls donning traditional Chinese costumes.

In order to enjoy Disneyland as the company intends it to be, visitors should be familiar with Disney—its characters, the stories behind them, and the values of Disney. They will enjoy Disneyland more if they are familiar with Disney films, cartoons, comics, and merchandise. An older local couple was overheard in the park saying they did not know how to enjoy the park; a Disney employee responded by pointing out the *Golden Mickeys* show. However, it is doubtful this couple would find the show meaningful if they were unfamiliar with the characters. The show would be more enjoyable if the viewer had knowledge of songs from Disney movies, and if they knew both classic Disney characters (Mickey Mouse, Minnie Mouse, Goofy, Donald Duck) and new Disney characters (Nemo, Little Mermaid, and the Hunchback of Notre Dame). Without knowledge about Disney, the *Golden Mickeys* show would merely be an entertaining spectacle.

Disney hopes that the mainland Chinese will be familiarized with Disney characters and its values before the company expands to the Chinese media market. The Disney Corporation seems to have miscalculated what little knowledge mainland Chinese hold in regards to the meanings of Disneyland. The Disney Corporation has also discovered that mainland Chinese visitors do not spend as much money as the company previously hoped and predicted they would; these visitors not spending money is not conducive to the company's goals. Nonetheless, there are a few reasons to account for this lack of interest in spending money. First, most mainland Chinese tourists do not spend one full day in the Disneyland theme park; due to travel restrictions, many of them only visit Hong Kong for a few days. Therefore, these tourists attempt to travel to as many places in Hong Kong as possible; packaged tours usually include a trip to Disneyland. The visitors stop by Disneyland briefly in order to avoid paying extra. Second, many mainland tourists prefer taking photos to going on the rides; some only walk around the park and spend their few hours taking pictures for memories. On many occasions, Disneyland employees have had to wait for tourists to finish taking pictures before they were able to start the rides. Because Disneyland is obsessed with effective management, the management finds these delays unacceptable. Third, mainland Chinese tourists are generally reluctant to buy souvenirs and to eat at the restaurants. The few hours spent in the park does not result in them wanting to buy a souvenir to "take a piece of memory home."

In order to remedy mainland visitors' reluctance to consume in Disneyland, the management issued a brochure and ran a television advertisement in the mainland. The purpose of these advertisements was to educate the mainland Chinese on how to enjoy Disneyland and why Disneyland is enjoyable (Fowler and Marr 2006). The television commercial featured a starry eyed girl who sees the magic that Disneyland brings. Reflecting China's one child policy, the girl is surrounded by her parents and grandmother. Although Disneyland is advertised as family entertainment, most mainland Chinese visitors to Disneyland are adults that joined a tour which included Disneyland as a stop. This, again, demonstrates the discrepancy between how Disneyland is being viewed by mainland Chinese and how it is supposed to be viewed (in the eyes of the Disney Corporation).

If most mainland Chinese tourists do not enjoy Disneyland as it is intended to be, then why do they keep visiting the park? In an earlier study, we reasoned that mainland Chinese tourists visit Hong Kong and Disneyland in order to experience modernity and "the West on Chinese soil" (Fung and Lee 2009). In the eyes of the mainland Chinese, Hong Kong, as a former colony, represents to them the exotic and the western. Disneyland has come to Hong Kong for mainland Chinese to experience the West; they ultimately do not have to travel to Europe or North America to gain this experience. Some mainland Chinese have said that they found Europe and North America to be boring during Christmas time because most locals stay at home during the cold winter. On the other hand, they view spending Christmas in Hong Kong as very festive because the majority of the locals are out celebrating in the agreeable weather. Clearly, these mainland Chinese do not care if Christmas is "authentic" or not in Hong Kong.

The images promoted by Hong Kong Disneyland through their website illustrates what westernized Chinese should look like. In one advertisement, young Chinese girls dressed up as princesses surround Snow White, who is modeled by a Caucasian woman. Another advertisement depicts a Chinese boy dressed in a sweater and button-down shirt—he interacts with Buzz Lightyear with a Caucasian couple visible in the background. An advertisement for the Disneyland hotel features Chinese parents with their only children. In all instances, the men are wearing formal clothing; they all don dress pants and dress shoes and either wear a polo shirt with a sweater draped over their shoulders or a dress shirt. Contrarily, the models featured on the American Disneyland website dress much more casually. This discrepancy also exists between how Hong Kong Chinese and mainland Chinese dress when they visit the park. The locals generally dress casually in denim jeans and sneakers. On the other hand, the mainland Chinese visitors dress formally; men wear suits, leather shoes, and sometimes carry briefcases while women walk around the park in high heels. Do the images on the Disneyland website influence how Chinese visitors dress when they visit the park? It can be suggested that Hong Kong Chinese, who identify themselves as westernized and modern, view a trip to Disneyland as entertainment and relaxation. To the mainland Chinese, however, visiting Disneyland allows them to experience what the west is like; dressing in formal western attire may help them feel like they are becoming more modernized and westernized.

Modernity in Japan

Japan opened its doors to the west during the Meiji Restoration. In turn, many Japanese adopted and integrated western fashion, education, and art into their lives and society. Western ideas arrived on the island mainly through educated Japanese nationals who returned home and spread these ideas, and also through western missionaries, and westerners living in Japan (Tobin 1992). However, the American post-war occupation of Japan had a more direct and pronounced influence on Japanese society. Some scholars believe that Japan's defeat in World War II demonstrates "modernity gone wrong"; therefore, Japan needed to embrace modernity the correct way in the post-war era (Gluck 1993). Iwabuchi argues that Japan endeavored to create a distinction between themselves and the rest of the Asian region.

> While the West played the role of the modern other to be emulated, Asia was cast as the image of Japan's past, a negative portrait which illustrates the extent to which Japan has been successfully modernized according to western standards.
>
> *Iwabuchi 2002*

52 Micky Lee and Anthony Y.H. Fung

Ultimately, the West has served as a reference point for Japan's modernization process.

Due to rapid economic development, post-war Japan was constructed as a "middle-mass society" (*shin chūkan taishū shaki*); trade surpluses in the 1960s and 1970s transformed Japan into an affluent society (Tobin 1992). In a 1993 survey, 90 percent of Japanese identified themselves as part of the middle class; the media have helped Japanese to construct their social classes. The national television channel NHK is widely consumed by Japanese, and it has helped in promoting Japan as a modern consumer society (Ivy 1993). Prior to World War II, Japanese consumers sought after goods sold in western-style department stores. Western luxury goods have become the prime objects of desire after the Japanese became more affluent. In addition, the soaring real estate price in Tokyo prohibited many from owning a house or apartment; they instead turned to the purchase of western luxury goods and high-tech products (Mitsuhiro 1994; Tobin 1992). Notably, the French luxury brand Louis Vuitton had the largest market in Japan.

Some scholars have argued that despite Japanese's clear appetite for western products, they do not merely copy and take from western ideas. Instead, they appropriate western ideas and transform them into something uniquely Japanese (Atkins 2007; Iwabuchi 2002; Tobin 1992). One illustrious example is the Japanese dish curry hamburger rice—it is a dish that blends ingredients from Indian, American, and Chinese cuisines. Often enough, Americans cannot identify the appropriated western goods, food, and images. American celebrities such as Madonna, Cameron Diaz, and Brad Pitt have appeared in Japanese advertisements. Yet, those advertisements are only shown in Japanese media. Japanese companies are willing to lavish money on American icons, but they want to promote the celebrities in a style that conforms to Japanese ideas. Oftentimes, these images are too "clean" for American consumers. Correspondingly, Iwabuchi suggests, "what is experienced through Japanese popular culture is actually a highly materialistic Japanese version of the American original" (Iwabuchi 2002). Others suggest that the foreign is a commodified sign of reassurance (Ivy 1995); the Japanese need to transform the foreign into a manageable sign of order. Ultimately, Japan "Americanizes" its society in order to "exoticize" itself: "when Japanese consciously or unconsciously make themselves into, or see themselves as, the object of Western desire and imagination," they are "self-orientalizing" themselves (Tobin 1992).

During the 1970s and 1980s, Japan National Railway (JNR) carried out two large advertising campaigns entitled *Discover Japan* and *Exotic Japan*. The idea behind the campaigns is that in order for Japanese to find home (the countryside), they need to leave "home" (the city). Critics see Tokyo as the "west" of Japan whilst the Japanese countryside is the "real" Japan (Tobin 1992). The JNR campaigns encouraged Japanese urbanites to discover Japanese heritage and history through a journey to a Confucian and Chinese-influenced Japan. The journey is "a Japanese self (re)discovering its authenticity by moving through original landscapes" (Ivy 1995).

Tokyo Disneyland

Opening its doors in 1984 at the height of Japan's economic boom, Tokyo Disneyland was the first Disneyland to be built outside of the USA. The theme park is owned by the Oriental Land Company, which aimed to replicate the original Disneyland in the Japanese city of Tokyo. Oriental Land Company promoted the park as a comfortable and calm place outside of the city (Brannen 1992). Furthermore, Tokyo Disneyland is promoted as a place where Japanese can enjoy a foreign vacation at home. The opening of the theme park gave the Japanese a sense of achievement and completion (Mitsuhiro 1994). Although Japan experienced a decade-long economic recession in the 1990s, Tokyo Disneyland remained the most profitable Disney theme park.

Even though Tokyo Disneyland is said to be a copy of the original Anaheim Disneyland, it is evident that much effort has been put into localizing the park, making it familiar yet exotic to Japanese (Brannen 1992). Because international visitors only account for six percent of all visitors (Yoshimi 2001), the main language used in the park is Japanese. Most of the signs are in both Japanese characters and English, but the employees are only fluent in Japanese. In addition, many games such as *Stitch Encounter* and live shows such as *The Golden Mickeys Show* are featured in Japanese only. The most popular restaurant in the park, the Great American Waffle Company, only provides a Japanese menu. From our observation, there is only one instance where another language (Mandarin) is used in the park; it is to announce the height requirement for racing cars. Employees who are hired overseas (such as glassblowers and watchmakers) only speak English. The craftspeople are part of the localization strategy because the original Disneyland does not employ this feature; its primary function is to convince visitors that they are not in Japan. It does not matter if local tourists do not fully understand what the craftspeople are saying as long as they remain and sound foreign.

Tokyo Disneyland was built on the Japanese imagination of what America is supposed to be like. Mitsuhiro believes Disneyland provides "the visitors with a single interpretive context in which they make sense out of their narrative experience" (Mitsuhiro 1994). How Japanese make sense of the park is illustrated by the name changes of some iconic Disneyland locations. For example, Sleeping Beauty Castle became Cinderella Castle, as Japanese visitors tend to associate Cinderella with Disney. In another instance, Main Street USA became the World Bazaar. This name change occurred because Japanese tourists probably do not fully understand Walt Disney's nostalgia for the small midwest American town and they do not know what small-town America stands for. On the other hand, the World Bazaar implies a shopping center with goods from all around the world, which does not require a specific cultural understanding. Furthermore, Frontierland became Westernland. Although Japanese are familiarized with western culture through film and television, they may not know why the American west used to be called the frontier. It is not Disney's job to offer visitors a lesson on US history

54 Micky Lee and Anthony Y.H. Fung

and geography. As long as the attractions resonate with Japanese vision of America, Tokyo Disneyland has achieved its goal.

Other localization efforts are evident: employees in the Tokyo theme park put their last names in addition to their first names on their name tags (Brennan 1992), unlike American employees who only use their first names. Additionally, there are few food stalls in Tokyo Disneyland because it is impolite to eat while standing in Japanese culture (Watson 2006). The park management of Tokyo Disneyland is more permissive of local behavior in the park than it is of its counterpart in Hong Kong. For example, it is common for Japanese visitors in Tokyo Disneyland to sit on the curbside watching the Disney parades. Some visitors even bring Disney stuffed toys and line them up on picnic cloths during the parade (Yoshimi 2001). Contrarily, Hong Kong Disneyland does not allow visitors to sit on the floor as it is associated with the behavior of the "uncivilized" mainland Chinese.

Why is the Tokyo theme park more localized than the Hong Kong theme park? A political economic perspective assumes that the ultimate goal of Disneyland is to maximize profit. The Disney management understands that Japanese visitors were keen consumers even before Disneyland opened its door in Tokyo; in fact, Disney movies were exported to Japan as early as the 1940s. Furthermore, the Disney management also understands that Japanese spend more money inside Tokyo Disneyland than Americans do in the American Disneylands (Brannen 1992). Tokyo Disneyland houses 48 shops and 49 restaurants, which is a large number given the small size of the park.

One region, two modernities

According to Giddens, modernity is inherently western (Giddens 1990); the modernity project is oriented towards the future. When political and business leaders suggest that the region of Asia will be the next major global power, they assume that Asia will be modernized and become more like the West; some worry that the cultural differences between the East and West will be effaced. The analyses of the behavior of the visitors of the Hong Kong and Tokyo Disneylands show that these visitors are far from adopting American behavior. However, it is clear that Chinese and Japanese generally aspire to be more westernized—to be modern is an avenue to becoming like the West. However, the West is an imaginary concept rather than a concrete reality; the locus of the West is not anchored in one single country or in one single culture.

A comparison of the conditions of modernity under which Hong Kong Disneyland and Tokyo Disneyland were built shows a few similarities between the parks. First, both cities of Hong Kong and Tokyo experienced foreign occupation under which a western style government, economy, and education were imposed upon the local population. In the case of Hong Kong, the local Chinese did not have a sense of modernity until the colonial government designed a western, modern, Hong Kong Chinese identity for the locals. Second, the condition of modernity is interdependent with economic development. The local populations in Hong Kong and Japan were encouraged to work hard to raise their own living standards. Economic development led to soaring real estate prices; city dwellers do not harbor hopes of becoming home owners and, in turn, want to spend money elsewhere. Third, both places look to the West for recognition and affirmation of their modernity. Unlike the French, the Hong Kong and Japanese locals welcomed Disneyland to their cities; they see recognition by Disney as an acknowledgment of the modernity of their cities. As mentioned earlier on, Hong Kong's former Chief Secretary Anson Chan stated, "one cannot put a price on Disney picking Hong Kong as the location of the third overseas Disneyland." Furthermore, when the Hong Kong press condemned the behaviors of mainland Chinese in the park, they quoted the American management for affirmation.

Nevertheless, the modernities of Hong Kong and Japan are different, and the Disneyland theme parks in Hong Kong and Tokyo reflect this claim. Hong Kong is at present a special administrative region of China; the political future of Hong Kong remains uncertain. Currently, the Hong Kong government promotes Hong Kong as "Asia's world city". The Globalization and World Cities Research Network included Hong Kong in their top ten list of alpha world cities.[1] However, the Hong Kong government is ambiguous as to whether Hong Kong is already a world city or whether Hong Kong is only aspiring to be one (Flowerdew 2004). The building of Disneyland may be confirmation that Hong Kong is indeed already a world-class city.

Hong Kong Disneyland differs from Tokyo Disneyland in that the Hong Kong government manages the park the "American way"; it is eager to learn how to manage a theme park from the management sent from Disney Headquarters. Hong Kong Disneyland is a faithful replica of the original Anaheim Disneyland as it attempts to present to mainland Chinese what the west is like. Additionally, the Hong Kong park depends on overseas visitors for its success. The submission of the Hong Kong government to the American Disney Corporation allows the company to strategically use the park in training mainland Chinese visitors to be reliable consumers. The Disney management has previously stated that it needs to hold the hands of Chinese in order to teach them how to enjoy the park (Marr and Fowler 2006). Evidently, Disney attempts to impose American behavior on mainland Chinese visitors. For example, Americans are not supposed to have a fixed time for lunch and snacks, and Americans are not supposed to sit on curbs (*Oriental Daily* 2005). Mainland Chinese visitors experience the west through Hong Kong Disneyland through various ways: they visit the park, dress up in formal clothing, and take pictures inside the park. Nevertheless, these visitors are more thrilled at seeing non-Disney elements in the park such as Chinese New Years festivities that include attractions such as dragon dancing and the God of Wealth (Fowler 2008).

In comparison, Tokyo Disneyland is much more localized than the Hong Kong one. The management at Tokyo Disneyland changed the names of many features to suit local tastes. It also expects visitors to speak Japanese and does not require employees to be proficient in English. The Japanese credit card (JCB) is the only credit card accepted in the park. Tokyo Disneyland has more freedom to localize due to the consumption power of Japanese. Yoshimi argues that Japanese have come to see Disneyland as their own and, in turn, believe that they are characters of the theme park by participating in it (Yoshimi 2001). On the Tokyo Disneyland website, there is no image that shows a family enjoying the park together. The Disney Corporation does not mind how the Japanese view the park; they may not use the park like Americans, but as long as they consume Disney images and products, Disney has achieved its goals.

The ethnographic discoveries of Disneyland in Hong Kong and Tokyo are in accordance with Watson's findings of McDonald's fast-food restaurants in Hong Kong and Japan (Watson 2000). Since McDonald's "golden arches" arrived in Hong Kong in 1975, Hong Kong locals have not seen McDonald's as an outlet of American culture. Instead, the locals utilize and localize the restaurant in various ways. McDonald's has become a public space where not only retirees linger but also one where young students hang out after class for many hours. The locals associate McDonald's as a place for cheap food, but not necessarily one that is for lower classes only. McDonald's' recent arrival in big cities throughout China proved to be successful among middle-class parents because they view McDonald's as a tool for their children to learn about the outside world (Yan 2007). Also, even if adults do not particularly enjoy the food at McDonald's, they enjoy the atmosphere and the clean environment. Many Chinese adults believe McDonald's represents what modernity stands for.

One topic that can be further explored is how the Chinese learn and derive modernity from the Japanese. Iwabuchi suggests that the rapid economic growth of select Asian countries has pushed Japan to rediscover Asia (Iwabuchi 2002). For a long time, Japan distanced itself from Asia as they viewed the region to be stuck in the past. Iwabuchi further states, "the significant role played by Japanese civilization is evident in its diffusion of western material civilization through the production of affordable commodities for Asian markets" (Iwabuchi 2002). It is undeniable that Japanese popular culture has had a significant influence on Hong Kong popular culture. Prior to the opening of Hong Kong Disneyland, many Hong Kong residents had already visited the Tokyo park; in the eyes of many Hong Kong locals, the Tokyo park is the original Disneyland. Hong Kong locals compare their Disneyland to the Tokyo Disneyland; perhaps Hong Kong Disneyland is viewed as the "original park" to the mainland Chinese and will be the main park to compare the Shanghai park to. In order to become more modernized, Asians (the Japanese, Hong Kong Chinese, and mainland Chinese) experience the West as an imaginary concept. The West is an image that can be experienced and consumed on the soil of Asia.

Note

1 This list can be found at http://www.lboro.ac.uk/gawc.

Bibliography

Atkins, E.T. (2007) "Popular Culture," in W.M. Tsutsui (ed.) *A Companion to Japanese History*, Malden, MA: Blackwell.

Brannen, M.Y. (1992) "Bwana Mickey: Constructing Cultural Consumption at Tokyo Disneyland," in J.J. Tobin (ed.) *Remade in Japan: Everyday Life and Consumer Taste in a Changing Society*, New Haven, CT: Yale University Press.

Davis, S.G. (1996) "The Theme Park: Global Industry and Cultural Form," *Media Culture Society*, 18: 399–422.

Flowerdew, J. (2004) "The Discursive Construction of a World Class City," *Discourse and Society*, 15: 579–605.

Fowler, G.A. (2008) "Main Street, HK: Disney Localizes Mickey to Boost its Hong Kong Theme Park," *The Wall Street Journal*, 23 January, B1.

Fowler, G. and Marr, M. (2006) "Disney and the Great Wall," *The Wall Street Journal*, February 9, B1.

Fung, A. and Lee, M. (2009) "Localizing a Global Amusement Park: Hong Kong's Disneyland," *Continuum: Journal of Media and Cultural Studies*, 23: 195–206.

Giddens, A. (1990) *The Consequences of Modernity*, Stanford, CA: Stanford University Press.

Gluck, C. (1993) "The Past in the Present," in A. Gordon (ed.) *Postwar Japan as History*, Berkeley: University of California Press.

Ivy, M. (1993) "Formations of Mass Culture," in A. Gordon (ed.) *Postwar Japan as History*, Berkeley: University of California Press.

Ivy, M. (1995) *Discourses of the Vanishing: Modernity Phantasm Japan*, Chicago: University of Chicago Press.

Iwabuchi, K. (2002) *Recentering Globalization: Popular Culture and Japanese Transnationalism*, Durham, NC: Duke University Press.

Lee, M. (2009) "Constructed Global Space, Constructed Citizenship," *Javnost – The Public*, 16: 21–38.

Marr, M. and Fowler, G. (2006) "Chinese Lessons for Disney," *The Wall Street Journal*, 12 June, B1.

Mitsuhiro, Y. (1994) "Images of Empire: Tokyo Disneyland and Japanese Cultural Imperialism," in E. Smoodin (ed.) *Disney Discourse: Producing the Magic Kingdom*, New York: Routledge.

Mosco, V. (2005). *The Digital Sublime: Myth, Power, and Cyberspace*, Cambridge, MA: MIT Press.

Mosco, V. (2009). *The Political Economy of Communication* (2nd edition), Los Angeles, CA: Sage.

Oriental Daily (2005) "Restaurants Popular," September 2, A26.

Orwall, B. (1999) "Walt Disney Set to Unveil Park in Hong Kong," *The Wall Street Journal*, November 2, B11.

Slater, J. (1999) "Aieeyaaa! A Mouse!" *Far East Economic Review*, 162: 50–51.

Tobin, J.J. (1992) "Introduction: Domesticating the West," in J.J. Tobin (ed.) *Remade in Japan: Everyday Life and Consumer Taste in a Changing Society*, New Haven, CT: Yale University Press.

Turner, M. and Ngan, I. (1995) *Hong Kong Sixties: Designing Identity*, Hong Kong: Hong Kong Arts Development Council.

Wasko, J. (2001) *Understanding Disney: The Manufacture of Fantasy*, Cambridge: Polity.

Wasko, J., Phillips, M., and Meehan, E.R. (2001) *Dazzled by Disney: The Global Disney Audiences Project*, London: Leicester University Press.

Watson, J.L. (2000) "China's Big Mac Attack," *Foreign Affairs*, 79: 120–134.

Watson, J.L. (2006) *Golden Arches East: McDonalds in East Asia*, Stanford, CA: Stanford University Press.

Yan, Y. (2007) "Of Hamburger and Social Space: Consuming McDonald's in Beijing," in J. Watson and M.I. Caldwell (eds) *The Cultural Politics of Food and Eating: A Reader*, Malden, MA: Blackwell.

Yoshimi, S. (2001) "Japan: America in Japan/Japan in Disneyfication: The Disney Image and the Transformation of "America" in Contemporary Japan," in J. Wasko, M. Phillips, and E.R. Meehan (eds) *Dazzled by Disney? The Global Disney Audiences Project*, London: Leicester University Press.

Young, R.J.C. (2003) *Postcolonialism: A Very Short Introduction*, Oxford: Oxford University Press.

4

COMIC TRAVELS

Disney publishing in the People's Republic of China

Jennifer E. Altehenger

Introduction

In 2004, Michael Eisner, then CEO of the Walt Disney Company, described Disney's sponsorship of the first NBA games in China as "an important cultural milestone for the Chinese people." The "magic of Disney", he continued, would "open the doors to entirely new worlds of fantasy, imagination, and adventure" (Walt Disney Company Press Release 2004). Such a statement revealed a naïve confidence that the Chinese people would unconditionally accept the magic of Disney. Moreover, Eisner did not take into consideration Disney's long, if controversial, history in China. By 2004, the company could look back on some 70 years of efforts to permeate mainland Chinese society.

Disney's history in China began in the early 1930s, when popular magazines in the Republic of China debated Walt Disney and his new "black cat" Mickey Mouse (*Linglong Magazine* 1931, Issue 37). Chinese feature films of the mid-1930s showed couples enjoying a date at the cinema, watching Disney animated cartoons. In 1938 Disney's first feature animation *Snow White and the Seven Dwarfs* screened in Shanghai and Beijing cinemas. After the founding of the People's Republic of China (PRC) in 1949, all Disney products were banned and publicly defamed as symbols of capitalist imperialism. It was not until 1986, some ten years after the Great Proletarian Cultural Revolution of 1966–1976 had formally come to an end, that the company was permitted to enter China again; this time through a regular television broadcast of short comics tightly controlled by the national media supervision system. By 1986 however, Mickey Mouse had also become a propaganda icon in campaigns to counter urban rodent plagues (Wasserstrom 2003).

From the late 1970s onwards, with Deng Xiaoping's "reform and opening" economic policies, foreign firms were allowed and encouraged to enter the Chinese market. But the PRC government's cultural authorities continued

60 Jennifer Altehenger

to tightly control national media. Only beginning in the 1990s did the government permit joint foreign media ventures. In the wake of these policy changes, Disney quickly became one of the first international entertainment corporations that sought to bring its products to the PRC. Feature films such as *The Lion King*, *National Treasure*, and *Pirates of the Caribbean* were screened in Chinese cinemas (Chandler 2005).[1] *Dragon Club*, a spin-off of the US *Mickey Mouse Club* and a joint production of Beijing TV and Disney, was introduced to PRC television in 1994 and has since been aired on more than 40 stations across the country, reaching an estimated 60 million households (Chandler 2005). The most recent, most visible, and much discussed example of China's "Disneyfication" has been the opening of Hong Kong Disneyland in 2005. Nevertheless, Disney's presence in China is still minor compared to its market share in European and Latin American markets as Chinese cultural authorities continue to scrutinize and restrict Disney's operations. Though the Disney corporation may have succeeded in becoming one of the best established foreign entertainment companies in the People's Republic, longwinded negotiations with Chinese authorities continue (ICMR Case Studies and Management Resources 2009).

Disney's attempts to permeate new international markets have attracted much journalistic and scholarly attention (Chandler 2005; Fowler and Marr 2005; Ressner 2005; Stajano 1999/2000; Wasko *et al.* 2001; Wasko 2001; Yunker 2005). These recent analyses focus either on Disney's TV and film divisions or on the development of national and international theme parks. One division of the "Disney universe" has gone almost unnoticed: Disney Worldwide Publishing. Yet, promoting Disney print publications has been a key component in the company's business strategies and operations in the People's Republic. Disney comic books were deliberately selected as one of the first products to be sold in the PRC. They were expected to increase brand recognition, familiarize people with Disney's trademark cartoon figures and thus pave the way for other Disney products to follow (Disney Consumer Products 2004). Disney comics therefore play a significant role in marketing the Disney brand to Chinese consumers.

Administratively, Disney Worldwide Publishing forms part of the consumer products division of the Disney corporation. Unlike other divisions of the Disney corporation, however, the coordination and production of Disney print comics was outsourced several decades ago. As early as the 1930s, the company transferred large segments of its comic production to Europe, in particular to the Mondadori publishing house in Italy and to Egmont publishing in Denmark by 1948 (Stajano 1999/2000).[2] Bound to Disney by complex licensing agreements, these companies continued and developed the legacy of Disney comics. Soon, European Disney comics were reimported into the USA for publication with Disney run US publishers (Drotner 2001). Though Disney print comics are commonly perceived as American products, they are in fact mostly produced in Europe. In 1994, Egmont and the PRC Post and Telecommunications Press (*Renmin Youdian Chuban Gongsi*) established one of mainland China's first media joint ventures, Children's Fun Publishing (*Tongqu Chuban Gongsi*), in

Beijing. For the past 16 years Disney print media has been administered by a Sino-European joint venture. Therefore, the case of Disney publishing and its transnational chains of artistic production complicates the study of Disney's global business operations. This chapter thus joins those who argue that it is no longer possible to think of the travels of Disney products to other countries merely in terms of the "Americanization" of non-US countries (Raz 1999; van Maanen 1992; Wasko *et al.* 2001). Although this lens of Americanization is convenient and has often been utilized by the media to criticize Disney's international activities, it cannot alone account for the complexity of Disney comics' transnational production, dissemination, and consumption.

This chapter is divided into three sections. The first section briefly discusses the main issues at play in the interpretation of Disney's venture to the PRC. The development and usage of concepts such as globalization and Americanization are important to understanding the global framework within which Disney has been commonly analyzed. The second and third parts focus on Disney print media and, in particular, on two comics marketed by Children's Fun Publishing: *Ultimate Fans of Mickey Mouse (Zhongji Mimi)* and *W.i.t.c.h. (Moli)*. *Ultimate Fans of Mickey Mouse* has successfully established itself in the PRC youth readers market. Conversely, *W.i.t.c.h.* never attracted a sufficiently large readership and ceased publication after a few years. Together, these case studies illustrate that Disney's "Americaness" is but one, often flexible, factor in the company's own advertising strategies, albeit an important one. The localization of Disney in the People's Republic has as much to do with middle-class consumerism and rising demands for diverse entertainment products as it does with economic nationalism.

A global Disneyfication?

Following World War II, Americanization was a term commonly used to describe the influence of US corporations and their products on other countries. Moreover, the term demonstrated the dominance of US cultural products in the growth of European consumer cultures (de Grazia 2005; Pells 1997). During the 1970s and 1980s, especially with regard to Latin American case studies, some scholars held that the ubiquitous process of Americanization proved the cultural imperialism thesis and argued that some Western countries had come to dominate cultural consumption globally (Ritzer 1995). Such discussions posited Disney as an entertainment company seeking to export the "magic of Disney," taken to be one prolific version of the "American way of life," to the people abroad (Debouzy 2002; Tomlinson 1999). Indeed, as part of the post-war economic miracle during the 1950s and 1960s, Walt Disney's entertainment empire had been so successful internationally that Disney and Donald Duck were described as "world diplomats" (de Grazia 2005). Walt Disney, their creator, was awarded the US Presidential Medal of Freedom for effectively disseminating the "American way of life" (Watts 1997). The theoretical paradigm of cultural imperialism thrived as a part of this Cold War discourse.

62 Jennifer Altehenger

Scholars of literary and cultural theory, however, criticized what they believed to be Disney's promotion and push of US capitalist ideology and the corporation's attempt to impose this imagery and its covert political agenda onto other countries (Budd and Kirsch 2005; Dorfman and Mattelart 1975; Giroux 1999; Schickel 1968; Smoodin 1994; Ward 2002). Many of these criticisms were written with equally politicized agendas in mind. Dorfman and Mattelart, for example, composed their famous writings on Disney as a left-wing propaganda leaflet that sought to expose Disney's support for the Chilean Junta. Cultural criticisms thus abounded. Most of these writings, moreover, were exclusively concerned with the cultural and ideological value of Disney products. Few traced how Disney actually operated abroad. They seldom examined whether there were differences in the consumption of the diverse Disney products and how consumers responded to and accommodated these products into their everyday lives. The Americanization paradigm left little space for such questions as it assumed a clear distinction and a hierarchical relationship between those who were dominating and those being dominated. Until today, terms such as the "Disneyization" (Bryman 2004) or the "McDisneyfication" of society (Paterson 2006) highlight the influences of such an approach.

Renewed attempts to deal with the complexities of an increasingly global economy and with the cultural consumerist homogeneity it seemed to impose guided those scholars who propose concepts of cultural globalization. Cultural globalization succeeded notions of cultural imperialism as an explanatory framework for the increasingly global integration of cultural practices and the concurrent rise of local variations and diversification (Robertson 1992). Emphasis was now placed on understanding the "shifting nature of transnational power in a context in which intensified global cultural forms have decentered the power structure and vitalized local practices of appropriation and consumption of foreign cultural products and meanings" (Iwabuchi 2002). Localization became the common frame of analysis emphasizing local practices of consumption over global politico-economic processes (Appadurai 1990; Friedman 1990; Hannerz 1992; Howes 1996; Tobin 1992). In these studies, Disney and its products did play a role. Nonetheless, the export of Disney products continued to be seen as a linear process of bilateral cultural exchange between the US and other countries. Projects such as the Global Disney Audience Project attempted to address this shortcoming, examining how Disney was consumed, appropriated and adapted across the world, thereby letting go of the familiar paradigm of cultural homogenization (Wasko *et al.* 2001).

However, the comparative neglect of Disney's transnational travels arguably also resulted from the Disney company's own attempt to create the appearance of global cohesiveness and an image of the unique, global universality of the "magic of Disney." Consequently, research mostly centered on how this magic of Disney was perceived, not how it may have changed or was being changed. In many ways, the corporation was utilizing its Cold War image as a beacon of US culture. Disney was therefore seldom examined in the same manner as, for example, McDonald's.

In the case of McDonald's, attention was quickly drawn both to the processes of localization by consumers in East Asia as well as to the McDonald's franchise's own efforts at localization as part of an international marketing strategy (Watson 2006). In the case of Disney, however, the export of the "American way of life" and the "magic of Disney" remained a common discursive and analytical framework in scholarly but also particularly in popular reviews.

This framework also dominated the evaluation of Disney's operations in mainland China. Given the company's Cold War legacies, international media quickly turned reports of Disney's business in the PRC into a case study for the alleged clash of Chinese communism and US capitalism. With the PRC remaining one of the only countries governed by a Communist political system after the collapse of the Soviet Union in 1989, the imports of American products to the PRC were readily interpreted within the antagonistic framework of resistance to the encroachment of US culture. Disney's youth entertainment exports were expected to spark controversy in the PRC, where youth culture had traditionally been closely linked to educational concerns and state propaganda. As a result, Disney products were seen as a likely antagonist to Communist Party controlled readings. As Koichi Iwabuchi has illustrated, such an antagonistic approach leads to a foreign cultural presence being "interpreted as a threat to national identity and/or to the national interest, or as a sign of the foreign country's status as an object of yearning in the recipient country." He concludes, "In either case it marks the foreign country's cultural power" (Iwabuchi 2002: 32).

Stark polarizations that emphasize alleged cultural superiority, however, understate instances of cultural and business cooperation such as the publishing joint venture, Children's Fun Publishing. They cannot help explain why, out of all media companies, the Danish publisher Egmont was chosen as the only suitable partner to bring Disney to China with the help of a media joint venture company. Finally, they give no voice to the diverse agents—publishers, magazine vendors, and different consumers alike—who are involved in the process of disseminating and consuming Disney products. Consequently, instead of widening our perspective, Cold War legacies have sometimes impeded closer analyses of creative local adaptations of Disney products, though these have been crucial to the brand's transnational success. Moreover, Disney products cover only one part of the local youth culture market. In fact, youth products from other East Asian countries such as Japan, Korea, and Taiwan dominate popular culture in the People's Republic. Accordingly, Disney has had to contend with a formidable competitor (Chua 2007; Iwabuchi 2002). This background is crucial to understanding the case studies of Children's Fun Publishing and two of its publications, *Ultimate Fans of Mickey Mouse* and *W.i.t.c.h.* These case studies help examine the role Disney print media play in the PRC publishing world and in popular culture. They also shed light on some of the strategies selected to promote Disney comics.

64 Jennifer Altehenger

Two comics and their transnational travels

China's Children's Fun Publishing distributes all Disney print media on the basis of licensing agreements. Just as Egmont does in Europe, Children's Fun Publishing also markets other non-Disney children's titles. Today, Children's Fun Publishing has a diverse portfolio of titles including *Mickey Mouse and Donald Duck, Princesses, Thomas the Tank Engine, Teletubbies, Barbie, Winnie the Pooh, Baby Einstein*, and more. Since its founding, Children's Fun Publishing has successfully enlarged its readership. Between 2008 and 2009, the company registered a profit increase of 30 percent (Egmont Annual Report 2009). The company mainly targets affluent urban middle-class families who are able to purchase the various weekly, fortnightly, and monthly publications, and who are willing to spend a substantial amount of money on entertainment and education for their children. This growing middle-class is an increasingly powerful force in promoting consumer culture in the PRC and it accounts for at least a third of the PRC population (Gerth 2010). Since its founding, Children's Fun Publishing has been able to profit from the development towards this active consumer culture. The company's product range has been steadily enlarged and diversified. As a result, there are now numerous publications for boys and girls at different stages of their childhood and teenage years.

In the immediate years following its establishment in 1994, Children's Fun Publishing focused on the publication of comic magazines and educational children primers. One of the first Disney products to appear on the shelves of magazine vendors and bookstores in 1994 was *Mickey Mouse Magazine*, a spin-off of the successful international fortnightly comic magazine of the same name. Soon, *Mickey Mouse Magazine* became Children's Fun Publishing's bestseller, selling up to 350,000 issues per fortnight. This amount, however, was still fairly small given that the average urban area in China accommodates several million inhabitants (Croll 2006). In 2002, a new comic called *W.i.t.c.h.* was launched, and was marketed as a twin publication to *Mickey Mouse Magazine*. As part of this new launch, the promotion strategy for *Mickey Mouse Magazine* was adapted and the magazine was now advertised as a publication for young boys between 9 and 14 years of age. *W.i.t.c.h.*, in turn, was advertised as a magazine for girls between 9 and 14 years old. In doing so, Children's Fun Publishing intended to enlarge the variety of products on offer for boys and girls, thus raising sales numbers and profit margins. In 2006, two new monthly comic books were added to the fortnightly *Mickey Mouse Magazine* and *W.i.t.c.h*: *W.i.t.c.h. Comic Book* and *Ultimate Fans of Mickey Mouse* (*Ultimate Fans*). Unlike the fortnightly magazines, which range between 30 and 40 pages each, the monthly comic books have some 150 pages and feature extended stories of 40 pages or more.

The international context of both comic books' production played a significant role in their promotion across the People's Republic. Both were adaptations of European publications. While *W.i.t.c.h.* was a Chinese translation of a recent newly launched European Disney publication, *Ultimate Fans* was the most recent addition to a long line of *Mickey Mouse* comic books worldwide, all of which were modeled on a comic book first developed in Italy in 1949. When it was launched in the early 1950s, the comic book *Topolino* (Italian for Mickey Mouse) was an innovation on the continental European market.[3] It took its lead from the US *Four Colors Comics* series (often also referred to as *One Shots*), a comic book anthology published by Dell Comics from 1939 to 1962. From the outset, the Italian *Topolino* was published in the format of a pocketsize, handy paperback (Stajano 1999/2000). The new comic book format was accompanied by a set of new protagonists and an image change for Mickey Mouse as well as the Duck family. Mickey Mouse was increasingly associated to his role as an aide to the local police of Duckburg,[4] or as a lead character in comic adaptations of historical events or literary works. The Duck family was either featured in classic adventure stories (similar to those first developed in the US), or also made the protagonists of historical or literary adaptations. In the 1930s and 40s, *Four Colors Comics* had successfully introduced this style of adaptations. However, the editors at the Italian *Topolino* refined and elaborated these adaptations to the extent that they soon came to be commonly seen as a European format of comics. From adaptations of Richard Wagner's opera *The Flying Dutchman*, or of Robert Louis Stevenson's *Dr. Jekyll and Mr.Hyde*, to comic adventures that explained why Napoleon Bonaparte always kept his left hand hidden in his coat, or investigated what really happened to Jules Verne's Nautilus, these stories took their readers on literary and historical journeys through time and across cultures.

In the 1950s, at the same time as Mondadori was promoting *Topolino* in Italy, the Danish publisher Egmont became active in the production of comics and started building up an in-house production workshop. Many of the comic stories that have since appeared in European Disney comic books were thus either produced in Italy or Denmark. While Italy's Mondadori was the first to promote pocket-size comic books on the European market, Egmont was pivotal in disseminating these new comic books across a wide geographical network, including Scandinavia, the Netherlands, Eastern Europe, and Russia. Within this network, Egmont-Ehapa, Egmont's German subsidiary, successfully turned the *Lustiges Taschenbuch* ("funny comic book") into one of Germany's most popular youth publications. Introduced in 1967, *Lustiges Taschenbuch* today has a print-run of approximately 300,000 copies monthly, an above-average brand recognition, and numerous fan groups across all age groups. These comic books have become collectors' items. They can be found at most magazine vendors and are as prominently read as the German fortnightly *Micky Maus Magazin*. As advertisements in China illustrate, *Lustiges Taschenbuch* served as a blueprint for the making of *Ultimate Fans* – the layout is identical and the monthly cover designs of *Ultimate Fans* are all reproductions of past *Lustiges Taschenbuch* cover designs.[5] When *Mickey Mouse Magazine* and *Ultimate Fans* were launched in 1994 and 2006 respectively, they both formed part of an extensive transnational chain of publications that originated in the USA, but bore the imprint of European post-war entertainment culture and a "Europeanized' version of US culture.

The trajectory of *W.i.t.c.h.* was very different. *W.i.t.c.h.* was developed in Italy in 2001 as a joint production of Disney Italia and the newly founded subdivision of Egmont, Egmont Manga, and Animé. This new comic's story structure follows the Japanese "magical girl" (*majokko*) genre, a part of the Japanese Shojo-manga, which denotes manga written for a female audience. *W.i.t.c.h.* tells the story of five teenage girls, Will, Irma, Taranee, Cornelia, and Hai Lin, all of whom possess supernatural powers. Each of the girls commands one of the four elements while the fifth girl unites all four elements to a powerful whole, and together they guard the "meta-world." Each *W.i.t.c.h.* issue contains several episodes of the storyline and each episode tells of some dangerous crisis that needs to be averted with the help of the heroines. At the same time, all five girls are caught in everyday problems of school, work, parental trouble, and romance. The comic therefore tries to capture the imagination of young girls dreaming of the possibility of supernatural powers in everyday teenage life.

The *W.i.t.c.h.* comic book was designed specifically with an international audience in mind. As a result, a key characteristic of *W.i.t.c.h.* is the diversity of the heroines' ethnic backgrounds. Will, Irma, and Cornelia are Caucasian but each has a different hair color (red, brown, and blond), Taranee is depicted as Afro-American, while Hai Lin is Chinese. Moreover, the choice of a manga format indicates that *W.i.t.c.h.* was an attempt by Disney and Egmont to develop a global comic that could answer to the recent manga and animé craze in Europe and beyond. To date, *W.i.t.c.h.* has been translated into 20 languages and has been received positively across Europe. In 2004, the comic was awarded the German Max-und-Moritz prize for the best German language comic publication for children and teenagers. Owing to its success on the European market, *W.i.t.c.h.* was introduced to China in 2002, only one year after its European launch.

When they were launched in China in 2006, the two comic book series were marketed as twin publications, one aimed at teenage boys and the other at teenage girls. The strategies employed to promote both products, however, differed substantially. *W.i.t.c.h.* was a comparatively young comic embarking on a transnational travel soon after its first publication in Italy. *Ultimate Fans*, conversely, was a classic of European youth entertainment culture. While the publicity on *Ultimate Fans* remained firmly dedicated to the comic's alleged US American origins, Children's Fun Publishing promoted *W.i.t.c.h.* as a European manga in an attempt to profit from the currents of economic nationalism and anti-Japanese sentiments. As a result, those transnational chains of production that had led to the two European publications becoming available in the PRC were manipulated and partly obfuscated in the process of localizing *Ultimate Fans* and *W.i.t.c.h.*. Unlike *Ultimate Fans* and *Mickey Mouse Magazine*, however, *W.i.t.c.h* ceased publication in the summer of 2009, without any official statement to explain the publisher's reasons for this business decision. Rather than coincidental, the success of the one comic book and the failure of the other was closely linked to the demands of Chinese consumers who had a very clear idea of what they desired.

Localization strategies

In 2008, the director of Children's Fun Publishing, Hou Mingliang, stated in an interview that his company, 14 years into its founding, was now actively seeking to adapt Disney print media to the taste of its customers in mainland China. Hou explained that Mickey Mouse, Donald Duck, and countless other Disney comic figures, would have to be localized. Clearly, localization had become an openly acknowledged business strategy of Disney's licensed publisher. Yet, even if not publicly stated in the past, localization had been a crucial component of Children's Fun Publishing's business strategies from the start.

When Children's Fun Publishing was established, a media joint venture with a government-controlled PRC publisher was not an easy alliance. In the 1980s, despite the quickly increasing growth in consumer cultures, publishing had remained an industry sector that was carefully guarded by the government's cultural bureaucracy. Children and youth publications were considered to be one of the most volatile publishing sectors since children and youth reading matters were to serve both an educational mission as well as provide entertainment to the next generation. Entertainment as well as educational readings could both have a direct impact on the intellectual upbringing of the party-state's future citizens.[6] Seen from this perspective, this sector was not a likely candidate for a pioneering media joint venture. The trajectory of Children's Fun Publishing however, illustrates that the contrary came to be the case: children and youth publishing were purposefully advocated by the government's cultural bureaucracy as a sector for a Sino-foreign joint venture for two reasons. First, it was a strategic move on the part of the cultural bureaucracies to answer to middle-class parents' growing demand for foreign youth products. Second, these foreign products, at the same time, provided entertaining educational materials which could be closely linked to the study of English as a foreign language, thus promoting the goal of educating the globally-versed future PRC citizen.

The interplay of education and entertainment is central to understanding the popularity of Disney products in the PRC. Children's Fun Publishing states on its website that it understands its role mainly as a publisher of educational materials. To the company, education is intricately linked to enjoyment and entertainment. The publisher hopes that its products will help young readers to grow into adults with the "correct attitude to the value of human life" (Children's Fun Publishing website, www.childrenfun.com.cn). The company continues to state that through this approach, parents, children, and Ministry of Education will "join hands." While in the US the Disney Company is very careful to publicize any claims to educating children through entertainment, Disney in China has had to adopt a policy of publicly advertising its reading materials as beneficial to youth education. Entertainment without an educational purpose was insufficient to enter the PRC market. At a time when Disney is criticized in the US for its clandestine, subversive policy of "edutainment" (Giroux 1999), parents and cultural authorities in China accept Disney precisely because it provides entertaining education.

68 Jennifer Altehenger

One of the reasons why classic Disney comics such as *Ultimate Fans* became acceptable to Chinese cultural authorities was the argument that Disney comics, comic figures, and Disney imagery might be convenient tools to teach Chinese children American English (Donald 2005: 68). In the PRC, knowledge of American English is considered a career advantage. As working in economically profitable businesses is one of the most popular career paths that affluent Chinese parents envisage for their offspring, these parents are often determined to provide their only child with the best possible education. This includes fluency in American English, to be acquired at an early age (Donald 2005). Readings such as *Ultimate Fans*, although in Chinese, should therefore be seen as complementing other, more conspicuous, educational efforts, such as the recently opened Shanghai Disney English School (*Shanghai Daily*, 2008). While *Ultimate Fans* is in Chinese, it familiarizes children with the Disney characters and the world of Disney that they will meet again in their English classes.

Purely entertaining comic books are thus tied into a larger advertising strategy that places a premium on entertaining education. Complementing these efforts, Children's Fun Publishing also offers Disney English summer camps for different age groups in urban China. In these camps, children are given all sorts of Disney paraphernalia such as Mickey Mouse backpacks, writing utensils, and Donald Duck caps, and spend several hours of the day learning English with the help of comic and picture books. These strategies of offering entertaining education have provided a solution for China's urban middle-class eager to provide their children with the advantage of learning a foreign language at an early age. In 2005, the Chinese Communist Youth League and Children's Fun Publishing carried out a joint project to encourage children's literacy in local schools. Schoolchildren were encouraged to dance Mickey dances, sing Mickey songs, and draw their own Mickey Mouse cartoons (Hing 2007a and b). The government's cultural authorities have sanctioned these efforts as a recent example of Disney's proliferation in the People's Republic.

This, however, does not mean that China's urban middle-class, along with China's mass organizations, have been Americanized. Nonetheless, Disney comics and comic figures have continuously been seen as a product of US culture and as such have been criticized for their inherent capitalist ideological message by critics within and outside of China. This capitalist ideology, critics argue, reveals itself in several elements, all of which are central to Mickey Mouse and Duck family storylines: a dichotomy of good and bad, absence of any kind of sexual relations, a notion of success tied closely to accomplishment and riches with a corresponding notion of the lazy, perpetually unsuccessful losers, and finally, a clear division of race. This supports an illusion of innocence intended to keep the reader in a perpetual state of childhood fantasy (Giroux 1999). Although these criticisms are partly correct in their descriptions of Disney imagery, they only skim the surface of Disney stories, especially of those produced in Italy and Denmark. In these storylines, Donald Duck, a confused and clumsy figure, turns into a superhero at night, triumphing over his uncle Scrooge in a final twist of moral righteousness. In

European Disney comics featured in *Ultimate Fans*, Donald is thus a loser during the day and a hero at night (Stajano 1999/2000). The comics promoted in the PRC therefore often differ substantially in their portrayal of Disney characters from the original comic strips published in the United States during the 1930s and 1940s.

Disney's promotion of and emphasis on family and moral values is commonly seen to represent its advocacy of an "American way of life." This fact has been an important element in Chinese parents' acceptance of Disney, as evident in analyses of the Disney company operating in the PRC. For example, Chinese consumer reception of the feature film *The Lion King* was largely positive; Chinese parents valued the film because "it tells a universal story of family renewance... of the importance of one's native land ... and of the danger of the Other" (Donald 2005). Mickey Mouse and Duck family comics are based on the same storylines, but such moral principles are not solely American. Rather, Disney releases "morally upright fables" to answer to consumer needs for comforting entertainment. As such, Disney stories may represent traditional Chinese notions of family and morals as much as they represent morals and values of other readers across the globe.

However, European Disney storylines, too, were adapted as part of their import to Chinese markets. When Egmont's German *Lustiges Taschenbuch* was translated into Chinese, a number of editorial changes were made in order to make the comic more attractive to Chinese readers. In the European edition, as described above, adaptations of historical events and literary works figured centrally each month. Initially, this structure was adapted for the Chinese market as well. The fourth issue of *Ultimate Fans* even featured an 80 page adaptation of Homer's *Odyssey*. After six issues, though, emphasis was increasingly placed on featuring adaptations of recent Hollywood feature films instead, such as *Indiana Jones* in Issue 33, and *James Bond* in Issue 20. While the format of *Lustiges Taschenbuch* was easily and successfully translated, translating the content was not as simple. As a result, the storylines were stripped of certain classic elements and brought closer to the global entertainment storylines that were promoted by Hollywood but shaped by transnational artistic collaborations. *Ultimate Fans* stories are now a compromise between adaptation techniques developed in Italy and Denmark, recognizable feature film storylines, and original 1930s Duck family adventure plots. This illustrates that the Disney corporation is a global entertainment culture that has successfully incorporated transnational chains of production and dissemination while simultaneously allowing for local adaptations and patterns of consumption.

Although Disney stories of Mickey Mouse and Donald Duck are identified and labeled as American, simply because they have been successfully produced and disseminated by Disney, the perceived Americaness of these products seems to matter only to selected aspects of product marketing, such as the promotion of entertaining education. Here, Children's Fun Publishing imposes the Disney product's identity as uniquely American in an attempt to answer to consumers' requirements. Thus, the product identity of *Ultimate Fans* and *Mickey Mouse Magazine* as authentically American is but one element in the process of localizing Disney products in China. In moments when this element is considered profitable to the dissemination

70 Jennifer Altehenger

and promotion of a Disney product (such as in advertisement strategies), explicit reference is made to the American Disney Company (Meiguo Dieshini Gongsi) as the origin of the product in question.

In other moments, however, the American nature of Disney is downplayed. The promotion of *W.i.t.c.h.* is a case in point. This comic was explicitly advertised as a European product, even though it was just as American or transnational as *Ultimate Fans* and *Mickey Mouse Magazine*. The comic book was supposed to appeal to girls because it combined popular elements. US television series such as *Charmed*, and older sitcoms such as *Bewitched*, proliferated and popularized the plotline of young girls with supernatural powers. Naoko Takeuchi's *Sailor Moon*, the successful Japanese animé and manga series of the 1990s that gained international fame, may have also provided a blueprint for *W.i.t.c.h.* In *Sailor Moon*, five teenage heroines vested with the powers of the moon and the planets fight against evil while wrestling with normal teenage issues. As a result, when they were promoted in the PRC, *W.i.t.c.h.* comics came up against the competition of Japanese manga which were already very popular among young Chinese readers. This led Children's Fun Publishing to opt for an entirely different advertising strategy than it had pursued in the promotion of *Ultimate Fans*.

In promoting *W.i.t.c.h.*, Children's Fun Publishing attempted to appeal to economic nationalist sentiments among it potential young Chinese readers and their parents. In recent years, Japanese manga have become extremely popular in China. They are readily available on the Chinese market, either as licensed publications at newspaper stalls, or as fake copies offered at the street side (Wang 2005). Thus, unlike other Disney comics, which are called *katong* (cartoons), *W.i.t.c.h.* was advertised as a *manhua* (manga). Moreover, *W.i.t.c.h.* was labeled a European manga, or *Ouzhou manhua*. The fact that *W.i.t.c.h.* was also a product of the American Disney Company was not mentioned. The case of *W.i.t.c.h.* therefore stands in striking contrast to the "American" *Ultimate Fans* comic book. Unlike *Ultimate Fans*, misleadingly labeled as US American, *W.i.t.c.h.* was marketed as uniquely European, even though the choice of genre, that of a "magical girl" manga, further meant that *W.i.t.c.h.* was based on an adaptation of an Eastern, specifically Japanese comic technique and logic. As a result, it was a Europeanized manga reimported into Asia.

That the European origins of *W.i.t.c.h* were markedly emphasized in its dissemination underlines Children's Fun Publishing's intentions to promote the comic as an alternative to Japanese manga. This strategy builds on economic nationalist sentiments and on the notion that reading Japanese manga as a Chinese citizen constitutes an unpatriotic act. In the past years, upsurges of economic nationalism have repeatedly accompanied political conflict between the People's Republic and Japan. Such smaller political conflicts have frequently played on legacies of the Sino-Japanese War in the mid-twentieth century resulting in popular anti-Japanese demonstrations (Gerth 2010). A recent internet controversy is one prominent example for such sentiments. In 2006, an article in the *Global Times* (the overseas edition of the mainland *People's Daily*) entitled "Beware of Japanese Manga

Misleading the Next Generation," triggered a discussion regarding the importance of Japanese manga's nationality (*Global Times*, June 2, 2006). The article cautioned against the consumption of Japanese cultural products, arguing that manga might exert a dangerous influence on young readers who could not clearly distinguish the implicit criticism of Chinese culture and the denial of Japanese war crimes from the enjoyment of reading manga. It was republished in the online version of the *People's Daily* (the Chinese Communist Party's prime daily publication; *People's Daily*, June 6, 2006). Shortly after, the *Global Times* featured a lengthy discussion of the initial article, again reprinted in the *People's Daily* (*Global Times*, June 6, 2006; *People's Daily*, June 8, 2006). This discussion was very critical of the original article's radical propositions and rejected them. However, the underlying argument, that readers should exercise care when consuming foreign cultural products, remained. The controversy caused a stir across numerous net portals where fans debated whether reading manga really was an unpatriotic act.[7] Although most consumers writing on the blogs agreed that their patriotism for the PRC was not at odds with their liking for Japanese manga, many did state that economic nationalist concerns were not unreasonable and should be taken into account.

Mickey Mouse Magazine and *Ultimate Fans* could profit from their alleged American appeal and answer to a demand for entertaining educational materials in China. The strategy to promote *W.i.t.c.h.* as an alternative to Japanese manga, however, was eventually unsuccessful. Even though fan communities across the internet questioned the claim that it was unpatriotic to consume Japanese manga, Children's Fun Publishing advanced *W.i.t.c.h.* as a compromise product for those manga fans, or parents, guided by nationalistic considerations. With the PRC predominantly dependent on the import of foreign (mostly Japanese) manga to meet the demands of consumers of comics, this approach may have initially seemed promising (Chua 2007; Donald 2005; Iwabuchi 2002). But the localization of *W.i.t.c.h.* was ultimately less successful than the localization of *Ultimate Fans*. Although *W.i.t.c.h.* gained readership in urban China, it was unable to establish itself as a strong competitor to Japanese manga imports, despite being promoted as a European comic. Japanese products such as *Doraemon*, one of the most popular children's mangas in China (Wang 2005), have proved more durable and easier to popularize. The demise of *W.i.t.c.h.* was therefore the result of several factors. First, it was much too expensive in comparison to Japanese manga; second, unlike Japanese products, *W.i.t.c.h.* was not available widely enough; and third, the comic's Chinese translations from the original Italian were often unidiomatic. Even though *W.i.t.c.h.* was a Disney product, it was not a sufficiently strong competitor to its Japanese contenders. Therefore, the simple fact that a product is associated to Disney is insufficient to make it desirable for Chinese consumers. Instead, Disney and Children's Fun Publishing have had to face a strong, influential "East Asian popular culture" (Chua 2007) and have not always been in the dominant position.

72 Jennifer Altehenger

Conclusion

Disney is a global, transnational, and local company. The Disney brand and its most famous figures such as Mickey Mouse and the Duck family are icons of an apparent global youth culture. Yet, as the above examples of *Ultimate Fans* and *W.i.t.c.h.* illustrate, this global appearance is mostly the result of complex transnational travels, to and from the US, Europe, and East Asia. What is perceived as a monolithic company with a linear development is in fact a complex cluster of international divisions and operations characterized by cross-cultural exchanges. In analyzing the travels of Disney products, we must therefore examine the cultural specificities of global processes (Ong 1999: 5). The Disney company is represented in different countries by different products. In the US, Disney represents television, films, media, and theme parks. In Europe, Disney print comic culture still accounts for a fair share of brand recognition. In the PRC, Disney provides entertainment as well as education with an emphasis on films, print products, and brand merchandise.

The study of smaller local case studies of Disney products illustrates that the Disney company is made up by the sum of its parts. As the two examples *Ultimate Fans* and *W.i.t.c.h.* have shown, each of these parts may undergo very different trajectories. Success or failure depends on the consumers and their demands in the respective target countries. *W.i.t.c.h.*, a comic specifically designed to answer to the preferences of global readers, failed in the PRC, while *Ultimate Fans*, with its American–European heritage, succeeded in gaining a hold on the Chinese market. To understand such a development, analyses of Disney in China should take into account inter-Asian exchanges of cultural products and the cultural specificities of the target country. Even flexible and adjustable product identities together with the Disney label may not suffice to make a Disney product competitive if the market is saturated. The static model of global Americanization cannot account for these diverse responses to Disney products. Analytical frameworks of cultural homogenization or of the supremacy of US cultural products therefore cannot help explain the dynamics of local responses to the increased availability of regional and global entertainment products, not even in the case of Disney. While Disney has certainly contributed to the growth of consumerism across the globe, it does not follow that the growth of consumerism has also led to the dominance of one superior culture over another. The global Disney brand has indeed induced several changes in PRC entertainment culture. Nonetheless, many of these changes are distinctly local.

Notes

1 Only 20 foreign films are selected for screening in PRC cinemas each year. Foreign films on DVD, however, have become easily available across the People's Republic for purchase either in licensed stores or as pirated copies.
2 "Disney historiography" has all but deleted the influence of Italy and Italian writers. Stajano, however, points out that the first Disney cartoons already appeared in March

1930 in the Italian weekly *L'illustrazione del Popolo* only two weeks after Walt Disney and Ub Iwker first published their comic strips in daily newspapers through the King Features Syndicate.

3 Mondadori publishing's first magazine in 1935 was also named *Topolino*. Closed during World War II, the format change was introduced with the reopening of the publishing house in 1949 (Stajano 1999/2000).

4 Different to the initial Walt Disney comics produced in the US, European Disney comics have the "Ducks" and "Mouses" all living in Duckburg. Thus, European Disney comics also feature stories in which Mickey Mouse and the Duck family interact.

5 It is possible to compare European cover designs for Disney comics on http://inducks.org.

6 The traditional Chinese children's book is, in fact, expected to be a primer with predominantly educational purposes rather than entertaining reading (Farquhar 1999).

7 For an overview of related articles, see http://www.comipress.com.

Bibliography

Appadurai, A. (1990) "Disjuncture and difference in the global cultural economy," *Theory, Culture and Society*, 7: 295—311.

Bryman, A. (2004) *The Disneyization of Society*, London: Sage Publications.

Budd, M. and Kirsch, M.H. (2005) *Rethinking Disney: Private Control, Public Dimensions*, Connecticut: Wesleyan University Press.

Byrne, E. and McQuillan, M. (1999) *Deconstructing Disney*, London: Pluto Press.

Chandler, C. (2005) "Mickey Mao," *Fortune Magazine*, April 18.

Chua, B.H. (2007) "Configuring an East Asian Popular Culture," in K.H. Chen and B.H. Chua (eds) *The Inter-Asia Cultural Studies Reader*, London: Routledge.

Croll, E. (2006) *China's New Consumers: Social Development and Domestic Demand*, London: Routledge.

Debouzy, M. (2002) "Does Mickey Mouse Threaten French Culture? The Debate About Euro Disneyland," in S.P. Ramet and G.P. Crnkovic (eds) *Kazaaam! Splat! Ploof! The American Impact on European Popular Culture, since 1945*, London: Rowman & Littlefield.

de Grazia, V. (2005) *Irresistible Empire: America's Advance through Twentieth Century Europe*, Boston, MA: Harvard University Press.

Disney Consumer Products (2011) *Publishing*. Online. Available at: https://licensing.disney.com/Home/display.jsp?contentId=dcp_home_ourbusinesses_publishing_us&forPrint=false&language=en&preview=false&imageShow=0&pressRoom=U.S.&translationOf=null&region=0.

Donald, S. (2005) *Little Friends: Children's Film and Media Culture in China, Asia-Pacific Perspectives*, Maryland: Rowman & Littlefield.

Dorfman, A. and Mattelart, A. (1975) *How to Read Donald Duck: ImperialistIdeology in the Disney Comic*, New York: International General.

Drotner, K. (2001) "Donald Seems So Danish: Disney and the Formation of Cultural Identity," in J. Wasko (ed.) *Dazzled by Disney*, London: Cassell.

Farquhar, M.A. (1999) *Children's Literature in China: From Lu Xun to MaoZedong*, New York: M.E. Sharpe.

Friedman, J. (1990) "Being in the World: Globalization and Localization," *Theory, Culture, and Society*, 7: 311—329.

Fowler, G. and Marr, M. (2005) "Disney's China Play," *The Wall Street Journal*, 16 June.

Gerth, K. (2010) *As China Goes, So Goes the World: How Chinese Consumers Are Transforming Everything*, New York: Hill and Wang.

Giroux, H.A. (1999) *The Mouse That Roared: Disney and the End of Innocence, Culture, and Education Series*, Maryland: Rowman & Littlefield.

74 Jennifer Altehenger

Global Times (2006) "Why Accuse Japanese Manga?" June 6. Online. Available at: http://world.people.com.cn/GB/1030/4447167.html.

Global Times (2006) "Beware of Japanese Manga Misleading the Next Generation," June 2. Online. Available at: http://world.people.com.cn/BG/1030/4438178.html.

Hannerz, U. (1992) *Cultural Complexity: Studies in the Social Organization of Meaning*, New York: Columbia University Press.

Hing, B. (2007a) "Taking the Mickey," *The Diplomat*, March 28.

Hing, B. (2007b) "Disney Appeals to China's Youth," *BBC News*, September 23.

Howes, D. (1996) *Cross-Cultural Consumption: Global Markets, Local Realities*, London: Routledge.

ICMR Case Studies and Management Resources (2009) *Disney Strategies in China*. Online. Available at: http://www.icmrindia.org/Short%20Case%20Studies/Business%20Strategy/CLBS089.htm.

Iwabuchi, K. (2002) *Recentering Globalization: Popular Culture and Japanese Transnationalism*, Durham, NC: Duke University Press.

Ong, A. (1999) *Flexible Citizenship: The Cultural Logics of Transnationality*, Durham, NC: Duke University Press.

Paterson, M. (2006) *Consumption and Everyday Life*, London: Routledge.

Pells, R. (1997) *Not Like Us: How Europeans Have Loved, Hated, and Transformed American Culture Since World War Two*, New York: Basic Books.

Pink, S. (2007) *Doing Visual Ethnography: Images, Media and Representation in Research*, 2nd edition, London: Sage Publications.

Raz, A. (1999) *Riding the Black Ship: Japan and Tokyo Disneyland*, Boston, MA: Harvard University Asia Centre.

Ressner, J. (2005) "Disney's Great Leap into China," *Time Magazine*, July 11.

Ritzer, G. (1995) *The McDonaldization of Society: An Investigation into the Changing Character of Contemporary Social Life*, California: Pine Forge Press.

Robertson, R. (1992) *Glocalization, Social Theory and Global Culture*, London: Sage.

Schickel, R. (1968) *The Disney Version: The Life, Times, Art, and Commerce of Walt Disney*, New York: Simon and Schuster.

Schiller, H.I. (1976) *Communication and Cultural Domination*, New York: International Arts and Sciences Press.

Shanghai Daily (2008) "Learning English the Disney Way in Shanghai," October 22. Online. Available at: http://shanghaidaily.com/sp/article/2008/200810/20081022/Article_377672.htm.

Smoodin, E.L. (1994) *Disney Discourse: Producing the Magic Kingdom*, London: Routledge.

Stajano, F. (1999/2000) "Disney-serier i Italien," *NAFS(k)uriren* 30–32.

Tobin, J.J. (1992) *Re-made in Japan: Everyday Life and Consumer Taste in a Changing Society*, New Haven, CT: Yale University Press.

Tomlinson, J. (1999) *Globalization and Culture*, Cambridge: Polity Press.

van Maanen, J. (1992) "Displacing *Disney*: Some Notes on the Flow of Culture," *Qualitative Sociology*, 15.

Walt Disney Company (2009) *The Walt Disney Company increases presence in China with sponsorship of country's first NBA Games*, Press Release, July 18. Online. Available at: http://corporate.disney.go.com/news/corporate/2004.

Walt Disney Company Press Release (2004) "The Walt Disney Company increases presence in China with sponsorship of country's first NBA games," July 28, http://thewaltdisneycompany.com/disney-news/press-releases/2004/07walt-disney-company-increases-presence-china-sponsorship-countrys.

Wang, Y. (2005) "*The Dissemination of Japanese Manga in China: The Interplay of Culture and Social Transformation in the Post-Reform Period*," unpublished thesis, Sweden: Lund University Center for East and Southeast Asian Studies.

Ward, A.R. (2002) *Mouse Morality: The Rhetoric of Disney Animated Film*, Austin: University of Texas Press.

Wasko, J. (2001) *Understanding Disney: The Manufacture of Fantasy*, Boston, MA: Blackwell.

Wasko, J., Phillips M. and Meehan, E.R. (2001) *Dazzled by Disney? The Global Disney Audiences Project*, London: Leicester University Press.

Wasserstrom, J. (2003) "A Mickey Mouse Approach to Globalization," *Yale Global Online*, 16 June. Online. Available at: http://yaleglobal.yale.edu/content/mickey-mouse-approach-globalization.

Watson, J.L. (2006) *Golden Arches East: McDonald's in East Asia*, 2nd edition, Stanford, CA: Stanford University Press.

Watts, S. (1997) *The Magical Kingdom: Walt Disney and the American Way of Life*, New York: Houghton Mifflin Company.

Yunker, J. (2005) "Disney in China: How Local is Too Local?" *Going Global*, June 21.

5

SAVING FACE FOR MAGAZINE COVERS

New forms of transborder visuality in urban China

Eric Kit-wai Ma

The concept of cultural transfer through global capitalism has historically been studied through discourses of cultural imperialism, international communication, and diffusionist modernization (Tomlinson 1999; Stevenson 1992). These early linear theses have recently been replaced by a proliferation of studies on cultural globalization, which propose more dialectic and multifaceted cultural exchanges between "the West and the rest." These recent studies emphasize the domestication, glocalization, and transculturation of dominant western cultural forms (such as Hollywood movies and transnational news) that have been appropriated in foreign countries (Chan 2002; Cohen 2002; Robertson 1995). In turn, global to local cultural exchanges are seen as one of the many global consequences perpetrated by western modernity (Giddens 1990); this is the concept of multiple modernities, a concept arguing that western modernity has been appropriated in foreign countries in various different forms (Eisenstadt 2000). Supporting these general arguments of cultural multiplicity are specific case studies of Japan, Taiwan, Singapore, Korea, Hong Kong, and China—they are seen as alternative cases of capitalist modernity that highlight unevenness, contradictions, contingencies, and contextual differences (Berger 1988; Ma and Zhang 2011; Rofel 1999; Yeh 2000).

In my previous studies, I proposed the concepts of satellite modernity and translocal spatiality (Ma 2001, 2002) in an attempt to enrich existing theories discussing cultural multiplicity in processes of globalization. In contrast to the dominant discourses that discuss global to local cultural flow, I instead stress the importance of intermediate satellite links as well as local to local cultural transfer in the global network of modern capitalism. In this chapter, however, I will refine cultural globalization theories by focusing on the transfer and subsequent repackaging of visual images across cultural borders. Popular images and visual styles journey across the globe and are consequently intertwined with emerging ways of life among middle-class consumers worldwide. When popular images travel from one destination to the next, they are repackaged in order to appeal to local audiences. This visual transfer and subsequent repackaging, or transborder visuality, is often reworked by local cultural intermediaries (such as journalists, movie directors, advertisers, and designers) who scour the global pool of image resources to find ones that can be used and locally adapted.

Arguably, capitalism is moving away from the economy of material production to an economy of signs and symbols (Lash and Urry 1994). In turn, consumer societies are experiencing a visual turnaround, in which visuality is one of the prime motivators of consumption (Davis 2011; Mirzoeff 2002; Mitchell 1994). This chapter will therefore aim to fill in the details as well as connect and integrate the cultural and social practices of visual production into the theoretical map of cultural globalization. By focusing on this small area of study, we will find that a significant link emerges; this link shows how pools of images flow from consumer societies of high modernity, to newly developed cities of satellite modernities, to developing countries aspiring towards a modern, urban, city life. In the case of urban China, large consumer markets are so quickly and forcefully building up that global visual cultures are beginning to cater to the specific demands of Chinese consumers (Curtin 2007); these transborder visual flows demonstrate strong reactive currents quite different from the scenarios depicted by popular globalization theories. For example, it is not the familiar case of a dominant global culture taking over a local indigenous culture, but a process whereby the rapidly expanding and developing Chinese market is exploiting global resources to build up national consumer markets.

Ethnography in a "lifestyle factory"

This chapter is a small part of an ethnographic study that focuses on magazine publishing in Beijing. Based on four months of field work in Trends Group, a publishing corporation, I trace how international, regional, and local images of visual cultures are repackaged in mainland China to provide the public and the consumers similar, yet different, patterns of cultural formations. Trends Group is a Chinese media corporate with a dozen lifestyle magazines under its wings including Chinese versions of international titles such as *Esquire, Cosmopolitan, Men's Health, National Geographic, For Him Magazine (FHM), Bazaar,* and more. These magazines have undergone different levels of localization but have all been very successful in capturing Chinese readers, due to their introduction of the foreign and having the correct combination of local and foreign content.

In 2006, Trends Group moved their offices to Trends Tower, a new building that was named after the corporation; the new headquarters towers over the high rises in the central business district of Beijing. I visited the construction site of Trends Tower in the summer of 2006 and began to consider the potential of the tower as a research site and theoretical metaphor. As a research site, it is a place where the local and the global collide, through intense and frequent sociocultural interactions; it is a place where cultural ideas and images flow in a concrete place where ethnographic observation is feasible. Theoretically and metaphorically speaking, the site is a factory that produces signs, symbols, and identities for the rising Chinese middle class. The Trends Tower will ultimately allow us to explore the modes of production and consumption in the new "sign" economy of urban China.

In the summer of 2007, my research team and I (consisting of two research assistants and a visual artist) were granted access to Trends Tower and worked in the research and development unit for four months. During this time, we were free to move around and interview editors, photographers, marketing officers, and the two heads of the corporation. This chapter will focus on the changes of the magazine covers throughout the years, utilizing a few specific examples to highlight the processes of visual appropriations and adaptations.[1]

Lifestyle factory: a metaphor

In the early stages of modernity, the factory was the cornerstone of a consumer and producer society; it was symbolic of modernity. In manufacturing economies, the factory was the site that fostered localized working and middle-class communities. Today, in the later stages of modernity, where is our "factory"? Where is the factory of the sign economy where emotions, identities, and aesthetics are formed? There has been a rough consensus on the formation of late modernity (differing from the social configuration of early modernity), which has been termed as liquid, reflexive, mediated, and a sort of second modernity (Bauman 2000; Beck and Beck-Gernsheim 2002; Giddens 1990; Ma and Zhang 2011). In this day and age, the Fordist mode of materialist production has been largely replaced by a post-Fordist mode of production in which information, symbols, and signs are the most important components. Using China as a case study complicates this theoretical description; China's fledgling modernity can be characterized as compressed and hybridized in the sense that it is rapidly catching up with different modes of modernity (Chan and Ma 2002; Lee 2000; Yeh 2000). China undoubtedly benefits from the effects of accelerating temporal-spatial compression of information technologies, while also remaining connected to early forms of assembly line capitalism. The factories of China provide and sustain transnational capitalism with its competitive and seemingly unlimited labor base. Therefore, in the context of China, Trends Tower can be seen as a high-power "factory" located in the center of Beijing. Trends Tower is a factory that relays international visual resources and translates these images into localized identity products, thereby satisfying the desires of Chinese urbanites to connect to the imagined urban life of affluent global elites.

High-speed and high-powered urbanization are accompanied by the messy processes of the de-skilling and re-skilling of everyday urban routines (Giddens 1991). Among the creative teams working in Trends Group, there has been a strong collective motivation to construct new urban identities through their magazine publications. Our interviews with these creative teams have demonstrated that they are eager to lead by example and share with the rising Chinese middle class their journeys of connecting to the global urban culture.

In the staff manual, Trends Group is defined as a lifestyle and attitude that emphasizes the importance of material and spiritual well-being; Trends' magazines are for those in pursuit of individuality and humanistic values. The term "trends" has been popularized in China and is the term for leading a "trendy lifestyle." Two interesting observations should be noted. First, the Chinese term for trends inherently suggests that humanistic values are relevant and significant in leading a trendy lifestyle, unlike the English term "lifestyle" which could signify something more materialistic and consumerist. Second, those working in the Trends Group along with the general public do not have a stable conceptualization of what the term "trends" really means, as our interviews and focus group discussions show. Seemingly, the trends culture is in the beginning stage of a discursive formation; meanings and boundaries have yet to be mapped out. Though western culture is at times a major reference to the formation of the trends culture, Chinese culture and literary heritage is also greatly influential.

Early dialectics of glocalization

The process of "glocalization," or the hybridization of the global and the local (Robertson 1995), has been used indiscriminately for many years in discourses concerning cultural globalization. This general and frequent use of the term, however, has not helped in defying a homogeneous thesis of global cultural flow. By using Trends Group as a case study in this paper, we will be able to see a more concrete and refined model of glocalization, from which a dynamic and process-sensitive perspective can be conceptualized.

Since 1993, Trends Group, like all other commercial media operations in China, has been working under a commercial publishing model while also being officially attached to a state-owned bureau; this dual arrangement is commercially flexible as well as politically safe. Trends Group conceptually came into being when two civil servants from the National Traveling Bureau, Wu Hong and Liu Jiang, decided that they wanted to run a commercial magazine on their own. Trends Group began with a small editorial team of local managers and journalists that published a local magazine entitled *Trends*. Since then, *Trends* has branched out by publishing a wide range of lifestyle magazines. Ultimately, *Trends* helps to construct niche markets in China by bringing local and international magazines with segmented market differentiations to Chinese consumers.

This study will look at the front covers of past issues of selected magazines—*Trends*, *Cosmopolitan*, *Esquire*, *Men's Health*, and *FHM*; the changes in visual styles on the covers will be explored in order to understand the sequential development of glocalization. Particular attention is paid to when these magazines began to first, promote international brand names and, second, use mainly local and regional celebrities as cover models.

In early *Trends* publications, the creative and editorial teams endeavored to engage Chinese locals by interviewing local celebrities and introducing to them new and various leisure activities and consumer goods. In the first issue of *Trends*, founder Wu Hong prefaced that *Trends* is not just about shallow, pretentious, and conspicuous consumption, but about real "trendy" living through material and spiritual well-being. *Trends*, he believed, should be connected to the deep humanistic values of the Chinese culture. Nevertheless, these humanistic Chinese characteristics in *Trends* were largely overshadowed by dominant visual styles, appropriated by cutting and pasting from foreign (mainly American and British) magazines. The so-called global content of *Trends* was undeniably taken from the hegemonic consumerist cultures of a few major developed centers and their regional satellite cities. In fact, many early front covers featured medium shots of foreign, well-dressed models and movie stars while the content was taken mainly from English sources and translated into Chinese for *Trends*. Furthermore, it was evident that the editors of *Trends* preferred local interviewees with transnational connections; stories and images of Chinese men and women traveling, studying, and working abroad were, and to some extent still are, preferable.

During the magazine's early years, Chinese readers were fascinated with *Trends*; many older and longtime readers recalled the powerful influence the magazine had upon them. These readers vividly recalled specific covers and stories, emphasizing their importance as lifestyle references during a time when consumer information was extremely limited. *Trends* was ultimately able to connect readers to the modern world that was found overseas, and not in China. Though some critics label *Trends'* early period as their copycat period, the company has since stressed the need to strike a balance between global vision and local engagement. Fundamentally, foreign companies have been unable to have the final say on the style and content of magazines published by Trends Group; Trends Group is an atypical example where the global dominant culture has not been able to take over the local indigenous culture. For example, many international labels have become interested in partnering with Trends Group. The reason various partnership proposals were unsuccessful was ultimately due to governmental policy against foreign media control or internal insistence on autonomy.

From collaboration to localization of the global

Since the late 1990s, Trends Group has been aggressively lining up agreements with overseas (mainly American) labels. The original *Trends* magazine has since branched out into two separate magazines entitled *Trends* and *Trends Gentlemen*; the former for female readers and the latter for men. Furthermore, Trends Group has also successfully negotiated deals with Hearst, bringing two leading American magazines, *Cosmopolitan* for women, *Esquire* for men, to China. This sort of cooperation between Trends Group and Hearst is mutually beneficial. On one hand, Hearst is non-intrusive of *Trends* as long as the Chinese versions of *Cosmopolitan* and *Esquire* are selling well. On the other hand, by adopting international labels, magazines under Trends Group acquire a global outlook, rein in more international advertising money, and are more resourceful in adapting images and content from international sister magazines. Through examining when the covers of Trends' magazines became "internationalized," newly acquired labels were heavily promoted by eye-catching slogans and add-on leaflets. Editors have confirmed that once international labels were secured, transnational products have been more willing to place their advertisements in the magazines.

During those stages of collaboration, transborder visual exchanges were frequent and intense. The editors of Trends Group's magazines were flown to the Hearst headquarters for training before they could launch the collaborated issues; Chinese editors from Trends Group recalled the culture shock of those training sessions. The styles, formats, and layouts were synchronized with each other, past issues of the Chinese versions of the magazines critically analyzed, and new ways of packaging were suggested. Additionally, the works of top photographers from the mainland were heavily criticized by their American partner. In one instance, photos of good food were shot in a very professional style that was approved and up to the standard of the Chinese editor, but the American editor criticized the photos, saying though the photos were pretty, the photos would not stimulate a reader's appetite. Photos from American magazines were shown and the tricks of the trade were discussed in great details.

> They have been doing this for many years; their magazine market is sophisticated and their publishing skills have come of age. We are just beginners in the field ... Chinese trends [lifestyle] magazines are just infants compared to them [American magazines].
>
> *Yin zhixian, senior editor; interview quote*

Ultimately, this stage of collaboration demonstrated that transborder visual flows were not just limited to the cut and paste of visual styles and content. Transborder exchanges became more technical and operational while the processes of visual design, production, and experimentation were brought to full scrutiny. Ultimately, the American team served as a mentor and as guidance for the Chinese team.

Though *Cosmopolitan* and *Esquire*, the two flagship magazines of Trends Group, had already coordinated with international labels in the 2000s, they began to seek out more partners. The Chinese versions of *Men's Health*, *For Him*, *Good Housekeeping*, *National Geographic Traveler*, *National Geographic*, and *Bazaar* were launched one by one, rendering Trends Group the most globally networked lifestyle publishing house in mainland China. Training programs, annual gathering of international partners, contents trade, and advertising and marketing exercises have become more frequent. There is a strong mutual learning effect among the dozen of magazines within Trends. The international standards on visual styles, such as clear and stable format, clean and neat design, glossy printing, controlled sexual appeal, and punch line tactics, have quickly been acquired.

In the 1990s and early 2000s, Trends' covers continued to be dominated by well-known stars from overseas. International collaborations have provided Trends' magazines with a huge pool of visual resources. Up to the early 2000s, stylist covers, proved to be working internationally, had been "imported" directly from affiliates.

Marketing wisdom was based upon this interview quote: "sales depend on covers, and, covers with western faces sell." In the late 1990s, *Cosmopolitan* experimented with local cover girls and failed in sales. At that time, western stars were more convincing as "spokespeople" of fashion and living trendy lifestyles.

Saving faces for magazine covers: case studies

The key to sales for a magazine is its cover, which, to a large extent, positions the niche of the magazine and attracts a specific group of readers. There are hundreds of lifestyle magazines in China, all of them trying to stand out at the newspaper stands on busy streets and metro-stations by featuring eye-catching covers. In this keen competition for readers' attention, movie stars, pop singers, and celebrities are safe bets. They are the spokespeople of trends and fashion; in China, a considerable part of their income is generated from being the models and spokepersons for trendy products. Lifestyle magazines need stars and, in return, stars need media platforms to sustain their visibility.

In the mediated world, events are almost invisible for the general public if they are not covered by the media. The aura of pop stars is conferred to them by the media; there will be no stars without mediation. Reciprocally, in China, if lifestyle magazines are not endorsed by stars, they are not marketable at all. The irony of this symbiosis is that, as the editors in this study pointed out, there are very few pop stars in China to satisfy the huge demand for magazine modeling, ending up with a few familiar faces dominating the magazine industry. In an interview with me, one editor stated, "Look around you, who can you find? Good looking and well dressed male movie stars can be counted by numbers. I bet there are no more than ten." Perhaps this editor was exaggerating. It is the reality, however, that editors in the mainland need to look for cover models in Hong Kong, Taiwan, South Korea, and Japan, where entertainment businesses have had a longer history. On the other hand, they can also reproduce directly from the American partners if they have collaborative agreements.

Articulating the celebrities featured in Trends

A senior editor from *Cosmopolitan* told us that there are generally two kinds of arrangements concerning celebrities and artists for cover shooting. First, after a regular feature interview for the magazine, if the editors find that the artist is suitable, they will invite him or her to appear on the cover, and then seek a fashion sponsor from among major labels. Second, if a movie star is already the spokesperson of a big label, and that label is placing a major advertisement in the magazine, then, as a packaged deal, the star will also be invited to be the cover model. Furthermore, there is the assumption that the image of the star is compatible with that of the magazine. Once in a while, there will be agents of artists recommending their artists for cover shooting; however, as a general policy of protecting the image of the Trends Group, these self-recommendations are usually declined.

Similar to other lifestyle magazines, *Cosmopolitan* will pick celebrities according to talks of the time. For instance, when Haige Chen launched his film *The Promise*, it was in the month of February, around Valentine's Day. Trends' editors invited the lead actor Dong-Gun Jang and lead actress Cecilia Cheung of *The Promise* to be the couple featured on the cover. "We cooperate with Chen, with a huge poster from the movie and the two lead artists. They are well known and their images fit in with us," said the editor. In actual fact, featuring a couple on the cover would violate the norms of the Hearst's *Cosmopolitan*; normally, *Cosmpolitan* only features one female artist for their covers. In doing so, the Chinese company was testing the limitations of the American headquarters.

In fact, quite a number of the Trends magazine covers have been criticized by the head offices of their overseas partners as being out of line with the overseas versions. An obvious violation is the subversion of gender stereotypes, and these "new moves" sometimes generate intense public discussion, which has been good for the brand building of Trends Group. In the following sections, I will select and analyze a few Trends covers to discuss the process of transculturation (Chan and Ma 2002), whereby the Chinese are producing their own versions of international labels.

Men's Health

In the early 2000s, Feng Wang, the then editor of *Men's Health*, made an editorial decision to use mostly Chinese or Asian (whether local, regional, or overseas Asian) models and celebrities on the covers of *Men's Health* magazine. "Stay healthy and care for your body" is the motto of *Men's Health* magazine; its covers are mainly comprised of masculine men showing off their healthy bodies. However, in the August 2004 issue, the cover of *Men's Health* featured famous Chinese model Hu Bing, smiling, half naked, with oil all over his body. This ambiguous image caught the attention of the American headquarters, who read it as an invitation to gay readers. Subsequently, the American office immediately warned the Chinese editors for violating their agreement as to magazine formatting. Some Chinese readers also raised the same criticism. Nonetheless, it must be noted that there is a discrepancy in the visual codes of homosexuality in the United States and in China. For Americans, homosexual codes are more stable; for the Chinese, these codes have been ambiguous as gay culture is still invisible in popular media. For the American managers, the cover was obviously homosexual; however, for the Chinese readers and editors, the cover was ambiguous.

In an interview with me, Jiang Liu, the then vice president of Trends retorted, "we should not discriminate against homosexuals. People even discuss homosexuality even on CCTV [China Central Television]. It is not illegal to talk about the topic and we are among the first to touch on this topic." Some readers complained that this was merely a commercial gimmick, and that they were making Chinese males too "girlish." Homosexuality is a social phenomenon and media practitioners need to pay attention to that fact. Although the American head office interpreted Hu Bing's image as overtly homosexual, one should not discriminate against the notion of homosexuality. First, Hu Bing is a famous Chinese artist and at the top of the model business. Second, even if he is homosexual, he is a local Chinese celebrity and has the ability to draw readers in. Nevertheless, criticisms have been persistent. Featured on the wall of the *Men's Health* American headquarters, there are editions of *Men's Health* from all over the world. The head office maintains that it is a magazine for mainstream male readers, therefore the aberrant style of the Chinese version was a heresy. As a gesture of disapproval, the American headquarters tore down the cover of the Chinese version from their hall of international partners.

Because of the lure of the huge Chinese market, *Men's Health* international still maintained a working relation with Feng Wang, the "heretical" Chinese editor. The relations between the American and Chinese team was repaired when Feng Wang was internally transferred to serve as the chief editor of *Esquire* in 2005. The new editor of *Men's Health*, Wenqian Li (originally from Taiwan), has switched to a more cooperative and professional mode of glocalization, while maintaining the policy of using Chinese and Asian cover models.

Esquire

In 2005, Feng Wang took up office in *Esquire* and started the same process of localization as he did for *Men's Health*. Chinese celebrities, movie stars, intellectuals, directors, writers, entrepreneurs, and sport stars from mainland China, Hong Kong, Taiwan, and Korea were been invited to appear on the covers of *Esquire*. In our interview with him, Feng Wang expressed a clear determination of localizing and regionalizing Chinese lifestyle magazines.

> The cover of a magazine is comparable to the face of a person ... it is the most important platform for a Chinese magazine to tell people about the spiritual outlook of us Chinese. It is a shame to let westerners sit on our chair. We will lose face if we keep continuing to do so!

Wang's undertone is arguably nationalistic. What is most significant to note is that this switch was done in good timing; in the mid-2000s, Chinese readers had grown and become more receptive to local icons.

Overseas versions of *Esquire* front covers generally feature successful males in their prime. In June 2007, the Chinese version of *Esquire* featured a famous Chinese artist who was over 80 years old. The cover story was entitled, "Mr. Trendy, Huang Yongyu, almost a fairy." Wang, with his work wear, becomes Mr. Trendy the Senior. In our interview with him, Feng Wang, the then chief editor of *Esquire* at the time, explained his decision:

> We do not buy into the idea that an "Esquire" gentleman has to necessarily be good looking, young, with good fashion sense. Mr. Huang, with his colorful

life experience, has turned himself into a cunning and wise old man. He is certainly a role model of our time, someone with progressive thinking, taste, and creativity. He is certainly "Mr. Trendy," judged by whatever standards. If we take this one step further, our magazine will go beyond the ordinary, and its content will be more substantial.

During this time, Wang had prepared for a drop in sales for the issue featuring Yongyu Huang. However, the copies of that issue sold out on newsstands of Chiang-an street in just three days.

Though Wang was fully aware of the marketing risk from the beginning, he believed featuring Yongyu Huang was worth a shot. Sales were initially shaky when Wang made his big changes, but have since been stabilized. Evidently, the Chinese version of *Esquire* also deviates from the American version by featuring cover personalities with a variety of age ranges. Hearst initially did complain, but as the growing commercial significance of the Chinese consumer market has become undeniable, the Chinese editors have been left to conduct their own affairs in Chinese *Esquire*.

Cosmopolitan

Similarly, the head office of *Cosmopolitan* had also criticized their Chinese counterpart for violating the "gender code" of their magazine. Featured on the front cover of the February 2006 issue of Chinese *Cosmopolitan* was Korean male superstar, Bae Yong Joon. This was the first time since the inauguration of *Cosmopolitan* (in 1998) that a male celebrity was featured on its front cover. The Chinese editor defended this cover, arguing that it was suitable as a Valentine's issue, and that young females adored Bae Yong Joon. Nevertheless, the Chinese editor and team received strong condemnation from the American head office.

Shirley Zhang, assistant publisher of *Cosmopolitan* and *Esquire*, recalled in our interview with her that George Green (the international director of Hearst) personally called her to give her a stern warning after the February 2006 issue was published. Green remarked to Zhang, "Shirley, this is your first time, and your last time!" Before making the decision, the Chinese editors of *Cosmopolitan* had asked for Zhang's opinion, as they knew she herself was a fan of Bae Yong Joon. Though Zhang did not initially buy into the idea of featuring Bae Yong Joon on the front cover, out of respect for the editorial staff, she left the editors alone to make the final decision.

Nevertheless, *Cosmopolitan* was, and still is, doing very well in terms of sales; clearly, a few violations of the norms of the brand have not hurt sales. On the contrary, these violations may even bring surprises to the readers and become a point of discussion amongst the general public.

> The result was that that particular issue did drop a bit in term of sale. But it did well. We … didn't defend ourselves and accepted the criticism. To be honest,

advertisers wouldn't care, because it was not a long-term change, just a one-off experiment. The good thing about publishing magazines in China is that here we can work miracles. What matters is whether you have the courage to do it. Of course there will always be a second opinion; there will be arguments and disagreements. Anyhow, you have to actually try things out before you know how the market responds.

Shirley Zhang, assistant publisher; interview quote

FHM

It is clear that the production of magazine covers involves advertising revenues, image building of the artists, sales and marketing, and magazine branding as a whole. Therefore, good planning and tactful negotiation are much needed beforehand. I chose *FHM* as one of the test cases for detailed observation. *FHM* caught my attention because it generates a lot of interest, discussion, and debate both within the Trends Group and among the general readers. The Chinese version of *FHM* deviates significantly from the original version of *FHM* published in the United Kingdom; the UK version and other international versions are arguably soft pornography for men. However, the Chinese version of *FHM*, for various reasons, experiments on issues of gender, sexuality, and power. More often than not, the covers of Chinese *FHM* feature sexy models with an analytic bent. These covers bring up progressive themes by exploiting the sexual appeal of female models; *FHM* policy for cover models is for them to be sexy, open, and frank. Indeed, some cover stories have aroused intense public interest and these controversial covers have, in turn, built a name for the magazine. Therefore, the publisher puts many resources into shooting substantive cover stories, creating a conceptually and visually challenging cover photo.

I conducted interviews as well as observations in the production of *FHM* cover stories during my stay in Trends. Jacky Jin, chief editor of *FHM*, told us that during the 1990s, describing a woman as sexy carried the connotations of being horny and promiscuous. "Female friends would find it offensive," he said. Today, however, times have changed; a regular office lady would be elated if someone described her as sexy, as being sexy has become admirable.

The chief editor also noted:

> The *FHM* cover with the artist Aduo as the feature model has become the most talked about cover of a Trends magazine. It was bold. Look at the visual treatment of that particular issue; though you cannot see any sensitive parts of her body, Aduo is still seen as "naked" in the eyes of the public. Aduo is making a statement, stating frankly that her body belongs to her; it is herself that will make the decision to show her body or not. For the Chinese people, this concept is challenging. In the past, us Chinese have not taken getting to know our own selves seriously; now, we understand that we have the right to express ourselves.
>
> *Jacky Jin, chief editor, FHM; interview quote*

According to Jacky, allowing people to freely and frankly share their life is the key to regaining the "rights to privacy and bodies" in China; this would be a huge leap forward for Chinese society. Undeniably, recent history of Socialist China has seen the public (the state) suppressing private expressions. In Jacky's words, "the political was swallowing the personal." Part of *FHM*'s success is due in part to the popular trend of reprioritizing one's body and private life in China.

While shooting the front cover, the editors of *FHM* and actress Aduo worked on four to five different potential treatments. For example, one of the options was to dress her in the uniform of a fireman, depicting her as a sort of masculine female in control of her own life. According to Chen, one of the editors of *FHM*, uniforms are sexy in the eyes of some. Nevertheless, it proved difficult in getting the uniform as well as the fire truck; additionally, it was winter during the shooting of the cover, and the cover would have had to be shot outdoors. Chen then came up with the idea of featuring Aduo as a chef. It was visually a competent idea, and Aduo was positive about the idea of a sexy chef. Nonetheless, *FHM* cover stories have to have a theme that can be seen as explorative.

> *FHM* has to have a theme in which readers can dig deeper, uncovering cultural meanings attached to the cover. People may ask—why does she have to take off her clothes? Why does she have to be sexy? Therefore, a good design is not good enough; it may work for other magazines, but not for *FHM*.
>
> Chen, editor, FHM; *interview quote*

Underlying this is the fact that mere pornographic pleasure is not officially allowed in China. To project connotations of being a magazine that explores important societal issues is in fact a tactic for staying away from unwanted accusations and censorship.

Finally, the creative team decided on the final option; they wanted to show females as an expression of power, and show that females are in control of their own world. Aduo also wanted to be extreme, to be in control of everything, like a goddess—she idolized Madonna and used her as an inspiration. Chen also recalled:

> Aduo was very confident, but had reservations about how explicit the photos would be. For instance, one of the original options was to dress her in quite a revealing outfit. However, we had to keep the magazine in mind—having too sexy a cover might imply difficulties in securing distribution outlets.
>
> Chen, editor, FHM; *interview quote*

As a comprise, the creative team used a belt to cover Aduo's underwear. The limit of explicitness is a matter of scale, and also a matter of latent values. Despite the fact that *FHM* is targeted at young male readers, the editors also insist that the cover story should not be offensive to female readers.

One of the editors noted, "I think if a dirty idea is visualized, men will find it interesting. But for women, it may be offensive. To make it simple, what we do is produce sexy images with style and class." Therefore, on the front cover, Aduo wore a workman's uniform and had a camera in her hand. When a woman is working and showing her body unintentionally, it is not viewed as overtly sexy, but subtly sexy, classy, and healthy.

With its explicit and bold covers, *FHM* is not the ideal magazine for all Chinese artists to promote their image. Chen said:

> We will not talk unwilling and skeptical artists into shooting [with us]. We would rather work with artists who identify with us. If they are willing to work with us, the questions of how sexy, of what the topic is, and how we are going to shoot—questions like these, can all be dealt with easily.
>
> *Chen, editor,* FHM; *interview quote*

Since *FHM* has been recognized by their peers in the magazine industry, there are indeed many artists who want to be featured on the front covers of *FHM*. Many artists consider it as a good way to reposition themselves. In 2007, Aduo was given the honor of being the most popular cover girl of the year—Aduo's particular issue was extremely successful, especially in terms of sales. *FHM* subsequently invited Aduo to be the cover girl for the December issue. Since being featured on *FHM*, Aduo has established herself as a sex symbol in China.

In order to understand the production process better, my research team and I participated in shooting the September 2007 issue of *FHM*. The task turned out to be more difficult than anticipated; however, this is not uncommon when producing magazine content that explores sexuality in China. The original plan of the *FHM* team was to feature actress Qin Hailu on the front cover. Chen, chief editor, explained, "I was interested in her because everyone says she is a 'not so pretty' actress. I wanted to challenge myself and the photographer by giving this 'best actress' a special treat."[2] The shooting was supposed to take two days, and was supposed to be shot at South Luogu Lane. Wuyi Zhang, my research assistant, woke up at 6:30am on July 24 and arrived at the Trends Tower studio at 7:30am that same day. At the Trends Tower studio, there were a few makeup artists and hairdressers, but not one person from the *FHM* production team; Zhang subsequently called the editor but nobody answered the phone. Only at 9:15am, when Zhang called Lin, the fashion editor, did Zhang find out that the boss of Qin Hailu's agent pulled out last minute, citing the shooting plan as being "too sexy" for the actress.

The editorial staff had found a replacement in great haste; they contacted Taiwan actress Pace Wu that night and discussed a new shooting plan. This time, the editor invited veteran photographer Zhun Chen to help. When Wu, the editors, and the photographer met up, Wu insisted she would not appear on the cover in a bikini; however, Chen believed that if Wu was not in a bikini, the cover photo story would look too plain. Unsurprisingly, the meeting came to a dead end. A few days later, another attempted collaboration, this time with actress Yili Ma, also failed. Finally, the editorial team secured Haizhen Wang, a model who skyrocketed to fame due to her alleged affair with movie director Yimou Zhang.

At 9:00am on the day of the shoot, my team and I arrived at a photo studio, Image Base Beijing, just outside the East Fourth Ring Road. Inside the park, there are torn down factories in which a few shooting studios are housed. When we arrived, Haizhen Wang had already arrived, and the stylists and *FHM* staff were busily arranging props and sets. When all the tedious preparation work was completed, it was already noon. The first shot, featuring Haizhen Wang in a bikini, was carried out smoothly. The editor Chen had told us that more often than not, the stars for *FHM* need some time to warm up and adjust; most of them are more comfortable taking off their clothes only after a few hours into the shooting session. But Haizhen Wang, being a professional model, played her part with ease. She had just taken a two-year break from the entertainment industry after giving birth to her child, and she had wanted to launch her comeback—being featured on the front cover of *FHM* was precisely what she believed her career needed at that moment.

The goal of *FHM* is to transform sexuality into something distinctly and uniquely Chinese; Wang's cover shooting is an illustrative case. After the lunch break, the photographer talked to the editors—he had done a web search right before the shoot and had come up with a theme connecting Wang to the classic Chinese text, *The Emperor's Private Script*. However, he wanted to transform it into something of his own entitled, *The Emperor's Heterodox*. The photographer's idea was to suggest that seeking visual pleasures in appreciating the female body and physique is the imperial way to foster well-being and health. The *FHM* editors, on the other hand, disagreed. Their worry was that the cover story would be too controversial; critics would slam *FHM* for messing with such a famous classic, Chinese text. In addition, the editors and the photographer himself did not know enough about *The Emperor's Private Script*; it would be difficult to write the content of the story. Nevertheless, the photographer was unrelenting. The final title of the cover story, after much discussion, became "The Sensual Imagination of the Emperor's Heterodox: An Urban Expression of Visual Styles." Arguably, the theme of the cover story was more of a gimmick than art that had real substance. The photos mostly displayed Wang's body against various street scenes as the background. This small case study illustrates the ways in which an international magazine for men (that had been deemed soft pornography) has been reshaped in China to become a popular magazine exploring sensitive cultural issues. The Chinese version retains the sexual appeal of the international label, but also transforms it into a seemingly cultural magazine on fashionable, bold, urban lifestyles.

Other Trends magazines started to use a few local cover personalities in the mid-2000s, but were not as extensive in their use as *FHM*, *Men's Health*, and *Esquire* were. These Trends magazines are carefully monitoring market signals to see whether or not Chinese readers are receptive to Chinese celebrities. These bold moves across different Trends magazines signals a transition from a strong desire to copy foreign visual culture to a new stage in which the local is actively appropriating the global on its own terms. High-profile international stars are still prime movers in global capitalism. However, in the case of China, because of huge market potential, the creative workers of Trends are now capitalizing on the

90 Eric Kit-wai Ma

cultural resources of their international partners. They are not being homogenized by the foreign but, instead, are turning foreign visual elements into local sentiments. This, however, is no simple glocalization. The consumerist ideologies of global capitalism may be prominent in international lifestyle magazines, including those published by Trends—nonetheless, the front covers of Trends' magazines are undeniably Chinese and Asian. It is clearly a departure from the 1990s, when white males dominated the front covers of Trends' magazines. The turning point for Trends' magazines came in the mid-2000s.

The Trends Group provides a good case for theorizing the relations between the growing local economy and the development of transborder visuality. As indicated in the beginning of this chapter, theories of cultural transfer in global capitalism have been modified from linear formulations to more dialectic approaches of glocalization, with culture-specific configurations embedded in various forms of modernities. We are now at a theoretical stage where patterns of glocalization need to be spelled out in concrete terms; the case of Trends adds a new dimension into the discussion. In the past decade of so, we have seen in the operations of the Trends Group a shift from a subordinate mode of transborder visuality, in which western consumer culture was hegemonic and dominating, to a more glocalized mode, in which Trends has been developing a strong editorial stance of reprioritizing the local and national.

Chinese visual culture, as exhibited in Trends' magazines, is far from autonomous. Officially, Trends Group is still a governmental unit. The managerial staff could be replaced at any time by state order, if the content became too far off from state endorsed limits. All Trends magazines are still dependent upon the powerful transnational networks of advertising and resources circulated around hegemonic cultural centers such as London, New York, and Los Angeles. However, despite the fact that consumerist ideology is winning consent easily among cultural producers and consumers, visual contents have changed to more localized and regionalized forms. Because of the large and still growing consumer market in China, Trends has great bargaining power in the global–local dialectic to work out their own cultural expressions, without having to yield to warnings and/or complaints from their international partners.

Exploiting the global: concluding remarks

In this chapter, the term visuality has not just conceptualized as an assembly of images. Visuality fundamentally also includes the production and consumption of visual products, their social and cultural contexts, the visual competence of the populations, and the social practices of viewing, judging, and producing visual hierarchies. Visual culture can be defined as the visual practices in which users seek information, meaning, and pleasure in an interface with visual technology (Davis 2011; Mirzoeff, 2002). Theoretically speaking, visual culture is constitutive of cultural networks, which produce social relations and practices. In visual culture, "how to see" and "what to see" are the strategies to know in order to exercise power. In short, visuality is not just mere images; it also involves complex networks that facilitate the production of modern, stylish, flexible, and sophisticated visual images.

Increasingly, visuality cannot be isolated from transborder flows. Images travel, as well as the tricks of visual production and consumption. There is a rough consensus that these flows are not linear, and are not necessarily predominated by a global to local logic, as proposed in various versions of critical theories. At a time when China is undergoing modernization in its most aggressive stage, popular images travel to China and reappear in highly altered forms in various national and regional scales. The Trends Group is an illustrative case that can enrich the debate on cultural globalization. Seeing the Trends Tower as a metaphor for a factory in the compressed modernity of urban China, the space is itself symbolic of a place where new identities are mediated and produced—it is a visual, spatial, and conceptual expression of transborder connections. Global visual resources are circulated across these lifestyle factories among all sister media groups around the world. Transborder exchanges include mutual referencing and learning, selling of images and contents, as well as technical and operational collaborations.

Since its inception almost 20 years ago, the magazines of the Trends Group have gone through different modes of transborder visual exchanges; from the early years of aspiring for and borrowing from the global, to a stage of deep collaboration, and, more recently, to a new stage of reprioritizing the local and capitalizing on the global. In this transitional stage, a heterogeneous mix of visual codes, global and local, is deployed to cope with the rising and multifaceted demands in the production and consumption of cultural products in urban China.

A few observations can be made here for discussion and further theoretical development. First, Trends can be seen as a case not of glocalization, but what I tentatively label "exploiting the global." With a growing bargaining power supported by strong domestic demands, Trends' leaders are able to ride on the cultural capital of western labels and exploit global marketing resources (image banks, visual expertise, technological transfer, and joint projects) for brand building and market consolidation. The "global" is no longer a dominating power, but a resourceful partner for flexible domestication. Nevertheless, there are complications. The Trends package might have a more national face than before, but is ultimately still following the consumerist logic of international counterparts. It is important to note, though, that Trends is not a subordinate in the transborder flows mapped out in this chapter.

Second, the Trends case demonstrates a shifting hierarchical hybridization through the mixing and matching of regional resources. Again, this is a tentative theoretical speculation based on a single case. In the 1990s, transborder flows flowed from the West to China, with satellite links relaying matured consumerism in Japan, Hong Kong, and Taiwan. Into the 2000s, urban visuality in China, as expressed in the Trends package, is not just a Sino–West collaboration, but a hybridization of Chinese and Asian signs and symbols. The flows have shifted from a "West to Asia to China" pattern to a complex and dynamic hierarchy, with a more powerful Chinese style domesticating western and regional styles.

Third, it demonstrates the role of the agency factor. The Trends case tells a story of developing visual competency, both from production and consumption ends. Producers and consumers have both acquired a more sophisticated visual language. It would be naïve to say that agency is autonomous, free from the structural constraints of late capitalism on a global scale. Trends' leaders and editors exercise their growing autonomy based on the rising personal wealth and expanding consumerism of the urban middle class. It is the editors' choice to localize Trends' covers and shift the editorial lines of international labels (the case of *FHM* is most indicative of this fact). Trends' magazines adopt a "Chinese look," capitalizing on Chinese, Hong Kong, Taiwan, and pan-Asian celebrities, with a mix of western icons. The editors of Trends are aware of the marketing positions of their local competitors, especially those headquartered in Shanghai that focus on Japanese style models. Trends' emphasis on Chinese and Asian models is a conscious marketing choice to differentiate themselves from their competition.

In conclusion, this chapter presents a complex transborder cultural map in the Sino–West context that demonstrates that in the current era, it is no longer simply cultural flows that flow from the west to China, with satellite links such as Hong Kong, Taiwan, and Japan. The case I selected for in-depth analysis is empirically and theoretically significant in the sense that it demonstrates that since the early 2000s, the rise of the Chinese consumer market and changes in consumer tastes have created more interactive and multidimensional transborder flows in urban China.

Notes

1 A full research report has been published in Chinese (Ma 2012).
2 Qin Hailu won the award for best actress at the 20th Hong Kong Film Awards.

Bibliography

Bauman, Z. (2000) *Liquid Modernity*. Cambridge: Polity Press.
Beck, U. and Beck-Gernsheim, E. (2002). *Individualization: Institutionalized Individualism and its Social and Political Consequences*. Thousand Oaks, CA: Sage.
Berger, P. (1988) "An East Asian Development Model?" In P. Berger and M. Hsiao, eds. *In Search of an East Asian Development Model*, New Brunswick, N.J.: Transaction Books, 3–11.
Chan, J. M. (2002) "Disneyfying and Globalizing the Chinese Legend Mulan: a Study of Transculturation: a Reinterpretation of Cultural Globalization." In J. M. Chan and B. T. McIntyre, eds. *In Search of Boundaries: Communication, Nation-states and Cultural Identities*, Westport, CT: Ablex.
Chan, J. M. and Ma, E. (2002) "Transculturating Modernity." In J. M. Chan and B. T. McIntyre, eds. *In Search of Boundaries: Communication, Nation-States and Cultural Identities*, Westport, CT: Ablex.

Cohen, A. (2002) "Globalization Ltd: Domestication at the Boundaries of Foreign Television News." In J. M. Chan and B. T. McIntyre, eds. *In Search of Boundaries: Communication, Nation-states and Cultural Identities*, Westport, CT: Ablex.

Curtin, M. (2007) *Playing to the World's Biggest Audience: The Globalization of Chinese Film and TV*, Berkeley: University of California Press.

Davis, W. (2011) *A General Theory of Visual Culture*, Princeton, NJ: Princeton University Press.

Eisenstadt, S. N. (2000) "Multiple Modernities." *Daedalus: Journal of the American Academy of Arts and Sciences*, 129 (1): 1–30.

Giddens, A. (1991) *Modernity and Self-identity: Self and Society in the Late Modern Age*. Cambridge: Polity Press.

Giddens, A. (1990) *The Consequences of Modernity*. Stanford, CA: Stanford University Press.

Lash, S. and Urry, J. (1994) *Economies of Signs and Space*. Thousand Oaks, CA: Sage.

Lee, L. (2000) "The Cultural Construction of Modernity in Urban Shanghai: Some Preliminary Exploration." In W. H. Yeh, ed. *Becoming Chinese: Passages to Modernity and Beyond*, Berkeley: University of California Press.

Ma, E. (2012) *Trends Factory: A Visual Ethnography*. Shanghai: Fudan University Press (in Chinese).

Ma, E. (2002) "Translocal Spatiality." *International Journal of Cultural Studies* 5 (2): 131–152.

Ma, E. (2001) "Consuming Satellite Modernities." *Cultural Studies*, 15 (4): 444–463.

Ma, E. and Zhang, X. (2011) *Mediated Modernity: A Dialogue Between Communication and Social Theories*. Shanghai: Fudan University Press (in Chinese).

Mirzoeff, N. (2002) *The Visual Culture Reader*. London: Routledge.

Mitchell, T. (1994) *Picture Theory: Essays on Verbal and Visual Representation*. Chicago: University of Chicago Press.

Robertson, R. (1995) "Glocalization: Time-Space and Homogeneity-Heterogeneity." In M. Featherstone, *Global Modernities*, London: Sage.

Rofel, L. (1999) *Other Modernities: Gendered Yearnings in China after Socialism*. Berkeley: University of California Press.

Stevenson, R. (1992) "An Essay: Defining International Communication as a Field." *Journalism Quarterly*, 69 (3): 543–553.

Tomlinson, J. (1999) *Globalization and Culture*. Chicago: Chicago University Press.

Yeh, W. H. (2000) *Becoming Chinese: Passages to Modernity and Beyond*. Berkeley: University of California Press.

6

CULTURAL CONSUMPTION AND MASCULINITY

A case study of GQ magazine covers in Taiwan

Hong-Chi Shiau

The global rise of men's fashion magazines

Established in the United States in the 1930s, *Esquire* and *GQ* were the first magazines to be designed with a male audience in mind. Subsequently, other nations in the West began to follow this trend and men's magazines were established in various other western nations; this development followed different paths and consequently had different outcomes. The concept of masculinity being constructed and presented in men's fashion magazines increasingly seems to be the work of global capitalist agents reconfiguring, reshaping, and redefining the concepts of masculinity and what masculine bodies should resemble (Iwabuchi 2002; Tam *et al.* 2009). The recent rise in popularity of men's fashion has undoubtedly accelerated the commercialization of so-called masculine male bodies in the East Asian region, following a historical trajectory similar to the West's (Tanaka 2003). The year 1954 oversaw the establishment of the first men's fashion magazine in Asia; *Men's Club* was established that year in Japan. Since 1954, many more men's fashion magazines have been added to the Japanese market. Though Japanese men's fashion magazines were the first of their kind to emerge in Asia, it still remains an ambiguous category. While magazines exist that target fashion-conscious and fashion-forward males, magazines that solely target females are always defined by the gender of their readership and are referred to as "women's magazines." When Black and Coward examined in 1990 the emergence of men's fashion magazines as a subcategory of women's magazines, they suggested that magazine publishers took such action to enable males to be able to represent themselves as non-gendered; magazines targeting men were classified on the basis of content, while those targeting women were classified by gender. This theory is seemingly in line with previous critical analyses that ultimately confront the status of the establishment of masculinity and images of the male as the norm, from which images of women and femininity deviate (Tanaka 2003).

Men's fashion magazines in Taiwan emerged as a subcategory of women's magazines, despite the masculine and consumer-oriented society of Taiwan. Only in the 1990s did Taiwan see the establishment of a distinct market for men's magazines; this was successfully capitalized upon and developed due in large part to foreign investors acquiring local Taiwanese publishing firms. Significantly, *GQ* launched in Taiwan in October of 1997, while *Men's Uno* was launched one year later in 1998; during the following decade, eight more magazine titles of similar content followed suit.[1] The Magazine Business Association of Taipei (MBAT) recognized the significant growth of what was termed as the "new, urban, young male" segment of Taiwan's magazine market and subsequently proclaimed the men's fashion magazine to be a distinct genre and market of its own. As aforementioned, men's magazines were initially categorized under "women's and fashion" magazines; however, the growth of men's fashion magazines in numbers and market size disrupted this method of classification. Men's fashion magazines in Taiwan have managed to defy the near universal trend of a decrease in the magazine advertising market, as is evident in the following statistics. *GQ* grew by 8 percent in 2004 and 10 percent in 2005, while *Men's Uno* fared even more impressively in those two years, growing at 44 percent and 25 percent respectively (MBAT 2006). Moreover, in the past decade, the advertising revenues for *GQ* and *Men's Uno* have grown at an exceptionally rapid pace, even though the Taiwanese magazine industry has been on the decline due to the popularity of digital trends. In the past decade, men's lifestyle magazines in Taiwan have gone from being an invisible magazine category to the fastest-growing magazine category, with a scale nearly comparable to the well-established category of women's fashion magazines (MBAT 2006).

Global consumerism and the concept of masculinity

Features of masculine consumerism and consumption first began manifesting themselves in late-nineteenth-century Britain, developing into a mass, hedonistic, masculine consumer culture during the 1950's consumer boom. The appearance and advance of the American middle class during this era propagated a new cultural habitus whereby material consumption meant expedition and facilitation of pleasure and personal liberation (Osgerby 2001; Osgerby 2003). This new class challenged the traditional American concept of masculinity, which was founded upon on the "breadwinner" archetype, or the production-oriented ethos characterized by the pursuit of enterprise, productiveness, and temperate respectability (Rotundo 1993). While feminine connotations of consumer desires and practices remain consistent and persistent, the preoccupation of men with such hedonistic pleasure has perpetuated an archetypical presentation of masculinity since the 1980s. This has been identified as a "narcissistic masculine consumer culture" or a "new man culture," and has often been associated with various new lifestyle magazines and advertisements. In line with the rise of this new man culture, the boom in men's fashion magazines has, in part, resulted from global publishers expanding their operations by exploiting opportunities in new and related sectors as a response to saturation in women's fashion publications (Edwards 1997; Nixon 1996). Since the 1980s, global capitalists advocating male consumerism have reshaped the popular scene, helping lead to the formation and emergence of aesthetically conscious young men worldwide.

In spite of the strong reactions and subsequent changes in recent decades over post-capitalism, literature that would help to understand hegemonic cultural constructions of masculinity outside of the West remains confined (Connell 1987; Hanke 1990). Owing to the global commercialization of culture, Taiwanese society has, in the last few decades, witnessed a nascent cultural orientation that has ascribed increased significance to the adaption of male consumption of fashion goods, laying the ground for a subsequent transformation. However, in the early 1990s, scholars analyzing the emergence of men's consumption often framed such changes in relation to various social movements, particularly the gay civil rights movement in Taiwan. With the emergence of new media technologies, the gay civil rights movement in Taiwan has become interconnected with the adoption of new media and consumption alliances related to identity. As Chou stated, "Taiwan's gay movement is also a movement of media" (Chou 2000: 159). Scholars of the Taiwanese gay movement claim that the emergence of the Taiwanese gay community in the 1990s and accompanying changes of the gender political scene can be attributed to computer-mediated communication. This new media helps to liberate the gay community and renders the formation of gay subjectivity tangible (Chou 2000; Martin 2003). In this context, a repositioning of gays and lesbians in commercial panoptic formations further transformed the fashion magazine industry as well as the representation of masculinities in Taiwan. During the 1980s, magazines were launched that targeted the interests of gay men and mixed fashion with consumption; these magazines were widely used by international publishers as a barometer for testing the prevailing social atmosphere.

Unlike the USA and Japan, the emergence of men's fashion magazines in Taiwan has been closely related to the proliferation of symbols and practices that celebrate subjectivities among sexual minorities, as well as the allegedly large, but unexplored, "pink economy." In the 1990s, the perceived desirability of lesbian, gay, bi-sexual, and transgender (LBGT) groups as a niche market triggered the development of many local men's fashion magazines. Thus, the formation of *GQ Taiwan* in 1997 occurred in a broader cultural context in which the nascent local men's fashion discourse was nearly non-existent, as they were dominated by women's fashion and/or so-called "queer" magazines. Desperately seeking another niche, global marketers and capitalists exploited the western imported notion of "metrosexuality" to sidestep the pink market and thereby expand their share of the local market.

The inception of Taiwan's *GQ* came in close proximity with the emergent pink market, and resulted from the larger social transformation linked to the gay civil rights movement. Similar to its American parent, *GQ Taiwan* contains articles unrelated to fashion and positions itself as a general men's magazine in competition with *Esquire*, another American men's magazine in Taiwan. Moreover, Taiwan's *GQ*, like other international editions, was launched as a regional adaptation of the

US editorial formula. The Taiwanese magazine market has long seen fierce competition between magazines. This is due to the growth in the number of magazine titles occurring in the context of a wider recession in magazine publishing. While adapting and adjusting international brands to fit the local environment is necessary, the entry of GQ to Taiwan as a business project can be understood as a "brand competition" between America and Japan. First, GQ is a general men's magazine with an American flavor whose main competitors are a few Japanese men's fashion magazines. While GQ was well known in the US, the general "men's magazine" was a completely new idea in Taiwan prior to its arrival. Having long been mixed with women's fashion magazines, Japanese style men's fashion magazines, on the other hand, were well established among the Taiwanese gay community. Bringing GQ into the Taiwanese market required answering numerous questions: would this American brand sell in Taiwan, and how far should GQ localize? Second, the Taiwanese public has long perceived men's fashion magazines to overlap with gay magazines. Thus, Taiwan's GQ faces the problem of distancing itself from the growing number of gay-related fashion magazines, as well as from its own gay readership. Another important challenge for the multinational corporation that owns GQ is how GQ Taiwan should strategically leverage the assets of its global parent. For example, should the Taiwanese edition always feature a standardized American male on its cover? While GQ succeeded in pioneering and extending a market segment, one of its fiercest local competitors in Taiwan, Men's Uno, has also been successful. As a new local men's fashion title, Men's Uno has successfully differentiated itself from GQ. As the subsidiary of Conde Nast, GQ aggressively capitalized on the new western aspiring, fashion-conscious readership as a successful pioneer in men's fashion media. In a sense, GQ's strong affiliation with its American counterpart inspired Men's Uno to turn to Japan as an alternative source of inspiration. The circulation of Men's Uno grew rapidly and, consequently, the magazine has become one of the top 20 magazines in Taiwan in terms of sales.[2] In this research, GQ and Men's Uno was used as a representative sample of the broader category of men's fashion magazines due to their importance and significance in the Taiwanese market.

Featured male cover models on *GQ Taiwan*: an analysis

Indicative of who wields power and influence in a certain field, magazine covers are products of editorial decisions mediated by the interplay of political, economic, and aesthetic forces (Johnson and Christ 1988). This study focuses solely on magazine covers and their featured models in order to make the study manageable. While earlier monolithic representations of masculinity have attracted criticism, alternative masculinities presented in global men's fashion magazines have reshaped the media environment, offering a fertile site for us to examine the changes and continuities of masculinity in a capitalist culture that reconfigures masculine bodies. This study therefore poses questions regarding three areas. The first set of questions (Q1a, b, c) is more descriptive than interpretative; these questions examine the frequency of non-locals, and the frequency in which non-locals are covered in order to gauge the extent of which western symbols have been appropriated and consumed in different contexts. The second and third sets of questions examine the institutional process of appropriating a non-local symbol and continues to examine why and how these symbols serve the objectives of Taiwan's *GQ*.

Q1a: How frequently has Taiwan's *GQ* featured non-locals on its covers?
Q1b: What were the ethnicities and countries of origin of these non-local cover models?
Q1c: How has the representation of non-locals in Taiwan's *GQ* changed over time?
Q2a: How frequently has Taiwan's *GQ* featured males on its covers?
Q2b: How has the representation of males in Taiwan's *GQ* changed over time?
Q3a: How has desirable masculinity been narrated in the cover stories of Taiwan's *GQ*?
Q3b: How has Taiwan's *GQ* changed over the past decade?

GQ's strong American affiliation is evident in its global parent, Conde Nast Publication, acquiring a local publisher (formerly also a strong local fashion magazine player) in 1996. Since its inception, *GQ Taiwan* has been a regional adaptation of the US editorial formula. Through the global expansion of *GQ*, global *GQ* can offer economies of scale to its 24 global subsidiaries (as of 2009), mostly by cutting operating costs through standardization. Content analysis of the magazine helps to understand what types of non-locals were chosen as cover models. Since this study focuses on how these non-local symbols were appropriated, the second stage of the study analyzes the narration of the cover stories and their rhetorical functions. Special attention was focused upon how unconventional, subordinate masculine attributes are negotiated and repackaged; these attributes are repackaged in order to render a sense of "situated masculinity," which is desirable to content producers in reaching out to their targeted readers. To understand more, I also conducted in-depth interviews with five key informants working for men's fashion magazines in Taiwan. Notably, I interviewed An Ko Chiang, the former editor-in-chief of *GQ* who is an outspoken gay rights activist, in 2010. The other four interviewees comprise of a *GQ* writer, a *GQ* part-time model, a *Men's Uno* writer, and, finally, the *Men's Uno* editor.

The sample period ran from 1998 to 2009, covering 12 years and 144 issues. The number of sample models exceeded 144 because *GQ* sometimes featured two or more models on the cover page, in which case, multiple models featured on a cover are measured simultaneously. Table 6.1 lists the frequency breakdown between 1998 and 2008.

To more clearly analyze the cover model sources, this study consolidates the sources into three items, which includes locals (Taiwan), non-Taiwanese Asians (East Asia), and non-Asians. Table 6.2 summarizes the trends in percentage form.

Regarding the cover models' ethnicities and countries of origin, men's fashion magazines in Taiwan featured more non-locals than Taiwanese. As shown in

Consumption and masculinity **99**

TABLE 6.1 GQ cover models: countries of origin and gender

	1998	1999	2000	2001	2002	2003	2004	2005	2006	2007	2008	Total
Non-Asian	12	11	10	5	6	3	6	5	5	0	2	65
Taiwanese	0	1	0	7	2	11	2	7	6	13	9	37
Chinese/HK	0	0	2	2	3	1+3	4	1	0	2	1	17
Japanese	0	0	0	1	1	1	1	0	1	0	0	5
Korean	0	0	0	1	0	0	0	0	0	0	0	1
Male	9	10	11	14	7	14	12	9	6	5	4	101
Female	3	2	1	2	5	5	1	4	6	10	8	47

TABLE 6.2 GQ cover models: locals versus non-locals

	1998	1999	2000	2001	2002	2003	2004	2005	2006	2007	2008	Total
Non-Asians	100	92	83	42	50	25	50	42	42	0	16	51
Non-Taiwanese Asians	0	0	17	33	34	17	33	8	8	17	7	19
Taiwanese		0	8	0	25	16	58	17	50	50	83	75	30

Table 6.2, 70 percent of models were non-locals, and most, in fact, were non-Asians. In the non-Asian category, white Caucasians make up 96 percent of all non-Asians, while Blacks and Latinos make up the remaining 4 percent. Arguably, in the men's fashion world as projected by Taiwan's GQ, non-Asian is nearly synonymous with white Caucasian. While numerous Black and Hispanic males have been featured on the covers of the American editions of GQ, only one Black and one Hispanic model has been featured on the covers of GQ *Taiwan*. This phenomenon deserves a closer look. In 1999, the June edition of GQ *Taiwan* featured Smith Wells, and the July issue that followed featured Ricky Martin. Though Ricky Martin is Hispanic, his appearance resembles that of a white Caucasian male; the cover story explicitly positioned his ethnic background as Hispanic and simultaneously stressed the sexual desirability of Latinos. Similarly for Smith Wells, the editors also emphasized his ethnic background and declared, "it is time to see a Latinos – a new ethnic face" (An 2010, personal interview). Therefore, both cover stories insinuated that Blacks and Hispanics had previously been underrepresented on their magazine covers. Nevertheless, there has never been another Black or Hispanic cover model since then.

When we look at the countries of origin of the white Caucasian models featured in 63 issues of Taiwan's GQ, we see that 42 models were from North

100 Hong-Chi Shiau

America (67 percent), 10 models were from England/Ireland (15 percent), six models were from continental Europe (10 percent), while five models were from Australia/New Zealand (eight percent). An intermediating factor explaining the employment of Caucasians as cover models is institutional: as the first men's fashion magazine in Taiwan, promoters of Hollywood films realized that *GQ Taiwan* had huge potential to become a key venue for promotion. Between 1998 and 2002 in fact, approximately 70 percent of western cover models featured in Taiwan's *GQ* were related to Hollywood. The accompanying cover stories often told of the movie roles played by cover models and divulged behind-the-scenes stories regarding upcoming Hollywood blockbusters.

Table 6.3 shows that all of the 10 male cover models that were featured multiple times were from English-speaking countries, six out of 10 were American, and David Beckham was the only model that had no affiliation with Hollywood. The initial preference for Hollywood actors as cover models was part of a conscious effort to brand the magazine as American. (An 2010, personal interview). For example, Tom Cruise's career was at its peak during 2002 and, during these years, he became very well known to Taiwanese locals. When asked why Tom Cruise was featured for three consecutive years between 1998 and 2000, the former editor-in-chief commented that Cruise was the first actor that would pop into peoples' minds during that time. Although the *GQ* production team was uncertain about whether such a focus would be able to sustain a strong Taiwanese readership, Tom Cruise, along with many other Hollywood actors, fulfilled their initial mission to brand the magazine as an American-oriented western publication. "As we pitched to western-aspiring advertisers in the category of men's fashion products, they were convinced" (An 2010, personal interview). Ultimately, Hollywood

TABLE 6.3 Demographic data on cover models featured multiple times on *GQ Taiwan* covers

Cover model	Country of origin	Times featured	Profession
Tom Cruise	USA	5	Actor
Brad Pitt	USA	3	Actor
David Beckham	UK	3	Athlete
Leonardo DiCaprio	US	3	Actor
Jude Law	UK	2	Actor
Harrison Ford	USA	2	Actor
Keanu Reeves	USA	2	Actor
George Clooney	USA	2	Actor
Tom Ford	USA	2	Fashion designer/film director
Orlando Bloom	UK	2	Actor

movie stars are used to portraying an American brand and image; the focus on western males fitted the needs of advertisers at a time when men's fashion was a nascent category. The tacit consensus among the editorial team was to offer "heavily American flavored" covers, which was critical to attracting advertisers in men's fashion. Meanwhile, those promoting Hollywood movies had long been seeking new advertising venues in Taiwan. Therefore, the direct adoption of American *GQ* covers featuring male Hollywood stars onto the Taiwanese *GQ* covers was a good match for Hollywood film distributors, who were key advertising buyers at that time. Additionally, as *Men's Uno* and *Men's Style*, two major Japanese-influenced men's fashion magazines, competed to seize a gradually increasing audience share in the late 1990s, *GQ* found that its strengths lay in its strong association with American brands (Hung 2010).

GQ Taiwan's shift from featuring predominantly American and/or Caucasian males to featuring a mixture of western, local, and regional males demonstrates the manifestation of numerous socio-economic institutional forces, as explained below. First, despite the popularity of Hollywood movies, the pool of famous Hollywood actors was limited; most of those well-known actors were soon exhausted (An 2010). Second, from the perspective of the Taiwanese editors, featuring Tom Cruise would be a better gamble than featuring other Hollywood "nobodies." Asides from the limited pool of famous Hollywood actors, multifaceted pressures from advertisers appeared to be the key in changing *GQ*'s target readers from young men to middle-age men. Since the year 2000, *Men's Uno* and *Men's Style* successfully captured a narrower male readership, comprising of the 20-something, highly fashion conscious males who closely referenced the featured products. While the use of western male cover models prior to the year 2000 successfully positioned Taiwan's *GQ* as an American-style magazine, this positioning was strongly challenged by advertisers. There was a significant purpose of using Hollywood actors as cover models during this period; *GQ Taiwan*, at the time, was desperately attempting to position itself as an American brand. By using these Hollywood models, *GQ* could convey a sense of aspiration and glamour in order to cater to local readers. However, the western cover models fell somewhat outside of the experiential terrain of local readers. As the editor of Taiwan's *GQ* eloquently noted, "While looking for men's fashion, *GQ* readers eventually came to seek local elements to which they could relate; Hollywood is another planet for our readers" (An 2010; Chen 2010). This belief was well substantiated as some advertisers yanked placements due to the lack of local male models; they argued that while local readers may enjoy Tom Cruise movies, they cannot relate him to their personal lifestyles. There was yet another intermediating institutional factor that was fundamentally related to the advertising-driven media environment. The increasing reliance on advertisements meant that the fashion goods advertised could be promoted through local male models on the cover and in the feature stories, creating a cross-sectional synergic effect that advertisers found important and desirable. Nevertheless, similar product placement would not be suitable if a western actor were employed.

Promoters of western fashion products and luxury goods promulgated their localization project by increased employment of locals; this was in tandem with the significant rise in East Asian market shares regarding luxury goods (particularly China). International luxury brands such as Gucci and Armani began endorsing their products with local Taiwanese celebrities, gradually replacing the traditional western celebrities. Godfrey Gao, a Taiwanese–Canadian model, the first East Asian model for Louis Vuitton, represented the start of a major trend. This process of localization in luxury brand advertising has made using East Asian males as models increasingly desirable.

Furthermore, there is an economic aspect for using local males as cover models: the employment of American models on *GQ* covers involves paying copyright fees, while many local males will appear on the cover for free, in exchange for a feature story. Locals are also more attractive because Taiwan and East Asia as a region is becoming a significant player in the international men's fashion market; Taiwan's *GQ* envisions a more balanced, multilateral, global exchange. Previously, it had been the norm for Taiwain to use cover models from Japan or the USA. In years to come, perhaps we may see a reversal in the flow of cover models with Taiwanese models being featured more prominently in Chinese, Japanese, or American editions of *GQ*. Using local models on *GQ* covers expands the repertoire for *GQ*'s global parent, while supplementing *GQ* covers in other markets. As An, former editor-in-chief of *GQ*, stated in a 2010 interview, "as an imported magazine, why don't you leverage your in-house resources and expand your publishing scope?" (An 2010). In Chinese markets, Asian models featured on front covers were largely from Hong Kong, and only in 2004 were models first imported from China. This trend echoes the increasing integration and accelerated cultural exchanges across the Taiwan Strait, particularly resulting from the new political stance towards China promulgated by President Ma since 2008.

The rise of local models, however, forced *GQ* to negotiate its position as a localized American magazine, begging the question of how *GQ Taiwan* differs from other local men's fashion magazines. East Asian male models, mainly Taiwanese, Japanese, and Korean, have long been utilized by *Men's Uno* and other magazines; yet, *GQ* is somehow distinctively different in several aspects. First, *GQ* tries to position itself as an upscale men's lifestyle magazine; it is a taste-oriented magazine that educates one on how to appreciate a wide spectrum of luxury goods. Thus, *GQ* male cover models are featured not so much in a fashion context, but rather in the context of a wider pattern of choices and preferences. The editor of *GQ* has even criticized his competitors such as *Men's Uno*, stating that they are too juvenile and technical in simply using ordinary, non-professionals in demonstrating to readers how to dress fashionably.

To summarize, *GQ Taiwan* initially employed a larger number of foreign models than *Men's Uno*. *Men's Uno* exclusively features only Japanese and Korean models while *GQ*, the Taiwanese subsidiary of a global group, uses models from rather diverse countries of origin. This trend, however, has been changed since the implementation of a localization project in 2006.

Consumption and masculinity **103**

Transformation of gender over time

The covers that were examined include roughly twice as many males as females (68 percent versus 32 percent), as listed in Table 6.4.

Examined chronologically, females as cover models has been on the rise since 2006; this represents a recent development in GQ. Originally, both GQ and *Men's Uno*, both men's fashion magazines, for the most part featured males on their cover pages. As listed below in Table 6.5, however, beginning in 2002, GQ began experimenting with using females as cover models. According to a former GQ editor, this auspicious local experimentation with voluptuous scantily clad females on front covers secured a number of best-selling issues. Subsequently, a drastic change was implemented the following year; this is listed in Table 6.5, with Taiwan's GQ largely featuring local women, alternating with local men every two or three issues.

The number of female models recently featured in GQ and on GQ covers has increased exponentially. In 2008, the last year that was analyzed by this study, a total of only four men were featured on GQ covers. Although not covered by the data analysis in this study, a quick review yields a clear trend: in 2009 and 2010, only two males were featured on the cover of GQ. The increasingly heavy coverage of women represents an important aspect of localization as a function of competition within the emerging genre, following a different social trajectory with different local ramifications. On the other hand, it has become extremely rare for a female bikini model to appear on the cover of the American version of GQ. The increase in female cover models, mainly dressed in a revealing and seductive manner, has repositioned GQ as a *Playboy*-like men's lifestyle magazine. "This is what Taiwanese readers want" (An 2010). These local female models that are being

TABLE 6.4 GQ covers by gender and frequency

Gender	Frequency	Percentage
Male	101	68
Female	47	32
Total	148	100

TABLE 6.5 GQ *Taiwan* cover models: frequency of males versus females

	1998	1999	2000	2001	2002	2003	2004	2005	2006	2007	2008	Total
M	9	10	11	14	7	14	12	9	6	5	4	101
F	3	2	1	2	5	5	1	4	6	10	8	47
M (%)	75	83	92	85	57	72	93	69	50	33	33	70
F (%)	25	17	8	15	43	28	7	31	50	67	67	30

featured on *GQ* covers are, in male model Jesse Chen's words, generally "second-tier stars, trying to make their way to the top, so they modeled almost for free" (Chen 2010).

Originally, the gay community represented a large percentage of the readership of men's fashion magazines. Since the late 1990s, however, numerous magazines have competed for this niche market. The heavy employment of female cover models by *GQ* is "a symbolic gesture to a broader, mainstream, fashion-conscious and male readers" (An 2010). While resistance to male nudity among heterosexual male readers remains prevalent, informal surveys have found that the readers of *GQ Taiwan* are particularly homophobic. Partially due to the nature of the *GQ*'s target readers—middle age, wealthy, urban, and somewhat conservative Taiwanese men—Taiwan's *GQ* found it necessary to look "more straight." Featuring female cover models would conveniently signify that Taiwan's *GQ* was not intended for the gay readership; many heterosexual male readers of *GQ* wished to distance themselves from the gay community. In 2006, *Men's Uno*, the chief competitor of *GQ*, became more clearly aligned with a gay readership. Only then did *GQ Taiwan* decide to depart from the style of its American parent by featuring female cover models; the distinction between gay and straight readers was purposefully made as *GQ* became wary of being classified as a gay quarterly.

GQ cover stories

Between the years of 1998 and 2002, when cover models were frequently Hollywood actors, the corresponding cover stories mainly told of their movies; the stories would often relate the development of the movie characters to the real-life actor. Cover stories revolved around storylines and characters, and most of this content was translated from news articles in American *GQ* (Ying 2010). Therefore, *GQ* cover models and stories generally served as a marketing venue to promote Hollywood movies. Between 2000 and 2004, the second phase of the study, male cover models became more diversified and included more local males. Even the content inside of the magazine had become rapidly localized. The cover stories of the local males featured manifested greater feminine and untraditional aesthetics than previously seen before, which can be related back to the notion of metrosexuality in men's fashion. During this time period from 2000 to 2004, the discursive construction of men's identities was driven by "commodity capitalism," a notion sustaining that global advertisers must standardize consumption patterns on a global scale which, in turn, enables the capitalist drive for constant economic growth (Giddens 1991: 196–197). These narratives in Taiwan's *GQ* offer an insight into how transnational fashion giants have become the most easily recognizable agents that impose media and commercial cultures on consumers in different markets (Gerhson 1997). Furthermore, the featured men in Taiwan's *GQ* from 2000 to 2004 frequently recounted how they had become consumers of fashion and style products that were seen as "feminine." Facilitating the capitalist drive for constant economic growth was the fact that since local models were now being sponsored by advertisers, most cover stories promoted consumerism. However, despite narratives describing these models' consumerist lifestyles (such as collecting material items such as jeans, shoes, and stuffed animals), the main themes in these stories still perpetuate the conventional role of the man as the breadwinner. This argument is supported by the following numbers: among the 48 covers that featured males, 35 cover stories raised feminine issues. For example, 25 commented on menswear and grooming, 11 discussed cosmetic products, weight reduction, and rejuvenation/anti-ageing, and six mentioned unconventional hobbies such as doll collections. These seemingly unconventional qualities were, at times, strategically used to overcome crises in their personal lives. Alternatively, feminine qualities often functioned as auxiliary side stories, and are non-essential for these males and their identity construction. One example is the GQ issue that featured Show Luo (Luo Zhi Xiang) as the cover model; stuffed animals were strategically placed in his photos to suggest his innocence when audio-visual footage showed that he had participated in an adult chat room. Show Luo spoke of his life and his hobbies in an almost infant-like manner, and portrayed himself as a victim of a "filthy and polluted adult world" (GQ 2008 October edition). GQ also featured four stories that recommended products such as moisturizers and facial masks for male use. On one hand, the featured men admitted that their heavy use of cosmetic products contributed to their youthful looks. On the other hand, these men also acknowledged that men would undeniably look more youthful if they were consistently responsible and confident, reflecting the construction of hegemonic masculinities. Either way, these tips were usually accompanied by reminders that "feminine" practices such as the use of cosmetic products could only be brought up after traditional concepts of masculinity had been successfully attained and maintained. Consequently, campaigns sponsored by advertisers were meticulously placed in the stories only to advance the male standing in the rankings of consumerism.

After 2006, the number of males featured on the covers of GQ *Taiwan* dropped dramatically. Excessive female nudity during this period gave off the sense that GQ was becoming a *Playboy*-like magazine, which I have deemed the "heterosexual hedonist phase" of GQ. Although less males were featured on its covers, the males featured inside GQ were always meticulously well dressed and well accessorized. Content on fashion-related products, including what to wear and how to groom, has not been dismissed as trivial, but their coverage has clearly been significantly reduced since 2006. Meanwhile, GQ has been increasingly featuring commodities such as fast cars, motorcycles, and alcohol. Ultimately, these discussions are supposed to appeal to the new target audience of heterosexual hedonists—a group that is described as high-brow, urban, and cultured with large disposable incomes—a demographic group that is crucial to the business of GQ.

This study selects the two cover stories of Jay Chou and Kevin Tsai in order to illustrate and contextualize how GQ cover stories were open to negotiations among non-hegemonic and traditional qualities. The June 2005 cover story featuring singer Jay Chou associated Chou with various subordinate masculine attributes. For example, Chou was described as being very attached to his mother, as well as being highly sensitive to music whilst growing up. Chou was moreover characterized as a loner who enjoyed fantasizing and daydreaming. While these characteristics are arguably perceived unflattering for a superstar, the story nevertheless also portrayed Chou as having the sense of masculinity that is preferred in Taiwan. One of most redeeming qualities that compensate Chou for his "feminine attributes" is his love for sports; this portrays him as inherently masculine. The story also recounted how Chou's fondness for basketball cost him an injury and hospitalization; Chou had suffered continuing spinal inflammation following the injury, and was therefore exempted from Taiwan's compulsory military service. The narrative focused on Chou's unattainable fame and success—he had the ability to extend his ambition to penetrate the music markets in China. Another aspect highlighting Chou's desirable masculinity was his versatility, as seen in his omnipresence throughout Chinese media; Chou emerged as a singer, but was also a composer and musician who could play a variety of musical instruments. As Chou's stardom progressed, he advanced his career through the pursuit of filmmaking and acting, even starring in a Jiang Yi Mou film. Finally, Chou's cover story also recounted his interest in flirting with women, and told of his desire to polish his English so he could date Caucasian women, yet again demonstrating his masculine attributes. Thus, this feature story on Chou showed *GQ* to be a more typical men's publication, one that was for heterosexual men.

In December of 2005, *GQ* featured Kevin Tsai on its cover, an openly gay celebrity with considerable media clout. Due to Tsai's significance in Taiwan as a gay icon, an exploration of how Tsai was featured and portrayed in *GQ* should be useful to this study; Tsai's story represented as well as renegotiated subordinate masculine qualities. Tsai's interview began with a rhetorical question: they asked him who, other than himself, could be surrounded by more naked Taiwanese women? The *GQ* editor framed this question as something that "all Taiwanese men are dreaming of, and are hoping to live up to" (An 2010). Therefore Tsai, with his obvious homosexuality, is portrayed as a male that is in an ideal position to educate males in what women like. Tsai's cover story, entitled "Top Secrets to Understanding Tsai's Success," avoided questions regarding Tsai's own relationships, despite the rhetorical question at the beginning. The article instead focused on Tsai's philosophy regarding how to lead a carefree life, which he learned from his achievements and accumulation of wealth from the Taiwanese television industry. Despite readers' assumptions that Tsai's homosexuality would be an inevitable topic of discussion, given Tsai's public relationship with his boyfriend and outspokenness on gay activism in Taiwan, the story ultimately ignored Tsai's homosexuality.

New agents in a global and local nexus

The construction of metrosexuality is reliant upon a series of commodities and consumerist practices and intensely advertising-media driven, as much sense of continuity here. Those who attempt to create new masculine identities arguably are not passive objects of structural and/or material changes in society. Rather, the socio-economic agents, or the gridlock network of local and global advertisers in particular, are the ones who are involved in the generation of cultural currents. This study attempts to shift the attention to global–local negotiations taking place in the media institutional processes, instead of viewing these cultural currents as being circumcized by hegemonic masculinities in a post-capitalist society with the ultimate goal to introduce auspicious consumption and consumerism. The increasingly localized GQ in Taiwan could exemplify a case of how transnational corporations take a pragmatic view of globalization, attempting to seek a market share and survive increasingly fierce competition. Similar to Fung and Lee's 2009 analysis on Hong Kong's Disneyland, transnational corporations do not hesitate to localize products and business practices in foreign markets. Through the three phases of Taiwan's GQ localization project, this chapter demonstrates how new actors, whether local or global, have come to play a central role in Taiwan's popular culture, aiding the construction of the concept of masculinity. Perhaps Taiwan's GQ can serve as a global context for diverse pursuits of markets, pleasures, and profitability in local contexts in Taiwan as has been discussed in other areas of East Asia (Chan and Ma 2002; Fung 2008, 2009).

With respect to gender representation on the front covers of Taiwan's GQ, this study largely affirms that the situated masculinities were similar to that of Connell's four hegemonic features of masculinities: power, ambivalence toward femininity, domination and objectification of nature and the psyche, and the avoidance of emotion (Connell 1983, 1987, 2000, 2002, 2005). On the other hand, subordinate masculinities such as homosexuality were greatly suppressed. The discursive construction of the role of the male in Taiwanese society may manifest itself in a negotiated form of subordinate and hegemonic masculinities. With the breadwinner role commonly emphasized in Taiwanese society, diligence and perseverance often juxtapose hedonist pleasurable pursuits; they manifest themselves as a form of high social upward mobility to celebrate new forms of localized consumerism and masculinities. It should be noted that the stories of GQ Taiwan have most likely been influenced by Buddhism and Confucianism, and have often contested the idea of "domination and objectification of nature and the psyche" (Connell 2000, 2002), with "zen" as the new buzzword accompanied by a great level of appreciation of co-existence with the nature.

Seen as a logical outcome of post-modernist trends in which human bodies are transformed into visible representational surfaces (Iida 2005), this chapter attempts to follow up this line of argument by linking important issues together, such as the notion of metrosexuality in global marketing campaigns with the gendered representation of the self in relation to hegemonic and subordinate masculinities. Though potentially subversive to conventional masculine values and ideals upheld by the phallocentric hegemonic discourse, this chapter, however, shares a similar caution along with many other scholars that the objectification of male bodies cannot be simplistically and optimistically interpreted as a step toward greater equality between representations of men and women (Bordo 1999; Dotson 1999;

Darling-Wolf 2003, 2004). Rather, men's fashion magazines have often been seen as an interplay among forces of global and local commodity consumption that has permeated in middle-class masculine cultures.

Though *GQ Taiwan* initially emphasized unconventional male activities such as dieting, the use of cosmetic products, and indoor exercise, this has now been exonerated. However, the concepts and presentation of metrosexuality, coherent with what has been propagated in the West, is running back to back with a sense of homophobic paranoia. Most themes of feminine dress codes and social etiquette presented in Taiwan's *GQ* ought to be adequately compensated by success in so-called masculine activities such as on sports fields, in the gym, and in the bar; these activities ultimately can be achieved via the consumption of men's fashion. Conventional discussions featured in women's fashion magazines, such as interpersonal/romantic relationships, astrology, grooming/clothing/cosmetics, and any housekeeping issues that were often a focus in women's fashion magazines, were extremely rare. As a response to the 1980's feminist movement in the west, the emergence of Taiwan's *GQ* appeared to follow a disparate route. *GQ Taiwan* was unlike some men's fashion magazines that were accompanied with earlier new man iconography that evolved after the West's feminist movement, which on one hand championed the new but increasingly localized "consumption masculinities," while on the other hand, rarely responded to or affirmed any assertions of the new man identity.

Notes

1 They drew their inspiration from Japan. For instance, Japan's *Huge, High Fashion* and *Men's Joker* all have copycats in Taiwan.
2 According to a billboard from Taiwan's Golden Stone bookstore, a widely used barometer of performance is the absence of a credible auditing system.

Bibliography

An, K.C. (2010) Personal interview, 24 November.

Black, M. and Coward, R. (1990) "Linguistic, Social and Sexual Relations: A Review of Dale Spender's Man-Made language," in D. Cameron (ed.) *The Feminist Critique of Language: A Reader*, London and New York: Routledge.

Bordo, S. (1999) *The Male Body: A New Look at Men in Public and Private*, New York: Farrar, Straus and Giroux.

Chan, J.M. and Ma, E. (2002) "Transculturating Modernity: A Reinterpretation of Cultural Globalization," in J.M. Chan and B.T. McIntyre (eds) *In Search of Boundaries: Communication, Nation-States and Cultural Identities*, Connecticut: Ablex.

Chen, C.C. (2010) Personal interview, 22 December.

Chou, W. (2000) *Tongzhi: Politics of Same-Sex Eroticism in Chinese Societies*, New York: Haworth Press.

Connell, R.W. (1983) "Men's Bodies," in R.W. Connell (ed.) *Which Way is Up?*, Boston, MA: Allen and Unwin.

Connell, R.W. (1987) *Gender and Power: Society, the Person and Sexual Politics*, Cambridge: Polity.

Connell, R.W. (2000) *The Men and the Boys*, Cambridge: Polity.

Connell, R.W. (2002) *Gender*, Cambridge: Polity.

Connell, R.W. (2005) "Globalization, Imperialism, and Masculinities," in M.S. Kimmel, J. Hearn, and R.W. Connell (eds) *Handbook of Studies on Men and Masculinities*, California: Sage Publications.

Darling-Wolf, F. (2003) "Male Bonding and Female Pleasure: Refining Masculinity in Japanese Popular Cultural Texts," *Popular Communication*, 1: 73–88.

Darling-Wolf, F. (2004) "Virtually Multicultural: Trans-Asian Identity and Gender in an International Fan Community of a Japanese Star," *New Media and Society*, 6: 507–528.

Dotson, E. (1999) *Behold the Man: The Hype and Selling of Male Beauty in Media and Culture*, New York: Haworth.

Edwards, T. (1997) *Men in the Mirror: Men's Fashion, Masculinity and Consumer Society*, London: Cassell.

Fung, A. (2008) *Global Capital, Local Culture: Transnational Media Corporations in China*, New York: Peter Lang.

Fung, A. (2009) "Globalizing Televised Culture: The Case of China," in G. Turner and T. Jay (eds) *Television Studies after TV*, London: Routledge, pp. 178–188.

Fung, A. and Lee, M. (2009) "Localizing a Global Amusement Park: Hong Kong's Disneyland," *Continuum: Journal of Media and Cultural Studies*, 23: 195–206.

Gerhson, R.A. (1997) *The Transnational Media Corporation*, New Jersey: Lawrence Erlbaum.

Giddens, A. (1991) *Modernity and Self-Identity: Self and Society in the Late Modern Age*, California: Stanford University Press.

Hanke, R. (1990) "Hegemonic Masculinity in Thirty-Something," *Critical Studies in Mass Communication*, 7: 231–248.

Hung, Y.C. (2010) Personal communication, 11 June.

Iida Y. (2005) "Beyond the Feminization of Masculinity: Transforming Patriarchy with the Feminine in Contemporary Japanese Youth Culture," *Inter-Asia Cultural Studies*, 6: 56–74.

Iwabuchi, K. (2002) *Recentering Globalization: Popular Culture and Japanese Tranationalism*, Durham, NC: Duke University Press.

Johnson, S. and Christ, W. (1988) "Women Through Time: Who Gets Covered?" *Journalism Quarterly*, 65: 889–897.

Magazine Business Association of Taipei (2006) *An Advertiser's Guide to Magazines in Taiwan*.

Martin, F. (2003) *Situating Sexualities: Queer Representation in Taiwanese Fiction, Film and Public Culture*, Hong Kong: Hong Kong University Press.

Mort, F. (1996) *Cultures of Consumption: Masculinities and Social Space in Late Twentieth Century Britain*, London: Routledge.

Nixon, S. (1996) *Hard Looks: Masculinities, Spectatorship and Contemporary Consumption*, London: University College London.

Osgerby, B. (2001) *Playboys in Paradise: Masculinity, Youth and Leisure-Style in Modern America*, New York: Berg.

Osgerby, B. (2003) "A Pedigree of the Consuming Male: Masculinity, Consumption and the American 'Leisure Class'," in B. Benwell (ed.) *Masculinity and Men's Lifestyle Magazines*, Oxford: Wiley-Blackwell.

Rotundo, E.A. (1993) *American Manhood: Transformations in Masculinity from the Revolution to the Modern Era*, New York: Basic Books.

Takana, K. (2003) "The Language of Japanese Men's Magazines: Young Men Who Don't Want to Get Hurt," in B. Benwell (ed.) *Masculinity and Men's Lifestyle Magazines*, Oxford: Wiley-Blackwell.

Tam S.M., Fung, A., Kam L. and Liong M. (2009) "Re-gendering Hong Kong Man in Social, Physical and Discursive Space," in F. Cheung and E. Holroyd (eds) *Mainstreaming Gender in Hong Kong Society*, Hong Kong: The Chinese University of Hong Kong Press.

Ying, C.H. (2010) Personal interview, 11 June.

PART II

Global discontinuity

The local absorption of global culture

7

AN UNLOCALIZED AND UNGLOBALIZED SUBCULTURE

English language independent music in Singapore

Kai Khiun Liew and Shzr Ee Tan

Introduction

Reflecting upon the cultural basis of Singapore's bilingual education policies, Singapore's elder statesman Lee Kuan Yew stated in his memoirs:

> The irony was that I was keen and anxious as anyone to retain the best features of Chinese education. When I acted as legal adviser for the Chinese middle school student leaders in the 1950s, I was impressed by their vitality, dynamism and discipline and social and political commitment. By contrast, I was dismayed at the apathy, self-centredness and lack of self-confidence of the English educated students.
>
> *Lee 2000*

An Oxford alumni, the first Prime Minister of Singapore is ironically one of those English educated students. Lee's scathing assessment of his country's English-speaking milieu epitomizes an iconic state of postcolonial unease in Singapore; the perceived negative impact of westernization arising from the state's efforts to successfully integrate itself into the global political economy. While vernacular and regional immigrant cultures of the populace are seen by Singapore's anglicized officialdom to be technologically archaic and suspected to be potentially ethnically divisive, culturally unmediated exposure to the indulgent individualism of the west through the English language as a matter of national policy has also been seen as leading to an indulgent and individualistic people constantly attempting to mimic "undesirable and antisocial" western lifestyles. This negative label of deculturalization and its connotations of susceptibility to cultural imperialism have been described of Singapore's "indie" music scene; of bands who have appropriated the highly introspective, melancholic, experimental, and folksy British-based, post-rock, and post-punk music genre.

Such an image, however, is easily contestable as a stereotype—many self-identified indie musicians speak of claiming a deterritorialized and postmodern sense of "new" locality, one that is not so much situated within western culture, than within the trope of an acultural, antimainstream dialectic. By consciously staying aloof from the commercial "local," and being unable to penetrate into the global stage, the Singaporean indie artist becomes a conceptual aberration to the scholarly understanding of the hybridizing and popularizing tendencies of popular culture in Asia in engaging the forces of globalization. Although the politics of the global language of English pervades all Asian countries, the fundamental issue with Singapore lies in its use as the principal rather than the dominant mode of communication. While English is widely used in the former Anglo-American colonies such as India and the Philippines, local or native languages continue to legitimately pervade both their political and popular cultural economies. By contrast, from language to culture, the local in Singapore is persistently overshadowed by regional and western influences. Yet, as this article will explain, especially in regard to the indie music scene, it would be difficult to either dismiss the local indie music scene as being typecast cases of colonial mimicry or indigenization of external influences. Nevertheless, notions of the mainstream, now relocated in postcolonial and distinctively socially engineered Singapore (away from the original genre's beginnings in the proverbial West) become harder to define. In musicological terms, style is either disarticulated as a deliberate result due to an act of cultural economic resistance, or by political default—from ethics, context, and taking sociopolitical stances. While it is tempting to categorize all manifestations of western music (even alternative rock/pop) under the umbrella of "the establishment" from the perspective of Chinese-speaking communities, other views engendered through the lenses of consumers versus practitioners, or national ideology versus grassroots causes, create fresh definitions. Evidently, cross-cutting strands and tensions permeated by different perspectives and demands of group and sub-group identification have to be teased out in consideration of Appadurian-style "scapes" carved out by economics, government policy, and language marking (Appadurai 1996). On this front, even as the indie community in Singapore seeks to move away from the trappings of national ideology and ethnic labeling, its members have also played a part strategic, part default persuaded game of consciously aligning with the larger forces of economic circumstance and governmental co-option.

Most of the complex machinations behind the indie scene find a larger background in Singapore's history as a proverbial Malay fishing village. Singapore became a British administered trading post largely populated by immigrant settlers from South China and India who, together with indigenous Malay inhabitants, worked toward eventual independence in 1965. A recurring trope stigmatizing the island's glaringly short history since its official founding in 1819 and its 1965 claim to independence is how the unlikely coalition of deterritorialized migrants has been articulated; Singaporean artist Kuo Pao Kun describes how the postcolonial norms of British governors came to be adopted by a conglomerate of "cultural orphans." Against this backdrop, the principal use of the English language in the songs of many indie bands can be understood to reflect a post-independence generation that is (predominantly) taught in English.

> You see the moon and the stars
> Look how far we have come
> Look around our faces we shine brightly in the sun
> With our hopes and dreams
> Imagine what tomorrow may bring
>
> *What Do You See?* (Electrico 2009)[1]

In 2009, Electrico, a Singporean indie band, was selected to compose and perform an official theme song for celebrations held in honour of the Republic's annual independence day celebration. These celebrations come together in the National Day Parade (NDP), a public pageant held in a sports arena that serves as a hegemonic tool for manufacturing cultural and political legitimacy on the island (Phua and Kong 1996). The song, entitled *What Do You See?*, reminded Singaporeans of their country's achievements, motivated them to greater heights, and give the so-called apathetic, self-centred, and self-doubting, English-educated populace a role in nation building. At the same time, the song also provided strategic street credence to a government campaign that would have otherwise been looked at by members of the general populace as a kitsch exercise in blatant propaganda (Tan 2005, 2010).

Musically speaking, *What Do You See?* exhibits a superficial resemblance to styles conventionally associated with genres of British popular music and British indie music, found in British acts such as Coldplay and Keane. Key musical markers include "lo-fi," simple but textured guitar riffs enhanced by a light drum and keyboard setup. Additionally, restrained emotionally and performatively endothermic vocals are applied to the song. However, the lyrics and visual content found in the music video of *What Do You See?* seem to deviate significantly from the darker, socially introspective basis of its emulated foreign-derived genre. In this sense, this particular work from a Singaporean act affirms the state's narrative of progress.

Unlike scenes of social alienation or moody sentimentality often presented in indie acts of the West, *What Do You See?*'s official music video is set against images of Singaporean modernity: skylines of the financial district, panned shots of the Esplanade (Singapore's premier cultural district), and panoramas of the recently developed Marina Barrage (a dam that converts the bay into a scenic freshwater lake). Such video interweaving of visual icons demonstrate the Singaporean state's desire to reengineer its society as a place for cosmopolitans within mainstream, global, socio-economic, and culture flows (Yeoh 2004). Contrasting with the melancholic environments of standard indie music videos of the west, the sequencing of *What Do You See?* is an interesting one. The video begins at dawn, moves enthusiastically to broad daylight, and climaxes with the band singing to a receptive and family friendly mainstream audience. Ultimately, the song's lyrics, together with its music video, represent a microcosm of the incongruous tensions brought about by simultaneous pressures acting on Singapore's English language indie music scene. This is shown during a time when the indie music scene is attempting to position itself within the triangulations of the global West, its own nation state, and its own local vernacular.

Discussions on globalization have commonly been associated with the concerns of cultural homogenization and cultural imperialism according to the dictates of the Eurocentric neoliberal order of the international political economy. The resulting response has ranged from resistance to appropriation of this order. Using the case of the indie music scene in Singapore, this paper attempts to position such interactions as more of a socially layered, postcolonial cultural process. This process involves the mediations of an Anglicized bohemian class uneasily sandwiched between the hegemonic discourses of the western-educated elite, the parochial conservatism of the heartlands, state-endorsed cultural ideology, and, finally, their idealistic search for musical individualism against the presupposed cultural and stylistic blank slate of Singapore's "orphaned" immigrant cultural makeup. Singapore indie music, primarily composed in the English language, has generally been suspicious of the state-imposed ethos of modernity as well as claims of ethnicized identity politics of the working classes.

Apart from the reluctance of localization for local Singaporean indie groups, this paper also articulates the socio-political psychosis of how it is not simply a case of superficially appropriating the material trappings of global capitalism. Even as the local indie music scene derides liberal western values, state and society in Singapore still yearn to reside in the centres of global cultural productions and celebrate citizens who have made international headways, whether in the classical music or transnational Mandopop (Chinese popular music based in Taiwan) entertainment scenes. Even as most local indie pop productions seem to be cleansed of local references and are thus rendered indistinguishable from their British counterparts, Singaporean musical acts have yet to gain acknowledgement and reciprocity from the latter group, which demonstrates that this genre is still an exclusively white European undertaking. Indie music in Singapore, therefore, becomes a unique case study of an appropriated western cultural practice that is neither adequately localized nor sufficiently reglobalized. In the context of Kuo's trope of Singapore's cultural orphanage and short national history, indie music fan Eva Wong states:

> I do not think we are a country that is yet comfortable in our own skin, and shows through in our music. And when there is not even a language barrier or unfamiliar musical style for an excuse, listeners will be even less forgiving.
>
> *Wong 2010*

As Wong alludes, indie music, in any sense of a "label," thrives on the identity of anti-identity politics even as it seeks an active presence in the liminal space of a consciously defaulted existence.

No record (and other) labels: defining against which establishment?

Perhaps a useful place to start would be in defining what the term "indie" means and signifies in Singapore. Casual surveys among key members of its self-identified community (which includes an overlap of performers and fans) reveal a plethora of varied and contested imaginings. These definitions range from "any band with no record label that fiercely promotes their music" (Soo 2010), to "anything produced in Singapore right now with the exception of Mandopop that gets exported to Taiwan ... you have to struggle for eardrums against the mainstream" (Chow 2010), to "locally produced English music" (Wong 2010), to "an attitude ... a DIY spirit" (Ching 2010), to "any rock music that doesn't sound too polished or commercial" (Hadi 2010), and, finally, it has been defined as a musical style or genre.

The classic problem of ontology shows up here in how definitions are less often articulated positively than made as negative identifications against "the other"; in this case, the mainstream. One may point out, however, that the concept of a mainstream culture in Singaporean musical life is unclear to begin with—there is not one mainstream, but several mainstreams. In turn, these mainstreams are delineated by different cross sections of community and sub-community perspectives, and each have their own individual histories. Should the mainstream, for example, be understood in terms of consumption or in terms of creation of musical content? Are they two spheres that operate on completely different cultural and economic levels? What would the mainstream constitute for different social strata of English and Mandarin speakers that are identified so strikingly and separately, as illustrated by statesman Lee Kuan Yew? How do general music production and their distribution lines operate within Singapore in the context of larger (and different) Southeast Asian and Taiwanese dominated Mandopop frameworks? Such issues are further complicated by the fact that Singapore's self-identified indie scene has also existed long enough in recent memory to have acquired diversified aspects, that include a sense of changing historical trajectory, a sub-genre (often marked by class and/or ethnicity), and, finally, transnational and globalized manifestations.

A wider historical context to the origins of indie music in Singapore must first be located in the country's earlier days of post-war colonial, independent governance, during the first influx of mass mediated, western popular music. During this era, pop/rock music genres emerging in the United States and United Kingdom were similarly heard on fledgling Singaporean radio networks and media distribution channels. Well-known international acts such as Elvis Presley, The Beach Boys, and The Beatles hit the airwaves and record stores, taking up so much listening space that early Anglo-American pop/rock become one of the island's primary musical cultures. As Singapore's economy developed at a rapid pace in the 1960s and 1970s, entertainment, as an activity and as a concept, became more accessible, in particular to a larger strata of the burgeoning middle class. For example, Beatles and Beach Boys aspiring Singaporean bands such as The Quests and Naomi and The Boys were formed, playing on national television in "talentime" showcases, alongside regular live gigs in lounges, bars, and entertainment venues. Many of these early local acts went on to acquire huge followings in the country, and continue to retain fans today (even among members of the indie crowd) in the name of nostalgia.

This early flush of a postcolonial, western-aspiring, Singapore-made pop scene did not last through the 1980s and early 1990s, as popular music trends in the West itself branched off into genres such as punk and glam rock, among others. While the latter style proved to be too sexual for the moral climate of Singaporeans, the former was too anarchic to be adopted by an increasingly state wary public. In the early 1990s, Singaporean maverick punk and experimental rocker Chris Ho began releasing subversive singles, but was only celebrated in the country among a small minority as a lone and eccentric (if not highly charismatic) cult figure. Meanwhile, the relative dearth of interesting local pop acts during the punk, glam rock, and hard rock era prepared the framework for the Singaporean birth of an indie scene paralleling the rise of the genre in the United Kingdom.

However, throughout the 1970s and 1980s, imported English language slow rock and easy rock did, in fact, continue to occupy prime positions in the island's postcolonial popular music soundscape. What was even more significant though was the sustained arrival of a nascent Cantopop and Mandopop scene directly from post-war and postcolonial Hong Kong and Taiwan. Evidently, the gradual establishment of a new, multiple dialect, Chinese language musical mainstream in Singapore can be traced to earlier historical influences. These influences include the music found in imported Chinese films, television theme songs, imported Cantonese opera films, local Chinese language and/or mixed language variety shows, and the Singapore-based, Chinese language radio station, Reddifusion. In terms of the economic reality, the Cantopop and Mandopop scene did not truly take off in Singapore as an industry and sizeable market until the early 1970s. Once these music scenes were entrenched into Singaporean society, its influence was felt significantly amongst all walks of Singaporean life; it became a major force that shaped the popular music soundscape of Singapore from the 1980s onwards. This music trend allowed Singapore to eventually develop its own stars, such as Stefanie Sun and Tanya Chua, allowing the island to acquire a small but significant economic stake in the Chinese diasporic and transnational music machinery.

Against this backdrop of interweaving postcolonial and Chinese diasporic trajectories, the rise of indie pop music in Singapore as a "defined against" genre has to be reconsidered. Was indie music in Singapore merely a musical style, an ethic, or a code of production? Was it defined by the nationality of individual band members, vis-à-vis their economic apathy? Did it change alongside the development of the genre internationally, or was indie really only a social class marker? The default imaginaries of "no record label" and "anything that is not commercial rock" as referred to by members of the scene echoes the parallel ethic of the indie scene in the United Kingdom. As Hesmondhalgh describes, the indie music scene is small-scale music production, that is rooted in anti-commercial stylistic practice, and vested in cheap technology (Hesmondhalgh 1999). Where commercial and mainstream practice in Singapore is defined according to shifts in ethnic/language marking, community, class, and consumer perspectives, grey areas of shared artistic and socio-economic practice elide and overlap. This is made further complex by the fact that the term indie has also come to be appropriated for different meanings over time on the international arena, where an originally "DIY," ethic dominated scene has extended to being a slick and professional "genre, often used interchangeably with alternative" (Chan 2010).

English speaking natives: cultural transmission, postcolonialism, and international capitalism

A prominent force shaping the perspectives of indie music production and appreciation can be found in the English–Chinese language divide of postcolonial Singaporean society. Such appreciation of the cultural discourses of contemporary forms of globalization (in particular, the Singaporean indie music's definition against Mandopop) must be taken within the context of the appropriation of European colonial modernity by developmental nation-states as they pursue economic and technological advancement. Here, postcolonialism, alongside postmodernism, plays a significant role in shifting the directions from a political and economic orientation to that of a cultural position. This occurs even if the concept of culture is still seemingly tied to anthropological and positivist models rather than deconstructive or hermeneutic ones (Krishnaswamy 2008).

In this respect, postcolonial criticism becomes useful in repudiating powerful meta-narratives and also shifts discourses from essentialism and national origin to that which is relational and subject position (Dirlik 2005). Being connected to the circuits of globalization has not, however, been an unproblematic undertaking; complicated and contradictory processes of cultural filtering, mediation, and imposition often occur. Not limited to manifestations of state building from public infrastructure to state policies, this experiment by postcolonial nations penetrates even the realm of cultural aesthetics as each realm relates, responds to, and repenetrates the mainstream.

It is imperative that the indie scene in Singapore should not be discussed in a vacuum, given that contemporary social contentions in a state has colonial lineages and associations (Holden 2008). Inheriting the legacy of British colonial governance, the People's Action Party (PAP), which has governed Singapore since 1959, sustained the use of English as the official language of (educational) instruction. Regional languages have become reduced to the symbolic category of "mother tongue" education for the dissemination of traditional cultural values to a rigidly defined and racialized multicultural populace of Chinese, Indian, Malaysians, and others. Localized expressions from Chinese provincial languages and dialects, along with creolized English or "Singlish," have become highly discouraged by the Singaporean state as they are now eager to ensure that Singapore maintains a connection and understanding with the rest of the world. This has led to the dichotomization of the linguistic landscape in Singapore along Asian mother tongues and western economic and technological languages (Bokhorst-Heng and Wee 2005), favoring the latter while the former continues to be tokenized.

Singapore's post-independence social engineering project to render the functioning of the state possible by systematic Foucauldian codification and classification of local relations of power (Dean 1994) has reaped significant cultural repercussions. Here, language policies have become part of the larger fracturing and emasculation of organic social networks and cultural flows that are overshadowed by state-led modernization. According to Wee,

> The state's petit-bourgeois, philistine modernity, with its objectifying, analytic and pragmatic modes of thought, meant that high art or mass art, history and memory at best played a weak role in transforming society ... the PAP state reorganized the body of cultural and symbolic significations for the logic of the commodity, while denying the importance of that body of meanings.
> *Wee 2007*

Following this observation, in its denial of the importance of the "body of meanings," the Singapore government effectively presents itself as the primary agent of connecting Singapore society to the networks of global capitalism and western modernity.

Departing from the position that Singaporean citizens are passive subjects of the neocolonial instrumental logic of the PAP state, recent scholarly works have turned towards exploring the varied strategies of response. "The challenge is to transcend the literal and symbolic violence done to the realm of culture, and even to transcend the nation-state that practices such violence" (Wee 2003). In the area of popular music, recent research has unearthed the persistence of subaltern socio-linguistic identities in using popular music genres from Cantopop (Liew 2003), Bhangra (Bal 2009), Xinyao, which is locally composed, independent Chinese language popular music (Kong 1996), to heavy metal (Fu and Liew 2007; Dairianathan 2009), and rap (Tan 2009), in order to platform otherwise repressed articulations and unacknowledged transnational vernacular interactions. Collectively, these popular flows resist the arbitrary subordination and continued denigration of ethnic minorities and working-class narratives sidelined by narratives of the predominantly Anglicized, ethnic Chinese, heterosexual male elite in Singapore.

The English-based indie pop scene in Singapore, however, appears to take a more ambiguous political position. Linguistically speaking, most members of the scene come from highly Anglicized educational and social backgrounds. In fact, in a scenario from Haraway's story of a cyborg created by dystopian capitalism, the English indie music scene has arguably emerged as an unexpected result of the expansion of English language education originally aimed to enable its workforce to serve international and industrial capital more efficiently. Because almost 50 percent of households in Singapore cite English as their primary language (Singapore Government 2005), general linguistic proficiency in the nation has begun to extend beyond basic English. Singapore's post-independence population therefore is able to access western cultural modernity more intimately. Rather than consuming and replicating cover versions of Britpop culture, Singaporean citizens are now producing their own indie music. From this mainstream emerged a subculture of discontent Anglicized Singaporeans, cynical with the elitism of the Oxbridge mandarins as well as the dilettante of proletarian mass culture—be it from Hollywood or Hong Kong. "Indie rock supplies a space in which artworks seem to exist outside the conditions of their production, and a bastion from which the cultured few may fend off the multitude" (Hibbert 2005).

In Singaporean terms, this meant that adopting stylistic allusions towards Cantopop and Mandopop (one half of the language divide and highly popular mainstream soundscape) was taboo for practicing indie musicians; Singapore had already become an embedded part of the Hong Kong–Taiwan music production network. Under this framework, rising Singaporean stars such as Stefanie Sun and Tanya Chua are regarded as commercial Mandopop artists as opposed to true indie artists. Aspirations toward western mainstream genres (in addition to the indie's Britpop-derived and American alternative scene) are a slightly more ambiguous matter as the English language Singaporean music scene is not sufficiently globalized to reap the economic benefits from an international or transnational context. This thereby allows for any music produced in Singapore by Singaporean musicians, by dint of its economic unviability, to be default classified also as indie.

In the words of The Straits Times' music critic Boon Chan, "it is so rare and difficult for something to be completely new and original … some form of imitation, or referencing if you like, is inevitable" (Chan 2010). Furthermore, indie musician and chronicler Joseph Tham speaks of indie artists' varied approaches at taking stands of philosophical resistance on cultural platforms:

> In the past (late 1980s and early 1990s), indie was not just a musical genre, but a stand which stood for the "us versus them" dichotomy in the general political and cultural setting in Singapore. But today, it is more defined as a genre than anything else; melodious, fey, whimsical even and most important of all confining to the traditional song form structure musicologically.
>
> *Tham 2010*

Tham's ideas on changing attitudes towards stylistic and artistic resistance are worth looking at in greater depth, and within a wider context. During the 1980s in Britain, indie was used to define a new phase of counter-hegemonic alternative cultural politics against Thatcherism; indie in the west first became synonymous with resistance against loud commercial exhibitionism of electro music and hip-hop (Hesmondhalgh 1999). Existing in the domestic rather than commercial scene, the "do-it-yourself" (D.I.Y.) independent music scene originally challenged the high-tech recording studio in attempting to offer a pure, unmediated interaction between artist and listener. Its music therefore seeks to abstract from the trivial and mundane, emphasizing on the downwind rather than the uplifting. In live performances, this is evident in the deliberate muting of charisma and minimal showcasing of rhythm tracks by dress-down bands who place greater emphasis on lyrics that are sensitive and clever (Hesmondhalgh 1999). Here, the early emphasis on individuality, autonomy, and experimentation, over that of commercialism and propaganda in indie rock, provided great inspiration for Singaporeans.

The paradox of claiming a defaulted and anti-establishment space within the island nation's postcolonial and developmental context, however, necessitated that indie had to be identified by its practitioners with a new kind of "white" culture. The meaning of white did not pertain to the genre's ethnically marked Anglo-American origins but, rather, was speaking in terms of a pure and unblemished canvas, untouched by commercial enterprise and artistic influences produced on behalf of music industry hegemonies. Indie, in its anti-commercial stance, thus provided a deceptively utopian platform which superficially did away with Singapore's postcolonial baggage in the face of transnational influences (in the form of resistance against diasporic Mandopop influences as well as mainstream imported western rock/pop). It swept the issue of Singapore's cultural orphanage neatly under the carpet whilst celebrating originality, uniqueness, individuality, and the voice unbound by tradition on an artistic, acultural, and apolitical blank slate.

Nevertheless, a simultaneous and ironic reality also presented itself in the blank slate. In its hidden, western standardized, and parallel "whiteness," was co-opted into musical reification a fundamentally hegemonic and Anglo-American originated musical framework. Ultimately, indie music as an international genre in changing worldwide markets quickly became subsumed into global capitalist markets as sub-streams of resoundingly mainstream sectors. In regards to utopia, Dyer stated that such self-serving and paradoxical expressions of entertainment "provide alternatives to capitalism which will be provided by capitalism" (Dyer 2002). In one sense, the indie musical style in Singapore was now deliberately disjunctured and decontextualized from indie music's political ethic, in the same way that underground bands in Beijing of the 1990s and 2000s achieved market success in China and abroad based on their anti-market stance and labeling.

In Singapore, the debate over what a true local indie ethic is becomes confused when successful Singaporean bands have been accused of selling out to the market, as is with the controversial case of Electrico, a national indie band. Electrico, the indie group that fronted a national song campaign in 2009, was not only criticized by members of the indie music circle for allowing its popularity to be blatantly co-opted by state ideology, but were also derided as empty copycats of Britpop groups; they were seen as fast leaving their early alternative status behind for commercial success. Indie fan and bass guitarist Clara Chow relates:

> I think that [the state's] benign neglect is good. People should make indie music because they want to, and not so that they can receive funding and set up an arts group that makes art nobody likes. As for Electrico, I wish they would stop trying to ape Coldplay. And the NDP song, born out of generic "need to be cool" artificial means, was naturally and inevitably bland.
>
> *Chow 2010*

However, Electrico's place within Singapore's indie music scene is not necessarily always so castigated, as is shown by its group of growing Singaporean supporters. These supporters, many of whom are not necessarily tapped into the local underground indie scene, have lauded Electrico's achievements and success as evidence of a local indie Singaporean group that has found mainstream success. Even within the self-identified indie music community, opinions vary. Sound artist and experimental singer Analog Girl highlights the uneasy alliances and symbiotic tensions existing between state directive, artistic integrity, and economic savvy: "I am glad Electrico got to write the last NDP song. They did the local indie scene very very proud, and the song is catchy and updated" (Analog Girl 2010). Jacklyn Soo of The Travellators echoes Analog Girl's sentiments: "proper financing and management should be appropriated. Electrico's song for NDP appeals to the crowd as we are moving ahead with youths on the nation's grooming of its identity" (Soo 2010). With the recent development of an annual well-paid and well-attended indie band platform called Baybeats (held at the Esplanade national arts centre since 2001), a more congenial relationship between indie musicians and state arts organizations has begun to evolve. Now, indie bands are sold on supporting local artists, as opposed to their anti-establishment value alone.

To be sure, such contradictions of political, economic, and stylistic intent are not only to be found in indie music scenes outside of the Anglo-American circuit. Despite its anti-commercial and anti-populist posturing, indie music worldwide has also ridden on the circuits of capitalist globalization. Record labels, both independent and mainstream, have begun to penetrate new markets outside the neighborhood with productions in which Frith's notorious notion of "authenticity" remains in doubt. Increasingly, close knit indie communities are sprouting outside the original core of the United Kingdom, in American and Australasian cities. These communities are inspired to live the "desired social experience", in sharing the same opposition and fluidity residing in the genre's aesthetics (Rogers 2008). In the non-western world, the localization of indie becomes a more problematic act of deterritorialization, especially where identity politics between the local and the global intersect. In his case study of Indonesia, Luuvas found the country's indie scene to be one with a

> destabilized sense of locality, in which Indonesian youth have not yet succeeded in constructing a coherent or consistent conception of where they stand on the world stage, nor established themselves as significant players in a transnationalized field of cultural production. They remain, as one of my informants put it, "di tengah-tengah," or "in the middle," no longer willing to uphold the markers of ethnic, cultural, or national identity as an intrinsic part of who they are, and yet not fully integrated into a cultural economy of the global.
>
> *Luvaas 2009*

Returning to the "white" political reading of indie music in Singapore, similarly defaulted and liminal articulations of identity can also be understood in terms of cultural resistance by reverse stereotyping. Singaporean pioneer and pop guru Dick Lee has been described as practicing "a domesticated rap style befitting Lee's pro-west resistance to the West" (Mitchell 1996). Mitchell further commented, that here was a

> positive, reverse sense of Edward Said's term describing western exoticization of the Orient in asserting (in English) an Asian identity that aims to demon-strate that the new Asian ready for the twenty-first century must be assertive, and combat caricatures, stereotypes, and "token yellows".
>
> *Mitchell 2002*

In reality, indie music in Singapore functions as a superficially Britpop aspiring sonic space that is as contested, multi-faceted, tensioned, and as it is liminal in its political, social, and aesthetic claiming of cultural identity. Marked by its "anti-whatever" stance and its refusal to be ghettoed by ethnic marking in the spirit of Rey Chow's 1993 diatribes against cultural essentialization, the indie scene staked its default ground positively around multiple borders. It has been marked by national ideology, western and transnational–Asian imported musical main-streams, the political establishment, and capitalist commercial practice.

Aesthetic dissidents: in search of the ethnically unmarked and the apolitical

From a Bourdieuan perspective (Bourdieu 1984), it would be easy to assume that such a crucibled, liminal space claimed by indie music practitioners would auto-matically align musicians with Singapore's governing elite and the (mainly ethnic Chinese) middle classes. Nonetheless, most participants in the indie music scene are not actively involved in either state building or middle-class formation. As members of the indie community are more intimately exposed to western cultural trends, their appropriation of the occident comes from cultural rather than tech-nocratic starting points. In fact, for most members, it could be argued that it was precisely the "petit-bourgeois philistine modernity" of the Anglicized political elite that provided the impetus in driving musicians to look for alternative narratives and spaces. Some teasing apart of the notion of aesthetic and political dissidence practiced in the name of an anti-establishment indie stance has to be undertaken.

Until the recent co-option of Electrico, alternative narratives expressed by more adventurous musical acts in Singapore were not welcomed by the state; the state has associated such acts with what it considers to be a hippie and decadent lifestyle of drugs and promiscuity. Such lifestyles and worldviews, in their eyes, produced a sense of hypersubjectivity at the expense of commonality with others (Chua 2005) and, in turn, threatened productivity and family (Phua and Kong 1996). From the 1960s until the 1990s, these anxieties were further shown as the state restricted the circulation, production, broadcast, and performance of "morally objectionable" western literature.

Nonetheless, these "objectionable" activities persisted and thrived in "fanzines" (fan magazines), tape demos, and live shows, which were local and foreign produced. The landmark year for Singapore's local indie scene was the year when *Big O*, a monthly alternative music magazine, became a formal publication. Initially consisting of photocopies clipped together, *Big O* eventually became a key portal in disseminating news and information on the Anglo-American indie and pop music scene. Furthermore, *Big O* became an integral part of helping rising local bands in promoting themselves through larger public forums; *Big O* would feature interviews, music reviews, as well as announce release dates of demos, albums, and public performances. In regard to live shows, underground and cult venues such as Nutz, Crazy Elephant, The Substation, and Moods came and went as they accommodated audiences ranging from 40 people to 400 people. In more recent years, higher-profile and yuppie-oriented venues such as Timbre, the Home Club, The Gashaus, and the Esplanade have moved into the scene, hosting single band bills, multiple band bills, and music competitions.

In the 1980s and 1990s, during the more formative years of the indie scene, the following bands were arguably the most prominent: Zircon Lounge, Humpback Oak, The Pagans, Sugarflies, The Oddfellows, The Boredphucks, The Padres, Concave Scream, Nunsex, Global Chaos, Force Vomit, Astreal, and Plainsunset. In more recent years, indie bands such as Electrico, The Observatory, Analog Girl, Great Spy Experiment, I Am David Sparkle, B-Quartet, and Lunarin have risen to the top of the scene. Oftentimes, artists move between different groups, indicating the limited pool of participants within the indie music scene, as well as demonstrating a highly networked and tight knit community in which both musicians and fans operate.

Fans and musicians of the indie music scene tend to view their scene, as a whole, as inspired by (or even imitating) the British indie scene; in particular, the late 1970's to early 1990's acts such as Joy Division, The Smiths, Pink Floyd, and The Cure. However, individual interviews reveal a more diverse range of influences, including North American artists such as Cat Power, Alanis Morissette, Joanna Newsom, and Patrick Watson, European artists such as Bjork, in addition to regional genres that include Thai rock, Japanese anime music, Asian techno, and groove and sound art.

Ultimate homage to Britpop, however, remains a long-running theme and has to first be situated within the early days of international pop imports into Singapore. Unlike with American music albums, imported British music was not commonly sold in mainstream Singaporean retail outlets. Instead, specialty record shops (such as Da Da Records, Roxy Music, and Sembawang Music) helped develop a growing niche market by offering these imported products as well as the merchandise of local bands and fanzines. What has being witnessed since the 1980s is a quiet level of globalization and cultural transmission away from the mainstream into an alternative music scene. Instead of a lock, stock, and barrel operation of McDonaldization, the spread of indie music involves a comparatively more nuanced transmission to a smaller and specific segment of the populace, which increasingly finds greater resonance and affiliation with the agenda and aesthetics of imported sounds.

As is evident by the names of local indie bands, the appropriation of global indie music trends serves as a local response by Anglicized Singaporeans to the paternalistic imposition and contradictions of a developmentalist party state. The subtleties of the post-punk and post-rock music genres have given English-educated Singaporeans the template for framing counter narratives and counter aesthetics to the dominant political culture. These genres are able to paint a more dysfunctional and dystopic vision (if not a more egocentric introspection) into their music. This ultimately challenges, however indirectly, the progressivist optimism of the Asian economic miracle upon which the Singaporean state has faithfully reiterated in their efforts to reinforce its dominance over civil society.

Concave Scream underlines their societal discontent by personalizing the impact of oppressive social structures into desolation, helplessness, and rage through their song *Prey*, released in 1997.

> Say a prayer
> Before you close your eyes
> Your consciousness is far beyond
> The realm of my existence
> I saw you there
> Corner of my dreams
> Standing at the edge of nowhere
> Heed the voices deep within
> And I can feel you calling out
> In desolation
> The fire's dying in your eyes
> And I held my hands out
> But you're out of reach
> The fire's dying in your eyes
> Holding on to nothing
> Holding back your pride
> The screams you hear
> Are tearing at your soul
> The greatest of your fears is calling
> Out your name, don't listen.

Prey (Concave Scream 1997)

On one hand, the lyrical content of many songs from local indie music seemingly reflects a deeper struggle for the recognition of an autonomous subjectivity and space against collective social pressures of the mainstream. On the other hand, most song lyrics steer clear of direct references to state affairs, politics, or traditionally sensitive issues of race and religion. Instead, they focus on more generic subjects such as social alienation, love, the inequities of relationships, and the general state of the human condition. Analog Girl clarifies:

I think there are more cultural differences than musical style differences. Singaporean musicians are probably more conservative in terms of subject matter and how they convey their message—it is more subtle, poetic, and not as provocative. That could be seen as a crutch but that's what moulds our identity as artists—characteristics that international audiences would find refreshing.

Analog Girl 2010

In this respect, alternatives in vernacular popular culture are also problematic for the indie scene in disdaining the commercialism, communalism, and conservatism of mass culture. This mass culture in Singapore is highly racialized along the ethnic lines as defined by the state. In many cases, involvement in the (English-speaking) indie scene has been a reaction to the imposition of mother tongue languages, which many citizens found oppressively alienating. This sentiment comes from a general reluctance of the Anglicized segment of the ethnic Chinese populace to have cultural markers of "Chineseness" imposed upon them; specifically, a Mandarin language education. Mandarin, though branded the Chinese "mother tongue," is alien to Singaporeans that have a mainly Southern Chinese linguistic heritage that includes Cantonese, Hakka, Techeow, and Hokkien dialects. Arguably, this echoes Chow's views on the subject of postcolonial ethnic stereotyping in Chinese diasporas (Chow 1993). To these Singaporeans, the emphasis on "Asianness" has been a false but systematically oppressive measure of indigenization.

Hence, when Singaporean indie artists and fans are not being able to speak Asian languages, it is indicative of resistance rather than manifestation of colonial penetration and erasure. In musical terms, this is further reinforced by the deliberate adoption of Euro-American derived musical styles constructed from diatonic major and minor scales and functional harmony. This is in opposition to traditional stratified polyphonies of Chinese-derived regional chamber ensembles, "Asianized western" and "pacific pop" pentatonic harmonies of Mandopop and Cantopop (Hamm 1995; Iwabuchi 1998; Ho 2003). While the latter genres have often been classified as "Chinese-sounding," the Anglo-American low-fi setup featuring drum kits, a sparsely strummed guitar, grooved keyboard, and restrained vocals has been classified not as western, but as modern, cool, and contemporary.

Consumers versus producers: an ethnic and class marked divide?

With little intention of "Asianizing" their linguistic and musical expressions, indie musicians in Singapore would have been regarded as the colonial petty-bourgeois who make up the chorus of those accepting the "fatalistic logic" of the position of European languages in the non-western literary world (Thiong'O 2005). Complicating the positionality of European languages and musical styles is the refusal of the Singaporean public to recognize its authenticity and legitimacy in the performance realm even though it is already completely internalized in the business and government realms. Matter has observed the tendency of majority Singaporean consumers (as opposed to niche crowds) to be prejudiced against locally produced English language popular music productions, viewing them as inferior to their Anglo-American counterparts (Mattar 2009). There is an innate difficulty for Singaporean, English language, indie music practitioners to become intimately localized, even though English has become Singapore's first language, rather than an additional institutionalized language. Nonetheless, from a postcolonial perspective, the representation of the English language in Singapore, by Singaporeans, is considered to be at the outer circle, in line with India and the Philippines, in contrast to the inner circles of Australia and New Zealand (Kachru 2005). Under such circumstances, indie musicians who aim to gain a larger regional public sphere may need to switch their language focus. This, for example, is seen in the case of Tanya Chua, who is a rocker turned Mandopop star. Chua began her professional music career as a singer in the English language music scene until she altered her career track by restyling her musical voice and joining the Taiwan-based, regionally entrenched, and well-distributed Mandopop industry.

The refusal of the Singaporean public to formally acknowledge the ownership of the English language manifests itself through poor sales for these productions in the mainstream market as well as within the local indie scene, where fans display greater enthusiasm for established British bands over that of their local counterparts. Another affliction of local indie artists is the reluctance of commercial radio stations in Singapore to provide greater airtime for their songs, although this has been changing in recent years. The Lilac Saints, a moderately successful indie band (nominated by a local radio station in 1996 for best local band) laments that the mainstream broadcast media are disinclined to play local indie songs, and songs from musical acts not signed onto major record labels. It seems, however, that bands themselves are not too eager to embark on commercializing, or selling out through systematic engagement with mainstream media, rather than a few cases of bands trying to push through a couple radio friendly tracks to allegedly unfriendly radio stations (Wong 2004).

These emerging divides between performers and audiences, as well as between producers and consumers, have situated indie as an economically asymmetrical genre. The consequences of apparent double standards of practice among Singaporean indie fans are evident in the collective marketing and internal self-identification and sub-identification of bands. This is confirmed by Analog Girl:

> In the global sense, Indie music has taken on a new face, fast becoming a genre on its own. So Indie does not necessarily define against the mainstream for me. Indie music can equally be mainstream now. For example, Electrico are mainstream, so are the White Stripes.
>
> *Analog Girl 2010*

In turn, many local acts along with their supporters (mainly between the ages of 20 to 30 years), automatically adopt a collective and community bolstered genre identity and branded stance of indie that is irrespective of style, influence, or social agenda. Indeed, Singaporean bands that would (musically) otherwise slip into established mainstream Anglo-American genres of pop, standard rock, rap, and hip-hop are, by default, often tagged as indie by nature of their relatively unknown profiles, or at least a relative lack of appreciation by local consumers. Elsewhere, the even more underground cult genre of Singapore-produced "sound art" has also been subsumed within the higher-profile label of indie, even though it has pooled audience, fan, and community resources with a sister sub-stream scene. The result, again, is a dislocation and shearing of actual musical style and musical content from social context; it does not matter what it sounds like, as long as it looks esoteric enough on paper, or if it is produced in Singapore, it will be labelled "indie." Indie fan and performer Clara Chow relates, "anything that is struggling for eardrums" could be effectively regarded as indie in Singapore, given its difficulty in selling on the mainstream market. Nonetheless, there remains, to some extent, interaction between the indie scene and the larger public in Singapore (including the media). The republic's main newspapers have sought to provide greater coverage for the local indie scene, announcing shows and album releases, while some radio stations have given airtime to long-running indie musicians, such as Chris Ho, in order to introduce alternative music to the greater public.

Hence, unlike the other ethnic and vernacular popular music followings by the Singaporean public, indie music is unable to mobilize grassroots and communal solidarity and support from the heartland of Singapore that supposedly has less affinity with the English language. For Fanon, the "moment that we can speak of a national literature" comes when a native of the land progresses from producing a work to be read exclusively by the colonial oppressor to producing one that addresses his own people. This contact with the new public should give rise to a new rhythm and imagination in the form of national consciousness (Fanon 2005). Being largely disconnected from the "ground," indie music continues to be marginalized not just from local society, but also from the regional mass market, which includes Singaporean consumers. The regional mass market, in particular, includes the transnational popular Chinese entertainment industry, or what has been called "Pop Culture China" (Chua 2001) or, conversely, "Asianized western" (Iwabuchi 1998).

If the local and the national are neither possible nor desired, what about claiming an affinity with the global western? With increasing recognition that global mass culture has been painted with so-called third world ideas and styles, we suggest that in the present situation of global complexity, the idea of home has to be separated analytically from the idea of locality (Robertson 2003). Local organizers and venues have seen a surge of demand for live performances by Anglo-American indie bands, including less prominent groups such as Florence and the Machine, Death Trap for Cuties, and Amiee Man (Thia 2010). Local indie fans are eager to see western indie acts perform in their country, whereas local indie bands hope to perform in the West in order to gain cultural acknowledgment and recognition from their compatriots. Though Singaporean indie bands have performed in music

130 Kai Khiun Liew and Shzr Ee Tan

festivals and are occasionally mentioned in the mainstream media, indie bands from Asia have yet to sign on to indie European record labels. Considering that even mainstream East Asian artistes with huge industry support such as South Korea's BOA and Taiwanese American Coco Lee and Machi have not made successful headways into the North Atlantic music industries, the tasks for these significantly less prominent Asian indie artistes would be substantially more daunting. While a recognized characteristic of indie culture is in its obscurity, there is also a simultaneous desire for expansion and wider recognition. Vivian, a member of Singaporean indie band, The Observatory, reflects:

> Success is subjective. To us, success isn't measured by good reviews, platinum sales, massive airplay, or getting signed to a major label. Ultimately, we need to be happy with what we're doing. Being able to sustain working together in the long term will give us the biggest satisfaction. Of course, it would be excellent if we can get something, in whatever shape, form, or contract, that allows our music to reach farther shores of listeners. That is a connection we will always seek.
>
> *Wong 2005*

However, unlike Singaporean artists who have made prominent headways in the ethnically presupposed Asian popular entertainment industries of Taiwan and Hong Kong, the prospects for commercial success in the west for Singaporean indie bands have been less certain. Even as post-industrial cities in the British Isles (such as Manchester) are marketing their indie heritage as part of urban regeneration and tourism (Botta 2009), the indie scene remains exclusively dominated by English males (Bannister 2006). For European consumers, the non-western world remains entrenched within the pre-modern oriental musicological spiritual imagination articulated in ethnicized world music rather than the urban angst of the post-industrial world. In other words, Singapore-based, English-language indie bands would not be able to satisfy the colonial fantasies produced through world music and its orientalist and exoticized domain of truths on the colonized (Barret 1996). In the same way, Cantopop and Mandopop, while reaping huge economic results in East Asia, are not sufficiently racially marked to constitute world music. While western indie bands are seen as too western to become localized and nationalized, the Singaporean English language indie bands become, by contrast, too "wannabe" and too "Asianized western" to be globalized in Europe or America.

> It is no longer simply the "first world" Orientalist who mourns the rusting away of is treasures, but also students from privileged backgrounds Western and non-Western, who conform behaviourally in every respect with the elitism of their social origins, but who nonetheless proclaim dedication to vindicating the subalterns. They choose to see in others' powerlessness an idealized image of themselves and refuse to hear in the dissonance between the content and manner of their speech their own complicity with violence.
>
> *Chow 1993*

Speaking on the "already deterritorialized nature of Indie music and pop/rock as a whole" (Chow 2010), she articulates:

> With globalization, I don't think there is much difference between Singapore English music and those from other places anymore. It's the same with music originating from other parts of the world. I don't think it's necessarily a bad thing to ape music and styles from western countries. Singapore, being an importer of a lot of things, has always been able to draw from everywhere, not just from the UK and US.
>
> *Chow 2010*

Finally, Eva Wong states:

> How distinctive can our sound be, if we're not nomads on the plains of the Silk Road or some reclusive subculture? We're not Asian enough, nor western enough, nor do we have strong artistic or aesthetic roots anywhere. We're a diluted people with a blank slate. The good thing is, we're [still] available for history to be written!
>
> *Wong 2010*

This difficulty in authenticating, identifying, and locating Singapore's indie music is also evident in the responses of Lim Cheng Tju, who has been an active columnist at *Big O* magazine:

> I have wondered about this over the years. When we started championing indie music, it's championing the things we like. Music we think is good and should be played on the radio. For some [punks], it's a way of life. We didn't think much about how it can or should represent us or our identity as Singaporeans or Asians. But after reading Said, etc. it does become an issue. So maybe Dick Lee or even the Kopi Kat Klan is more "authentic."[2]
>
> *Lim 2010*

While recognizing the absence of territorial consciousness behind the productions of the indie music scene, Lim is also reluctant to acknowledge the more "culturalist" English-language productions that are endorsed by both state and academia in Singapore.

The form of cultural displacement, however, does not imply that the indie music scene has no significant role in global, national, and local societies and cultures. On the contrary, the English-language indie music scene in Singapore has served in extracting and distinguishing the bourgeois bohemia from the Anglicized elite. Although seemingly obscured by the hegemony of the state and also by the dominance of vernacular mass cultures, the indie scene has ultimately proved to be quite influential on Singaporean society. When speaking solely about the music of the indie scene, it has provided the impetus for the articulation of more radical discourses in both the cultural and formal realms of politics. Rather than an isolated space, this sonic music sphere, in its exciting, fast-changing, and dynamic tensions effected on behalf of its very liminality, has engendered a complex network of interactions between musicians, artists, activists, and even the state.

Though it may appear that the indie scene is dominated by ethnic Chinese Singaporeans, many significant figures in the scene come from other ethnic minorities, and also foreign nationalities. Far from being an isolated sub-culture of bourgeois bohemia, the scene is plugged into multiple stages, disseminating agents, histories, communities, contexts, and networks. In other words, Appadurian scapes of activity within and without Singapore, prefixed by their ethnic, media, technology, finance, and idea-driven directives.

It has been observed that most local indie performances share a stage with local heavy metal bands, which are generally fronted by ethnic Malays; for example, this has taken place at venues such as the Substation, one of Singapore's greatest venues for fringe arts. Asides from the music scene, Philip Cheah, a pioneer of the Singaporean indie scene and the editor of *Big O*, is also responsible for establishing the Singapore International Film Festival; Cheah created this in 1987 to provide Singaporean audiences with independent films produced regionally and world-wide. Other interdisciplinary performers of the arts such as Zai Kuning, George Chua, and Yuen Chee Wai move casually between the indie music scene and performance arts, such as sound art. As aforementioned, singer-songwriter Tanya Chua began her career singing in English as a rock artist but eventually found fame and fortune in the Mandopop and Cantopop world. However, Chua occasionally reappears in the indie music scene to put on a live show. Additionally, English language indie music groups have been instrumental in supporting the revival of Singaporean films from the 1990s. A clearcut case of this is seen in Eric Khoo's 1995 feature film, *Mee Pok Man*; the soundtrack to this film was performed by the Lilac Saints while Joe Ng from The Padres starred in this film.

There has been a reluctant acknowledgment by the state of the aforementioned activities, as the state is seeking to socially reengineer its populace towards the cultural economy by moving the country into a post-Fordist economy. In recent years, Singapore's premier theatre, the Esplanade, has been used as a venue for indie performances that would have been scoffed at a decade ago. In many ways, the very existence of an indie scene in Singapore serves also as a political symbol. Indie musicians triumphantly claim an alternative space and potentially subversive social narrative on behalf of marginalized artists and the social activist community at large. These musicians, in turn, have been utilized and co-opted by the state in creating a positive international image for tourist promotion; they serve as evidence of the nation's arrival at cosmopolitan civilization.

While the Singaporean state has recognized the indie scene's contribution to cultural branding, the state has also been attempting to deal with the more radical politics that the appropriated indie genre has produced. Some younger, more vocal activists of the indie scene have been attempting to expose the true face of the state, which filmmakers have been a great part of. For example, filmmaker Seelan Palay

An unlocalized and unglobalized subculture **133**

endorses civil disobedience, while fellow filmmaker Martyn See continuously tests the censors' limits with his political films. To some extent, both filmmakers are acquainted with the indie music scene, as Palay is a drummer in a few indie bands, and See is a frequent audience member at indie shows. While Palay and See confront the state in the formal arena, another young activist, Chris Ho, challenges the structures of Singaporean society with his deliberate exhibitionism of non-conformity through a heavily tattooed body and angsty literary works influenced by punk culture. While aggressive actions by members of the indie community (such as open demonstrations or active verbal interactions with the public) are closely watched by the state, manifestations of their varied social stances through the mediated platform of music have been treated as political safety valves. Perhaps this is in the same manner as Avner's ideas of how humour, in its own state, and harmless "mainstream guise," can function as a "social corrective" (Avner 1988).

The globalization of indie pop has functioned in rearranging local social structures, involving the creation of a new bohemian class in Singapore that derives its energies from the fringes of popular culture rather than institutions of high art and education alone. Wilson wonders whether the "bohemian" in this appropriated form would invariably frame its politics of dissent along internal exile, rather than opposition, along with replacing transformation and revolution with resistance and transgression. Would it, for one (in tribute to the traits of disenchantment with society as demonstrated through the indie ethic) paradoxically challenge the bourgeois attitudes, but yet fatalistically accept the impersonal power structures of the global economy (Wilson 1999)?

The indie scene in Singapore is currently considered as politically moderate, subject to the absorption of the state and market, instead of mounting direct challenges to the impersonal power structures. It nevertheless remains to be seen how the indie scene will influence the aesthetics and politics of its fans, many of whom are civil servants, teachers, business executives, and housewives.

Finally, a return to historical trajectory can perhaps provide conclusive evidence on the indie genre's liminally bordered existence, anti-identity politics, and musical disarticulations. The Singaporean indie scene has existed for over 15 years now, and has maintained a long enough presence in local memories to allow for a developmental timeline, cultural nostalgia, and sub-scene trends to manifest themselves. Although there has been a tendency for local bands to strengthen themselves under the common banner of indie, distinct sounds and diverse styles are found; sound artist Yuen Chee Wai, Coldplay-aspiring Electrico, and heavy metal acts Slayer and Helloween are all classified as indie. The recent release of *Oaksongs*, a boxed set of retrospective albums by local band Humpback Oak, has generated a surge of interest among Generation-X-rebel-hipsters-turned-office-commuting responsible young parents. Humpback Oak's re-releasing of their 1990's recordings has allowed for these long-term indie fans to take a trip down memory lane, as well as follow Humpback Oak's evolution of musical style, as they moved from raw to professional.

Apart from defaulting against the strands of Mandopop, Cantopop, and mainstream western pop-rock imports along the English–Chinese language divide, one way of locating indie music within the historical development of Singapore pop is to see indie as an answer to a 1980's punk-deprived local scene that had been following parallel exploits of western popular music cultures. As indie music as an international genre continues to change and will ultimately become absorbed within the global mainstream, it will be interesting to see how the scene in Singapore will chart its own, already complex, courses.

A salient point to be made is how, in spite of Singapore's liminal definitions of indie music, incongruencies persist on the aesthetic, economic, and socio-political levels. As a new age of internet file sharing arises (with iTunes, CDBaby, MySpace, etc.), social media dominated platforms dawn, and the "no label" generic labeling of indie musicians will surely evolve into new and dynamic socio-musical scapes. Additionally, notions of originality, copyright, performativity, dissemination, and economic modeling will also be dramatically altered.

Indie's glocal oddity

> I see them in the pouring rain
> Laughing at me once again
> But it's them who are getting wet
> I'm up in the cloud & breathing fresh air
> But if you want me to come down
> My feet's on the ground
> I'll be there in a little while
> I'll be around
> I wonder if I'll ever see
> The day when everyone is free
> People tell me it could never be
> I'm up in the clouds & shouting out loud
> But if you want me to come down
> My feet's on the ground
> I'll be there in a little while
> I'll be around
> Well just today
> I was on my way when I saw the tears running down
> Joy and pain all rolled in one
>
> *Unity Song* (Oddfellows 2009)

A de facto anthem for the Singapore's local indie music scene, *The Unity Song* by the Oddfellows could be written anywhere in the English-speaking world, as it highlights little geo-linguistic and cultural references. It is a song of protest against conformity, and its lyrics are as socially relevant to the United Kingdom as they are to Singapore. The subtleties and simplicity of the lyrical contents are character-istic of the indie genre that emphasizes sarcasm, wit, and sublimity that are often layered with an eclectic musicological spectrum of acoustics from post-rock to experimental electronic music. Although indie traces its origins from the British Isles, they cannot claim exclusivity over the indie domain as the genre becomes increasingly diffused to the rest of the world, just as Oddfellows' music has shown. However, unlike Britain's Joy Division and The Smiths, Singapore's Oddfellows will probably never enjoy global recognition from the world market or even from its own mainstream national audiences.

As this paper has illustrated, Singapore's indie music scene presents a problematic arena in studying local appropriations of global trends that are predominantly diffused from the West. Indie music has penetrated Singapore through the socio-cultural fringe of Anglicized Singaporeans; a group that continues to find difficulty in identifying with both the paternal and developmental logic of the authoritarian, technocratic elite and the cultural conservatism of the vernacular masses. While this group of Anglicized Singaporeans may be the product of the primacy of the English language in postcolonial Singapore, their expressions have remained largely discouraged by the state for its resemblance of the excesses and indulgences of the west. Furthermore, these expressions have also remained unacknowledged by fellow countrymen due to notions of racial inauthenticity, and gone generally undetected in the global market. As Singapore's indie community becomes increasingly elevated due to post-Fordist Singapore's emphasis on the cultural economy, participants of the scene have nonetheless been resisting attempts to have their expressions vernacularized and ethnicized in order to make their music more local and authentic for audiences. As such, the conscious deployment of standard English becomes a manifestation of these politics.

Nevertheless, the local indie music scene's sense of denial and self-denial does not mean they have ideologically adhered to the genre's spirit of resistance against commercialism and the mainstream. Local performers have either been appropriated by officialdom into celebrating state power or absorbed by the regional, commercial Chinese popular music industry as songwriters, composers, and performers. In spite of indie music's relatively miniscule following, it would be premature to portray the aforementioned as evidence of the indie scene "selling out" to the state and market. Though it is linked with neo-liberal global capitalism, the indie music scene in Singapore ultimately remains located within the westernized bohemian fringe, detecting and appropriating new global aesthetics and politics to push the socio-cultural boundaries in the national and local realms.

Notes

1 This video, available online at http://www.youtube.com/watch?v=GKAMTOx0nNw, alongside other uploads of the same video, has gone on to garner more than a collective total of 80,000 views since its appearance on YouTube in 2009.
2 Copy Kat Klan had only produced a single album "Oi, Why so so like dat" (1987) whose colloquial title suggests the unrestrained use of pidgin English or "Singlish" that is widely spoken by Singaporeans on a more casual and informal basis.

136 Kai Khiun Liew and Shzr Ee Tan

Bibliography

Analog Girl (2010) Personal communication, March 21.

Appadurai, A. (1996) *Modernity at Large: Cultural Dimensions of Globalization*, Minnesota: University of Minnesota Press.

Avner, Z. (1988) "Humor as a Social Corrective," in L. Behrens and L.J. Rosen (eds) *Writing and Reading Across the Curriculum*, Glenview, IL: Scott, Foresman and Company, 356–360.

Bal, C. (2009) "Bhangra and the Reconstruction of 'Punjabi-ness' in Multiracial Singapore," in D. Goh *et al.* (eds) *Race and Multiculturalism in Malaysia and Singapore*, London: Routledge.

Bannister, M. (2006) "Loaded: Indie Guitar Rock, Canonism, White Masculinities", *Popular Music*, 25: 77–95.

Barret, J. (1996) "World Music, Nation, and Postcolonialism," *Cultural Studies,* 10: 237–247.

Bokhorst-Heng, W. and Wee, L. (2005) "Language Policies and Nationalistic Ideologies: Statal Narratives in Singapore," *Multilingual*, 24: 159–183.

Botta, G. (2009) "The City that was Creative and Did Not Know: Manchester and Popular Music 1976–1997," *European Journal of Cultural Studies*, 12: 349–365.

Bourdieu, P. (1984) *Distinction: A Social Critique of the Judgment of Taste*, London: Routledge.

Chan, B. (2010) Personal communication, March 16.

Ching, P. (2010) Personal communication, March 19.

Chow, C. (2010) Personal communication, March 11.

Chow, R. (1993) *Writing Diaspora: Tactics of Intervention in Contemporary Cultural Studies*, Indiana: Indiana University Press.

Chua, B.H. (1995) *Communitarian Ideology and Democracy in Singapore*, London: Routledge.

Chua, B.H. (2001) "Pop Culture China," *Singapore Journal of Tropical Geography*, 22: 113–121.

Dairianathan, E. (2009) "Vedic Metal and the South Indian Community in Singapore: Problems and the Prospects of Identity," *Inter-Asia Cultural Studies*, 10: 587–608.

Dean, M. (1994) *Critical and Effective Histories: Foucault Methods of Historical Sociology*, London: Routledge.

Dirlik, A. (2005) "The Postcolonial Aura: Third World Criticism in the Age of Global Capitalism," in P. Leistyna (ed.) *Cultural Studies: From Theory to Action*, Oxford: Blackwell Publishing.

Dyer, R. (2002) *Only Entertainment*, London and New York: Routledge.

Fanon, F. (2005) "On National Culture," in G. Desai and S. Nair (eds) *Postcolonialism: An Anthology of Cultural Theory and Criticism*, New Jersey: Rutgers University Press.

Fu, K.S.Y. and Liew, K.K. (2007) "From Folk Devils to Folk Heroes: Tracing the Malay Heavy Metal Music Scene in Singapore," in G. Bloustein, M. Peters, and S. Luckman (eds) *Sonic Synergies: Music, Technology, Community and Identity*, Aldershot: Ashgate.

Hadi, E. (2010) Personal communication, March 25.

Hamm, C. (1995) *Putting Popular Music in its Place*, Cambridge: Cambridge University Press.

Hesmondhalgh, D. (1999) "Indie: The Institutional Politics and Aesthetics of a Popular Music Genre," *Cultural Studies*, 13: 34–61.

Ho, W.C. (2003) "Between Globalization and Localization: A Study of Hong Kong Popular Music," *Popular Music*, 22: 143–157.

Holden, P. (2008) "Postcolonial Desire," *Postcolonial Studies*, 11: 345–361.

Hibbet, R. (2005) "What is Indie Rock," *Popular Music and Society*, 28: 55–77.

Iwabuchi, K. (1998) "Pure Impurity: Japan's Genius for Hybridism," *Communal Plural: Journal of Transnational and Crosscultural Studies*, 6(1): 71–86.

Kachru, B. (2005) *Asian Englishes Beyond the Canon*, Hong Kong: Hong Kong University Press.

Kong, L. (1996) "Making Music at the Margins? A Social and Cultural Analysis of Xinyao in Singapore," *Asian Studies Review*, 19: 99–124.

Krishnaswamy, R. (2008) "Postcolonial and Globalization Studies: Connections, Conflicts, Complicities," in R. Krishnaswamy and J. Hawley (eds) *The Postcolonial and Global*, Minneapolis: University of Minnesota Press.

Kuo, P.K. (1995) *Images at the Margins: A Collection of Kuo Pao Kun's Plays (1983–1992)*, Singapore: Times Books International.

Lee, K.Y. (2000) *From Third World to First: The Singapore Story: 1965–2000*, Singapore: Times Media.

Liew, K.K. (2003) "Limited Pidgin Type Patios? Policy, Language, Technology, Identity, and the Experience of Canto-Pop Music in Singapore," *Popular Music*, 22: 217–233.

Lim, C.T. (2010) Email interview, March 26.

Luvaas, B. (2009) "Dislocated Sounds: The Deterritorialization of Indonesian Indie pop," *Cultural Anthropology*, 24: 246–279.

Mattar, Y. (2009) "Popular Cultural Cringe: Language as Signifier of Authenticity and Quality in the Singaporean Popular Music Market," *Popular Music*, 28: 179–195.

Mitchell, T. (1996) *Popular Music and Local Identity: Pop, Rock and Rap in Europe and Oceania*, London: University of Leicester Press.

Mitchell, T. (2002) *Global Noise: Rap and Hip-Hop Outside the USA*, Middletown, CT: Wesleyan University Press.

Phua, S.C. and Kong, L. (1996) "Ideology, Social Commentary, and Resistance in Popular Music: A Case Study of Singapore," *Journal of Popular Culture*, 30: 215–231.

Robertson, R. (2003) "Globalization or Glocalization?' in R. Robertson and K. White (eds) *Globalization: Critical Concepts in Sociology*, London and New York: Routledge.

Rogers, I. (2008) "You've Got to Go to Gigs to Get Gigs: Indie Musicians, Eclecticism, and the Brisbane scene," *Continuum: Journal of Media and Cultural Studies*, 22: 639–649.

Singapore Government (2005) *General Household Survey (Education and Language)*, Singapore Government Statistics. Online. Available at: http://www.singstat.gov.sg/pubn/popn/ghsr1/chap2.pdf.

Soo, J. (2010) Personal communication, March 10–21.

Tan, S.E. (2005) "Manufacturing and Consuming Culture: Fakesong in Singapore," *Ethnomusicology Forum*, 14: 83–106.

Tan, S.E. (2009) "Singapore Takes the Bad Rap: A State Produced Music Video Goes Viral," *Ethnomusicology Forum*, 18: 107–130.

Tan, S.E. (2010) "National Songs Revisited: From Propaganda to Pop, to Anti-Cool Kitsch," *s/pores*. Online. Available at: http://s-pores.com/2010/03/national-songs-revisited.

Tham, J. (2010) Personal communication, March 25.

Thia, S. (2010). "Mainstream Music? Nah. Singapore Loves its Indie," *CNN Asia*, 5 February.

Thiong'O, N.W. (2005) "The Language of African Literature," in G. Desai and S. Nair (eds) *Postcolonialism: An Anthology of Cultural Theory and Criticism*, New Jersey: Rutgers University Press.

Wee, W.L. (2003) "Creating High Culture in the Globalized Cultural Desert of Singapore," *The Drama Review*, 47: 84–97.

Wee, W.L. (2007) *The Asian Modern: Culture, Capitalist Development, Singapore*, Singapore: National University Press.

Wilson, E. (1999) "The Bohemianization of Mass Culture," *International Journal of Cultural Studies*, 2: 11–32.

Wong, E. (2010) Email interview, April 21.

Wong, M. (2004) "Strange Lullabies: The Observatory Interview," *Ageing Youth*, August 8. Online. Available at: http://www.agingyouth.com/?p=469.

Wong, M. (2005) "Climbing up the Blank Wall: An Interview with Observatory," *Ageing Youth*, 15 June. Online. Available at: http://www.agingyouth.com/?p=332.

Yeoh, B. (2004) "Cosmopolitan and its Exclusions in Singapore," *Urban Studies*, 41: 2431–2445.

Discography

Concave Scream (1997) *Erratic*. Springroll Creative Entertainment.

Oddfellows (2009) *+65 Indie Underground*. Universal Music.

8

"ONLY MIX, NEVER BEEN CUT"

The localized production of Jamaican music in Thailand

Viriya Sawangchot

Introduction

> Hey! What kind of song is this song? People listen to it and do not understand where it comes from … who knows where this song comes from? Why do some call it reggae, while some call it ska?
>
> *Ska Variety* (2009) OK Mocca

Released in early 2009, *Ska Variety* by OK Mocca immediately became a hit song among the younger Thai generations. *Ska Variety* was written by OK Mocca's 24-year-old percussionist, Surachet Rattanan; the lyrics curiously stated, "what kind of the song we are playing now? Is it reggae or ska?" These questioning lyrics are perhaps related to the fact that Thailand had, in 2009, around 20 new Thai bands pop up, who play both reggae and ska music; that year, Thailand also held four reggae and ska music festivals. Moreover, at the March 2009 reggae and ska festival Hit and Tist Number One, OK Mocca performed a version of *Ska Variety* that was mixed with "Mor Lum," a traditional northeastern Thai folksong; not only did OK Mocca mix the musical styles of reggae, ska, and folk, they also integrated these elements into their performance style. For example, the beat of Ok Mocca's *Ska Variety* stayed true to the ska genre, but the band made sure the rhythm could be combined smoothly with Mor Lum. Though OK Mocca may have been questioned about their style of music (whether it was reggae, ska, or Mor Lum), they need not question themselves anymore because the band ended up leaving behind *Ska Variety* as their only hit song.

Also in 2009, *The Guitar Magazine*, Thailand's longest standing and most popular music magazine, dedicated a special issue to the reggae and ska styles in the local Thai music scene; it argued that OK Mocca, along with other Thai ska and reggae artists such as T-Bone, Job 2 Do, Kai Jo Brothers, Gold Red, Zom Amara, Buddha Bless,

140 Vinya Sawangchot

Tamon, Teddy Ska Band, Skalaxy, and the Super Glasses Ska Ensemble, attempted to appropriate Thai popular and folk music into their reggae and ska music.

If the reggae and ska genre originated from Jamaica, but is now making sense in the globalization of music culture and industry, how has it affected/how is it affecting the Thai popular music industry and culture? How do popular Thai music artists re-negotiate reggae and ska to stand up on the global level? Rather than assuming that reggae and ska is an invasion of Thailand's music culture through the globalized flows of music culture and media, this chapter aims to explore how Thai music artists appropriate and contest global music styles. In particular, this study explores the introduction of reggae and ska into Thailand, which originated from Jamaica in the 1950s and, subsequently in the 1970s, became a popular global music style due to localization and freer markets. Finally, this study will examine patterns in Thai music culture (from the 1980s up until today) that have emerged due to the introduction of reggae and ska into the country.

Globalization, reggae, and Bob Marley

The concept of globalization is frequently associated with structural and institutional changes in financial markets, trade, security, as well as telecommunication and culture (Robertson 1990, 1991; Tomlinson 1999; Giddens 2009). First, this chapter will serve to create an understanding of globalization and, second, will examine why globalization matters through the exploration of Jamaican popular music (particularly reggae music). Therefore, the focus in the first part of this chapter will be on the dimensions of the aforementioned structural changes; in particular, their interactions with global media and culture and, more specifically, on reggae music and its industry.

In order to understand globalization not only in economic and political terms, but as a multidimensional process, Appadurai argues that the globalization of culture is often discussed in terms of global/multidirectional flows, regional/cultural interaction, and the locality linked (Appadurai 1991). Frith contends that musical styles are a simple example of globalization, and demonstrates how local producers and consumers negotiate through global media flows (Frith 1989). During adds that the globalization of culture can take on many forms and has various effects, some of which work in the opposite direction to the original source (During 1997).

Nevertheless, before our current era of globalization, popular music in Jamaica (particularly in the ska and reggae genres) in the 1950s was related to politics, ideology, and spirituality and religion; however, the globalization of culture sprung up during the 1970s with Bob Marley's songs (Giddens 2009). Therefore, this study will focus on examining the globalization of these musical styles and other related and shared meanings that trace back to the origins of ska and reggae in Jamaica from the 1960s to the 1970s.

Barrett contended in his book that the ska and reggae genres in Jamaica (whether a musical genre or musical discourse) were born out of post-World War II frustrations, due to the dominance of American popular music (Barrett 1997). During that time, Jamaican popular music came into contact with American popular music, particularly the genres of jazz and rock and roll. These two popular music cultures combined together to create a traditional Jamaican musical style, followed by new musical forms unique to Jamaican popular music. Ska began to emerge in Jamaican popular music during the 1950s and, a few years later, the rock steady genre, which had a slower groove than ska, also emerged on the music scene. Also, reggae was initially established in the Jamaican popular music scene during the 1960s, but this was only after the establishment of ska.

The earliest ska musicians in Jamaica were strongly influenced by modern jazz, African-American R&B, as well as rock and roll. Reggae, on the other hand, though developed from ska music, is dominated much more by the sounds of bass and drums, rather than guitar and vocals; its beats are also slower than that of ska music. In late 1960's Jamaica, the reggae genre gained more popularity than the ska and rock steady genres. However, the crucial difference between ska and reggae lies not in musical style, but in the so-called "rastafarian spirit." To clarify, Rastafari is not a religion, but was actually related to the political motivations of Jamaicans against British colonizers during the 1900s. It should also be noted that reggae is widely accepted as the creative expressions of Rastafarians, the group of people who believed in Rastafari. Though Rastafarians may refer to a number of different people groups, beliefs, and attitudes, all of them share a common African heritage. Whether one believes it or not, historical anthropology has proved that Ethiopia is the birthplace of all humanity; thus all humans come from African roots. Moreover, all Rastafarians share a common belief in "Haie Selassie," the emperor of Ethiopia who ruled from 1930 to 1973; this emperor was believed to be God returning to earth to create a kingdom of God in Ethiopia (Hebdige 1987, 2003; Barrett 1997; Stolzoff 2000).

As aforementioned, early Rastafarians did not have a musical style of their own, but gradually adopted reggae through observation and imitation of Jamaican youth. After Jamaica was granted independence, the idea of Rastafari became defined as a form of cultural resistance that signified power, freedom, and defiance in asso-ciation with reggae music (Barrett 1987). Indeed, the dreadlock hairstyle of long, uncombed locks worn by males signified someone that was perhaps wild, danger-ous, and dreadful; it was used to identify those that were Rastafarians and reggae musicians. Though there are Rastafarians who do not keep their hair long, the true symbol of Rastafarians is their long-haired appearance; some believe it to be an imitation of Ethiopian tribal warriors (Barrett 1997). Nevertheless, not all reg-gae artists consider themselves Rastafarian—some of them agree with Rastafarian ideas while some of them do not (Stolzoff 2000). Among Rastafarians, there has been no official leader or priest since the early years (Hebdige 1987; Barrett 1988). Therefore, in order to construct themselves as Rastafarian, most Rastafarians sig-nify in some manner that they live life on the outer fringes of society and promote radical changes, spiritually and materially, in the world (Giddens 2009).

Although reggae became the primary form of musical expression for Rastafarians due to the influence of prominent Jamaican musicians (such as Joe Higgs), the growth of the reggae music genre should nevertheless be largely attributed to the music of the deeply charismatic Robert Nesta Marley, widely known as Bob Marley (Barrett 1997). In the early 1970s, Marley released his world famous album entitled *Natty Dread*, which included hit songs such as *Natty Dread, Revolution, No Woman No Cry*, and *Rebel Music*. Bob Marley extended his success to the global music markets in the early 1970s; by then, his music and personality were already well known in Jamaica. What made Marley's songs unique were his lyrics; though many of his songs spoke of injustice in Jamaican society, they could be related to and paralleled to other injustices in other societies. Most of his lyrics, as is evident in many of his hit songs such as *I Shot the Sheriff, Get Up Stand Up*, and *Redemption Song*, were also dedicated to helping the oppressed stand up to injustice and resist this injustice whenever and wherever it showed up. With four successful albums and several successful tours around America and Europe from the mid-1970s to the 1980s, Marley initiated the popularity of reggae music as well as the Rastafarian spirit. Ultimately, Bob Marley was Jamaica's first reggae artist who successfully publicized reggae and Rastafarian ideals both in Jamaica and abroad; this began in the 1960s and lasted up until his untimely death in 1981.

During the post-Marley years in the 1980s and 1990s, reggae music and the Rastafarian movement extended globally to places such as the USA, England, France, and Japan, among other areas. However, as aforementioned, not all reggae musicians present themselves as part of the Rastafarian movement. One prime example would be the English reggae band, UB40, who found huge commercial success in the 1980s in both England and the world music market with hit songs such as *Labor of Love* and *Red Red Wine*.

Asides from Bob Marley, other Jamaican reggae artists did not become international stars or Rastafarian icons like Marley did. Jamaican reggae bands such as Big Mountain and Third World had limited commercial success during the late 1980s, particularly in American markets; they produced a few hit songs such as *Reggae Ambassador* and *Baby I Love Your Way* respectively. It is interesting to note that Musical Youth, a Jamaican diaspora reggae group in England, composed the hit song *Pass the Dutchie*, which helped to enable dialogues on class, national, and diaspora communities in England (Lipsitz 1994). During the 1980s to 1990s, though many reggae songs became popular throughout the world, market shares of reggae music in the global market were far smaller than other popular genres of music such as rock, pop, soul, and disco. In addition, reggae was not considered part of the "world music" genre that was originally established in the mid-1980s (Taylor 1997).

Reggae is one moment of black music history; it is an idiom of post-colonial Jamaica and has been a central part of Jamaican youth since the 1960s. Nevertheless, in the 1970s, with the help of Bob Marley and his popular songs, reggae music and the Rastafarian spirit became global platforms of world markets and movements respectively. Surprisingly enough, though Bob Marley became a world-renowned reggae artist, in Jamaica he is not given as much credit as he should be (Niaah 2010).

In the following section, I will examine the global and local productions of meaning regarding reggae music and the Rastafarian spirit in Thailand. On one hand, I will demonstrate how the global found the way to cultural absorption of both international and Jamaican reggae into the local. On the other hand, I will demonstrate how local Thai artists have established their own musical styles internationally as well as locally by producing their own songs.

The production of localized reggae in Thailand

In the 1980s, there was political stability and high economic growth rates in Thailand (these were known as the "semi-democracy years"), and the state endlessly promoted the national tourism industry (Pongpaichit and Baker 1995). Moreover, Thailand was becoming a key market in global markets, and the discourse on the "borderless world" proved to be a keyword of globalization in Thai public debates during this era (Reynolds 2002). With high national growth rates, Thailand was also fast approaching NIC (newly industrialized country) status. Undoubtedly, all these factors together fundamentally contributed to the Thai entertainment and media industries.

During the 1980s, the musical and entertainment landscapes of Thailand were undergoing a process of dramatic transformation. First, Thai musical artists and groups began to write, compose, and play their own songs. Second, the Thai broadcasting media and the establishment of giant Thai record companies such as RS Promotion, Grammy Entertainment, Nithithat Promotion, and Music Train benefitted and supported the already established Thai music industry (Siriyuvasak 2000). The interest in the reggae genre was originally generated by both Thai record companies and live music houses; this began in the 1980s. The next section will examine reggae music as a type of relation between the globalization of media and cultural flows and its localized consumption and production in Thai popular music. Three Thai reggae artists will be utilized as case studies.

Pansak goes to the sea

In Thailand, Pansak Rangsipammanakul is the first Thai musician who wrote a reggae song; the song, *Pai Tae Kandeewah* (meaning "let's go to the sea"), was featured on his debut album that was released in 1984. During the time the song was released, Rangsipammanakul was 32 years old, and owned Media Company, an advertising agency where he worked as managing director. Prior to this, Rangsipammanakul began learning music at 11 years old through private courses; at 16 years old, he and his high school friends formed a rock band called Soul and Blue. Soul and Blue went on to win the King Phumiphol music award. However, after his high school years, Rangsipammanakul left Thailand behind to study fine arts at the University of Montevallo in Alabama.

In Alabama, Rangsipammanakul earned money to pay for school and living expenses by playing music in restaurants; he gradually became accustomed to and westernized by music cultures such as blues, folk, and rock. After graduation,

Rangsipammanakul stayed in Alabama to work in an advertising company before finally returning to Thailand in 1978. His experiences working at an advertising company essentially helped him become more knowledgeable about the music recording and production processes. In Alabama, Rangsipammanakul worked on a demo of songs written by himself, and he proposed this demo to Nite Spot Production when he returned to Thailand. Notably, Nite Spot was one of the first Thai media companies to work with radio broadcasting; they subsequently became a music house and then concert organizer. Rangsipammanakul later went on to work at Nite Spot as their music marketing manager. Nite Spot Production did, however, sign Rangsiammanakul after his return to Thailand and, in turn, he became the company's first artist. With the lack of quality recording studios in Thailand, Nite Spot Production sent Rangsipammanakul abroad to record his debut album; he returned to the USA, working with renowned American producer Hershey Reeves on his master recording at Wishbone Studio in Alabama.

It is evident that whatever creativities that Pansak had at that time, the production process of his music still had to rely on some the so-called "international." Released in March 1984, Rangsipammanakul's debut single, *Pai Tale Kandee Kaw* (also the name of his debut album title) immediately became a hit song among many FM radio programs in Thailand. The music video that went along with the single (which was the first music video that accompanied a popular song) aired frequently on music programs on Thai television channels, which greatly helped to boost its popularity. The songs on *Pai Tale Kandee Kaw* were unique and different from other Thai popular songs at the time, due to its musical and recording style.

It should be noted that Thai record labels, both major and small labels (initially established in the 1980s) used local studios and local producers to record their music; furthermore, they also used local media, particularly broadcast media such as radio and television programs, to expose their music productions on a larger scale.[1] Among these record labels, Nite Spot Production was a small but much more modernized record label due to their western music programs on radio and television, which aired hit western songs and music videos. When the company went into business producing and promoting Thai popular music, they did so by working with artists such as Pansak Rangsipammanakul, whose musical and aesthetic styles could be comparable to those of the West.

Arguably, during the 1980s, most young people in Thailand could easily sing along to *Pai Tale Kandee Kaw*. Ultimately, Rangsipammanakul's debut album enjoyed huge success in the Thai popular music market and, in turn, Nite Spot Production reaped great profit. However, the other songs on the album followed more of a pop rock musical style, and never became a hit song like the title song. Though *Pai Tale Kandee Kaw* is credited as the first Thai reggae song in the history of Thai popular music, Rangsipammanakul was never credited as the first Thai reggae musician. Perhaps this is due to his appearance and attire; Rangsipammanakul dresses like a businessman rather than a musician, and has never dressed in a manner that would represent one who adhered to the Rastafarian lifestyle. Furthermore, after his debut album, Rangsipammanakul never composed a reggae song again.

Why did Rangsipammanakul decide to write a reggae song in the first place? According to my research, it was actually Nite Spot Production that wanted to introduce new styles of popular music to the Thai popular music market; they wanted the songs they produced to become hits that could be competitive in the global popular music markets. As aforementioned, reggae music in the 1980s became a globally popular musical style; reggae bands such as Third World and Big Mountain were crowd pleasers, and the musical style of Rangsipammanaukul's *Pai Tale Kandee Kaw* were similar to these two bands, rather than the Rastafarian reggae styles of Bob Marley. In Rangsipammanakul's case, though he was creative and talented himself, he had Nite Spot Production, a business investment that helped him to create musical styles that integrated both global production and musical styles. Though he did not wear dreadlocks, look like a Rastafarian, or embody the Rastafarian spirit, Rangsipammanakul is still credited with composing the first popular Thai reggae song.

The arbitrariness of Pansak's song is frustrating, particularly for those who had heard reggae music before. Therefore, the authenticity of the reggae style of Rangsipammanakul's song was called into question by those Thai audiences who had previously listened to popular reggae music. These same Thai audiences were those people that frequented Bangkok's downtown pubs; this is where T-Bone, a young music group who was infamous for their Bob Marley covers, was discovered. The influence of T-Bone on the Thai music industry and culture will be discussed in the following section.

T-Bone joins the downtown pub

As this study previously mentioned, globalization is a multidimensional process that appears in various different forms and has a multitude of different effects. Perhaps T-Bone, a Thai reggae cover band, can be useful in explaining the phenomenon of globalization of reggae music and the Rastafarian spirit in Thailand.

In the mid-1980s, T-Bone was formed by the Teerapenun brothers, Jadsada and Nakarin, in addition to a few of their college friends. The young band started out playing many live music shows, incorporating blues, rock, and reggae music at pub venues such as Bluemoon Pub and Kasorn Road in downtown Bangkok. However, T-Bone eventually earned themselves the reputation of being a Bob Marley cover band. Why did T-Bone choose to cover so many Bob Marley songs at their live shows? Nakarin Teerapenun, the band's lead signer and guitarist, has stated that he wished to play reggae music and believed Bob Marley to be the only international reggae artist that would be familiar to Thai audiences in the 1980s. Nakarin also believed that authentic rasta reggae music came only from Jamaica. Nevertheless, Nakarin was wrong; the Thai audiences familiar with western music in the 1980s became accustomed with reggae music not only through Bob Marley, but also from listening to other international reggae bands such as Big Mountain and Third World. Furthermore, Musical Youth, the young reggae band from England whose single *Pass the Dutchie* was released in 1982, became a big hit on

146 Vinya Sawangchot

the Thai radio charts. In 1983, Musical Youth performed a successful live show in Bangkok put on by Nite Spot Production. Moreover, reggae band 10 CC's single, *Dreadlock Holiday*, also received frequent airplay in Thai music broadcasts starting in the late 1970s. Though Bob Marley's cover of Eric Clapton's hit *I Shot the Sheriff* became a big hit among Thailand's Clapton fans, T–Bone preferred to perform Bob Marley's original songs for western tourists and nightlife audiences of Thailand.

Since the 1980s, the number of western tourists visiting Thailand has consistently increased and Bangkok has since become a tourist hub. For many tourists, Bangkok was the first destination before travelling to other areas in the Asian region. Since T–Bone audiences were mainly western tourists who knew Bob Marley's songs very well, the band was not only pressured to practice more, but also felt the need to create a Rastafarian image for themselves. Thus, T–Bone began donning dreadlocks and dressing in the three colors of reggae—red, yellow, and green. Whether or not the members of T–Bone were initially interested in rasta and reggae, the band had to adopt these styles musically and aesthetically in order to entertain their audiences and earn profit. New downtown pubs in Bangkok such as Saxophone Pub invited T–Bone to regularly play live shows; T–Bone performed on Friday and Saturday nights at Saxophone Pub, the two nights that were mainly filled with western audiences. Though Saxophone Pub was known as a blues and jazz pub, T–Bone still attracted audiences by playing Bob Marley covers. Although T–Bone was seen as a band that attempted to blend reggae into the music of Thailand's pub culture during the 1980s, reggae music, seemingly, was more suited to the tastes of western audiences and was incorporated to please them, and not Thai audiences.

What is surprising to note, however, is that even though T–Bone frequently played shows at many of Thailand's famous pubs, they received minimal pay in comparison to Thai rock and pop bands who played songs from the top charts, or blues artists who played classic blues tunes. When Prapas Chonsaranon, the managing director of Muzer Records, a Thai record label, lightheartedly asked Nakarin of T–Bone if they would like to be superstars, there were no signs of refusal from Nakarin. After ten years of being solely a pub band, T–Bone landed a record deal and had the opportunity to release their first reggae album in the early 1990s. T–Bone's debut album, aptly entitled *T-Bone*, was released in 1992. Following the steps of Thailand's major record labels, Muzer Records oversaw the whole production process of *T-Bone*, the songwriting to studio production processes were fully controlled by the record label's production teams; in fact, none of the songs on the album were written by band members. However, T–Bone gained popularity through a hit song on their debut album named *Thor Hen Tong Fah Nun Mai?* (meaning "have you ever seen the sky?"); Muzer also produced a promotional video for this song, and it received great radio airplay. The song's sweet lyrics and beautiful music video propelled it onto Thailand's popular music charts and familiarized the Thai public with T–Bone. Ultimately though, the song was undeniably unrelated to the reggae and rasta inspired music T–Bone had played before; it was a melodic pop song that was similar to other popular songs in the Thai mainstream popular music market.

"Only mix, never been cut" **147**

Finding success with their debut album, T-Bone subsequently recorded a second album entitled *Khun Nai Sa-ad* the following year in 1993. Though Muzer Records was again behind the production of this record, this second album by T-Bone did not prove to be successful. Muzer Records came to its dissolution in 1994, and T-Bone effectively signed with WEA, an international record label. Through WEA, T-Bone released their third album, *Lek, Chin, Sod* in 1994, which proved to be a success like their debut album. Through *Lek, Chin, Sod*, the band was able to oversee the production process themselves and slowly began the evolution of their musical style from reggae to ska. Nakarin had learned that the root of reggae music was derived from ska; therefore he wanted to compose, produce, and integrate ska music into the popular music styles of Thailand. In this third album, there were two ska songs, *Pipop Mudjurat* and *Smacom Chua Lok Hang Prathad Thai*, which quickly became hit songs in Thailand. In fact, *Pipop Mudjurat* was the first popular Thai ska song ever written and released by a Thai band.

In 1997, T-Bone released their fourth album entitled *Godd*, which was produced by yet another record label, Sony Entertainment Thailand. Nevertheless, *Godd* never found market success; its failure was due to the boom of alternative music in Thailand at the time, which dramatically altered the country's popular music scene. In addition, the alternative music trend can be attributed to the introduction of music sharing into the Thai popular music market. Basically, the Thai reggae music that T-Bone produced was not popular in the Thai music markets anymore, despite their large fanbase.

Although T-Bone produced four albums and a few hit songs, the production of their albums was not unique in that they were just like other Thai artists' albums, produced by the production teams of major record companies. The music produced by T-Bone under major record labels did not come close to the unique reggae and rasta music of Bob Marley that the band had previously played at pubs. The music released by T-Bone on their albums should, however, be credited with creatively expanding Thai pop music; they incorporated reggae and rasta into Thai popular music styles. After the *Godd* album, the band took a break from studio recording and moved forward to find success on the international stage. Having researched the roots of Jamaican music, T-Bone in 2003 released an EP called *Mon Pleang Ska*, which subsequently led them to be classified as a Thai reggae/ska band. Even though after the release of their albums T-Bone still performed at Saxophone Pub, they can no longer be solely identified as a pub band. On one hand, the band renegotiated the reggae styles of Bob Marley and other symbols of Rastafarian culture into local popular musical styles and the local popular music market. On the other hand, however, Thai record labels such as Muzer Records played a significant role as local producers adamantly resisted the globalization of musical styles.

It is ironic to note that it was only after T-Bone became an unsigned band again that they successfully penetrated the international music markets with their reggae/ska songs. In 2005, the band played a concert for the tsunami benefit in London and played at the Glastonbury Music Festival in the same year. The year that followed was a successful one for T-Bone, as they played at WOMAD Singapore, and played a sold-out show in Bangkok. In 2007, the band yet again received an opportunity to play at the Glastonbury Music Festival.

In short, during the years from 2005 to 2007, the band performed many successful shows both inside and outside Asia, and consequently received a reputation as a successful Thai reggae and ska band. From 1998 to 2004, the band did not record or release any studio albums, only EPs and DVD concerts, as a few members of the band had created their own record label, Hualumpong Limdin. This record label, mainly run by Nakarin Teerapenun, signed and produced the albums of Thai indie rock bands such as Photo Sticker Machine. Interestingly enough, Hualumpong Limdin never signed any Thai reggae bands to their label.

T-Bone, to many, was a musical group that attempted to blend together the styles of reggae and ska (both musically and aesthetically), and project this style onto the Thai popular music scene. Arguably, T-Bone had two platforms of reggae: one of which was closer to popular mainstream music in Thailand, and another, which was more reggae and rasta musically and aesthetically. Job 2 Do does this quite differently and presents and projects reggae from his soul and his songs.

Job 2 Do lives by the sea

Bunjob Pon-in, commonly known as Job 2 Do and/or Job Bunjob, is the man who is behind the huge popularity of reggae and rasta in Thailand in recent years. In contrast to the members of T-Bone, who portray an image of Bangkok youth, Job Bunjob is seen as a wild country boy from Thailand's south. The south of Thailand has two coasts, one along the South China Sea and the other along the Andaman Sea, which is similar geographically to the Caribbean Sea. In Thailand, Bunjob is also viewed as the father of Thai rasta reggae, due to his iconic dreadlocks, dark skin, and southern dialect. Bunjob was born in 1953 in the Trang province in southern Thailand, living there until he completed high school. After high school, Bunjob relocated to Bangkok for work, and it was there that he met a westerner who invited him to go to Scotland. By 1981, Bunjob was living in Scotland, eventually started a family there, and lived there in total for about 17 years. During his tenure in Scotland, Bunjob frequently played street music and won an award for street music in 1995; at this time, Bunjob mainly appreciated and played blues and rock music, not reggae music. In the late 1990s, Bunjob and his family returned to Thailand and lived in the southern province of Krabi, at the invitation of his old southern friends.

In 1998, there was a huge influx of backpacking westerners into Thailand in search of Krabi, a city that had been advertised heavily as an amazing tourist destination. These tourists mainly congregated at Reiley Beach in Krabi province, which is best known as a prime location for cliff climbing and is mainly inhabited and dominated by local youth. Bunjob eventually came to live at Reiley Beach and began to play reggae music at Skunk Bar on the east end. With the large crowds of westerners at Skunk Bar, Bunjob became famous in this area by playing Bob Marley covers. Beginning in 1998, many rasta businesses such as reggae pubs, dreadlock hair kitting shops, and boutiques filled with reggae fashion and souvenirs were constructed at East Reiley Beach and, in 2000, it was established as a Rastafarian community.

During the tenure of his career, Bunjob always held performances in pubs located in tourist areas in southern Thailand such as Phuket Island, Pi Pi Island, Samui Island, and Phaghan Island. Though Bunjob was initially influenced by the music of Bob Marley, he eventually came to compose his songs with local instrumental styles and incorporated Thai southern dialects; this made his songs quite different from Bob Marley's. With his claim to fame already established in southern Thailand, Bunjob was granted a record contract with GMM Grammy (one of two major record labels in Thailand) and released his debut album, *Job 2 Do*, in 2000. Bunjob's music and image were not similar to any other artists that GMM Grammy had signed before; his dark skin, dreadlocks, and Rastafarian spirit set him apart from GMM's popular music stars. Unsurprisingly, his first album never received mainstream success in the Thai popular music market. Although there had previously been popular Thai reggae songs, there were never any popular songs that were sung in different dialects, as the majority of Thai pop songs were sung in the central Thai language. In fact, in Thailand, there were few popular artists that did not sing their songs in the central Thai language; in Thailand if you cannot speak the central Thai language well, you will be looked down upon by most.

Though Bunjob's album was a failure in terms of sales and financial profit, he received a Season Award (hosted by *Season Magazine*) for best new Thai artist in 2000, the greatest Thai popular music award that an artist could receive. In 2000, Bunjob was already 46 years old; he may have even been the oldest artist who has ever won this award since its conception in 1990. The following year in 2001, GMM Grammy broke their contract with Bunjob and, after this, Bunjob never publicly mentioned or discussed his debut album again.

However, the failure of his debut album furthered Job Bunjob's desire to engage in reggae performances more directly, and he did so through various reggae venues in Thailand. In 2006, Bunjob played at the first ever Pai Reggae Festival as the main artist on the main stage; the Pai Reggae Music Festival was located in Mae Hong Son province in northern Thailand, and boasted over 70,000 attendees in the first year of the festival. Even without a record contract to a major record label, Bunjob released many successful live albums such as *PP Princess Paradise* (2004), *Tsunami Aid Concert* (2004), *No War* (2006), *YAN Unplugged* (2007), *Libong Live* (2007), and *Sapawa Log Lon* (2008); these albums were mainly produced by independent, local record labels originating from southern Thailand. In 2006 and 2007, he produced two songs, *Luem Mi Long Sauy Lak Sai* and *Dae Kon Chang Fun*, which were sung in a southern dialect making it quite different from other Thai popular songs in *Ploy*, a famous Thai film. These two melodic pop songs shot Bunjob to fame in the Thai popular music scene. Despite this fact, Job Bunjob did not sign a record label again as he did not want to be controlled by corporate capitalism anymore.

How did Job Bunjob respond to the Rastafarian reggae spirit? It was not only Bunjob's music, but also his image and charisma, that evoked the Rastafarian spirit and led him to be deemed as the father of Thai rasta and reggae. It was particularly the content of Bunjob's early songs, about freedom, the environment, sustainability, and the issues of southern Thai people, which should essentially be valued as a manifestation of the Rastafarian spirit. Bunjob also took action as a local activist to call upon his people to stand up and fight for the protection of the sea environment. In 2004, he wrote a song for UNESCO's documentary about the Sea Gypsies from the Andaman Sea area in the Indian Ocean. Bunjob's recent songs have engaged audiences through its meaningful messages to take action against worldwide war, global warming, and environment devastation.

If Giddens was correct in stating that reggae is the song of freedom fighters in the anti-globalization movement of the rastafari (Giddens 2009), Job Bunjob has done it successfully in Thailand. Ironically, most people of Thailand know Bunjob due to the frequent television airing of his hit ska song, *Do Ther Thum*, used in a healthy drinking water television commercial.

In comparison to Thai artists such as T-Bone, Job Bunjob unquestionably has been more influential in the Thai reggae and rasta scene, and clearly has more Rastafarian followers. Even though T-Bone is more internationally renowned as a Thai reggae artist than Job Bunjob is, Bunjob has become a famous Thai reggae artist among western tourists who have visited Thailand in recent years. Bunjob frequently played live reggae shows and lived a Rastafarian life. He used to say on stage, as a person from the south of Thailand, "I was a naturally born Rastafarian."

Globalization for everything, reggae for something

As we have seen above, Thailand has stood in the global flow of reggae music since the 1980s. Does the globalization of music necessarily need a western context? More specifically, in the case of reggae music in Thailand, we might ask how popular music and its culture of non-western contexts could be absorbed by the globalization of media and cultural flows; in this case, it is Bob Marley's reggae style in Thailand.

Pansak Rangsipammanakul is known as the pioneer of Thai reggae through his hit song *Pai Tale Kandee Kaw* released in 1984; nevertheless, this song, though classified as reggae, was also a ballad. At the time, this technique of composing reggae ballads was familiar to Jamaican and western reggae artists whose songs were popular on the global music charts. Also, since Rangsipammanakul's music was produced by American producers, his music was more analogous to western music, rather than the aesthetic of Jamaican reggae music. However, the advent of T-Bone in the Thai popular music scene is quite different. T-Bone brought to Thailand Jamaican "rasta reggae," to entertain and impress not only Thai middle-class audiences, but also western tourists and audiences that knew reggae music well.

However, Job Bunjob found success through a different path. Though he initially signed to a major record label, his debut and only album was a financial failure. Bunjob integrated localized Jamaican reggae music and local Thai elements such as local characteristics and southern dialect into his music. This factor, along

"Only mix, never been cut" **151**

with his 17 years of musical experience in Scotland, meant that Bunjob very much knew how to integrate the international into the local. Though Bunjob's music is influenced by global audiences (such as the western tourists that watch his live shows in Thailand), his music is not exactly the same as global reggae or Jamaican reggae. Arguably, Bunjob's music challenges the reggae styles of Bob Marley while inventing a new style of Thai popular music; he finds a way to avoid and absorb the cultural globalization of music, particularly in Jamaican reggae, and turns it into an interactive relationship between Thai mainstream popular music and non-mainstream local music.

The journey of reggae and the Rastafarian spirit across the globe has been occurring since the 1980s. Frith notes that, these days "all countries' popular music are shaped by international influences and institutions, by multinational capital and technology, and by global norms and values" (Frith 1989). The diversity of Thai reggae artists have created hybridized musical forms across boundaries, locally and internationally, in a similar way to how Giddens defines globalization as "the intensification of worldwide social relations, which links distance many miles away and vice versa" (Giddens 2009). Hall argues that globalization is not the simple concept of a "western invasion" anymore (Hall 1991); this idea serves the music practices of rasta reggae in the global popular music platform during the 1990s. What is happening now is an international music taste and a spirit of the "third world musician" that has gone beyond the dominance of global popular music.[1] Perhaps reggae is a musical form that has ambivalently routinized as being original (Barrett 1997), and subsequent globalization processes have increased the intensity of this style by easily integrating new styles into non-western local music (Robinson 1991).

Hence, the question should be raised whether the struggles over reggae styles can be understood in terms of globalization. How can we understand this struggle? Thai reggae does not only encourage resistance through its lyrical content; through its lyrics and musical style, Thai reggae purposely resists the conventions of local and international popular musical forms.

On one hand, we have seen that Thai reggae music was created through appropriating the musical styles of Jamaican reggae, international reggae, and Thai popular music. The question of what authentic reggae is has lead some Thai artists to represent themselves as Rastafarians. It can be contended that reggae became the primary musical expression for Thai musicians who wanted to not only explore new genres of music in the Thai music scene, but also the cultural politics of the Thai people. Essentially, among Thai reggae musicians, we are witnessing the concerned questioning of social, economic, and political issues of contemporary Thai society.

Conclusion

This chapter argues that the popularity of Jamaican popular music in Thailand, particularly reggae music, should be understood as an institutional embodiment of new local–global music cultural forms. In Thailand, though the interest in reggae

152 Vinya Sawangchot

was originally generated by Thai record companies and live performance houses in the 1980s, we have yet to fully understand this genre; like Rattananan sung, "why do some call it reggae, while some call it ska?"

It should not be assumed that the introduction of reggae and ska music into Thailand was an attempted cultural invasion of Thailand. The popular Thai reggae artists that have emerged in the last few decades, such as T-Bone and Job 2 Do, are complex cases; they are prime cases of reggae music that have fused with local music styles, spaces, and markets in an age of globalization. In recent decades, the global flows of popular music have been made possible by technologies such as the internet and satellite.

It is evident that Thai reggae music, as a musical genre and as a musical discourse, began to evolve in the 1980s, through appropriating a space between local and global music industries. The major and local independent record labels, local reggae artists, local pubs, and local music promoters have helped this progression and evolution of Thai reggae. However, what the Thai music scene has done to the reggae genre as a global musical style is to integrate it with local styles of music and introduce it to the local market; it does not want to be cut off from the globalization of media and cultural flows. Perhaps we have to redefine the context of globalization; through doing so, we also may be redefining the context of de-globalization. In the three cases of Thai reggae artists that we explored in this study, globalization appears to be something that was internal as well as external. There is little doubt that globalization matters, but what also matters are the conditions that globalization occurs under.

Note

1 When "world music" was booming and also being categorized by major record stores/labels in the mid-1980s, reggae music was surprisingly not being categorized as a discourse of world Music (Firth 1989; Taylor 1997).

References

Appadurai, A. (1991) "Disjunctures and Differences in the Global Cultural Economy," in M. Featherstone (ed.) *Global Culture: Nationalism, Globalization and Modernity*, London: Sage.

Barrett, L.E. (1997) *The Rastafarian*, Boston, MA: Beacon Press.

During, S. (1997) Critical Inquiry, vol 23, no. 4, pp.803–833.

Frith, S. (1989) *World Music, Politics, and Social Change*, Manchester: Manchester University Press.

Giddens, A. (2009) *Sociology*, London: Polity Press.

Hall, S. (1991) "The Local and the Global: Globalization and Ethnicity," in A.D. King (ed.) *Culture, Globalization, and the World System*, London: Macmillan.

Hebdige, D. (1987) "Reggae, Rastas, and Rudies," in J. Curran (ed.) *Mass Communication and Society*, London: Sage.

Hebdige, D. (2003) *Cut'n'Mix: Culture, Identity, and Caribbean Culture*, London: Routledge.

Lipsitz, G. (1994) *Dangerous Crossroads: Popular Music, Postmodernism, and Poetics of Place*, London: Verso.

Niaah, S. (2010) *Dancehall: From Slave Ship to Ghetto*, Ottawa: University of Ottawa Press.

Pongpaichit, P. and Baker, C. (1995) *Thailand: Economy and Politics*, Kuala Lampur: Oxford University Press.

Reynolds, C.J. (2002) "Thai Identity in the Age of Globalization," in C.J. Reynold (ed.) *National Identity and its Defenders: Thailand Today*, Chiang Mai: Silkworms.

Robertson, R. (1990) "Mapping the Global Condition: Globalization as the Central Concept," in M. Featherstone (ed.) *Global Culture: Nationalism, Globalization, and Modernity*, London: Sage.

Robertson, R. (1991) "Social Theory, Cultural Relativity, and the Problem of Globality," in A.D. King (ed.) *Culture, Globalization, and the World System*, London: Macmillan.

Robinson, D. (1991) *Music and the Margins: Popular Music and Global Cultural Diversity*, London: Sage.

Siriyuvasak, U. (2000) *The Political Economy of Thai Broadcasting Media* (in Thai), Bangkok: Chulalongkorn University Press.

Stolzoff, N.C. (2000) *Wake the Town and Tell the People: Dancehall Culture in Jamaica*, London: Duke University Press.

Taylor, T. (1997) *Global Pop*, London: Routledge.

The Guitar Magazine (2009) "Special Issue on Reggae and Ska's Time," Volume 40, April.

Tomlinson, J. (1999) *Globalization and Culture*, Chicago, IL: Chicago University Press.

9

POPULAR ONLINE GAMES IN THE TAIWANESE MARKET

An examination of the relationships of media globalization and local media consumption

Lai Chi Chen

Introduction

Since late 1990, online gaming (OLG) has become a form of popular entertainment in the East Asian market. In 2007, massive multi-player online role-playing games (MMORPGs) made up 60 percent of the market share in Taiwan, while casual games comprised the rest of the online gaming market (Liu 2008). The genre of MMORPGs in Asia can be categorized into several types, including adventure, simulation, and strategy games. Casual games are those games that are played competitively online without the existence of a persistent online realm; some casual games are as simple as online poker or Chinese Mahjong.

There are approximately four million online players in Taiwan, the majority of them aged between 12 and 25. In 2006, many diverse forms of foreign licensed games entered the Taiwanese market. At that time, most of the new game titles available in Taiwan originated from Korea. Significantly, these Korean-produced games expanded the game base of players in the Taiwanese market. According to data from the International Data Cooperation (IDC), Taiwan's online gaming industry has flourished since 2006 (MIC 2006). Today, Korean games, along with other foreign games produced in the US, China, and Japan, strongly appeal to Taiwanese gamers.

In 2007, imported licensed games, mainly from Korea and China, made up at least 70 percent of the market share (MIC 2008), while Taiwan's domestic gamemakers constituted the remainder. In 2008, the US's *World of Warcraft*, Korea's *Luna Online*, and Taiwan's *Wulin Online* were ranked as the top-three best-selling game titles in Taiwan. In Taiwan, each of these games can appeal to 100,000 people who access its server at any given time. Three very different types of games—western fantasy games, Asian cute games, and Chinese "wuxia" games—appeal to three separate groups of gamers. Offering different types of games also increases the structural base of gamers and has contributed to the growth in the size of the Taiwanese market. From 2000 to 2007, the OLG market expanded rapidly to an estimated $300 million (Brightman 2007) and to $380 million by 2010; it is set to expand at a steady 8 percent per year (Wan 2010).

The data above provides only a brief overview of the current state of the Taiwanese OLG market. This study aims to examine the relationship between globalization and the development of Asian media by focusing on popular types of online games in the Taiwanese online game market. Furthermore, it discusses the market structure of Asian online gaming, the characteristics of Asian game culture, and the game consumption by Taiwanese users. A deep analysis is utilized to ascertain whether established literature can fully explain the developmental trends of Asian popular culture, or whether other factors should be considered to in order explicate the characteristics of game consumption by Asian gamers.

Globalization, modernity, and regionalization

Globalization is a phenomenon carrying dimensions that have been revolutionizing arenas as diverse as media, culture, and social development. It has resulted in uneven economic development and also led to local, cultural, and social changes. This research attempts to discover how the market for a regional cultural product is formed and how local media has evolved under the climate of globalization. It will do so by examining different economic, social, and cultural-linguistic issues. The research also aims to clarify the relationship between global and local media, and the latter's usage.

Media globalization

Globalization not only affects trade and finance, but also culture, society, and politics. Media researchers use the concept of globalization to explain the situation when western cultural products enter foreign markets and are accepted by their respective audiences. At the same time, globalization is also an explanation for the acceptance of western cultural products by those in non-western nations; western cultural products may also be accompanied by western ideas of economy and politics. From the perspective of global media researchers, the west's dominating power in the cultural industry has formed a "West–rest" model (Robertson 1997). Hamelink (1993) contends that the globalization process undeniably affects the communications industry, as it extends its activities geographically in a move toward "statelessness," and towards an oligopolistic market where only a few global media firms are successful in developing.

For instance, the popularity of American popular culture (such as American movies, music, and television programs) in the global market can be seen as a good example in supporting the argument for media globalization. At the same time, it seems that cultural globalization is simply a synonym for Americanization (Hall 1997; Toynbee 2000). This in turn poses this question—why do so many US cultural products prove to be successful exports? The answer can, in part, be gleaned from the perspectives of the market and technology.

Externally, the USA can be seen as the dominant base for Anglo-European culture. Internally, however, many of the American cultural products are successful in the global markets because of their hybridization of native cultural roots with other cultures, as represented by late nineteenth- and twentieth-century immigration to the USA. One market aspect achieved by American cultural artefacts is their universalization, which cultural products from other nations have not undergone. The universalization of American products has been achieved through the absorption of various key cultural elements that appeal to diverse audiences in the home market (Straubhaar 2002). This universalization also explains why American cultural products can penetrate overseas markets quite easily, compared to other western cultural products. In addition, US-based and other global media conglomerates have aimed to be advanced technologically, culturally, and linguistically; they tackle the content issue by producing programs in local languages.

Cultural globalization cannot be explained using a simple system; the model of cultural globalization has been operating on a complex level. The global market encourages corporations to establish joint equity ventures in which the media giants all take ownership of a part of an enterprise, helping firms reduce competition and increase profitability. At the same time, the complex web of joint ventures and ownership includes links with foreign companies in order to avoid "arousing the ire of local governments" (Auletta 1998). Thomas' study shows that the operations of the transnational satellite channel, StarTV, is often carried out by locally owned cable stations (in Asia), ranging from neighbourhood entrepreneurs to large domestic firms with political affiliations (Thomas 2006).

Furthermore, there has recently emerged a trend towards a two-tiered global system, even though media firms operating in developing countries dominate in their own national and regional markets. For example, Mexico's Televisa, Brazil's Globo, Argentina's Clarin, and Venezuela's Cisneros Groups are among the world's 60 or 70 largest media corporations. At the same time, media firms in global competition admit that they have hardly resisted this trend in the global system. With the aid of their extensive ties to the US giants, second tier media firms have also established global operations that focus on nations speaking the same languages (McChesney 2004; Sinclair 2004). The model of cultural production exported from the US to the global market has therefore been established—a strong producer in a global city first dominates the local or national market. This will lead to the export of media programs, technology, and skills that may, in turn, shape the contour of channels in other markets. This provokes the hypothesis that the current configuration of a global, polycentric, media scene, sporting multiple established and emerging cultural linguistic markets, may be undermined in the future (Zhu 2008).

Modernity in globalization

Several prominent theories, including those of Giddens (1990), Friedman (1994), and Robertson (1995), have raised the need to consider modernity as a crucial aspect of globalization. The basic understanding is usually a neutral formulation, as described by Giddens (1990). Globalization can be defined as the intensification of worldwide social relations, which began in the first migrations of peoples and long-distance trade connections, and subsequently accelerated under particular conditions. The process of globalization can also be considered as a universal phenomenon that is transforming the entire world, extending the basis of communication and cultural exchange (Curran and Park 2000). In the later stages of the globalization process, modernity and globalization can be thought of as a factor accelerating the formation of global social relationships, and as a specific global momentum associated with a particular condition (Pieterse 1994). In addition, what emerges is often a strongly localized adaptation of what is considered modern in global patterns. Robertson (1995) was the first one to term the process of hybridization of the local and global as "glocalization."

Furthermore, scholars such as Eisentadt, Moore, and Lerner believe international communication to be a key part of the process of "third world" modernization and development. Modernization theory arose from the notion that international mass communication could be used to spread the message of modernity and transfer the economic and political models of the west to the newly independent countries (Thussu 2000). Researchers have previously pointed out that media helps to diffuse a value system that is favourable to innovation, mobility, achievement, and consumption, which originates from the concept of modernity that had been developed in Western Europe and North America. On gaining evidence of the role of media in national development, Lerner (1958) noted that it helps to break down the traditionalism that is an obstacle to modernity. This further raises expectations and aspirations, enabling people to imagine and desire a "better alternative" for themselves (McQuail 1987).

It is worth noting that modernization theory can be applied to the phenomenon of concepts of western modernity being spread from western to modern non-western nations and, also, from the latter to their regional neighbours. Using *Tokyo Love Story* as a case study, Iwabuchi researches and discusses why Japanese dramas have been popular in other Asian countries. In the modern era, most Asian countries have adopted the western free market economy and accepted and encouraged the formation of a middle class. The Japanese drama presents how modern youth live in urban settings. For example, one of the attractions of *Tokyo Love Story* to young Taiwanese viewers was its new style of portraying love, work, and the roles and position of women in society (Iwabuchi 2002). Furthermore, the "West–rest" model cannot be seen as a concept of the dichotomy between the central and the peripheral. Here, the current cultural dynamics of Southeast Asia can be seen as an instructive case. This case implies that it is no longer America, but Japan (in different circumstances) that is seen by Asian populations to offer more persuasive

158 Lai Chi Chen

models of modernity. However, there may be a multiplicity of modernities; a truth that "the rest" are capable of generating their own forms of modernity (Curran and Park 2000; Morely 2007).

Asian modernity can be termed as a phenomenon as most Asian nations have, as aforementioned, adopted the western free market economy, formed a middle class, and moved into modern social and economic development (Melody 1992). Most importantly, modern concepts can easily be disseminated within a regional market with the auxiliary of new technologies under the globalized system (Morely 2007). For instance, new technology plays an important role in aiding the export of Japanese popular culture to other parts of Asia. In the inter-Asian region, inexpensive video CDs (VCD) of Japanese dramas can be easily purchased and copied. VCDs can, therefore, be viewed as an "Asian technology" with globalizing significance; the pirating organizations in different Chinese locations (such as Taiwan and Hong Kong) having produced alternative centres of Japanese popular culture for transnational consumerism (Iwabuchi 2002; Hu 2004). In addition, the emergence of satellite television has helped Japanese programmes penetrate other Asian markets, such as Korea and Taiwan (Iwabuchi 2002; Shim 2006). This process has led the mass media and telecommunications (particularly the broadcast media equipped with the most advanced communication technologies) industries into becoming the most rapidly growing industries in Asia. This is beneficial from a cultural and economic perspective, since cultural products in one country can be transmitted transnationally to audiences in other countries. New technology has indeed brought about new contours in both regional and local markets.

Regionalization and geo-cultural proximity

The new global, cultural, economic order should be viewed as a complex and disjunctive order, although the media sector is considered to be the privileged preserve of North America. The researcher Kai Hafez (2007) has argued that the global media system is ill considered. Media markets are by no means characterized by complex interdependence, even if specific transnational linkages from the geo-cultural area of Europe and the USA are very advanced. In fact, local and regional capital continues to set the tone and is shielded by protectionist media policies (Hafez 2007).

The weakness of many globalization theories may lie in their focus on the power of the west, whilst ignoring the weight of other markets. Cultural–linguistic markets are emerging at a level smaller than the global, but larger than the national. They form in areas where audiences share the same or similar languages, or have intertwined histories and broadly overlapping cultural characteristics. It appears that people resident in these places tend to look for television programming, music, and internet sites that possess a greater cultural proximity to themselves (Sinclair *et al.* 1996; Hoskins *et al.* 2004).

It is a fact that cultural products are circulated within certain regional markets rather than around the globe. Huntington (1996) has hypothesized that there are a limited number of "civilizations" based on underlying religious, language, and cultural divisions. The Chinese market has expanded to a Confucian cultural influence sphere, and the large Arabic market has broadened to an Islamic market (Sraubhaar 2002; Morley 2007). It is worth noting that language and cultural factors appear to be more important than geographical factors when new technologies help media cross borders (Wildman and Siwek 1988). For instance, Televisa Mexico has grown to be the major media conglomerate in Latin America. Their unique access to a large market and geographical proximity to export territories has enabled the television station to position themselves at the centre of their respective international regions (Sinclair *et al.* 1996).

The rapidity of technological development and growing economic integration are the two factors that have sped up the formation of a cultural-linguistic market. For instance, the greater Chinese market is conducive to the development of this geo-linguistic region into an arena of television exchange, while certain types of programmes, such as comedies, gangster films, and action films with special effects, have formed a niche market within Chinese commercial cinema today (Chen 1996; Curtin 2007). The predominantly ethnic Chinese locations of the Asian region (Taiwan, Hong Kong, mainland China, and Singapore) have their own histories of popular cultural exchanges in different Chinese languages. They constitute a subset that may be termed as "Pop Culture China" (Huat 2008).

Today's global film and television market is indeed constituted of intricate relationships, which can be connected and strengthened due to technological, economic, and cultural factors. According to Joseph Straubhaar (2007), the regionalization of television and film has diverged from the established system of globalization. First, many national television systems have become an independent market where the localized produced programmes have become dominant. Second, a number of countries such as India, Japan, and Brazil, and media capitals such as Hong Kong, have moved beyond producing for their own markets to exporting cultural products that are able to compete with North American exports. Third, there are patterns that indicate that sub-national (such as Latin American nations and Francophone Canada) and local television broadcasting is growing (Straubhaar 2007).

In the following section, the research examines three popular game types in Taiwan and analyzes the factors that have led to their success within the local Taiwanese market. The findings should shed light as to whether the Asian popular game culture is part of the globalization process, or whether modernity is shaping the formation of a regional popular culture. The section begins by examining the reception and consumption of game products in the Taiwanese market.

Popular online games in the Taiwanese market

Today, online gaming is a popular form of entertainment in the Asian market; it should also be noted that particular game forms appeal specifically to East Asian audiences. According to the MIC's 2007 survey, 59 percent of Taiwanese users

160 Lai Chi Chen

prefer "cute games," 45 percent prefer medieval games, and 20 percent prefer Chinese "wuxia" games (Liu 2008). The different game genres are designed to attract a larger quantity of users, rather than limiting the game market to hardcore gamers. The medieval game is one of the mainstream genres in Taiwan and other Asian markets; the wuxia game primarily targets Chinese audiences, while cute games (originating from Japan) have become very popular with urban gamers in Asia.

In 1999, the Korean produced MMORPG, *Lineage*, was introduced to Taiwan. During that time, only three online game titles were in operation. *Lineage*, developed by NC Soft, was based on a western adventure story and appealed to hardcore gamers. It has been one of the top-selling game titles in the Taiwanese market since its introduction. In 2001, the company Chinese Gamer successfully developed the first Taiwanese oriented game, *Sango Online*, based on a Chinese historical story. It is worth noting that Taiwanese game firms were innovators; they created imaginary oriental worlds containing characters that adhered to Chinese cultural elements. This includes classic historical novels, wuxia and chivalric novels, and Chinese ancient legends. This was a different approach to that of western, medieval, adventure-based, fantasy MMORPGs, as wuxia games focus solely on Chinese cultural elements.

In 2005 and 2006, two different types of games were introduced to the Taiwanese market: the US fantasy game and the Korean cute game. First, Blizzard's global hit, *World of Warcraft* (*WoW*), entered the Taiwanese market and immediately attracted a large of number of hardcore users. To date it has amassed around 700,000 subscribers. Subsequently, distinct types of cute games originating from South Korea, such as *Maple Story* and *Kart Rider*, began to operate in Taiwan. According to an IDC survey, in 2006, the size of the Taiwanese market rapidly increased to 40 percent. While traditional MMORPGs are developed for hardcore users, the cute game attracted new users to join the virtual world, including young females and younger gamers. Korea, today, has become a base for the production of diverse game genres that target the Asian game market.

US fantasy games: World of Warcraft

Notably, the most popular game in the East Asian market originates from a US-based game firm. *WoW* has been ranked as one of the top three best-selling titles in the Asian market, including China, South Korea, and Taiwan. In addition, it has more subscribers in China than in the United States. *WoW* offers a fantastic world that is based on a western mythological storyline. Its success has partly been achieved due to its range and variety of fictional characters offered and its complexity of design. In order to attract more Asian players, the game developer looked for inspiration in Asian culture, using various Asian cultural elements when creating the game content. Shane Dabari, the producer of *WoW*, admits that *The Burning Crusade*, a new version of the game, has added more Asian cultural elements in areas such as weapon design and martial arts plots. Dabari emphasizes that the design of the inside of the dungeon in the game does not represent the typical western concept of a castle, but should rather be seen as a fantasy place that connects together western and oriental cultural elements.

Most of the western MMORPGs reconstruct a pseudo-historical, magical, and medieval realm, and offer players a selection of characters, moods, and atmospheres. This type of role playing game has evolved into multiplayer networked games, operating within a computer generated environment (Stern 2002). The researcher Eddo Stern (2002) terms this type of fantasy game "neo-medievalism," when describing the bonds of the magic age and new technology in a game world. Generally speaking, the western medieval epics, which were originally designed for hardcore gamers in the western market, attract both western and Asian males. Subsequently, the format of the western game has been transplanted to the Asian MMORPG, and has been adapted to fit the demands of Asian users.

In contrast to western gamers, Taiwanese players tend to spend longer periods within gameplay, with 44.6 percent of players spending at least two hours each day within the game world (MIC 2008). According to Martin Lee, the operator of *WoW* in Taiwan, many Taiwanese players attain the highest level possible during one month of intensive gaming, through fulfilling tasks and defeating monsters. In contrast, western gamers would probably take at least six months to a year to complete the same process. This is due to the fact that game play is seen purely as amusement in the West, while, in Asia, gaming is seen as an intense competition.

Korean fantasy games

South Korean produced games make up a large portion of the Taiwanese market share. Significantly, game designers in South Korea are experts in restyling MMORPGs into different formats and genres of games. There are two significant types of Korean-produced games, Asian style epic games and cute games; both well received in East Asia. Asian medieval epics borrow the western storyline, but, usually, contain content preferred by hardcore Asian gamers who are attracted to capturing territory and killing enemies. Cute games, on the other hand, provide family-friendly content and appeal to females and younger users, who are not familiar with complex manipulation normally used in hardcore computer games.

Fantasy topics can easily cross cultural borders, and are accepted by western and Asian gamers alike. Similar game formats have influenced Asian game developers because the medieval subject appeals to a great number of users. The Korean *Lineage* series has maintained its popularity in the intra-Asian markets, including the greater Chinese market, since the time of its release. Evidence of this can be seen in the user figures; *Lineage* claims an astounding 2.5 million to 8 million subscribers a month (Stern 2002). This fantasy MMORPG, released in 1998, features 2D isometric-overhead graphics similar to those of *Ultima Online* and *Diablo 2*. Korea picked Taiwan to be its first foreign market. Generally, *Lineage* attracts hardcore Taiwanese gamers; at its peak, it attained one million subscribers. Subsequently, South Korean games entered other markets and have become one of the most popular MMORPGs in the world. In 2009, the sales of the *Lineage* series attained $270 million USD; globally, it was ranked fourth place among other profitable MMORPGs, while *WoW* was ranked first place (*United Daily News* 2010).

The gameplay of *Lineage* was purely designed to fit the preferences of young, Asian, male gamers. The game is based primarily upon a castle siege system, which allows castle owners to set tax rates in neighboring cities and to collect taxes on items purchased in stores within those cities. It should be noted that player versus player combat (also known as PVP) is extensive in *Lineage*. Players can engage in combat with other player characters at any time as long as they are not in safe zones, such as cities. Different "blood pledges" (an association to unite players) allow them to become involved in castle sieges during wars. For instance, blood-thirstiness is encouraged in *Lineage*. Gamers can progress by killing other gamers, which is normally accomplished through completing a quest or slaughtering monsters in a virtual world. This design has overwhelmingly drawn the attention of young Taiwanese males as well as other Asian gamers.

Moreover, the design of the game has been modelled to fit the preferences of Asian gamers. For instance, the type of game characters in Korean fantasy games present a hero with Caucasian features, which is very appealing to Asian players. Players who want to make up for their own dissatisfaction in real life can perform a perfect representation in the virtual world; they wish to identify with perfect and strong characters. Western game protagonists, by contrast, present more flawed appearances, showing scars or obviously unattractive features which would not be acceptable to players in the Asian markets. Generally speaking, western players are more accepting of beast-like characters in games than are Asian gamers, according to an observation by Scott Lee, Vice President of Webzen.

Korean cute games

The concept of the "cute game" originates from Japanese video games, which are mostly designed to be aesthetically "cute." Originally, Japanese characters in cute games were designed to be culturally unrecognisable in order for them to cross geo-cultural markets (Iwabuchi 2002). Today, their formats, aesthetic designs, and the genres themselves have become templates for the replication of online video games. On further examination of the characteristics of the Asian cute game, it is evident that the cute game can be further subdivided into cute games for children and cute games for females.

Ragnarok Online (RO), developed by Gravity, provides cute, 2D representations and a 3D virtual space for navigation and exploration. Its storyline originates from western Nordic mythology. In 2003, *RO* was a big hit in Taiwan, with around 350,000 online users playing the game during peak times. Most importantly, 30 to 35 percent of users were females in their mid-20s; the structure of the audience differed greatly from traditional hardcore gamers, predominantly males between the ages of 15 to 25. The cute game was developed to emphasize social interactions and mutual aid. Teamwork is encouraged during gameplay, where users have to assist one another to receive upgrades. Furthermore, there are collective tasks to be fulfilled; they are designed to encourage the players to come to each others' mutual aid. The cute game designs of *RO* also appeals to female gamers in East Asia. In contrast to more serious games such as *Lineage*, which can be offensive, competitive, and complex, the lovable virtual world of *RO* is filled with cute artefacts, warm friendships, and pleasant tasks; therefore, it is highly favoured by urban, Asian females.

Since its introduction to the Taiwanese game market in 2005, Wizet's *Maple Story* has seen over 110,000 subscribers, the majority of whom are under the age of 15. The game concept is inspired by *Mario Brothers*, a Japanese, cute, adventure video game; this popular MMORPG makes use of 2D capacity scenarios and scrolling story lines. Players in "maple world" can experience an adventure journey where they can defeat monsters and develop the skills and abilities of their characters, just like in typical role playing games. Quests are comprised of varying tasks that players must perform in return for experience points and possible rewards.[1] Different from fantasy games, players jump up and down in a jungle adventure and earn experience points by making their avatar smash monsters designed as cute representations, such as mushrooms, rabbits, and snails. The world of *Maple Story* has successfully attracted new players to join online gaming because it introduced an easier way to play games. In addition, the kid's cute MMORPG has been a hit in the intra-Asian markets, in markets such as South Korea, Japan, Singapore, and Taiwan.

Chinese wuxia games

Within the Chinese cultural sphere, the wuxia genre of games accounts for at least 20 percent of the market in Taiwan, and more than half of the market in China. Wuxia figures prominently in the popular culture of Chinese-speaking areas by way of novels, manga, films, and television series. The Chinese wuxia game world presents a narrative texture rather than a fighting game, where the gamer creates a special identity based on Chinese history, traditions, and culture.

It should be noted that Taiwan's game developers were the pioneers of wuxia games; they were the first to adapt wuxia knight–errant martial arts tales for computer games in the 1990s. *Fighters of the Enchanted Sword*, developed by Taiwan's Software in 1995, was the first computer game based on a wuxia romance. This game was derived from an original story[2] and has become one of the most successful titles throughout the entire Chinese-speaking world, including Taiwan, mainland China, Hong Kong, Malaysia, and Singapore. This brings up the question as to why the wuxia topic holds such an irresistible appeal to Chinese speaking audiences. Wuxia-themed games provide a unique oriental fantasy world where traditional Chinese characters can be found, such as swordsmen, Buddhist monks, and Taoist priests; gamers can also choose to play the role of a chivalrous warrior whose aim is to become the martial arts champion whose fighting skills can knock out all other avatars.

While the wuxia topic has crossed over to the field of online computer games, it remains an accepted form for audiences in the Chinese cultural sphere. In order to guarantee commercial success, wuxia game titles are usually adapted from popular wuxia novels. In 2001, Taiwan's *Jin Yong Online*, based on Jin Yong's series of novels, gained popularity in the greater Chinese market. According to data compiled by the Taiwanese game developer, Chinese Gamer, there were 1.8 million users in Taiwan and 2.5 million users in China. In 2006, Chinese Gamer developed another popular selling wuxia game entitled *Huang Yi Online*, which was adapted from a famous wuxia comic book published in Hong Kong. With over 190,000 concurrent users, *Huang Yi Online* was not only popular in the Taiwanese market, but also in other Asian markets. In 2007, this game product was licensed to five eastern and southern Asian markets. Its huge success is partly due to Jin Yong and Huang Yi's work, which is highly regarded in Chinese-speaking society. The game's subject matter was, therefore, readily accepted by players in the Chinese cultural sphere.

Limited financial resources have meant that Taiwanese firms have not been able to provide enough self-produced game products to satisfy the demand of the domestic market. Moreover, China has become the biggest online gaming product consumption market, and has great capability for game production. Most of China's self-produced games are based on Chinese topics taken from Chinese popular culture, such as wuxia novels, television dramas, or films. Although this makes it difficult for these game titles to be accepted by players from different cultural and linguistic backgrounds, Chinese game products have found their market niche with Taiwanese users; these two markets can be deemed as cultural-linguistic markets.

Analysis

The popularity of online gaming in Asia began in South Korea and subsequently spread to other Asian countries and prospered in the Chinese market. However, the production and operation of online gaming needs the support of modern technological facilities. When Asian cities independently accepted this technological modernization, it paved the way for their acceptance of US cultural products. It is true that US-produced games can be marketed in both eastern and western markets. Undoubtedly, American pop culture still has a powerful influence on the Asian audience. At the same time, Asian modernity and new technology play key roles in accelerating the formation of regional popular culture. When we look at the case of Taiwan's online gaming consumption, we find that Asian popular culture consists of a very complex set of relationships, composed of a variety of game receptions.

Empirical evidence shows that the structure of the Taiwanese online gaming market reflects, at least, three levels of relationships. First, a global master narrative media system can be used to explain the case of *WoW*. The success of *WoW* in Taiwan and China implies that international products appeal to a certain group of users, who are largely male and between the ages of 18 and 35; most are college students or office workers, who mainly belong to a higher social class status. The US MMORPGs attract a mass of Asian hardcore users. *WoW* provides simplex content for global users, with the exception of localized language translation. Its global success can be seen as a result of the pre-existing video format, which has been available for more than ten years. This has contributed to product awareness and has led to significant investment in production and testing, allowing additional capital and time to be dedicated to research and development processes.

However, this case cannot sufficiently negate the fact that the earlier paradigms were not disjunctive in the wider contemporary world. The case of Taiwan's online gaming market indicates that international products appeal to a certain group of users, as mentioned above. In actual fact, Asian-oriented game products account for a large market share in Taiwan. Asian fantasy MMORPGs borrow western storylines, but provide the content preferred by hardcore Asian gamers. This type of Asian game is presented as a mediation, combining formats of American games with Asian popular culture. These titles have subsequently become a huge success in regional markets. Although fantasy topics were originally designed for young male users in the west, they have become a popular game genre that is accepted globally. Moreover, western formats have influenced Asian game developers, as the medieval subject appeals to a large number of global users. Consequently, both US and Asian medieval epic games have been able to cross cultural borders and become globally accepted. The significant difference between US and Korean games is that the latter's content has been specifically tailored to fit the demands of local users in the intra-Asian market, whilst US games stress their simple content and focus on the global market.

Second, the East Asian game market has a wider gamer base than the western market. For instance, while Korean fantasy games attract hardcore Asian gamers, Asian cute games, with their casual content and delicate artefacts, appeal to many different gamers, many of them new gamers. Cute games have unexpectedly formed a new niche market in Asia by appealing to younger players as well as female players. Attracting the young players in the Asian OLG market, kids' cute games borrow concepts from Japanese cute games that are based on adventure storylines. At the same time, girls' cute games stress the functions of social interactions and feature contemporary elements, which tend to attract young females. Whilst enjoying modern life, these young female users are attracted to creating virtual identities using good-looking characters and having frequent social interactions in a virtual world. Today, the cute game is a burgeoning sub-genre, with a large number of new users keen to enter their imaginary world.

Undeniably, a regional market exists, both in terms of the particular game forms that have a specific appeal to east Asian audiences, and the specialist skills that are needed to create and manage games within east Asian culture. The increasing diversity of Asian-centred online gaming (whether it is based on modern life or a historical, oriental world) are not only created for Asian users, but are also localized for different Asian markets. Now diversified, Korean game formats are designed to target different groups of Asian users. It has formed an active intra-regional flow of games from Korea to Taiwan and Japan and also even further to other southeastern countries, indicating a regional market paradigm.

Third, in contrast to fantasy games and cute games, which are designed to be market oriented, Chinese topic games are designed based upon the preferences and tastes of Chinese gamers. This has led to the formation of a Chinese market within the country's cultural sphere. The greater Chinese market has distinguishing geo-cultural features that are shaped by Confucian cultural influences. Chinese audiences express different attitudes toward cultural products, such as preferring products based on martial arts tales (Curtin 2007). However, Chinese topic games such as martial arts tales are only circulated within the greater Chinese market and are generally only accepted in Chinese diaspora communities in other Asian countries.

Taiwan and China can both be deemed as cultural markets, since Chinese topic games are inclusively accepted within the two markets. Undoubtedly, the Taiwanese market can be deemed as "sub-national"; it is also a niche market in Chinese culture. This can be explained both in terms of Taiwan's market structure and because of its market dependency. The wuxia games make up 20 percent of the online games played in Taiwan (if not more), indicating a large cultural unit. Taiwanese gamers have a preference for the Chinese topic games, demonstrating that the country's market structure is similar to China's, but different from those of other Asian countries. As Taiwanese game firms cannot afford to solely focus on satisfying the demands of the local market while also operating foreign licensed games, China has now become a major game provider (like South Korea has).

In short, this research has attempted to examine the existing set of theoretical claims about media globalization, modernity, and cultural proximity through the case of the Taiwanese online game market. While the fantasy game genre has become accepted globally, and the attraction of "cuteness" seems apparent and pervasive in the Asian market, the wuxia game is inclusively circulated within the greater Chinese market. The case of *WoW* can be seen as an example of media globalization, where a US cultural product obtains overwhelming dominance in both western and international markets. However, it cannot explain the current state of the Asian game market. The fact that different types of online games have found their market niches in Taiwan shows that online gaming in the country has become part of a localized popular culture; it appeals to a wide user base consisting of young males, females, and children. This movement can be seen as a process of transmutation within a sub-culture, wherein computer game consumption was previously dominated by young males. Two markets therefore exist simultaneously at a regional and global level, at least in the case of Taiwan. At the regional level, the popularity of Asian-style MMORPGs in Taiwan implies that the idea of "Asian-ness," as a commodity, has emerged from the intra-regional networked culture. At the sub-national level, the reception of Chinese topic games in Taiwan shows that the country can be included as part of the larger online game market in China.

Online games originating from the US are easily able to become global entertainment, as their content can be revised and customized to fit the demands of local users. In turn, this has resulted in the transformation of American games into regional cultural products. In short, Asian online games have been hybridized; they combine western templates along with the preferences of Asian audiences. Under further examination, the majority of Asian online games, such as fantasy games and cute games, can be seen as market-oriented products. These products were originally designed for the western market, before their format spread to the Asian market and became a significant part of the mainstream Asian game culture. The regional market, therefore, can indeed be regarded as a sub-global market.

It is worth noting that Asian modernity has helped overcome the limitation of time and space in order for other nations in the region to come to accept the same digital cultural content. First, the operation of online game products is fundamentally based upon a modern environment, and requires the support of advanced internet techniques and specialized customized service. There is no barrier for those Asian nations that have the capabilities to accept internet entertainment, since they have accepted a similar process of modern development. Asides from this, new technology, in regards to computer systems and internet techniques, also plays an important role in speeding up the circulation of cultural flows in the regional Asian market. For example, the same game title can be circulated and operated in many different Asian markets even though the game must undergo a process of localization before it enters different local markets. Second, and most importantly, this cultural flow has now expanded its circulation—first from South Korea to Taiwan, China and Japan, and has also recently expanded towards newly economically developed countries, such as Thailand, Indonesia, and Vietnam. Arguably, this is different from the circulation of Japanese popular cultural products in the 1990s, which were only circulated within a few East Asian countries. Today, Asian modernity is not only reflected in modern phenomena, with advances in infrastructure, economic and social development, but also in a more tangible way that affects contemporary culture in terms of media consumption and audience preferences. This can truly be termed as the era of postmodernity (Featherstone 2007).

The unique position of Taiwan

Though integrated as part of the regional market, Taiwan has truly become a dependent market importing a range of different types of online games that account for a large part of their market share. Notably, all imported Asian MMORPGs have had to be specifically customized to meet the tastes of Taiwanese users, irrespective of which Asian nation these games originate from. This process of localization, however, has involved more than just simple language translation. Some changes that are part of the localization process includes character adjustment, altering the design of specific events and manufacturing different virtual items. Also, it should be noted that games imported from China also undergo localization changes, even though Taiwan and China share the same language. Taiwan indeed can be seen

168 Lai Chi Chen

as a sub-national market, and clearly distinct from the Chinese national market. However, it is clear where these two markets diverge. Significantly, within the Chinese-speaking market, Taiwan is regarded as more sophisticated, wealthier, and more diverse, while China represents more of a homogenous national market. There is evidence to support this statement; it is reflected by looking at Japanese cute games, which are accepted by urban Asian gamers, but ultimately have been unpopular in the Chinese market.

Taiwan's market is also constituted by the fragmented structure of game players, as local users accept many diversified types of game genres. For instance, Keoi's *Nobunaga's Ambition*, a historical, Japanese, samurai game, is operational and popular in Taiwan. At the same time, Taiwan has become an important test market for other Asian game publishers who have intentions to expand to overseas markets. For example, *Lineage*, *Maple Story*, and *Ragnarok*, all Korean-produced games, first succeeded in Taiwan and were then, subsequently, licenced to other Asian countries. In short, the sophisticated features of the Taiwanese market demonstrates that it acts as a stepping stone for Asian game firms who wish to expand into wider regional and global markets.

Notably, some foreign licensed games have been even more popular in Taiwan than in their market of origin. For instance, in 2006, China's Perfect World Entertainment produced *Perfect World*, and adapted it into a free game. This allowed it to find great success in the Taiwanese market, and it was also successfully launched in the Japanese market. To date, this Chinese-oriented MMORPG has been exported to nations outside of Asia, to places such as Brazil and Russia. Interestingly enough, *Perfect World*'s introduction to the Chinese market in 2004 was a failure. This case illustrates that the characteristics of the Taiwanese online gaming market consumption is advanced, cosmopolitan, and closely linked with the consumer tastes of other modern Asian cities. Nevertheless, this uniformity of Asian popular culture has not been found in China. Users who are fond of Chinese game titles with Chinese cultural content are unlikely to be attracted by cute games.

Conclusion

The structure of Taiwan's online gaming market can be seen as the epitome of Asian game culture. The emergence of its sophisticated market characteristics cannot be seen purely as the result of globalization; these characteristics have arisen from an interwoven domain where cultural, social, economic, and geographic factors matter. Modernization provides a westernized paradigm for other countries to follow, and similar processes of modernity can be found in East Asia; in Taiwan, South Korea, China, and many more. Asian modernity has manifested itself in different ways, transforming its social, cultural, and economic structures. While analyzing this research from a local perspective, we see an active intraregional flow of games within Asian nations, which is, in turn, embedded into the global system. Asian game culture has evolved significantly from internet technology and western game formats, and has furthermore been developed into an integrated regional market. Asian popular culture is identified by a large consumer market—it is bigger than national markets but smaller than the global market, at least in the case of the Taiwanese online game industry.

Currently, a complex set of relationships—global, regional, and sub-national—coexists in the Taiwanese game market. American game products undeniably, still, have an overwhelming influence on the Asian market. *WoW* has ranked as the number one best-selling game since its introduction into Taiwan; this can arguably be cited as an example of the globalization of the market. It is evident that in Taiwan, the regional and the sub-national markets count more than the global market. At the sub-national level, the reception of the Chinese topic games in Taiwan shows that Taiwan can and should be included as part of the overall Chinese online game market. Also, there is a cultural-linguistic market that exists in Taiwan, which is larger than national markets. Additionally, it is worth highlighting the role of Taiwan as an intermediary in the regional Asian market—the sophistication of the Chinese market shows that diversified foreign games are easily accepted by Taiwanese players. Most importantly, these games that undergo localization processes in Taiwan are more likely to be extended to other Asian markets or even to the global market. Taiwan's unique place in the intra-Asian market is due to the Taiwanese market's possession of potential, not only to readily and easily accept and consume game products from abroad, but also to mediate and transform them into popular cultural formats that can be widely accepted in the intra-Asian arena.

Notes

1 There are over 100 different available quests, each with varying pre-requisites; most quests may require the player to have attained a certain level, or to have completed another specific quest.
2 The originality in game design means the game title is developed from innovative concepts. Meanwhile, more game publishers in the Asian market are seeking to secure ways to develop titles that have an inherent market awareness.

References

Auletta, K. (1998) *The Highwaymen*, New York: Random House.
Brightman J. (2007) "Taiwan Gets Online Gaming: The market for online games in Taiwan will exceed $300 million this year," *Business Week*, April 26. Accessed June 14, 2010. http://www.businessweek.com/innovate/content/apr2007/id20070426_642995.htm.
Chen, J.M. (1996) "Television in Greater: Structure, Exports, and Market formation," in J. Sinclair, E. Jacka and S. Cunningham (eds) *New Patterns in Global Television: Peripheral Vision*, Oxford: Oxford University Press, 126–160.
Curran, J. and M.-J. Park (eds) (2000) *De-westenizing Media Studies*, London and New York: Routledge.
Curtin, M. (2007) *Playing to the World's Biggest Audience: The Globalization of Chinese Film and TV*, Berkeley, CA: University of California Press.

Featherstone, M. (2007) *Consumer Culture and Postmodernism*, London: Sage.

Friedman, J. (1994) *Cultural Identity and Global Process*, London: Sage.

Giddens, A. (1990) *The Consequences of Modernity*, Cambridge: Polity.

Hafez, K. (2007) *The Myth of Media Globalization*, trans by Alex Skinner, Cambridge: Polity Press.

Hall, S. (1997) "The Local and the Global: Globalization and Ethnicity," in A.D. King (ed.) *Culture, Globalization and the World-system: Contemporary Conditions for the Representation of Identity*, Minneapolis, MN: The University of Minnesota Press, 19–40.

Hamelink, G.J. (1993) "Globalism and National Sovereignty," in K. Nordenstreng and H.I. Schiller (eds) *Beyond National Sovereignty: International Communication in the 1990s*, Norwood, NJ: Ablex, 371–393.

Hoskins, C., McFadyen, S. and Finn, A. (2004) *Media Economics: Applying Economics to New and Traditional Media*, London: Sage.

Hu, K. (2004) "Chinese Re-making of Pirated VCDs of Japanese TV Dramas," in K. Iwabuchi (ed.) *Feeling Asian Modernities: Transnational Consumption of Japanese TV*, Hong Kong: Hong Kong University Press, 205–226.

Huat, C.B. (2008) "Structure of Identification and Distancing in Watching East Asian Television Drama," in H.B. Chua and K. Iwabuchi (eds) *East Asian Pop Culture: Analysing the Korean Wave*, Hong Kong: Hong Kong Unversity Press, 73–90.

Huntington, S. (1996) *The Clash of Civilizations and the Remaking of World Order*. New York: Simon & Schuster.

Iwabuchi, K. (2002) *Recentering Globalization: Popular Culture and Japanese Transnationalism*, London: Duke University Press.

Lerner, D. (1958) *The Passing of Traditional Society*, New York: Free Press.

Liu, C.H. (2008) "The Behaviour Analysis of Taiwan Internet Entertainment in 2007," (Chinese edn) *Advisory and Intelligence Service Program Report*, Taipei: Market Intelligence Center.

McChesney, R.W. (2004) "The Political Economy of International Communications," in P.N. Thomas and Z. Nain (eds) *Who Owns the Media*, London: Zed, 3–22.

McQuail, D. (1987) *Mass Communication Theory: An introduction*, 2nd edn, London: Sage.

Melody, W.H. (1992) "Communication Policy in the Global Information Economy: Whither the Public Interest," in M. Fergusson (ed.) *Publication: The Imperatives: Future Directions for Media Research*, London: Sage, 16–39.

Market Intelligence Center (2006) *An Analysis of Asian online gaming market* (Chinese edn), Taipei: Market Intelligence Center.

Market Intelligence Center (2008) *An Analysis of Taiwanese online gaming market* (Chinese edn), Taipei: Market Intelligence Center.

Morley, D. (2007) *Media, Modernity and Technology: The Geography of the New*, London: Routledge.

Pieterse, J.N. (1994) "Globalization as Hybridization," in M.G. Durham and D.M. Kellner (eds) *Media and Cultural Studies Keyworks*, Oxford: Blackwell, 658–680.

Robertson, R. (1995) "Glocalization: Time-Space and Homogeneity-Heterogeneity," in M. Featherstone, S. Lash and R. Roberston (eds) *Global Modernities*, London: Sage, 25–44.

Robertson, R. (1997) "Social Theory, Cultural Relativity and the Problem of Glocality," in A. King (ed.) *Culture, Globalization and the World-system: Contemporary Conditions for the Representation of Identity*, Minneaplois: University of Minnesota Press, 69–90.

Shim, D. (2006) "Hybridity and the Rise of Korean Popular Culture in Asia," *Media, Culture and Society*, 28(1): 25–44.

Sinclair, J. (2004) "Geolinguistic Region as Global Space: The Case of Latin America," in R. Allen and A. Hill (eds) *The Television Studies Reader*, New York: Routledge, 130–138.

Sinclair, J., Jacka, E. and Cunningham, S. (eds) (1996) *New Patterns in Global Television: Peripheral Vision*, Oxford: Oxford University Press.

Stern, E. (2002) *A Touch of Medieval: Narrative, Magic and Computer Technology in Massively Multiplayer Computer Role-Playing Games*, Proceedings of Computer Games and Digital Cultures Conference, Frans Mayria Tampere: Tampere University Press.

Straubhaar, D.J. (2002) "(Re)Asserting National Television and National Identity Against the Global, Regional and Local Levels of World Television," in M.G. Durham and D.M. Kellner (eds) *Media and Cultural Studies Keyworks*, Oxford: Blackwell, 681–702.

Straubhaar, J.D. (2007) *World Television*, London: Sage.

Thomas, A.O. (2006) *Transnationl Media and Contoured Markets: Redefing Asian Television and Advertising*, London: Sage.

Thussu, D.K. (2000) *International Communication: Continuity and Change*, London: Arnold.

Toynbee, P. (2000) "Who's Afraid of Global Culture?' in W. Hutton and A. Giddens (eds) *Global Capitalism*, New York: The New Press, 191–212.

United Daily News (2010) "Three South Korean MMORPGs were Tanked as Top 10 Money Making Online Gaming Titles," July 7 (Chinese edn), *udn.com*.

Wan, H. (2010) "Taiwan's Online Gaming Market is Expected to Reach 12.5 billion in 2010," Feb 25 (Chinese edn), *funddj.com*. Accessed June 14, 2010. http://www.funddj.com/KMDJ/News/NewsViewer.aspx?a=4fd69ccd-351f-477a-8ffb-433e58841240.

Wildman, S. and Siwek, S. (1988) *International Trade in Films and Television Programs*, Washington, DC: American Enterprise Institute for Public Policy Research.

Zhu, Y. (2008) "Transnational Circulation of Chinese Language Television Dramas," *Global Meidia and Communication*, 4(1): 59–80.

10

THE RISE OF THE KOREAN CINEMA IN INBOUND AND OUTBOUND GLOBALIZATION

Shin Dong Kim

Only sensed by few people at the time, the Korean film industry underwent a silent revolution during the late 1990s. Heavily influenced by the gloomy outlook of the film industry for the majority of the 1980s, not many people in Korea were able to promote optimistic observations. By the late 1980s, the Korean film industry had reached a perilous point; dangers escalated and peaked at the end of the decade when international distributor United International Pictures (UIP) finally obtained permission to directly manage the distribution of American films in Korea. Deep fears of the total collapse of Korea's domestic film industry were common at this time. In turn, this fear provoked those in the film industry to protest against government measures, and to protest against foreign distributors in the Korean market, as major profits resulted from the import, distribution, and exhibition of Hollywood produced films. The protests, however, produced little impact and the Korean film market was opened. Nonetheless, this fear subsided in the next few years.

Though many in the Korean film industry were initially worried about the collapse of domestic film production, the industry began consecutively producing box office successes, which began with a Hollywood style Korean blockbuster entitled *Shiri* in 1999. The next ten years were arguably the golden years of Korean cinema; they were marked by continuing success for Korean film not only in the domestic market, but also, to some extent, in foreign markets and at international film festivals. This unforeseen success was a pleasant surprise for Korea as it was far from a planned achievement; nonetheless, people began taking it for granted. The transformation of the Korean film industry and cinema culture over the last decade has not yet been fully explored or explained. Though it may be too early to make a final assessment about the transformation, it is certainly worthwhile attempting to evaluate this transformation for retrospective analyses.

In the early 1990s, there began a series of significant changes in Korean film production. Though Korean new wave films in the 1980s led by directors such as Kwang Soo Park and Sun Woo Jang marked a turning point for Korean cinema, overall, there was an atmosphere of crisis in the domestic film industry. These new wave films were politically loaded and appealed to intellectuals, but were completely unsuccessful in commercial terms. Unlike the economy that developed at a rapid pace, the film industry in Korea looked to be lagging behind the overall progress of Korean society for decades while sticking to the traditional ways of the filmmaking business. Filmmaking was largely viewed as a risky business where modern and scientific management and planning would never find a chance to intervene. People believed that in order to produce a film, one must go to Chungmuro, a local vicinity in downtown Seoul where those connected to the film industry loosely but intensively gathered. Chungmuro was symbolic of the Korean film business for decades and secretly signified a "mind your own business" type of business practice. This downtown area was never a formal system of film production but it worked as if it was one; it had its own ethics, norms, and order. This quasi-system of film production and distribution worked well with authoritarian regimes from the 1960s up until the 1980s. Generally, money for profit and investment came from the distribution and exhibition of imported Hollywood films to Korean theaters. Domestic film production was weak, while state control upon the film business was strong. Ultimately, cinema was viewed as a potentially powerful medium of propaganda that could cause political instability and political dangers to Korea's dictators if not properly controlled. Therefore, political censorship of films was unrelenting; the state ensured Korean produced films would justify authoritarian regimes and aid in helping Korean nationals forget about their harsh realities through the fantasy worlds of movies. To many, it was better to stay away from the film industry in order to avoid unnecessary trouble.

Up until the 1990s, since the domestic film production in Korea was unable to equip itself with well-trained and well-educated producers, stable financial means, and perhaps most important, the freedom of expression, there was virtually little possibility of producing quality movies. Domestic productions were largely recognized as films that were low budget and that had a low quality of content that targeted a less educated audience. Besides from the content of the films, there lay a significant gap between domestic productions and high-quality imported movies, particularly in the area of creating visual narratives. Contrastingly, American and European productions were considered high quality and recognized as cultural films. Going to the cinema in Korea was considered a cultural activity rather than simple and mindless entertainment; however, this only applies to western films. Korean cinema, as well as regional cinema (such as Chinese martial arts films from Hong Kong), was regarded by local audiences as sitting in a different category from western films; they were low quality, low taste, and purely viewed for entertainment purposes. A dangerously unclear line divided the border between high and low, refined and crude, culture and entertainment in the public imagination. To domestic consumers of film, this division was seemingly unshakable. When the unprecedented success of Korean films (artistically and economically) came to light in the 1990s, this prejudiced division between imported and domestic films was shattered; it should be described as nothing short of a revolution in Korean cinema.

What, then, would plausibly and reasonably explain the transformation of Korean cinema from the 1990s onwards? What are the factors that made possible the transformation and subsequent success of Korean cinema? Only multiple answers would serve to answer these questions. The silent revolution of the industry was arguably due to all of the following factors: first, the restoration of the freedom of expression following political democratization in 1987; second, the globalization of domestic business practices post-1988 when Korea opened its market doors; third, the arrival of a new generation of producers and consumers in the 1990s; and, finally, state awareness and promotion of the culture industry since 1997.

However, not all these factors should be weighed equally in their contribution to the revolution in Korean cinema; some factors play a more direct role while others play an indirect role, but whose influence has lasted longer. The globalization of the Korean film industry, in particular, was a fundamental factor that exercised a great, immediate, and direct impact upon the nation's film industry. Therefore, this chapter is intended to elucidate the rise of the Korean cinema in the context of the globalization process. Any discussion on globalization instantly involves notions of localization, the nation-state, regionalization, and more; these issues will be considered one by one, in relation to the changes made in the domestic film industry as well as the culture of Korea. However, a brief overview on the current situation of the Korean film market in order locate it in a global context is essential. This will be followed by a theoretical discussion on the globalization of the culture industry in general, as well as in regards to the specific case of Korea. After that, this chapter will delve into how the globalization of business and the film industry was enforced in Korea since 1989, examining the opening of the film distribution business to foreign capital as well as changing the screen quota system in Korean theaters. Finally, the last section of this chapter will explore the outward globalization strategy of the Korean film industry and their prospects for the future.

Korean cinema today

For Korean nationals today, watching a movie is certainly one of the most common and popular leisure activities. Paquet, a diligent observer and reliable chronicler of Korean cinema, commented on the characteristics of the majority of moviegoers in Korea: "If you look around, you will notice that the crowd is overwhelmingly young (under 30), and mostly female" (Paquet 2001). Nevertheless, if it is a successful film that is playing at the box office, audiences are made up of both males and females from a wide age range. Going to the theater and watching a movie should be regarded as entertainment and a cultural activity; some movies are more for entertainment purposes while other movies display more cultural value. Either way, the Korean film market today is seemingly successful in meeting the film consumers' wide range of tastes and desires as the number of viewers has increased significantly over the last decade. Simultaneously, the domestic film industry and market rapidly developed and was ranked on the top ten lists of world cinema industry in the same period. A brief statistical overview on the Korean film market may provide an introduction to the current situation. The average size of the Korean film market from 2002 to 2007 was 1.3 billion US dollars, which made it the tenth largest film market in the world during that time period. The largest film market belonged to the USA, making an average of 33 billion US dollars per year. The United Kingdom, Japan, France, and Germany had market sizes between three billion and six billion USD. The film markets of India, Australia, Italy, Spain, and Korea rounded up the top ten, with market sizes falling between 1.7 billion and 1.3 billion USD per year. From these statistics, it is evident that the total sum of the top nine countries' film markets is much smaller than that of the American market alone. However, the top ten film markets account for over 70 percent of the entire global film market.

The film markets are composed of submarkets that are categorized through content distribution. On the global level, the largest submarket is comprised of home rentals (such as DVD rentals), followed by movies shown in theaters and, finally, online sales. However, the home video market in Korea is not proliferated. In fact, the home video market is shrinking, which has discouraged companies to produce and print movie titles using the DVD format. Interestingly enough, though, there is a high proportion of theatrical distribution of films in the Korean film market. More than 60 percent of sales are from theatrical distribution of films; only India's numbers are higher than Korea's, at an astonishing 92 percent. Notably, the lowest numbers come from the USA and UK, at 27 percent and 22 percent respectively.

Korea has roughly produced about 100 films per year during the five year period from 2002 to 2007, but has imported more than 100 foreign films. The imported films mainly originate from the USA, while the remainder come from Japan, France, and China (which includes Hong Kong and Taiwan). In the year 2007, Korea produced 112 movie titles, but imported 135 titles from the USA, 63 from Europe, 59 from Japan, 13 from China, and 11 titles from other countries. Though domestic productions comprised only 29 percent of films, they nevertheless claimed 45 percent of all viewership; this is significant in demonstrating the unexpected success of the Korean film industry. In 1998, a survey showed that seven to eight cinema viewers out of ten would choose to watch foreign imported films over domestic ones; this was more or less the reality in Korea from the 1970s to the 1990s. Domestic films, however, began to surprisingly capture the audience's attention beginning in 1999; the market during that time was divided between domestic productions and imported films. In the period from 2003 to 2007, domestic films, on average, attracted 57 percent of the annual viewership; this number only followed USA and India, where domestic films attracted around 93 percent of the annual viewership.

The growth of domestic film production and distribution in Korea is indeed an impressive one, but the increase in frequency of watching movies at theaters also

176 Shin Dong Kim

deserves consideration. In 1998, there were 50 million people that visited a movie theater, translating to one movie a year per Korean citizen. In 2007, almost a decade later, these figures inflated to almost 160 million people. Going to the movies has been constantly and rapidly growing in Korea, regardless of whether it is to watch an imported or domestic film. It is interesting to note though that the amount of imported films in Korean cinemas is gradually decreasing, while that of domestic films has grown to more than half of the total.

The landscape of Korean cinema has been fundamentally altered due largely to the emergence of new, local filmmakers. The emergence of these new storytellers visibly arose in 1996; Darcy Paquet effectively summarizes the phenomenon:

> However beginning in 1996, a new generation of directors began to take over the industry. Art house master Sang Soo Hong made his debut with the award-winning *The Day a Pig Fell Into the Well* (1996), which weaves the experience of four characters into a single story. In this and his subsequent films, Hong built a reputation for his honest depiction of the cruelty and baseness of human relations. The year 1996 also saw the debut of controversial filmmaker Ki Duk Kim, known for his rough but visually striking film style (largely self-taught) and his tendency to shoot films very quickly on a shoestring budget. Unlike most other leading Korean directors, Kim's films such as *The Isle* (2000) were first championed internationally, rather than by local critics. Then in 1997, Lee Chang-dong made his debut with *Green Fish*. A former novelist, Lee would eventually win a Best Director award at Venice for *Oasis* (2002), and also served as Korea's Minister of Culture and Tourism from 2003–2004.
>
> *Paquet 2007*

These are only a few successful leaders in a much larger pool of talented directors from the new generation. For example, Chan Wook Park, Jun Ho Bong, Jee Woon Kim, and Seung Wan Ryoo, among others, were considered to be a part of a new generation of directors that adhered to a style called "commercial auteurism"; this style blends auteur films with commercially successful techniques of shooting, editing, and storytelling. These filmmakers knew how to create nationally popular and profitable films while establishing their own styles in producing visual narratives (Jung 2008). Where did all these talented filmmakers come from? How did they suddenly emerge onto the Korean film scene? Are they different from their predecessors? If so, how are they different? These are all appropriate questions to be asked in order to create a better understanding regarding the development of contemporary Korean cinema, and will be explored in this chapter.

Something that may be critical to understanding the seemingly sudden rise of the Korean film industry and the technology of film production is directly related to the nature of these new filmmakers; the simplest way to put it is that these new filmmakers do not adhere to the old system of Chungmuro, or how the old generation did things. A more defined answer requires a longer explanation in regard

The rise of the Korean cinema in inbound and outbound globalization **177**

to the emergence of these new filmmakers and the socio-economic context from which they came. The following section will discuss this point as a precursor to the exploration of the Korean film industry's globalization processes.

New generation, new production and consumption, and cultural capital

Filmmaking is a laborious process that is highly technological; it involves technology that is tangible and visible such as computers, vehicles, and television, and also invisible technology (so-called "soft" technology) such as the mechanisms that are applied to almost every aspect of human life such as political, social, and economic institutions. From the small technique of one movement in a dance to the complexity and creativity of composing an epic, the progress of human society is deeply indebted to the invisible soft technologies of every kind. Correspondingly, filmmaking necessitates and is dependent upon intensive technology of all sorts. Just like James Cameron's technology intensive *Avatar* (2009), arguably, most films produced in the future will greatly rely on both hard and soft technologies. From this point of view, the quality of films produced is primarily decided by the creative technologies of the producers; the director, actors, cinematographer, screenplay writer, choreographer, lighting and sound crew, costume designer, make-up artists, hair dresser, financier, marketer, and so on, play integral roles. The creative quality of these producers is the core element of basic technology that filmmaking rests upon.

Where does quality arise from then? The new generation of successful Korean directors have undeniably been equipped with the cultural capital of the technologies of filmmaking. According to Pierre Bourdieu, the most basic and fundamental cultural capital exists in its embodied form (Bourdieu 1986). In other words, one needs to be educated and trained for an extensive period of time if there is the desire to transform external wealth into embodied cultural capital or an "internalized habitus"; additionally, this can only be achieved through one's own efforts. Directly related to the cultural capital that people accumulate within themselves are the technology and skills of filmmaking for producers, and media literacy for viewers. Cultural capital has also been conceptualized in terms of human capital as well as social capital (Becker 1964; Coleman 1988). The three notions of cultural capital, human capital, and social capital are useful in exploring a similar object of inquiry, which is a value figuratively inscribed on the human body.

Current contemporary Korean filmmakers are better prepared to deal with cultural capital than the filmmakers that preceded them. Most of these new and successful directors belong to the baby boomer generation, born between 1955 and 1964, and also belong to the post baby boomer generation. These new directors were generally given a relatively systematic and stable public education for the first time in the history of the nation. Four long decades of colonialism and exploitation along with the devastation and destruction brought on by the Korean War, Korea, at the start of the 1960s, was in deep economic and social deprivation and left with limited resources to deal with this crisis. In 1961, the first Five Year Economic Development Plan commenced under the authoritarian regime of the time, and the country began experiencing economic revitalization beginning in the mid-1960s. Social infrastructure was developed and implemented in full force, which included the education system. Subsequently, schools were filled with students, wealthy and poor students alike. Those who were born at the end of 1950s and throughout the 1960s are classified as the so-called "386 generation," denoting those who were born in the 1960s, went to college in the 1980s, and reached their thirties by the 1990s. What is unique about this generation is the way they enjoyed being educated qualitatively and quantitatively different from previous generations, and how they formed strong bonds of their own while living under the harsh dictatorships of the 1970s and 1980s, all the while struggling for democratization. The collective consciousness of the 386 generation did not harmonize with the Korean War generation, or the generation from the colonial period. Ultimately, the arrival of the 386 generation meant the arrival of the first affluent and well-educated mass in Korean society.

Based on this background, most of the new filmmakers were professionally educated and trained in filmmaking through specialized schools, either domestic or foreign. Unlike the previous generations of filmmakers that would have entered the film business through Chungmuro (where the skills of filmmaking were passed on through low-paying apprenticeships under already established directors), these new directors honed their skills through formal film schools and/or college film clubs. Directors of the 386 generation were free from conventional bondages and hierarchical pressures that hindered creativity and discouraged experimenting in film.

Another factor of critical importance in understanding the precipitous rise of the Korean film market lies in the preparedness of viewers and consumers. Film, as a medium, requires literacy on the part of the viewers; if the viewers are illiterate, no masterpiece will be able to find a place to survive and thrive. The readiness of the Korean audience to appreciate the film language of the new directors in the 1990s possibly provided the most fertile condition for the prosperity of the Korean film industry during the last two decades of history. The quality of viewership is, in fact, the most fundamental factor that dictates the destiny of the Korean film industry. This is due to the fact that the success and failure of a film is dependent upon the audiences' decisions; profit is derived from ticket sales, which comes from the viewers' wallets.

Theoretical issues

The most explicit shock that manifested itself in the transformation of the Korean film industry and market undeniably came from Hollywood. In 1988, Hollywood's major distributor UIP entered the film distribution business in Korea. When local resistance (through the form of protests) against the opening of the market proved to be futile, the domestic film business had to hurriedly find a solution to compete with the direct distributors. Old notions, conventions, and traditions of managing the distribution and exhibition of films through national theaters had to be dispelled and market operations had to become more transparent than ever before in order to introduce planned management and generate investment. However, the opening up of the market to foreign business, along with the reduction of the screen quota, which was for decades believed to be an effective protective measure for domestic film production, posed severe challenges to the local film industry.

These measures of opening the market and reducing the protective screen quota system were unavoidable, due to pressure from Hollywood through the General Agreements on Tariffs and Trade (GATT) and the World Trade Organization (WTO). There are numerous reasons as to why Hollywood studios aimed to extract more shares from the Korean market. First, since the mid-1980s, the earnings of Hollywood films came more from international sales than from domestic sales. The domestic market, at this time, was experiencing slow growth and perhaps even stagnation; the overseas markets provided a greater and easier route for expansion. Second, the Korean film market was growing rapidly alongside the general economic development of the nation. Hollywood movies have long been major suppliers in the Korean film market. For Hollywood businessmen, it was not only logical, but also desirable, to take a chance on the closed business practices in Korea and possibly gain better sales in the distribution of these Hollywood films. Details on these measures will be discussed in a later section; but first, a brief review of some pertinent theoretical issues is in order. The pressure on Korea to open their market originated from Hollywood and its businesses; it then spread to the White House and the United States State Department and, eventually, to the Blue House and the Korean ministries of economic and trade affairs. Essentially, the Korean economy has been export oriented since the development plans of the 1960s. The American market has long been the largest and most profitable destination for manufactured Korean goods that range from automobiles, to mobile phones, and even nail clippers. The United States government was determined to open the Korean film market, and mounted consistent pressure on the Korean government. If Korea did not open the film market, it was clear that the US government would have retaliated through anti-dumping accusations on the items that Korea was exporting to the US market.

"One world, one market"; this has been the prevailing slogan for economic globalization. Its use began centuries ago when colonial exploitations and exchanges were commonplace; however, the notion of fair trade belongs to national sovereignty, and sealing domestic markets from the outside has been a respected right of the sovereign state. From the last two decades of the twentieth century on, this assumption has nevertheless become groundless, due to the following factors. The "borderless world" as preached by Ohmae already reached completion, at least in terms of the global economy (Ohmae 1990, 1995). The "finanscapes," as described by Appadurai, were fully integrated worldwide (Appadurai 1990); for Harvey, the integration of the global economy was seen as inevitable in order to save capitalism from its rigid system of accumulation that would have induced a deadly sinking rate of profitability (Harvey 1990). Harvey and Appadurai's explanations of globalization are still persuasive even though their theories are over two decades old. On one hand, Harvey correctly theorized that the economic force is well behind, and is, perhaps, also on the surface of what we call globalization. On the other hand, Appadurai makes it clear that the globalization processes occurr unevenly among different junctures or "scapes." These scapes are unfolding in the areas of ideology, media, technologies, ethnicity, and finance in a relatively autonomous way; they are overlapping, interdependent, but also autonomous. Appadurai's ideas seemingly correspond with Althusser's ideas regarding the relative autonomy of the state apparatus and other social instances (Althusser 1971).

Appadurai's theory is particularly useful when looking into the history and current state of Korean cinema. The pressures of globalization that arrived in Korea in 1988 were purely economic. For nearly a century, however, films in Korea have been fully captured within the "ideoscapes" and "mediascapes" of Hollywood and of the West. In this sense, it is evident that globalization, as understood through Appadurai's "scapes," has already been in place for many decades. True to this claim, it was known before as cultural imperialism (Tomlinson 1991) and/or modernization (Lerner 1958), and is now designated as cultural hybridization (Kraidy 2005) and/or globalization of cultural identity (Friedman 1994).

Fung's study and analysis on transnational media corporations in China comes as an interesting and thoughtful theory in explaining the recent status of media globalization (Fung 2006). Fung's cyclic model of globalization and glocalization integrates the state and the national into the capital and global levels. This model emphasizes the attempts of the formidable Chinese state to interact with global media corporations, all the while retaining its control on domestic media and ideoscapes. The Chinese state initiates the process of localization (foreign cultures moving from the outside to the inside) in which hybridization and deglobalization remove some of its "foreignness" and the seemingly threatening elements; ultimately, the end result of localization is the nationalization of global culture.

For Fung, glocalization is the nationalization of imported cultures; in regard to Chinese society, it is not necessarily a new approach to processing cultures from the outside world. Undoubtedly, Fung's model of glocalization can, in part, account for the processes of cultural hybridization that occurred in the Korean film industry during the last century. One of Korea's leading filmmakers, Ji Young Jung, masterfully portrayed through his film, the *Life and Death of the Hollywood Kid* (1994), how Korean filmmakers learned from Hollywood movies on their own and how they borrowed tactics from American films. Whether knowingly or unknowingly, many Korean filmmakers integrated the foreign idea of filmmaking with local history and sentiments.

While Fung's model uncovers the cyclical nature of interactions between the global and the local, the dichotomy of the global/local hinders one's vision in seeing the fluid nature of the global/local nexus. His model posits the Chinese state and society as an object of globalization, or something that needs to be globalized; it regards the global cultures as the forces that globalize China. However, it is the Chinese state that hybridizes and nationalizes foreign contents and feeds these glocalized outcomes back to the global cultures; in other words, the Chinese state glocalizes global cultures through nationalization. The disturbing aspect of regarding the Chinese state as an object of globalization is the fact that it places the Chinese state outside of the global cultures, when, in fact, China itself is already a dominant actor in the global cultures. Fung's model arbitrarily treats western cultures as the global cultures; this portrays globalization as China opening up to the outside world. Perhaps this is true to the current, general situation of China, but the model does not show how China is already a major force of globalization.

Korean cinema has already gone through the glocalization processes in which both local producers and consumers educated themselves on the language of film, as well as the conventions of film, by watching movies from Hollywood and around the world. The language of Hollywood films is predicated upon its unique conventions and culture. It was not only the directors who were strongly influenced by Hollywood styles and aimed to produce films that perfectly fit the archetype of the conventional Hollywood film, but also the viewers that accrued the cultural capital of appreciating and interpreting films of diverse genres. The higher literacy level on the part of the audience, in turn, set a higher standard for filmmakers. With the arrival of a new generation of filmmakers and viewers, the Korean film market, by the 1990s, was ready to build a qualitatively different and upgraded film culture.

During the same time, the closed market of Korea was under severe pressure to open up. Paradoxically, this challenge turned out to be a positive stimulus in helping Korea discard their exhausted and inefficient ways of managing the film business, and helping to rationalize and modernize the country's film market practices. The growth and transparency of Korea's film industry also generated large amounts of corporate capital; investments in the production of domestic films soared, and one of the early successes was found in the 1999 drama, *Shiri*.

Globalization of cultural economy imposed

The globalization of the film market in Korea can be summarized in two main events: the opening of the domestic market to foreign capital and the reduction of the screen quota system. Initially perceived as threats to the already struggling domestic film industry, these two shifts, in the 1990s, worked more as catalysts for growth and development, change, and success, rather than as destructive factors. In this sense, the globalization of Korea's film market became positive forces that modernized the market structure and practices; there were many reasons and conditions that demonstrated globalization's contributions to the domestic industry and market. The decision by the Korean government to open the domestic film market was, in fact, one industry out of many to be opened up to foreign capital during the latter part of the 1980s. The pressure from global corporations to enter the Korean market through lowering the entry barrier increased after the Urguay Round of the GATT and the launching of the WTO. All kinds of

Korean industries were put on negotiation tables, and media-related services were no exception. Industries associated with advertising, television, and film, as well as telecommunications, were attractive to global corporations, but being perceived as politically and culturally sensitive meant that the level of opening markets was relatively low. The screen quota system, for instance, was consistently asked by global corporations to be eliminated whenever negotiation talks were held.

Following the opening up of the Korean film market, the market underwent a slow and inactive period for the next few years. With the inauguration of president Young Sam Kim, large Korean corporations, such as Samsung and Daewoo, jumped into the production business with products such as home video and films. Kim's administration set into place the initiation of cable broadcasting, which meant sizable expansion and privatization of Korea's television business. Thus, corporate capitals saw in Korea's film industry great investment and business opportunities; for the first time in the history of the Korean film industry, corporate investments were made. Byeongcheol Kim chronicled the development of the film industry in the early part of the 1990s and acknowledged that the entrance of corporate capital was instrumental in establishing the "packaged cinema" of the 1990s. In other words, packaged films are films produced with systematic market research and planning:

> Most notable is emphasis on and investment in prior research and marketing. In the stage of prior research, the target audience is determined roughly, a market survey on their needs is conducted, a scenario is written based on that, and marketing points are set. In this process, the scenario, which is the design of a cinema, is drawn up like designing a product to conform to the desire of consumers, rather than being written with the creative inspiration of an artist. In addition, marketing is planned systematically by dividing the production period into three stages, pre-shooting, shooting, and post-shooting.
>
> *Kim 2006*

Packaged cinema is significant as it signals a departure from the age old Chungmuro system of production and distribution. Corporations injected their business savvy into the Korean film industry; they contributed not only large amounts of capital but also other skills such as market analysis, viewer segmentation and targeting, and audience specific marketing. Moreover, corporate capital in the film industry also completely changed the theater system in Korea. Individually owned and locally owned and managed theaters were replaced with multiplex chains; today, most screens in Korea belong to one of the top three multiplex chains of CGV, Megabox, or Lotte Cinema.

Corporate capital entered Korea's film industry even as the windows of film distribution multiplied due to cable and satellite television, in addition to home video markets. In fact, the overall growth of Korea's media industry since the late 1980s was significant enough to attract corporate attention. Although both Samsung and Daewoo (both Korean megacorporations) withdrew from the film industry when the financial crisis hit Korea in 1997, they left behind a profound legacy. After the financial crisis, their places were soon filled by other large corporations. As the Korean economy recovered quicker than anticipated, the film industry was realigned alongside the logic of industrialization.

The so-called Korean wave in East Asian popular culture from the 1990s onwards is another significant factor contributing to rise of the film industry. The rise of the domestic film industry contributed to the Korean wave, yet the popularity of Korean films was also reliant upon the powerful wave in East Asian societies. Therefore, the globalization of popular culture (including cinema) came to a point where globalization did not necessarily mean a one way traffic of cultural goods. Ultimately, the idea of outward globalization emerged with the Korean wave; this will be elaborated upon later in this chapter.

Even after the opening of the Korean film market to Hollywood distributors, the screen quota system maintained in place until 2006. According to the screen quota system (which was initially implemented by Park's authoritarian regime of the 1970s), theaters in Korea had to reserve one-third of screening days to show foreign imported films. The intent of the system was to protect the domestic film industry, which, at the time, was competitively weak in comparison to Hollywood and foreign films. The screen quota system did, in fact, achieve its purposes, all the while contributing to the maintenance of the primitive Chungmuro regime. The new screen quota system implemented in July of 2006 reduced by 50 percent the amount of screening days that were required to show Korean films; this meant that previously, 146 screening days were reserved for domestic films while the new system reduced this to 74 screening days. This new system was rationally followed by the installation of the integrated computerized polling system, one that automatically generates data on all movie screenings. According to a survey conducted by the Cultural Solidarity for Screen Quota in 2008, Korean theaters were, on average, showing Korean films on 95.1 days, or 31.1 percent of the total screening days. Though this was 22 days more than the required number as listed by the new system, it was a significant decrease from the 192.1 days under the old screen quota system. This finding suggests two possible interpretations. First, it is possible that theaters purposely maintain a higher number of days screening domestic films than required (as long as they attract viewers), and Korean films showed that they were competitive enough to claim 30 percent of the total screening days, at least in 2007. Second, perhaps theaters now seek greater opportunities for profits from increasing screenings of foreign imported films; this would, in turn, yield a greater amount of viewers and ticket sales. For domestic filmmakers, this second theory would certainly constitute a threatening change, as they lose more chances in showing their films to the public, but ultimately for the exhibitors, this is an improvement to the business. Some in Korea have had doubts about the new system, warning that if it is contributing to the decrease of domestic films (by way of screenings and sales) in the long run, the impact of the new system would fundamentally be counterproductive for the local film industry and culture. If, however, the new system does not negatively affect the domestic film industry in terms of business and production, perhaps, then, it would demonstrate that the Korean film industry has stabilized itself to compete against foreign films. Ultimately, as the new screen quota system was only recently implemented, it is too early to make any reasonable conclusions; it will take many more years to find any stable patterns.

The new screen quota system and its reduction in the number of domestic films required to be screened each year is arguably a direct outcome of trade negotiations affected by economic globalization. Practically speaking, the current screen quota is no more than a nominal safety net for domestic production. This has symbolic and psychological repercussions, as it silently demonstrates that the government did not, in fact, abolish the quota system to protect Korea's cultural sovereignty against Hollywood pressure and competition. Some have argued that the new system is merely helping the domestic industry to seek easy assistance from the state rather than improving the quality of domestic cinema and building global competitiveness. Opposing opinions on the effectiveness of the screen quota system have become a great debate; some are predicting the complete removal of the system in the near future, but many more believe the system will be kept in place.

If globalization and glocalization of filmmaking, in terms of culture, have existed ever since the first film was invented, the globalization of the film industry as a market only manifested itself in recent decades. Contrary to worries regarding the opening of the Korean film market and the potentially destructive outcomes it would incur, the film industry of Korea fundamentally transformed the global competition into positive stimulus for industrial development. For example, Korea was able to build a new system of film production that departed from the old Chungmuro regime; nonetheless, there is growing apprehension that the new blockbuster system is ultimately leaving less room for independent cinema.

Outbound globalization or nationalist globalism?

"Think global, act local" has become guiding wisdom for many in the rising tide of globalization. However, the catchy slogan bears little use on the practical level and exposes many questions. Questions such as, what does it even mean to "think global"? Does it mean one is not nationalistic if they choose to purchase an imported automobile when their own national economy is on the downturn? What does it mean if a person travels abroad often and watches many foreign movies? The concept of globalization appears to be changing alongside the reality of globalization. As previously discussed in this chapter, scholars of globalization have conceived of complementary notions such as localization, glocalization, and hybridization in hopes of creating an improved conceptualization of globalization. Interestingly and also ironically in a sense, Fung argued that the nature of Chinese globalization is actually the nationalization of global culture (Fung 2008). Globalization is a process of "denationalization" in many aspects; nation-states are supposed to be losing their control and power over the cross-border flows of capital and labor. Moreover, Appadurai argues that finanscapes and ethnoscapes are expanding worldwide, while the state is finding its authority and negotiating power diminishing.

If this is true, why does the prominent trend of emphasizing the importance of national competitiveness in the face of globalization still materialize in our world today? Are these two processes even able to coexist or are they mutually beneficial and supportive of each other? On the abstract level, globalization may seemingly be lowering the borders of nation-states while increasing trans-border interactions in all regards. What is actually happening in tangible situations is actually quite different, according to the societies where there is a clash between global forces and local resistance. In some cases, the nation and national firms fare better by going global. At the same time, global competition between corporations and nations are intensifying as the interests of these groups conflict.

Whether a nation-state or private entity, stances toward globalization or anti-globalization are dependent upon the possibility of gaining profits and power from the globalizing process; however, these views are dynamic and shifting. When the Korean film market was forced to open up in 1988, most filmmakers and citizens, in general, believed that the globalization of a nation's culture and society was morally wrong and was merely a manifestation of neo-imperialism. This soon passed, as the national film industry found unexpected success and prosperity. When the Korean wave spread rapidly throughout the East Asian region, and cultural products originating from Korea were in high demand and exported in large quantities, the contradictory attitude of Korean nationals was exposed. In other words, Koreans generally were displeased if Hollywood exports sold well in Korea, but if Korean pop culture sold well in other parts of the world, Koreans were delighted. Evidently, nationalistic chauvinism spreads quickly. With the breakthrough of Korean popular culture and its proliferation to foreign markets, along with the decade long popularity of Korean pop culture (the Korean wave) in Southeast Asian societies, public sentiment among Koreans is easily turned into a inaccurate conception of cultural domination (in the Asian region); this has been especially manipulated by politicians and commercial media.

In a sense, the global/local dichotomy seems to be less realistic than the global/national dichotomy since the strength of nation-states has arguably been challenged by processes of globalization. From the beginning, perhaps an appropriate antonym for the global should have been national, rather than local, which is vague and abstract. Unlike the popular slogan, "think global, act local," globalization has not necessarily weakened the nation-state system much at all. An intensification of globalization has promoted in Korea, national competition in the integrated markets and has even turned the state into an active agent of competitiveness. For example, since 1997 under the Dae Jung Kim administration, Korean governmental initiatives have been crucial to the promotion of the culture industries. Specifically, Korea's film industry since the 1990s has had full governmental support, as it is regarded as one of the industries for growth (Shim 2002, 2010). Combined together with other sectors of popular culture, Korea's domestic film industry is now seeking more business opportunities in the global market. The strategies of the film industry have, in recent times, moved from defensive and protective to aggressive and outgoing; this signals a move towards globalism, which is arguably quite nationalistic in nature. Again, this demonstrates a sort of hypocrisy among Koreans as they have strongly voiced their opinions for the political protection of the domestic film market against Hollywood, while at the same time called for the promotion of the Korean culture and films in foreign markets.

The globalization of the Korean film industry forms two distinctive but interdependent processes. The first process is "inbound globalization," which is globalization under external pressures to open the domestic film market for global film businesses (most notably, Hollywood studios and their overseas operations). This notion of inbound globalization began in the latter part of the 1980s and resulted in opening Korea's film distribution business to UIP, a Hollywood corporation. The direct distribution of Hollywood films by UIP pushed the domestic film industry to restructure their system; they quickly retired traditional conventions regarding business practices and film production. Nevertheless, the event that profoundly altered the production, distribution, and exhibition of films in Korea was the arrival of national corporations into the film market during the 1990s. The notion of packaged cinema was born out of this new corporate management system, and was followed by the birth of the Korean style blockbusters at the end of the decade.

The second process is "outbound globalization"; in terms of this study, outbound globalization is a process initiated by the joint forces of the Korean state and the Korean film industry in hopes of expanding the domestic market and pushing domestic films to be globally competitive. Up until the early 1990s, the idea of exporting domestic films to the global market was so foreign that not many took this notion seriously. However, in the latter part of the 1990s, Korean films began receiving global recognition through international film festivals and overseas sales soared; the ensuing decade oversaw impressive growth in export sales as well. The increasing popularity of Korean pop culture and the rise of the Korean wave unmistakably paved the way for domestic films to reach international viewers; the films, in turn, contributed to the popularity of the Korean wave. In a sense, outbound globalization perhaps is based upon dominating nationalist desires, in both cultural and economic terms. Although the popularity of Korean pop culture is interpreted by most Koreans as global recognition of Korean culture, it should be noted that Korean produced pop culture (consumed nationally and globally) is a highly hybridized creation, which is marked by the deep influence of western popular culture. Ultimately, this does not matter to Koreans, as they are comfortable with the dynamic and hybrid popular culture that is the embodiment of their cultural life.

If inbound globalization provokes defensive and protective nationalist sentiment among the Korean population, due to fears of losing cultural identity and economic value, outbound globalization encourages Koreans to become more open and sensitive to other cultures in order to produce foreign accepted media products.[1] The dichotomy of inbound and outbound globalization may allude to a similar trend and phenomenon analyzed by Fung regarding the Chinese case. The intent of dividing the cyclical process of globalization into the inbound and outbound is to shed light on the unique and salient characteristics connected to each directional process.

Though defining globalization has become complex due to a multitude of diverse conceptions, in general, globalization means lowered national borders and increased cross-border flows, quantitatively and qualitatively. When the globalization of the film market was conceptualized and suggested in the 1980s, it was perceived as a death sentence for local cinema in the minds of most Koreans, filmmakers, and viewers alike; this was due to the fact that, in the past, the Korean film market was dominated by Hollywood imports as domestic movies were not of high quality and reaped little profit.

Looking at it from a different perspective, however, globalization has always gone along with the development of national cinema in Korea. Cinematography itself was an imported technology that found its way to Korea in the beginning of the twentieth century, while most films that Korean audiences watched were imported (mainly from Hollywood) from the very beginning. Culturally speaking, Korean cinema has been globalized for a long period of time. The composition of films in Korean national theaters has, in its history, been composed of foreign imports as well as domestic films; foreign imports from Hollywood, in particular, constituted a large part of cinema in Korea until the mid-1990s. In this regard, Korea's film market and consumption was already globalized in full scale; perhaps there was no room to further globalize Korean cinema when foreign films dominated and were unchallengeable.

In hopes of constructing a more explanatory story on the recent growth and surge in popularity of the Korean film industry, this chapter looked at the processes of development through the concepts of inbound and outbound globalization. Also examined was the emergence of the new generation of filmmakers and audiences in Korea, who embodied richer cultural capital than the generations preceding them, and how they were profoundly important in shaping the new film culture and industry. Learning from Hollywood, Korean society went through a period of silent and unrecognized preparation where cinematic skills and technologies developed and eventually flourished. When political democratization was achieved through democratization movements, Korean society encountered a new generation of creators and consumers who had accumulated great cultural capital that would contribute immensely to production and consumption. Though the globalization of Hollywood came first, it was succeeded by localization processes of local producers in the 1980s and 1990s. The successful localization and subsequent hybridization of techniques acquired from Hollywood promoted the rise of Korean cinema from the 1990s onwards, pushing the outbound globalization of Korean films. The birth of the Korean realism in the late 1990s is worth in-depth analyses and discussions from aesthetical perspectives, which goes beyond the range of this particular chapter.

TABLE 10.1 Market share of exhibited films in Seoul by country, 2001–2007

		Korea	US (direct dist.)	US (imported)	China/Hong Kong/Taiwan	Europe	Japan	Others	Total
2007	# of titles	112	60	75	13	63	59	11	393
	% of titles	28.5	15.27	19.08	3.31	16.03	15.01	2.8	100
	# of viewers	21,017,945	13,650,881	9,757,652	486,720	1,296,964	741,557	225,151	47,176,870
	Viewers per title	187,660	227,515	130,102	37,440	20,587	12,569	20,468	120,043
	% of viewers	44.55	28.94	20.68	1.03	2.75	1.57	.48	100
2006	# of titles	108	68	51	12	51	35	20	345
	% of titles	31.3	19.71	14.78	3.48	14.78	10.14	5.8	100
	# of viewers	30,521,843	14,525,094	3,136,935	634,979	393,722	1,201,988	135,830	50,550,391
	Viewers per title	245,870	199,237	61,348	52,915	7,674	34,343	6,792	132,159
	% of viewers	60.38	28.73	6.21	1.26	.78	2.38	.27	100
2005	# of titles	83	63	51	7	54	25	15	298
	% of titles	27.85	21.14	17.11	2.35	18.12	8.39	5.03	100
	# of viewers	25,832,185	13,225,750	5,004,166	676,252	1,075,998	926,083	236,974	46,977,408
	Viewers per title	310,174	200,740	87,592	96,607	18,635	14,721	15,762	151,494
	% of viewers	54.99	28.15	10.65	1.44	2.29	1.97	.5	100
2004	# of titles	74	72	47	9	33	28	5	268
	% of titles	27.61	26.87	17.54	3.36	12.31	10.45	1.87	100
	# of viewers	25,513,346	11,755,590	7,610,481	749,287	267,286	973,040	168,763	47,037,793
	Viewers per title	306,509	159,892	145,011	83,254	8,100	34,428	31,982	161,007
	% of viewers	54.24	24.99	16.18	1.59	.57	2.07	.36	100

		Korea	US (direct dist.)	US (imported)	China/Hong Kong/Taiwan	Europe	Japan	Others	Total
2003	# of titles	65	68	44	10	29	18	6	240
	% of titles	27.08	28.33	18.33	4.17	12.08	7.5	2.5	100
	# of viewers	21,780,462	11,852,060	7,238,731	1,100,280	650,097	1,263,861	62,591	43,948,082
	Viewers per title	317,109	167,192	144,663	110,028	22,323	70,215	10,432	172,585
	% of viewers	49.56	26.97	16.47	2.5	1.48	2.88	.14	100
2002	# of titles	82	74	57	6	24	13	18	274
	% of titles	29.93	27.01	20.8	2.19	8.76	4.74	6.57	100
	# of viewers	18,364,143	12,804,599	7,059,847	572,608	518,213	1,322,292	126,027	40,767,729
	Viewers per title	217,734	161,672	99,711	95,435	21,590	101,254	7,002	138,812
	% of viewers	45.05	31.41	17.32	1.4	1.27	3.24	.31	100
2001	# of titles	52	60	77	14	45	24	8	280
	% of titles	18.57	21.43	27.5	5	16.07	8.57	2.86	100
	# of viewers	16,131,887	10,704,585	5,528,493	276,307	1,824,380	489,759	27,806	34,983,217
	Viewers per title	310,229	178,410	71,799	19,736	40,542	20,407	3,476	124,940
	% of viewers	46.11	30.6	15.8	.79	5.22	1.4	.08	100

Source: **KOFIC** (2009)

TABLE 10.2 Number of imported films by nationality 2007

Country	Number of films	Total amount paid (US$)
US	162	54,887,703
Japan	120	4,819,389
France	30	2,156,985
UK	16	952,242
Germany	11	183,312
China	8	2,205,734
Italy	7	106,342
Hong Kong	6	610,248
Canada	5	70,290
Spain	5	198,050
Thailand	3	295,920
Mexico	3	46,675
Denmark	3	92,266
Czech	3	24,126
Taiwan	2	106,752
Russia	2	292,850
Australia	2	32,880
Singapore	1	53,684
Israel	1	17,950
Brazil	1	20,000
Argentina	1	31,738
Chile	1	13,056
Netherlands	1	128,590
Belgium	1	26,500
Swiss	1	10,500
Portugal	1	15,133
Hungary	1	8,200
Bosnia	1	14,230
Ireland	1	11,408
Romania	1	10,850
New Zealand	1	50,752
South Africa	1	25,500
Etc.	1	7,000
Total	404	67,526,855

Source: KOFIC (2009)
Translated and the order was modified according to the number of films imported.

TABLE 10.3 Number of films exhibited at theaters by year

	Domestic films		Imported films		
	Produced	Exhibited	Imported	Exhibited	Exhibited total
2007	124	112	404	281	393
2006	110	108	243	237	345
2005	87	83	253	215	298
2004	82	74	285	194	268
2003	80	65	271	175	240
2002	78	82	262	192	274
2001	65	52	339	228	280
2000	59	62	427	277	339
1999	49	42	348	233	275
1998	43	43	296	244	287
1997	59	60	431	271	331
1996	65	55	483	320	375
1995	64	62	378	307	369
1994	65	52	381	238	290
1993	63	51	420	215	266
1992	96	68	360	201	269
1991	121	86	309	176	262
1990	111	–	309	–	–
1989	110	–	321	–	–
1988	87	–	248	–	–
1987	89	–	100	–	–
1986	73	–	50	–	–
1985	80	–	30	–	–
1984	81	–	27	–	–
1983	91	–	23	–	–
1982	97	–	27	–	–
1981	87	–	32	–	–
1980	91	–	41	–	–
1979	96	–	31	–	–
1978	117	–	34	–	–
1977	101	–	42	–	–

continued

192 Shin Dong Kim

TABLE 10.3 Number of films exhibited at theaters by year (*continued*)

	Domestic films		Imported films		
	Produced	Exhibited	Imported	Exhibited	Exhibited total
1976	134	-	43	-	-
1975	94	-	42	-	-
1974	141	-	41	-	-
1973	125	-	56	-	-
1972	122	-	74	-	-
1971	202	-	75	-	-

Source: KOFIC (2009)

Note

1 As Korean media products were being sold in foreign markets, producers became sensitive to local responses and quickly acknowledged the need for localization to better meet the tastes of local consumers. Clearly, this is a Korean version of media localization, which ultimately pushed the producers to create content that was based more on universal values and tastes; this is partially discussed in Lee's 2010 study.

References

Althusser, L. (1971) *Lenin and Philosophy and Other Essays*, New York: Monthly Review Press.

Appadurrai, A. (1990) "Disjuncture and Difference in the Global Cultural Economy," *Theory, Culture and Society* 7: 295–310.

Becker, G. (1964) *Human Capital*, New York: National Bureau of Economic Research.

Bourdieu, P. (1986) "The Forms of Capital," in J.G. Richardson (ed.) *Handbook of Theory and Research for Sociology of Education*, New York: Greenwood.

Coleman, J. (1988) "Social Capital in the Creation of Human Capital," *American Journal of Sociology* 94: 94–121.

Friedman, J. (1994) *Cultural Identity and Global Process*, London: Sage.

Fung, A. (2006) *Global Capital, Local Culture: Transnational Media Corporations in China*, New York: Peter Lang.

Harvey, D. (1990) *The Condition of Postmodernity*, Oxford: Blackwell.

Jung, J.Y. (2008) *Bong Jun-ho*, Seoul: Korean Film Council.

Kim, B. (2006) "Production and Consumption of Contemporary Korean Cinema," *Korea Journal* Spring: 8–35.

Kraidy, M.M. (2005) *Hybridity, or the Cultural Logic of Globalization*, Pennsylvania: Temple University Press.

Lee, S.G. (2010) "Americanization in Korean Film Culture: Some Continuities and Discontinuities in the Era of Globalization," *Asian Communication Research*, 3: 103–112.

Lerner, D. (1958) *The Passing of Traditional Society*, New York: Free Press.

Ohmae, K. (1990) *The Borderless World*, New York: Harper Business.

Ohmae, K. (1995) *The End of the Nation State: The Rise of Regional Economies*, New York: Free Press.

Paquet, D. (2001) *Going to the Movies in Korea*. Online. Available at: http://www.koreanfilm.org/movies.html.

Paquet, D. (2007) *A Short History of Korean Film*. Online. Available at: http://www.koreanfilm.org/history.html.

Shim, D. (2002) "South Korean Media Industry in the 1990s and the Economic Crisis," *Prometheus*, 20: 337–350.

Shim, D. (2010) "Whither the Korean Media?" in D. Shim, A. Heryanto, and U. Siriyuvasak (eds) *Pop Culture Formations Across East Asia*, Seoul: Jimoondang.

Tomlinson, J. (1991) *Cultural Imperialism*, London: Pintor.

PART III

Cultural domestication
A new form of global continuity

11

POCKET CAPITALISM AND VIRTUAL INTIMACY

Pokémon as a symptom of post-industrial youth culture[1]

Anne Allison

Introduction

Since the launch of the Nintendo console 14 years ago (the video game device produced by the Japanese company worth $85 billion USD), two million Pokémon games for the Nintendo console have been sold. The so-called next generation of the Pokémon Black and Pokémon White video games for the Nintendo DS took Japan by storm in 2010, and hit American stores in 2011. The last Pokémon games produced, HeartGold and HeartSilver, sold more than 8.4 million copies worldwide. Pokémon, also known as Pocket Monsters, fundamentally symbolizes a world of imaginary relations and endless consumption. It offers entertainment in a variety of forms; it offers them through the forms of electronic games, trading cards, animated cartoons, movies, comic books (also known as manga), as well as tie-in merchandise. The basic premise of Pokémon is a virtual universe inhabited by wild monsters that players seek to capture and domesticate to use as tools in capturing more monsters. Inhabiting this playworld, with its magical topography of towns, forests, and caves, are the 151 original Pokémon (which has now expanded to 649 species of Pokémon); the goal of playing the games is to capture all the Pokémon. This process, known as *getto suru* in Japanese, and "gotta catch 'em all" in the US ad campaigns, is perhaps repetitive, but, nonetheless, increasingly complex. With its quest for continual accumulation, Pokémon mimics capitalism. However, countering this fact and also interwoven with it is an alternative agenda of interpersonal and cyborgian communication—building ties with others, both human and virtual, in order to reach your goal. Encouraging kids to befriend other players and monsters, and encouraging them to endlessly expand their control (by acquiring more monsters in hopes of becoming the world's greatest Pokémon master), Pokémon breeds compulsive acquisitiveness while fostering cooperation and intimacy.[2] This tension is at the heart of the game's logic, and at the heart of its seemingly universal appeal.

198 Anne Allison

Created in Japan, Pokémon was first released there in 1996. Within the next two years Pokémon had become a global craze; to date, it has become a media-mix empire, generating billions of dollars in revenue and setting global trends worldwide. With the success of Pokémon and other successful kid hits in the new millennium, Japan has emerged as a competitive producer of cutting edge and trendy goods in the market of global youth culture that was once long dominated by the United States. Japanese products designed for the global youth market are delineated to be both "cute" and "cool," while also technologically enticing; these products aesthetically identify as Japanese and globally cosmopolitan. As such, "coolness" forms a point of articulation for the dislocations of global capitalism and the flexible intimacies that can be built within it.

A sign of Japan's burgeoning "soft power," Pokémon is also a symptom of the anxious times that launched it. Japan's bubble economy, an era of runaway spending and skyrocketing investment, burst in 1991, which triggered a deep sense of unease across the nation. After the bubble burst, Japan was further hit by a severe recession that led to unprecedented layoffs, downsizing, rising unemployment, and mounting suicides. During this time, Japan was in the midst of a national identity crisis—an identity forged in the postwar era by a type of corporate capitalism ideologically built on deep-seated commitments to the company, family, and school. After rising to the rank of global industrial power in the 1970s, Japan is now faced with new fears about the country's future.

In this context, the anxieties and doubts of the crisis moment crystallized around the youth of the nation; the youth are the segment of the population that embodies, both literally and figuratively, the future. On the one hand, youth are pitied for having to endure the rigors of a social economy that pushes all its subjects to work intensely hard by continually performing at the highest levels, thereby sacrificing personal desires and friendships in the process. In a society geared toward academic achievement (known as *gakureki shakai* in Japanese), the pressure to study, succeed, and compete starts almost at birth. Concurrently, both the time and space allotted for leisure and play have diminished. Given that commuting time is also extensive, the Japanese population increasingly spends more time alone. The Japanese environment is one where everyone moves fast to accomplish more and more each day; the human connectedness (*ningenkankei*) once held as fundamental to society is said to be eroding, if not already gone. Children are particularly affected by an "orphanism" (*kojinshugi*) that characterizes contemporary Japanese society (Takeda 1998).

According to a 1997 study by the Hakuhōdō advertising agency, most youth from ages 10 to 14 return home after dark (the average time is 8pm), eat dinner alone, and are involved in intense exam preparation (44 percent attend cram school). The youth of Japan today are so-called "amenbo kids," children who, like water spiders, attach easily but superficially to multiple things (Hakuhōdō Seikatsu Sōgō Kenkyūjo 1997). In a 2004 study on the post-bubble generation, the kids that grew up in the 1990s, Hakuhōdō reported that these youth today lack ambition and goals for the future. Instead, they are unsure that hard work at school

Pocket capitalism and virtual intimacy **199**

will guarantee job security as adults (as it once did for their parents); the youth, particularly the females, are absorbed in the immediacy of the present. The study calls teenage girls today the "sugar generation" for their attachment to immediate pleasures (Hakuhōdō Seikatsu Sōgō Kenkyūjo 2004).

On the other hand though, Japanese youth are also blamed for the angst of the times. Throughout the 1990s, these youth have been the target of a moral panic fueled by mass media. In what is said to be a rash of social pathologies (refusing to go to school, living solitary existences in their bedrooms, causing havoc in classrooms, committing violent crimes, preferring part-time jobs to full-time jobs, and schoolgirls engaging in amateur prostitution to attain brand name goods), these youth symbolize the collapse of Japan's collective culture and the nation's excesses of materialist hedonism. Even more pointedly, the youth are further condemned for a lack of commitment towards creating a socially productive future for themselves, such as studying hard to enter a highly ranked university or working towards a corporate career (Yamada 2004). Indeed, daily newspapers are frequently filled with reports of how youth today are unwilling to embody, or are incapable of embodying the qualities of hard work, and commitment to their family, education, and career that has been the anchor of Japan's corporate capitalism for more than a half century.

Such a crisis of and for youth is hardly unique to Japan. Rather, it is symptomatic of the global mapping of neoliberalism, techno-informationalism, and migratory movements that mark the twenty-first century, what I call millennial capitalism. Japan's economy is one that has shifted from, according to labor, the central roles and values of society, to an economy that is centered around consumption—a speculative and presentist logic has replaced the modernist belief in progress organized by hard work and savings. Fortunes and futures are now pinned on what Comaroff and Comaroff deem occult economies: get rich quick schemes, gambling, lotteries, and magic (Comaroff and Comaroff 2001). Neoliberalism turns workers from investors in the future to spenders in the present (Rifkin 1995). Japanese kids today are in a crisis, caught in the middle of a struggle over what it means to be a modern nation; this is parallel to what Grossberg has argued for American teens, it is a time when youth experience deep anxiety about loneliness, isolation, and have an inability to connect to others, combined with an ardent desire to belong (Grossberg 2005). As their place and relations within the social order transforms, youth become the unintended consequence (Grossberg 2005: 106) of the radical change in the nature of modernity and its attachment to progress. Once the hope and embodiment of the future, kids are in peril under a neoliberal economy driven by speedup and risk (Giroux 2003).

Precisely because of such postindustrial conditions, which reorganize the conception of the future and therefore of youth itself, "children are uniquely positioned to symbolize the very possibility of a new social and economic order" (Grossberg 2005). It is this connection that lies behind the global fetishization of youth-identified trends and fads today that, repackaged into commodity form, sells wildly, even to adults. This is certainly true of Pokémon, a stupendous moneymaker that has been praised for the way it mimics contemporary times—a playscape that both reflects and reimagines contemporary conditions of speculation, fragmentation, and digitalization. Fans of the game reiterate how it offers them a space of their own and a constellation of flexible attachments, which lends intimacy to connections formed with other kids, electronic pocket monsters, and digital play itself. Yet, because of the new age qualities of Pokémon's play (also said to evoke an older Japan whose spirituality, communitarianism, and gift giving have now vanished) and the multifarious bonds it forms around acquisition (Ivy 1995), the game has been supremely successful in world markets, spreading across ever-more venues for sale and becoming a model of and for Japanese capitalism in the twenty-first century.

In these play products which are targeted at youth and constructed to appeal to the desires and anxieties stemming from their postindustrial living conditions, Japan has located a response to its anxiety over national identity and the post-bubble economic crisis. That is, the industry of youth goods and "cool" techno-trends that have been booming since the early 1990s, extends to the global marketplace, constituting what has been called Japan's GNC, or their "gross national cool"(McGray 2002). One of the few success stories in Japan's recessionary economy, kids' entertainment is earning the country much needed capital, both real (more that $15 billion USD by Pokémon alone in domestic and global sales between 1996 and 2003) and symbolic (an international reputation in popular cultural goods that is historically unprecedented). Increasingly, corporate and government leaders have come to recognize the importance of its GNC and actively promote "Japanese cool" today as a source of national soft power that will, they hope, restore the country's economic security and global prestige.

Ironically, the state of flesh-and-blood youth is still the source of much handwringing in public discourse for some of the very qualities—flexible versus long-term attachments and presentist play versus future oriented work—packaged so enticingly in so-called cool entertainment goods. In this chapter, I will examine the play structure and commercial property of Pokémon in these terms—as a fantasyscape that promises an alternative world of connectiveness but in which the logic of play also presumes, and socializes children into, a worldview of accumulation, competition, and consumption very much aligned with the problems of youth in millennial capitalism. Pokémon is both old and new in Japan, it is this doubled nature (flexible intimacies and virtual acquisitions) that account for the popular and globalized spread of Japan's millennial brand of cultural goods today.[3]

Pokémon's invasion of the West

Pokémon ("Poketto Monsta") was originally designed as a software game for Game Boy—the hand-held digital game console launched by Nintendo in 1989. Created by a young game designer, Tajiri Satoshi, and his staff at Game Freak for a Japanese consumer base of boys aged 8 to 14, Pokémon was bought by Nintendo and released in February 1996. Predictions for Pokémon sales were initially modest because Game Boy's 8-bit technology was on the wane in an electronic game-world that was becoming dominated by far more powerful machines. However, sales were far better than expected, in part because the game is simple yet catchy, and also because the hand-held Game Boy fit in with the time's portable (*keitai*) culture. Sensing the start of a fad, its marketers sought to expand Pokémon across a variety of media venues. In summer of 1996, Pokémon came out as a serialized comic in *Korokoro Kommiku*, read by half of all Japanese boys in fifth to eighth grade.[4] Playing cards, distributed by Media Factory, followed the comic in the fall. The television animation produced by Terebi Tokyo debuted the next year in April; in the same month, Tomy launched Pokémon toy merchandise, and, in the summer of that year, the first Pokémon movie hit the big screen. Along with these, there has also been an abundance of tie-in merchandise, such as the sheets and rice bowl used by the eight year old in the epigraph. Almost immediately, Pokémon was exported to other markets in 1997. Beginning in East Asia with Taiwan, Hong Kong, and China, Pokémon then entered the United States in 1998, followed by Australia, Canada, Europe, Latin America, Israel, and the Middle East. Under the current wave of cultural globalization in which western countries dominate, it was one of the few cases in which an Asian popular culture export has successfully migrated to, and even taken over, the West.

Months after its launch as a Game Boy game in February 1996, Pokémon gained fame in Japan not only as a commercial sensation, but also as what some experts were calling a new form of play and a social phenomenon. As described by Okada Toshio, a professor at the University of Tokyo and an expert on mass culture, Pokémon is play that goes beyond the world of the game itself (Yamato 1998); this was a description I heard often in the course of doing fieldwork. Its software is relatively simple, and the game can be played alone or with others. In this, Pokémon is somewhat different from the trend of video games, which have become increasingly complex since the late 1980s, demanding intense con-centration and single minded, often solitary, absorption. Pokémon's designer, Tajiri Satoshi, purposely crafted the game to feature not only battles (*taisen*), the competitive motif of trying to beat, eliminate, or kill an opponent (which is standard in action games today), but also exchanges (*kōkan*), cooperative nego-tiations with other players to trade monsters (Nintendo 1992). It was the latter concept, innovative in the gaming world, that attracted Nintendo to sign on the project in 1991 and to support development for the five long years Tajiri took to complete it. Though Tajiri was instructed by Nintendo not to take out the battles in gameplay (on the grounds that a game without battles would be boring for kids and sell poorly for Nintendo), Tajiri built Pokémon with two strategies for acquiring pocket monsters. Moreover, he programmed the game so that 11 of the 151 pocket monsters could be acquired only through exchanges with others (Hatakeyama and Kubo 2000).

In designing Pokémon, Tajiri stated that he had two major motivations. One was to create a challenging yet playable game that would spark the imaginations of children. The other was to provide to kids a means of relieving the stresses and pressures of growing up in a postindustrial society (Nintendo 1999). Born in 1962, Tajiri shared the opinion of many in his generation that life for children at the millennial divide had become overly regimented, fast paced, and solitary. Nostalgic for a world not yet dominated by industrial capitalism, he strove to create a kind of neo-traditional environment in the imaginary playworld of Pokémon. To bring up memories of the past (Nintendo 1999), Tajiri drew from his own childhood experiences in a town where nature had not yet been overtaken by industrialization. As a boy, his favorite pastime had been insect collecting; Tajiri was fascinated by the abundance and diversity of species in their natural environment and spent long hours collecting, studying, and raising bugs. It was through these activities involving interactions with nature (adventure, discovery, mastery) and culture (trading and sharing with others), that the game designer aimed to transmit to contemporary youth bereft of natural playgrounds and the age-mates that go along with them. For this postmodern insect collecting, Tajiri chose the virtual space; a medium that would be familiar to youth and conforming to their mobile and industrial lifestyles. A game junkie (*otaku*) himself since the age of 12 (when a video arcade with Space Invaders arrived in town), Tajiri became hooked on these virtual worlds, just as he was once hooked on nature. In the virtual game worlds, he rediscovered the same type of adventure, exploration, and competition he had earlier enjoyed through bug collecting. (Hiratsuka 1997). However, there was one main difference—whereas the latter opened a child up to horizons beyond the self, virtual games enclosed kids within their virtual constructions.

Interactivity and communication

Disturbed by the tendency toward atomism visible in gaming and in society at large, Tajiri designed Pokémon to promote more interactivity. He did this by, first, creating the game to be a challenge, but playable even by young children; the rules are easily grasped, and players can make progress as long as they are persistent. Given the surfeit of detail involved in Pokémon, however, kids are also encouraged to gather and share information with other children. This emphasis on information, making the gameworld something like a language whose acquisition and mastery promote communication, is an important part of Tajiri's design. In his vision, communication (*tsūshin*) is further stimulated by the exchanges that constitute a central feature of playing Pokémon. His hope was that exchanges would be perpetuated outside the parameters of the game itself and into currencies of other kinds. One example given by Tajiri was that a child might exchange one of his virtual Pokémon for a tangible bowl of ramen or a comic book, in a mixing of metaphors, economies, and pleasures (Nintendo 1999). As Tajiri intended, exchanges enmesh players in webs of social relationships; ideally the communications within Pokémon and by playing Pokémon would build both virtual and real communities of friendship.

Interactivity was crafted into this playscape in a third way, by giving children a fantastic world of imaginary monsters and virtual landscapes with which to commune, so to speak, with their imaginations. In the course of doing fieldwork, I heard repeatedly from marketers, commentators, and child experts that Pokémon provides youth a "space of their own" (Nakazawa 1997); even though this space is make believe, to the youth, it is emotionally real and cushions them from the daily grind of studying, test taking, and commuting. Typically, adults referred to it as a fake (Hori 1996) or fictional (Nakanishi 1998) environment, but children were more prone to describe Pokémon as a mix of reality and fantasy. The world is "like reality, only fake," with monsters that are "like animals but mutated and made up."[5] In creating the Pokémon, Tajiri instructed his staff to draw on childhood memories of insects, animals, and the outdoors, with the goal of capturing the fascination these things would hold for a child. His own childhood memories shaped his design of many Pokémon, one example would be Nyoromo, a rolypoly Pokémon with a translucent body, plug legs, and a tummy stamped with a big twirl, which was modeled after a tadpole (Hatakeyama and Kubo 2000).

The world of Pokémon is constructed to be playful, yet intricate. Superimposed onto digital grids, its landscape is an array of cute habitats and a series of pathways; the bridges, tunnels, and roads are the frontiers in which players seek out wild Pokémon. Typologized by the habitats they come from—the sea, mountains, fields, and sky—Pokémon have particular powers and traits. Each Pokémon is characterized by type, such as fire, water, and grass, which informs players' gaming strategies. In Pokémon battles, for instance, water trumps fire and fire trumps grass. To attain more pocket monsters, children must master the complex science of the details of Pokémon. The complexities cannot be understated; not only do Pokémon have multiple traits, but these traits also change. As these Pokémon win battles, they are strengthened and transformed, which, in turn, changes their traits. A complicated and fluid life form, pocket monsters need to be known in order to be caught; this requirement makes playing the game a pursuit of "pokémonology" (pokémongaku)—mastery over a wealth of information and manipulation of this information to create winning strategies.

Of course, children also study at school to master information, but school-based learning is pressurized and standardized, and performance is intrinsically linked to future success, career, and social status. As Masakazu Kubo, a producer of the Pokémon cartoons, comics, and movies emphasizes, kids today are beaten down by an educational system that enforces endless memorization of sterile facts to be regurgitated during stressful exams.[6] In his opinion, youth who are overly regulated by this stifling regiment are rejuvenated by the playworld of Pokémon, which is imaginatively rich, comes with a game course that anyone can navigate, and is customizable to one's own preferences. Because pocket monsters are imaginary, the stakes in playing Pokémon are different from those in school. Study is involved in both, but the facts in Pokémon are literally animated, producing in the player a commitment and bond that feels intimate. A player becomes personally invested in their monsters through assuming ownership of them, knowing them, and cultivating their strengths.

Such a socially utopian vision of Pokémon—unsurprising for this producer and marketer of the property—underplays its commercial and consumerist orientation that translates well to the capitalistic logic found also in the West. If it is true what Kubo has argued, that the school system fetishizes one kind of object, Pokémon certainly fetishizes another. Pokémon fans worldwide have been described as compulsive, in their pursuit to master Pokémon's encyclopedic storehouse of data. Additionally, this information is embodied in goods that are available in the "Pokeworld," which feeds a never ending desire to consume (that many parents have complained about). Even though the taxonomies in Pokémon are borrowed from nature, they can be transferred all too easily to the realm of commodity fetishism.

The practice of communicating through Pokémon encourages a subjectivity akin to what Fredric Jameson has recently called the "addictive capitalism" of the millennial era. Addiction to the rush of acquisition is part of the pleasure in playing Pokémon games. The desire to consume, enforced by the game, echoes what Ōhira Ken has described as the emergent Japanese subject in contemporary times—people who, inept at human relationships, are compulsive consumers and taxonomers of brand name goods in which they invest value and affection. Based on insights from his psychiatric practice, Ōhira calls them "people who speak things" (*mono no katari no hitobito*); he argues that attaching so much value to the acquisition of things does not correct the atomism of millennial times as much as extends it in a new and intimately consumerist direction (Ōhira 1990).

Cuteness: expanding the empire with imaginary kinship

Undoubtedly, Pokémon's success was completely unexpected. Never intended to be for the global markets, Pokémon was designed for only one audience in Japan, namely Japanese boys ages 8 to 14. Pokémon's immediate success on the Game Boy console prompted marketers to expand their horizons. Though Pokémon first branched out into comic books, trading cards, and toy merchandise, Pokémon was later developed in cartoon series and movie versions, which held the most promise for profit. There is conventional wisdom in the children's entertainment business that states that in order to become a flourishing trend, a successful toy or video game must be accompanied by a television show or film. In the case of Pokémon, in telling the story of how three kids travel to discover, catch, and attain more and more Pokémon, has altered and widened the scope of what started out as a mere video game. As the anime producer, Masakazu Kubo, explained to me, Pokémon Inc. is built on three main pillars: the electronic video game, the trading cards, and the movies and television cartoons (also serialized as comics). These components are comprised of a host of elements that appeal to diverse audiences; the overarching quality is what he called "cuteness" (*kawaisa*) or "gentleness" (*yasashisa*).

Speaking specifically of Pokémon and its success on the export market (such as becoming the top ranked children's show on US television when it launched on the Warner Brothers network in fall of 1998), Kubo added that the "cute element" gave Japan soft or cultural power, something that the Japanese are polishing in order to accrue overseas capital and prestige. Okada Toshio, a Japanese culture critic, has argued that cuteness is one thing that speaks to all audiences. In his mind, Pokémon is the embodiment and definition of cuteness, a cuteness that may be Japan's key to working foreign capital in the twenty-first century (Yamato 1998). Others have suggested that Japan's future in influencing and even leading global culture will come through three industries central to the business of cuteness: video games, anime (animation), and manga (comic books). The market for these three industries has surpassed that of the nation's car industry in the past decade, leading some economists to hope that these will pull Japan out of the red. As one economist noted, what Japan has, is an *animé komikku* game industry, which will be the root of Japan's new, twenty-first century culture and recreation industry (*Nihon Keizai Shimbun* 1999).

What makes Japan successful in its marketing and exporting of games, comics, and cartoons is not simply technological or business prowess, but what has been called the expressive strength (*hyōgenryoku*) of Japanese creators (*Nihon Keizai Shimbun* 1993). Identified through its portable convenience, dataized flexibility, and fantastic spirituality, this postmodern play aesthetic takes from Japanese culture and society, the old and the new. For example, an article in *Wired* magazine reporting on DoCoMo (a wireless internet service), stated that Japan is "putting its stamp on the times" in regard to consumer electronics (Rose 2001). The DoCoMo cell phone converts into a hand-held computer and a wireless e-mail receiver, and is sleekly designed, which makes it a fashionable accessory. It can also relieve a user's stress through downloadable games, and downloadable images such as ones of Hello Kitty that can be added as screen savers. "Gazing at Hello Kitty on their handsets, [users will] relax for a moment as they coo, 'Oh, I'm healed'." (Rose 2001). As the article states, the intent of the DoCoMo cell phone was to create a technology that is not only efficient and convenient, but also cozy and fun. Healing in times of rupture and individuation, technology doubles as a communication device and a gadget for play—it is a prosthesis with infinite and intimate possibilities, that can be both personal and social. The adjective that has been used most to describe this quality of technology, play, and consumer culture, is cute.

Pikachu as a global icon

Yasashisa, or the gentle aspect of cuteness, is precisely the word Japanese producers used to characterize the marketing of Pokémon in Japan.[7] As they pointed out, however, this was not Pokémon's original sensibility as it started out as a role playing action game targeted at young boys. The cuteness of Pokémon came with the story versions, particularly in the animated cartoon developed by Masakazu Kubo and his staff. As Kubo once stated in an interview, the overarching objective of this was to extend the audience of Pokémon to girls, younger children, and even mothers (who are vital in the marketing of children's entertainment in Japan). Giving narrative and characterization to what are only sketch lines on a Game Boy screen, the Pokémon cartoons also foregrounds a central figure (such as Mario or Mickey Mouse) that can ultimately serve as an icon for the entire phenomenon. Instead of choosing a character with human characteristics, a pocket monster was chosen, engendering a different imaginary bond of possession, companionship, and intimacy, key to the construction of *yasashisa*. This character chosen was Pikachu, the yellow, cute, mouse-like Pokémon. Though Pikachu was only one of the 151 pocket monsters in the original Pokémon game, Pikachu became the lead Pokémon in the television cartoon and, subsequently, also became a global symbol or icon similar to the likes of the Nike swish and McDonald's golden arches.

According to Kubo, a checklist was involved in making this selection. The criteria included a memorable but warm image (Pikachu has a squiggly tail, pointy ears, and sweet face), a noticeable but non-threatening color (yellow), a catchy name (Pikachu), an unforgettable refrain ("pika pika chuuuu," which is reproducible by even small kids and can be globalized without translation), and a face that cold be inscribed with a range of emotions, including tears, for the cartoon and movie versions (Kubo 1999). Most importantly, the creature had to be cute, an ideal that Pikachu has realized in spades, serving as the epitome of cuteness according to almost every person I interviewed regarding Pokémon.[8] As Kubo summed up, this character grabs people's emotions; its cuddly appearance delights children and makes mothers feel safe.[9] Nevertheless, what is equally important is the fierce powers that Pikachu holds despite its cute exterior.

When asked to characterize Pikachu, or pocket monsters in general, children invariably coupled cuteness with other features (namely strength), and spoke more of the relations they formed with their imaginary pocket monsters, rather than static traits. According to one ten-year-old boy in Tokyo, "Pokémon are imaginary partners, creatures that can be your loyal pet if you control them. They're companions until the end, sort of like animals that are real, except mutated." A seven-year-old girl in the United States declared, "Pokémon are like creatures that are made up. The creators got ideas from nature, but they turned nature around. People care a lot for their Pokémon, but they also use them to fight other Pokémon."

Fetishism of cuteness

At the heart of the "cute fetish" promoted by Pokémon, is a relation of usefulness and intimacy. Serving as its icon, Pikachu is also the vehicle by which cuteness was expanded from a relatively minor role in the game version into a more complex web of affective and utilitarian value through the story-based media of manga, anime, and movies. When Pokémon moved into media more reliant on storytelling, instead of focusing on strategies and battles of acquiring monsters (that the games emphasized), these stories exhibited dramatic subplots and elaborate adventures that almost always involved Pokémon and their multivalent relations with humans. As the iconic pocket monster, Pikachu figures heavily in these dramas; its development as a character was largely in terms of the complex bond it shared with Satoshi, its human owner, master, and friend.

In the localized US Pokémon stories, Ash (Satoshi in the Japanese version), a ten-year-old boy, is the lead human character who travels all around the Pokéworld in search of wild pocket monsters; his ultimate goal is to become the "world's best Pokémon master." Accompanying Ash in this mission are his two friends, Misty (also known as Kasumi), a ten-year-old girl, and Brock (also known as Takeshi), a 15-year-old boy, and Pikachu, his most trusted Pokémon. Ash and Pikachu first meet in the initial episode (of the cartoon and also the graphic comics) when, mimicking the structure of the Game Boy game, Ash is given his lead-off Pokémon by Dr. Oak. Upon seeing Pikachu, the cute yellow pocket monster, Ash is initially disappointed, assuming that Pikachu would be a weak tool for realizing his ambition of capturing all 151 Pokémon. However, Pikachu surprises him with a display of indomitable will; when ordered into the Pokeball by Ash, a monster by which all Pokémon are digitalized for travel, Pikachu refuses. By forcing Ash to carry it atop his shoulders, like a pet or young child, Pikachu acquires a badge of distinction. For, as the only Pokémon to remain outside the ball—and therefore the currency of equivalence into which all the other Pokémon are convertible—Pikachu never gets "pocketed" in the cartoon. Always appearing more monster than a thing, it is forever visible and cute; the material sign of use value in what is also a generalizable medium—monsters that, like money, stand for and generate wealth.

Engaged in what Roland Barthers deemed a "constantly moving turnstile" (Barthes 1972), Pokémon continually oscillate between meaning and form, full on one side while empty on the other. In this process, Pikachu serves as an alibi; it is the material sign of use value in what is simultaneously a system of exchange. Pikachu is the boy's property, possession, and tool, but also something much more in the cartoon—it is a free agent, loyal pet, and personal friend. This deeper relationship between the boy and the monster begins in the first episode of the cartoon. Having refused the monster ball, Pikachu is riding with Ash on his bicycle when the two are attacked bye killer birds overhead; Ash is knocked unconscious by these two birds. Pikachu, going into warrior mode, battles the birds on its own, thereby saving its master. Awakening seconds later, Ash is duly impressed by his Pokémon's bravery and skills. However, in a trope recurrent in the series, Pikachu then becomes at risk for injury and Ash risks his own life to save his Pokémon. In the first episode, when Pikachu is injured, Ash rides his bicycle through the birds in order to deliver Pikachu to the Pokémon Center, where it can be healed. In this drama of reciprocity, gifts of kindness are exchanged, establishing a social relationship.

The bond between Ash and Pikachu is referred to repeatedly as one of friendship in the text of the cartoon. For example, in one memorable episode when Satoshi is competing against the whiz kid at a cram school for Pokémon trainers, he refers to his monster as he nevertheless wins the battle by using Pikachu. After the battle, Ash's competitor concedes he had learned something new—that displaying kindness towards one's Pokémon actually strengthens its fighting abilities. This message reoccurs throughout the cartoon series; humans must act as masters but also as trainers, tending kindly to their Pokémon for moral reasons (maintaining an interpersonal relationship) and practical reasons (maximizing monster utility, hence value).

As morality and practicality converge, Pokémon are treated as objects as well as objects to have relations with; they are gifts as well as commodities. This convergence also demonstrates something feudal and futuristic. On one hand, the monster–human bond resembles that between vassal and lord; the Pokémon serve and sacrifice for their masters and, in return, are fed, tended to, and trained. On the other hand, monsters are commodities that fetishize the power of personal accumulation and interpersonal intimacy, even kinship, between a human and non-human. The pocket monsters are a flexible, fluctuating, and interchangeable currency, shifting between means and end, capital and companion, property and pal. Fluctuating between use value and exchange value, as an exchange value they also fluctuate between an economic value—acquisition of Pokémon leading to mastery and wealth—and a value of relationality—what we could call the spirit of (Pokémon) capitalism.

Culture and capitalist ideology

Thus, cuteness is expanded and rearticulated in the process of narration and brings together, in narrative formats, millennial alienation, along with a new, flexible intimacy. As it does so, the game's capitalist logic of acquisition merges with other communitarian and altruistic sensibilities. In one exemplary cartoon episode, the story starts as usual: the triumvirate arrives in a new place looking to discover and catch new pocket monsters. The scene depicted is a natural wonderland whose eco-balance has recently been disturbed by the invasion by a species of beetle into the habitat of another. The three kids are asked by a worried naturalist to put aside their desire to catch Pokémon for the time being and to help him restore order; in turn, the children selflessly get to work. In time, the kids discover the root of the problem and return the forest to ecological harmony. This task was extremely time consuming, however, and their scheduled stop is almost up. Preparing to leave without a single catch, Ash is approached by one of the rescued beetles, indicating that it wants to join his traveling band. The boy orders it to stay put with its own kind, but the beetle persists. Shrugging his shoulders, Satoshi throws his monster ball and, upon crawling inside, the beetle becomes the boy's latest capture. The objective of acquiring Pokémon has not been displaced so much as it has been contained within the greater agenda of helping others. As a reward for his kindness, Ash receives another pocket monster, part of his personal stock, but also what will become a kind of (interspecies, human/virtual) kin relation.

In this way, nature collapses into capital (the wild Pokémon become acquired valuable property) and capital collapses into culture (a relation of things into interpersonal relations). This ploy occurs often in the cartoons; touched by the altruism of humans, Pokémon frequently leave behind their own kind to join the worldly human mission to discover and catch more pocket monsters. Needless to say, the process of acquiring Pokémon is gentler than attacking wild monsters with Pokeballs or winning them in battle after they have been whiplashed, pummeled, or stung. It also reimagines the bond and bondage formed by freely entering into a system that will reduce them to living inside of a Pokeball. Here the representation mimics that of capitalist ideology; people who are voluntary laborers willingly contract work for wages in an economic system built on exploitation and reification—a phenomenon commonly shared among global culture. Implicitly, the monsters making this choice exchange the wilderness of natural habitats for something enticing (worldly travel and nomadic adventures) and also moral, in the Maussian sense (Mauss 1967). Exchanging a gift of human kindness for a gift of the pocket monster itself results in a storehouse of goods and also new age attachments and intimacies. The cuteness factor makes this whole operation appear childlike and sweet, with Pokémon such as Pikachu "cutifying" the relationship of acquiring Pokémon and simultaneously doubling as pets and pals, thereby normalizing the global capitalist logic.

The play logic goes global

In one of my interviews, I talked to a group of Pokémon fans in Greeley, Colorado—young boys and girls from ages 7 to 12, who were all Caucasian and middle class. Although their tastes and passions varied widely—some only played the Game Boy game, others only watched the cartoon, some loved the cute Pokémon, while others concentrated on strong monsters alone—the group as a whole shared the tendency to view this playworld in terms of affection, utility, warmth, and instrumentality. One seven-year-old girl put it this way: "I love the Pokémon. They are my friends, and they help me win more Pokémon." A nine-year-old boy added, "A Pokémon is loyal and your servant. I mean, it is mine, but I take care of it too." Only one child, a girl age seven, thought it odd that players had to continually put their Pokémon into battle, where they would be injured and maimed. "Why did the designers make it that way? Aren't Pokémon supposed to be our friends?" However, even this girl admitted to being an avid player of the Game Boy game. She was also, like most of the other kids, an impassioned Pokémon card collector who kept all her prized cards in a binder used to collect and trade with other kids. She eagerly displayed to me the cards she liked most, and listed these Pokémon's key traits. For this group of fans, value was calibrated in numerous ways: affection for the way a Pokémon looked, utility based on how a Pokémon could be played in the card game, and "market value" based on prices listed in unofficial card collector guides (which almost all of the kids owned). For example, this young girl's brother, when opening his pack of Pokémon cards that I had brought from Japan, exclaimed, "Hey dad! I got a 25 dollar card!"

Similarly, news coverage of this fad in the United States tended to fluctuate between its friendly and acquisitive aspects. At one end were the reports of the "buy and sell bazaar" (Healy 1999) atmosphere it fostered; kids traded with their friends or at malls on Saturday mornings with Pokémon collector albums tucked firmly under their arms. These children were turned into miniature salespeople, investing in their own form of stocks. Indeed, for its arousal of a market sensibility in kids, Pokémon was considered a kind of collector play by one commentator—it was a kid craze different from marbles, yo-yos, or Beanie Babies (Healy 1999). Certainly, this market sensibility is what led to acts of violence; incidents of theft, stabbings, and punch-outs (mainly over Pokémon cards) ensued. Even lawsuits occurred: parents sued Nintendo for inciting kids to buy endless packs of cards, expending hundreds, even thousands, of their parents' hard earned dollars (Halbfinger 1999). Yet despite some concerns about the addictiveness, acquisitiveness, and commercialism that Pokémon generated, the overall attitude toward the product was approval. Significantly, adults often praised the connections and friendships inspired by Pokémon, sometimes seeing "something notably Japanese here ... values that are admired but not always handsomely rewarded in American society" (Strom 1999).

In my mind, the cultural logic of inter-relationality attributed by some to a Japanese past does not, in itself, account for the global appeal of Japanese entertainment products today. What does, rather, is the intermixture of a market economy (trading, gambling, accumulating wealth) with fantastic monsters that double as portable property and friends. This sense of collapsibility or reversibility between gifts and things, relations and acquisitions, arguably, defines the essence of Pokémon. Does this represent a new playmode and a form of global capitalism? Perhaps the distinction here is more of degree than of kind. Hardt and Negri's depiction of a world today that is decentered from such modernist brokers and institutions of power as the family and the nation-state and is increasingly less organized in terms of clear cut distinctions is agreeable (Hardt and Negri 2000). This is the worldview that is reflected in Pokémon: a space populated by endless entities that break down into endless parts (of powers, strengths, attacks, values) that can also be acquired by players and variously (re)connected, offering various and flexible attachments for players as well.

Such play of acquiring and connecting can be comforting to kids, giving them something that feels personal and invites interpersonal relationships. Moreover, it also is part of a market economy, of a playscape that is bought and sold on the marketplace and of a play logic that mimics a marketplace of continually transacting and accumulating things. This is both the underside and the future of a play that doubles so closely with capitalism, a play in which the alternative space to postindustrial life at the millennium is simply another version ever-more intoxicating and compelling to kids. It is with such a logic that Japanese playgoods are making their mark in the global youth market, yielding vast profits and soft power in shaping the world, both virtual and lived, of postindustrial kids today. I urge those who criticize the presentism of youth, their disinvestment in futurist goals, the loneliness and rage that often accompany their addiction to consumerism, to focus instead on the conditions of empire and millennial capitalism that are so productive of, and that find so profitable, such youth behaviors of today.

Notes

1 This article is a modified version of the article published in *Figuring the Future* edited by Jennifer Cole and Deborah Durham. Santa Fe: SAR Press.
2 I use the terms kids, youth, and children interchangeably in this chapter to refer to the audience of Pokémon players who, in Japan and elsewhere, have a broad age range from about age two (as watchers of the cartoon) to mid-20s and above (as players of the video and Game Boy games and collectible card games). This elastic age range also pertains to global youth culture more broadly these days as the category "youth" has become something of a floating signifier, standing for and stretching to a wide body of behaviors, practices, and goods used or appropriated by an increasingly large segment of the population. One example of this is hip-hop. Its fans range across the entire age spectrum even though it still gets identified as youth based.
3 The height of the Pokémon fad occurred in 1998 and 1999. The fad is currently over. Yet in Japan and other marketplaces, such as the United States, the cartoon is still broadcast on TV, new movies are still being made (the most recent one was released in summer 2005), and new Game Boy games, as well as other electronic products, are still hitting the market. In this chapter, I therefore use both the past and present tenses to refer to the Pokémon phenomenon.
4 This figure was given to me by Masakazu Kubo, executive producer in the Character Business Planning section of Shōgakukan Inc., the publishers of *Korokoro Kommiku*. Kubo has been one of the most important figures in the Pokémon business in Japan. Masterminding the original comic book version, he has also been one of the main producers for the cartoon and movie series.
5 From interviews with Japanese children, November 1999.
6 In a personal interview, December 1999.
7 Personal interviews with executives at Tokyo Terebi, Shogakukan Production, ShoPro, and Tomy Company.
8 During my fieldwork on Pokémon, conducted in Japan and the United States (1999–2000), I interviewed producers, designers, marketing executives, teachers, parents, children, child psychologists, educational experts, scholars, reporters, and cultural critics.
9 Personal interview, December 1999.

References

Barthers, R. (1972) *Mythologies*, New York: Hill and Wang.
Comaroff, J. and Comaroff, J.L. (2001) *Millennial Capitalism and the Culture of Neoliberalism*, Durham: Duke University Press.
Giroux, H.A. (2003) *The Abandoned Generation: Democracy Beyond the Culture of Fear*, New York: Palgrave.
Grossberg, L. (2005) *Caught in the Crossfire: Kids, Politics, and America's Future*, London: Paradigm Publications.
Hakuhōdō Seikatsu Sōgō Kenkyūjo (1997) *Kodomo no Seikatsu* (*The Lifestyle of Youth*). September 9, no. 260. Tokyo: Hakuhōdō Seikatsu Sōgō Kenkyūjo.
Hakuhōdō Seikatsu Sōgō Kenkyūjo (2004) *Kodomo no Seikatsu*. May 11, no. 397. Tokyo: Hakuhōdō Seikatsu Sōgō Kenkyūjo.
Halbfinger, D.M. (1999, September 24) Suit claims Pokémon is lottery, not just a fad. *New York Times*, 5.
Hardt, M. and Negri, A. (2000) *Empire*, Cambridge: Harvard University Press.
Hatakeyama, K. and Kubo, M. (2000) *Pokémon Suto-ri* (*Pokémon Story*), Tokyo: Nikei BP Shuppan Centā.
Healy, M. (1999) Pokémon frenzy disrupting US schools. *Daily Yomiuri*, 27, October 21.

Hiratsuka, A. (1997) Tajiri Satoshi, *Antore*. July, 168–171.

Hori, T. (1996) *Nihon no omocha, anime wa kore de iinoka? (Are Japan's Toys and Animation a Good Thing?)*, Tokyo: Chirekisha.

Ivy, M. (1995) *Discourses of the Vanishing: Modernity, Phantasm, Japan*, Chicago and London: University of Chicago Press.

Kubo, M. (1999) Sekai o haikai suru wasei monustā Pikachu (Pikachu, a Japanese monster that is wandering the world). *Bungei Shunjū*, 21, 340–349.

Mauss, M. (1967) *The Gift: Forms and Functions of Exchange in Archaic Society*, New York: W.W. Norton and Company, Inc.

McGray, D. (2002) Japan's Gross National Product of Coolness. *Foreign Policy*, May/June, 44–54.

Nakanishi, S. (1998) Pokémon būmu to Pokémon shōku (The Pokémon boom and the Pokémon shock). *Kodomo hakusho (Children's Encyclopedia)*, Tokyo: Nihon Kodomo o Mamorukaihen, Sōdobunka, 273–279.

Nakazawa, S. (1997) *Poketto no naka no yasei (Wildness in the pocket)*, Tokyo: Iwanami Shoten.

Nihon Keizai Shimbun (1993) *Kabunushi no hanran--Juyaku ga sabakareru hi* (The revolt by shareholders – the day, directors get suited). Tokyo: Nihon Keizai Shimbun.

Nihon Keizai Shimbun (1999) Nihon anime kaigai ni eikyōryoku (The influence of Japanese animation overseas). *Nihon Keizai Shimbun*, 3, December 1.

Nintendo (1992) "Mario Kart" [Super Nintendo], Japan: Nintendo.

Nintendo (1999) *Nintendo jiseidaiki Happyō (Announcement About the Next-Generation Machines at Nintendo)*, May 12. Kyoto: Nintendo.

Ōhira, K. (1990). *Yutakasa no seishinbyōri (Pathology of abundance)*, Tokyo: Iwanami Shoten.

Rifkin, J. (1995) *The End of Work: The Decline of the Global Labor Force and the Dawn of the Post-Market Era*, New York: G.P. Putnam's Sons.

Rose, F. (2001) Pocket monster: How DoCoMo's wireless Internet service went from fad to phenom – and turned Japan into the first post-PC nation. *Wired*, May, 126–135.

Strom, S. (1999) Japanese family values: I choose you, Pikachu! *New York Times*, 4, November 7.

Takeda, Y. (1998) *Mienai kazoku, part 3: Ko to shūdan o yuragugeru infura o (The Family that Can't be Seen, Part 3: Shaking up the Space Between the Individual and the Group)*, Tokyo: Nikkei Dezain: 38–44.

Yamada, M. (2004) *Kibōkakusa shakai (The Society with Different Desires)*, Tokyo: Chikuma Shobō.

Yamato, M. (1998) Kūzen no hakai genshō "Pokémon" chō hitto no nazo (The Riddle of the Super Hit Pokémon that is an Unprecedented Social Phenomenon). *Gendai*, January, 242–249.

12

PLAYING THE GLOBAL GAME

Japan brand and globalization

Kukhee Choo

Japanese popular culture, including animation, video games, comic books, and other audio-visual media, has been circulating widely in the global market over the past two decades. Of the aforementioned popular media, Japanese animation and video games are arguably the most prominent examples of how mass-distributed pop culture can become major effective tools for the market economy as well as for other socio-cultural phenomena. The sudden surge in market sales abroad during the mid-to-late 1990s motivated the Japanese government to officially support the popular culture industries, also known as the "Content industry," at the turn of the new millennium, fundamentally believing that they had great potential to benefit the Japanese economy in the long run.

Emerging out of the incumbent Prime Minister Koizumi Junichirou's administration as the Intellectual Property Rights scheme in 2002, the plan to promote the Japanese Content industry developed into a full-blown national effort when the Content Industry Promotion Bill, or the Kontentsu Sangyō Shiensaku Hōan, was passed in June of 2004. It included six media industries at the time: animation, live-action films, manga, popular music, television dramas, and video games. In the late 2000s, a larger cultural spectrum was embraced in order to cultivate Japan's national promotion; non-media fields such as character goods, fashion, and food were added to the promotion list. Among the initial six industries, the government was particularly keen on promoting Japanese animation (anime) and video games. Japanese government officials stated that the motivation for their support of these industries was due to the sheer volume of increased video game and anime DVD sales in the United States since the late 1990s. Numerous Japanese governmental reports have referred to Japan's "Gross National Cool" (McGray 2002) and also referred to Joseph Nye Jr.'s concept of "soft power" (Nye 2004). Therefore, Japan's quest to build their own soft power has been guided under the banner of "Cool Japan" in their efforts to promote a new Japanese image and identity

214 Kukhee Choo

towards the western markets. In June 2010, the Ministry of Economy, Trade and Industry (METI) announced its new agenda to establish Japan as a culture industry nation. In turn, METI set up the "Cool Japan Division," which replaced the Content industry division established in 2004.

The Japanese government's support of popular national culture is one of the most drastic policy shifts since the Meiji era's cultural policies in the late nineteenth century. Being the precursor of globalization, nineteenth-century forces of westernization resulted in Japan's co-opting of Western logic (Anderson 2009) and resulted in Japan establishing self-orientalizing policies vis-à-vis western powers. Over a century later, we witness Japan in a new modality, this time dealing with larger forces of globalization. After two decades of post-bubble economy recession, the current Japanese government's pledge to develop soft power through the means of popular culture mirrors the Meiji era's late-nineteenth-century cultural policies targeting western audiences. This chapter will analyze the Japanese governmental support of the Content industry as a reactionary policy to the forces of globalization. Ultimately, this has not resulted in a disruption or contestation to global flows, but rather appears to embrace the institutional structure of Western capitalism in globalizing its popular culture to appeal to a broader global audience.

Transnational Japanese popular culture

The global flow of capital, power structure, and culture has positioned Japanese popular culture as a challenging alternative to western globalization. Some researchers argue that Japanese popular culture has become a new site of globalization; a counter force to the western, mostly American, cultural influence (Iwabuchi 2002; Befu 2003). Others argue that consuming Japanese culture in Asia reflects, though not fully, some Asian nations' former colonial relationship with Japan (Ching 2000). Conversely, whether positive or not, some western scholars convey the fear of being invaded by Japanese popular culture (Bosche 1996; Kelts 2007); this argument is oftentimes based on the essentialist binary structure of East versus West.

Scholarship on the international circulation of Japan's popular culture is also diverse. Though discussion on Japanese popular culture as a global medium is a recent one, Koichi Iwabuchi argues that as far back as the 1980s, audio-visual commodities of Japanese origin, such as the Walkman, karaoke machines, computer games as well as VCRs, were culturally influential in the global market (Iwabuchi 2002). Yet, Iwabuchi maintains that these commodities were essentially "culturally odorless," stripped of its any visible and conceptual ties to its country of origin (Iwabuchi 2002). Following the theories of Eiji Otsuka and Toshiya Ueno, Iwabuchi asserts the following, in regards to the nation-less, or *mukokuseki*, aspect of Japanese anime in the global market:

> However, it is quite another to say that this cultural influence and this perception of coolness is closely associated with a tangible, realistic appreciation

of "Japanese" lifestyles or idea. It can be argued that the yearning for another culture that is evoked through the consumption of cultural commodities is inevitably a monological illusion. This yearning tends to lack concern for and understanding of the socio-cultural complexity of that in which popular cultural artifacts are produced. This point is even more lucidly highlighted by the *mukokuseki* nature of Japanese animation and computer games ... It is argued that a sense of yearning for Japan is still not aroused in Asia, because what is appreciated, unlike American popular culture, is still not an image or idea of Japan but simply a materialistic consumer commodity.

Iwabuchi 2002

Though insightful, there remains a void as Iwabuchi's argument has not taken into consideration the effects and influence of past colonial experiences on individual Asian countries' identity formation as well as their consumption pattern. Iwabuchi deems Japanese products to be materialistic consumer commodities, but this concept may, in fact, present to us an embodied and imagined global hierarchy. Instead of asserting that Japan may merely be a replacement of western culture and influences to neighboring Asian countries, thereby erasing any traces of Japanese cultural influence or cultural imperialism, it is fundamental to understand and examine how Japan has presented itself to Asian countries as an alternative to western culture. In short, Iwabuchi's argument needs further inspection to better understand the broader Asian socio-historical context.

Furthering Iwabuchi's argument is Harumi Befu's concept of "anonymization," whereby Japan, in the process of production and consumption in foreign countries, is neutralized of positive or negative value (Befu 2003). Befu explains how sushi, karaoke, and anime have become a part of global culture through its creolization process (Befu 2003). Mirroring the rhetoric of American cultural imperialism, Befu overlaps food culture with media culture. Coca Cola, McDonald's hamburgers, Levi's jeans, Disneyland, and Hollywood films become a totalized agglomeration in the discussions of Americanization—similar to what Douglas Kellner describes as a spectacle in which postmodern cultural hybridity and global post-Fordism coexist (Kellner 2003).

What American products represent to the consumer may indeed be a modern lifestyle based upon hypercapitalism. Contrastingly, what sushi represents to the average consumer, especially western consumers, may simply be the notion of a type of expensive cuisine that is not based on any form of mass-production capitalist processes. The following question thus arises: Upon what premises do academics of Japanese popular culture base their totalization of anime and video games with traditional cuisine culture? McDonald's, Coca Cola, and Disney are all American brands that represent a mode of production and distribution network unequal to any other form of mass-production culture around the world. Today, the Japanese anime and video game industries are similarly following these modes of production and distribution through global distribution channels generated by high capitalist venues. If so, where does sushi production stand in this post-Fordist global network? The

216 Kukhee Choo

fervor associated with any form of global Japanese culture may proceed to an over-eagerness to converge those cultures and their global effects into a cluster.

Focusing on the capitalistic tendencies of Japanese popular culture, Anne Allison argues that the globalization of Japanese children's popular characters, such as Pokémon and Sailormoon, interact with capitalism and cultural flows that decentralize US hegemonic media (Allison 2006). Though Allison focuses on the neo-liberal state when explaining the Pokémon phenomena, in Japan's case it is evident that it is not just the neo-liberal capitalists who are guiding these globalization campaigns, but rather, the Keynesian attitude of governments playing "active and interventionist roles in the economy in order to ensure both growth and equity" (Woods 2010). Similarly, Christine Yano explains the global popularity of Hello Kitty through the concept of "pink globalization," where the so-called Japanese trait of cuteness, or *kawaii* as it is known in Japan, has become a global trait (Yano 2006). Yano additionally asserts the following:

> Whereas critics of Euro-American centered globalization have protested the cultural gray-out and buy-out of first McDonald's then Starbucks throughout much of the industrial world, the critics of Japan-based pink globalization express different kinds of concerns. They are not concerned with Kitty overtaking local cultures and economics; Sanrio's pink globalization does not threaten with that level of scale. Rather, Kitty's critics express a more subtle, yet no less emphatic critique. Some sneer that cute may have overstepped its bounds ... that Hello Kitty is no longer just kid stuff ... Others who monster Kitty find cause for alarm in the nature of what Hello Kitty stands for—that is, cute itself.
>
> *Yano 2006*

As Yano points out, unlike Iwabuchi or Befu's claim that Japanese culture is stripped of its identity and origin and becomes anonymous, critics abroad are concerned with the cultural implications of the representation of Japanese popular culture such as Hello Kitty. Yano concludes with a poignant remark that "the imaging of both product and nation-culture go hand in hand, and back and forth in shifting dialectics" (Yano 2006). In other words, Japan as a nation, instead of becoming nation-less, anonymous, and its products being stripped of its national origin and identity may, in fact, be imagined more through its popular cultural products in recent times.

Joseph Straubhaar, expanding on Iwabuchi's argument, asserts that the cultural proximity of Japan to its neighboring countries played an important role in the consumption of Japanese products and popular culture by consumers in the Asian region (Straubhaar 2007). Yet, this view does not adequately explain the explosive popularity of Japanese popular culture outside of the Asian region. Leo Ching further raises critical questions against the idea of Japan's cultural proximity being a factor of the consumption and influence of Japanese popular culture and products. Ching develops upon Arif Dirlik's argument that regionalism is a constituent of globalization, rather than a symptom of its process; it therefore becomes "complicit with the globalist project" (Ching 2001) rather than being an opposing force to globalization. Based upon this view, it can be argued that Japan as a region in the global mapping occurs not because of the process of globalization itself, but by strengthening Japan as a nation-state, Japan becomes a part of the flow that contributes to the formation of globalization. Therefore, strengthening rather than erasing the identity and image of Japanese culture is what makes it global in orientation.

While scholars such as Ulf Hannerz inspect globalization as a positive force where transnational connections create a cross-border global ecumene (Hannerz 1996), Ching's assertion seems to warn against the Utopian optimism that this global navigation will blur temporal and spatial boundaries. Ching further cautions us that "the moment Japan establishes itself as the only non-western colonial power ... the radical discourse of emancipation is inverted and reorganized as a justification for Japanese imperialism in Asia" (Ching 2001). The lingering fear among Asian countries that Japanese popular culture may take over their social values, and, in turn, repeat experiences of past colonialism, does in fact continue to exist (Yoshino 1999).

In short, the debate on globalization's cultural impact on local cultures is multifaceted and complex. In the case of Japan, being caught between the nexus of east versus west has created various tensions between Japan and the Western powers, in addition to tensions between Japan and neighboring Asian countries. For western nations, Japan becomes feared as an opposing and prominent force that may invade the western economies; Japan is also feared as a country that may hinder the process of decolonization of Japanese culture for Japan's former colonies. Examining the Japanese government's support and promotion of transnational popular culture, or promotion of its Content industry abroad, will ultimately provide a better understanding of how Japan has embraced the western capitalist mode of globalization in order to globalize, brand, and market its national popular culture.

The culturalization of commodities

In 2001, the annual profits generated from the Japanese Content industry was estimated at ¥11 trillion, only ¥2 trillion less than Japan's largest automobile company, Toyota's revenue that year. In the years of 2004 and 2005, the net profit of Toyota was US$15 billion and US$10 billion respectively. During this same period, the Japanese government envisioned their Content industry reigning in an annual revenue of ¥17 trillion by 2010 (METI, Strategies for Creating New Industries Report, May 2004; Table 12.1), showing the high expectations that the government had for the Content industry. Even after Japanese DVD sales in the US market declined over the course of the mid-2000s and the estimated annual revenue of the Content industry was ¥14 trillion, high expectations of the Content industry has not waned. By 2020, the Japanese government hopes the Content industry will earn ¥20 trillion annually (METI, Content Industry Development Research Group Report, May 2010).

218 Kukhee Choo

TABLE 12.1 Creating the seven new strategic industries for the twenty-first century

Seven new strategic industries	Estimated turnover by 2010*
Business support services (human resources)	107
Environment and energy-related appliances and services (promotes research)	78
Health and welfare-related appliances and services	75
Information home appliances	18
Content: stimulating international advancement	17
Robotics	2
Fuel cells	1

Source: METI, Strategies for Creating New Industries Report, May 2004
* Units in ¥ trillion

The Japanese government's optimism in developing and strengthening their Content industry was followed by a full-fledged effort to revamp Japan's national image under logo of "Cool Japan," when they passed the Content Industry Promotion Bill in 2004. With the boundaries of economic and cultural policies becoming blurred, Japan began embracing forms of popular culture that were once regarded as mediocre, over the historically favored and dominant traditional high arts culture (Nakamura and Onouchi 2006). The White Papers written throughout the twentieth century by the Ministry of Education, Culture, Sports, Science and Technology (MEXT) never declared or recognized Japanese anime or manga as part of the high arts culture; Kabuki theater, sumo wrestling, and traditional Japanese tea ceremonies prevailed and dominated the cultural scene. A number of scholars, mostly western, oftentimes analyze the aesthetics of anime and manga by linking their historical lineage to the traditional high arts culture; nevertheless, anime, manga, and video games have historically been viewed as vulgar and childish without qualities pertaining to the high arts culture (Nakamura and Onouchi 2006). MEXT's White Paper in 2000, however, officially oversaw government recognition of Japanese anime and manga as integral parts in Japanese traditional arts (MEXT White Paper, November 2000). Similar to George Yudice's notion of "culturization of economy" (Yudice 2003), the potential for Japanese popular media to become an important means of international communication and of channels of international cultural flow in today's information age further encouraged the Japanese government to elevate the status of privatized commercial commodities such as anime and manga to be labeled as part of the high arts culture, which I define as the process of "culturization of commodities".

The Japanese government's sudden strategic move to incorporate anime and manga under MEXT's cultural umbrella, which administrates cultural promotion domestically and abroad, is indicative of how the government is not only viewing the Content industry as potentially lucrative for the economy, but also as a powerful means to improve its national image in foreign, particularly western, eyes. To truly understand the Japanese government's multifarious approach towards popular media, which is historically unprecedented in its scope and velocity, it is important to discern how the promotion of the Content industry as culture masks the state's true motivation—namely, long-term economic incentives. Economic considerations for popular culture—the potential for the Japanese Content industry to become a lucrative commodity emerged only after J-pop (Japanese popular music), J-dorama (popular television dramas), manga, and anime in the 1990s gained region-wide acceptance throughout Asia. This extensive popularity of Japanese media in the Asian region was viewed as an important force that challenged the US-centric global media, resulting in a recentralization of global media flows in the region (Iwabuchi 2002; Befu 2003). Throughout the rest of the world, the popularity of Japanese popular culture spread and became global; Japanese popular culture and its market grew steadily from the early 1990s onwards and exploded into one of the largest conceivable markets for the Japanese economy.

The Japanese government began paying greater attention to the Japanese anime industries only after the explosive popularity of anime was evident; anime such as Sailormoon and Pokémon fared extremely well in US markets during the 1990s. The July 2001 METI White Paper further examines the successes of Pokémon and lists it as an exemplary case study for Japan's anime business. Moreover, major media companies in the US are now also paying attention to the successes of Pokémon. These aforementioned factors are indicative of the Japanese government's main motivations behind supporting the anime industry: the economic potential of the industry as well as the looming gaze and presence of the American market. Even though, since the 1960s, a sizable amount of syndicated television anime had been exported to Asian, South American, and European markets, anime was long considered a mere locus of transnational children's programs until the 1990s. Additionally, game consoles such as Nintendo and Sega were considered as simple home entertainment consoles for children at most. By the late 1990s, however, video game sales in the American market alone surpassed both the Asian and European markets combined (METI, Japan's Video Game Industry Report, May 2004).[1] The US market for anime and video games was not only important for its significant gross revenue but also, paradoxically, as one anime company CEO asserts, it was the only market that the Japanese anime industry, for over 30 years, could not successfully penetrate. Thus, the US market growth in the 1990s of the consumption of anime and video games provided much anticipation for Japanese policymakers.

Economic motivations were therefore already palpable during the early years of governmental planning for promoting the Content industry. In order to stimulate Japan's Content industry, METI sponsored various events throughout the years: the Tokyo Game Show since 1999, Tokyo International Anime Fair from 2002, and the Digital Games Research Association Conference from 2003. Currently, the largest

220 Kukhee Choo

event is the Japan International Contents Festival, also known as CoFesta, which has been held since 2007. Nevertheless, the Japanese government was prompted to encompass broader cultural fields, such as fashion and food under the national cultural umbrella when data from the mid-2000s showed an ebbing of anime DVD sales in the US, largely in part due to illegal internet downloading.[2]

Currently, popular commodities such as anime, manga, video games, television dramas, popular music, and films as well as food culture have been included in the official rhetoric of Japanese culture; each independent cultural field is compressed and presented under the name and totalized banner of Cool Japan. This means that global consumption of Japanese culture through the Content industry is fundamentally linked to the yearning for a Japanese lifestyle that can only be satiated through the consumption of anything that is associated with preconceived notions of what is "Japanese." In turn, Japan's national branding and marketing, which are manifested through the culturization of its commodities, have heavily focused on the national image of Japan. Therefore, first anime and manga, and progressively, fashion and entertainment icons have become the governmental focus in promoting Japanese culture overseas. To summarize, the Content industry that the government has focused on provokes in foreigners imagery of what is perceived as Japanese, and, in turn, stimulates global imagination of and yearning for Japan. Undeniably, this means that contemporary Japanese popular culture is filled with stereotypical images of their nation and Japanese cultural products are easily identifiable as Japanese; in other words, contemporary Japanese popular culture is "nation-full" instead of "nation-less."

Globalization of anime

Recent anime characters such as the ninja in 2002's Naruto and the samurai in 2004's Bleach have easily been identifiable as Japanese; however, early Japanese anime was arguably erased of any links and traces to Japan. The globalization of anime is not a recent phenomenon—the anime industry has, in fact, since the 1960s, been an important part of the global media flow. The recent surge in worldwide popularity of Japanese media, entertainment, and culture is based on three factors: first and most importantly, the rapid diffusion of television; second, the *mukokuseki* nature of early Japanese anime; and, third, the recent and rapid development and popular use of the internet. In order to understand how Japanese anime has integrated into international television markets, it is first imperative to comprehend the processes television went through to become the dominant medium throughout the world. Japan actually played an integral role in early television programming, providing cheap filler programs since the 1960s to the USA, as well as countries throughout Europe and Asia.

The advent of television has undeniably changed not only mass media topology, but also has fundamentally influenced economies throughout the world. For example, as Thomas Schatz summarizes, television in the US "quickly transformed the American media landscape" (Schatz 1997) which resulted in the decline of the old Hollywood system during the 1950s. As box office sales declined, film studios started to produce more features for television programming. With the increase of television stations throughout the US, acquiring programs "to feed TV's voracious appetite for programming" (Schatz 1997) was increasingly in demand. This massive void and frenzy to find programs to fill the empty time slots between television programs occurred not only in America, but also in virtually all other countries of the world; in turn, production and consumption of many other countries' products were stimulated. Most of the developing countries of the 1950s and 1960s therefore viewed television as an essential economic strategy (Thomas 2006).

The Japanese anime industry quickly seized upon this opportunity and produced programs, satisfying their own national appetite for television programming in addition to the demands of the global television market. In the beginning, however, Japanese animation was produced according to the simple equation of supply and demand, for television stations to attract sponsors, and also found attractiveness in being a package deal, where reruns and syndication were made easy (Tada 2002). By the early 1970s, the Japanese anime industry became a key producer for children's programming,[3] when they were in the business of exporting their programming at low costs to countries such as the US, Brazil, France, Italy, and South Korea. This perhaps explains why scholarly research on the Japanese anime industry has been delayed. Not only was anime considered a less than desirable aspect of Japanese popular culture but, also, there was a deep-rooted stigma of anime as only related to children's media; therefore, less scholarly study and academic attention was given to the subject in the context of the global media landscape. As Buckingham succinctly puts it, the "study of the institutional context of children's television production has been a relatively marginal concern within communications research generally" (Buckingham 2005).

As aforementioned, another important factor contributing to the global diffusion and dissemination of Japanese anime since the 1960s is the fact that early Japanese anime was not distinctively tied to its country of origin—it had a *mukokuseki* aspect, as Iwabuchi would put it. Therefore, children in various countries that Japan had exported their anime to had fundamentally absorbed Japanese anime and regarded it as their own media culture. Subsequently, the countries in the Asian region had no reservations or animosity towards anime's Japanese origin. As an "odorless" medium (Iwabuchi 2002), early Japanese anime was able to navigate easily through various countries' television programming. Even as early as 1964, Japanese newspapers wrote articles on how Japanese animation was popular abroad.[4] Even though Japanese anime did not generate significant financial revenue during this time, it was fundamentally and steadily integrated into the global media landscape.

One primary example is South Korea. Being the major outsourcing country to many Japanese anime production companies since the 1960s, many of the titles produced in Japan were therefore simultaneously broadcast in South Korea, and South Korean children grew up absorbing these programs as part of their national (television) culture. Though after World War II, the South Korean government officially banned Japanese culture from being imported into the country, there were, nevertheless, unofficial backdoors that allowed various forms of Japanese culture such as music, animation, and print material, including comic books, to enter the South Korean market (Otmazgin 2005; Choo 2009). Once these Japanese products entered South Korea, book publishers and broadcast stations would make the Japanese elements invisible in this media in order to evade governmental restrictions. In comic books, Japanese outfits were redrawn, and original Japanese text was pasted over with Korean dialogue. In animated TV programs, Japanese speech would be dubbed and voiced-over in Korean, and the theme songs kept their original tune and melody, but was replaced with Korean words.

South Korea's leading daily newspaper, *The Chosun Ilbo*, reported on July 28, 1998 about a significant soccer match between South Korea and Japan held in South Korea that year. The newspaper reported that during this soccer match, Japanese supporters attending the game were baffled to hear the South Koreans rooting on their national team by singing the theme song of a Japanese anime production, *Mazinga Z*. The Japanese supporters countered the Korean cheering by singing the theme song in its original Japanese form. South Korean media immediately rushed to criticize the ignorance of the South Korean soccer fans for singing a song that originated from the rival team's country. Additionally, numerous entries in web-based blogs surfaced, lamenting the lingering presence of Japanese culture due to its past colonial rule over Korea. Many South Koreans used the slang term *jjok palida*, or "losing face," to describe this incident. This soccer match incident is a clear demonstration of the *mukokuseki* nature of Japanese anime, and how it was internalized into South Korean culture. What is evidently problematic from this incident, for both the South Korean media and Japanese soccer fans, is their lack of critical understanding of how global media flow functions within a culture. Although US media imperialism has been a dominant discourse during the 1980s and 1990s, the advent of the concept of globalization has stimulated debates that illustrate the complexity of how media and culture navigate through the global ecumene (Hannerz 1996).

As mentioned previously, Iwabuchi furthered Straubhaar's notion of cultural proximity (Straubhaar 1991) and claimed that Japanese culture's popularity in Asia during the 1990s was the result of a narrowed temporal lag between Japan and Asia in terms of modernity, which then created a spatial affiliation by the latter (Iwabuchi 2002). Yet, Iwabuchi's speculation on the Asian desire to consume Japanese popular culture as a regional process of modernization does not adequately explain the popularity and high consumption of Japanese anime in the west throughout that same time period. Nissim Otmazgin asserts that the convergence of regional markets and communities in Asia created platforms that allowed regional consumers and producers to access the same forms of popular culture (Otmazgin 2008). Otmazgin goes beyond the view that deems the consumption of Japanese popular culture in Asia as a form of globalization that positions the region as both "receiver and indigenizer" *vis-a-vis* Japan that is "both indigenizer and mediator to the *global*," and instead argues that "intra-regional relations shape the circulation and consumption of cultural products" (Otmazgin 2008). In short, local regions become equal players in disseminating Japanese popular culture. Otmazgin's view perhaps better explains how the early *mukokuseki* anime was distributed throughout various regional markets, particularly beyond Asian markets, without even being considered to be receivers of Japan's globalization.

Asides from the global distribution of television, and the *mukokuseki* nature of early anime, the most recent and perhaps most influential factor in promoting Japanese anime is the global advent and dissemination of the internet during the twentieth century. Unlike traditional television programs or movies, technologies today have allowed contemporary anime to be able to be distributed, transmitted, and viewed instantaneously, regardless of one's location. This technological revolution in communications media has undeniably contributed greatly to the worldwide dissemination of Japanese anime. With the development of the network society and digital media technology, information and entertainment is transmitted quickly across borders, creating what Appadurai defines as the cultural hybridity of mediascapes (Appadurai 1996).

Anime now functions within mediascapes, where national boundaries are crossed and cultural meanings are mediated and negotiated. From this perspective, the *Mazinga Z* song that the South Koreans sang fundamentally cannot be viewed as the same *Mazinga Z* that the Japanese fans sang; it was not only sung in different languages, but also has been internalized differently into each respective culture. Through understanding the multi-layered and complex nature of cultures, perhaps we will be able to see how the broadcast of early Japanese anime in various countries globally led to the assimilation and internalization of anime into each country's local media culture. Given the diverse interpretations and scopes of negotiation across cultures, how can these hybrid global transactions be understood in the context of the twenty-first century when the Japanese government is attempting to brand anime as fundamentally and essentially Japanese?

Race to build culture industries

Throughout its history, independent of and alienated from governmental cultural policies, the Japanese animation industry existed as an exclusive business that self-sufficiently navigated throughout foreign territories; it never came by significant governmental support in the early days. Moreover, even though Japanese anime had been globally distributed and consumed since the 1960s, it historically has not been a major avenue of global cultural exchange or participatory in global flows of cultural products between nations. Only at the turn of the twenty-first century did the Japanese government embark on a full revamp of Japan's national image through popular culture. One governmental ministry, MEXT, became the overseer of ensuring anime was known as a fundamental part in traditional Japanese culture, promoting anime under the banner of Cool Japan. Another governmental ministry, METI, became the analyzer of global business trends in regard to anime, hoping to ultimately maximize Japan's own lucrative market share. According to David Throsby, in order for art and culture to be considered important in policy terms, economists establish economic credentials of art and culture by cultivating and shaping an image of it as a viable industry (Throsby 2001). By contrast, however, the Japanese government is promoting their anime industry as art, in order to ensure anime is taken seriously abroad.[5] Though government reports in the early 2000s emphasized the importance of anime succeeding economically abroad under the Cool Japan slogan, there has been a slow transition towards marketing Japan's national image through Japanese anime. Additionally, governmental interest in the potential to increase positive foreign sentiment towards Japan as a contingent effect of popular culture surfaced before the passing of the 2004 Content Industry Promotion Bill. A Japanese government report in 2003, for example, illustrates changes in attitude among South Korean students who were exposed and listened to popular Japanese music over a control group who only listened to popular western music (METI, Effects on the Content Industry Global Distribution Report, April 2003). According to the report, there was a notable increase in leniency towards Japan among the students who listened to popular Japanese music; their attitudes moved towards fully accepting Japan's apology to Korea for its colonial misconducts. The control group students who were exposed to popular western music, however, were steadfast on their opinion that Japan's apology was not enough. This report is significant in understanding the undeniable correlation between popular culture and national image. It is unprecedented in Japanese history for its government to further economic or cultural policies that implement image-centered strategies in order to bolster the economy. Furthermore, though the Japanese government's support towards potential economically beneficial markets is not new, what differs from past bubble-era governmental policies is the process of converging boundaries of economic and cultural policies.

For over a century, cultural policies in Japan fell under the responsibility of MEXT, and economic policies were managed by METI. During Japan's heights of economic success during the 1980s, the consumer products labeled "made in Japan" did not cross over to the cultural realm, as they were still limited to the tangible material-based industries such as automobiles and electronics. When Japanese popular culture in the forms of J-pop, J-dorama, manga, and anime proliferated throughout Asian markets during the 1990s, it was deemed unworthy for cultural promotion and the revenue generated was not significant enough for an economic push by the government. With the exception of live-action films, the Japanese government until the last years of the twentieth century neglected all the media industries currently included in the Content industry.

South Korea's passing of the Culture Industry Promotion Law in 1999 provided the most likely impetus in pushing the Japanese government to examine their own (digital) media industries. It has also been argued that Japan's focus on soft power has been motivated by the rise of the Chinese market economy (Lam 2007: 352). However, various Japanese government reports and Diet proceedings indicate South Korea as the primary motivating factor for Japan's concentration on building up their soft power. After Kim Dae-jung, the former South Korean president in 1999 proclaimed himself as *Munhwa Daetongryeong*, or the "culture president," he, in turn, initiated massive financial support and implemented various policies to build up the South Korean culture and digital media industries.[6] The involved industries supported by the government included the production of live-action films, animation, music, and video games. By the turn of the century, South Korea saw a sudden surge of consumption of their popular culture in various Asian countries, resulting in what is known as Hanryu, or the "Korean wave."

Additionally, in the various interviews conducted for this study, a handful of Japanese government officials admitted that South Korea's new policies towards their cultural media industries played a formative role in changes to Japanese policies. Correspondingly, when the South Korean government was in support of their live-action film industry, Japan decided instead to aim for its most competitive media in the global market: the anime and video game industries.[7] Moreover, unlike South Korea, whose nation-wide project involves direct financial support from the government on production,[8] Japan's anti-monopoly law prevents the government from directly funding their national industries. With only a few grants existing in Japan for anime production that is theatrically released, industry personnel are quick to point out the national government's contradictions in wanting to eagerly promote the anime industry. The awareness of the collaboration between the national government and film industries in South Korea has in turn created disputes and tension between Japan's national government and anime industry; some Japanese anime companies have even sought out cooperation and collaboration abroad in order to go beyond the governmentality of Cool Japan. This ultimately captures the complex dynamic of industry, national government and globalization; and the effects it has on governments through seeking alternatives in global networks and connections.

The challenge of globalization or "Japanization"

Even though earlier globalization of Japanese popular culture such as anime may have been considered to have a *mukokuseki* aspect, the current Japanese government promotion of their Cool Japan project leaves no room for the global audience to ponder upon whether anime is Japanese or not. As evident in how manga and anime have been absorbed into the broader sphere of traditional cultures by the Japanese government, or what Michal Daliot-Bul refers to as a neo-Japonesque strategy (Daliot-Bul 2009), Japanese popular culture in the global market can no longer be viewed as detached from a national image.

Once a national image is associated to a product, it may be hard to dissociate it from existing impressions, both positive and negative, of the country of origin. In a 1991 study by Laura Hein, the long-stemming, stereotypical notion of what was perceived as Japanese among American college students was analyzed. What Hein found was that students would "operate out of a paradigm that subtly reshapes the historical material into something of their own making," which stems from the western tradition of viewing Japan as an "exotic Oriental land" (Hein 1991). However, the students' view of Japanese tradition was very positive (Hein 1991). This may explain the Japanese government's motivation to promote anime and manga as part of traditional arts. Moreover, even though there are no governmental interventions regarding anime and manga production, the global market demand has led to an increased production of narratives and images that employ Japanese traditions over the popular science fiction narratives that dominated over previous decades.[9]

Yet, unlike the positive sentiment displayed towards Japan in Hein's study, negative images of Japan associated to World War II in Western media seem to persist even in the twenty-first century. These are evident in George W. Bush's rhetoric that tied Japan's bombing of Pearl Harbor to the September 11 attacks on the World Trade Center[10] and a *South Park* animation parody on Pokémon's popularity, in which a Japanese toy character named Chimpokomon (a Japanese reference to male genitals) turns out to be brainwashing American children to bomb Pearl Harbor for a Japanese emperor named Hirohito. Here, we witness the deep-rooted bias against Japan in the United States manifesting itself in utmost prejudiced depictions. Younger audiences of Japanese popular culture in the US such as children and young adolescents may not yet have the necessary media literacy or self-reflexivity to examine their own possible biases when consuming Japanese products.

The overall approach on analyzing globalization, culture, economy and policies has often focused on the hybridizing attributes of media and culture.[11] What is more, most of the studies done on economic policies and culture have been within the boundaries of the nation state. Colin Hines notes that either nation states or regional grouping of nation states react to globalization through the process of localization, which "reverses the trend of globalization by discriminating in favor of the local" (Hines 2000). The contemporary Asian governments, including Japan, have been taking on the form of Asian localization through strengthening policies on popular culture in a regional domino-effect development. After the South Korean government initiated its governmental project to create a digital content country in 1999, the Japanese government followed with the Content Industry Promotion Policy in 2004 and, currently, China has announced its national support towards their animation industry. In short, there appears a strong tendency of policy and culture industry convergence within Asia in relation to the merging economic, political, and cultural dimensions of globalization.

On the relationship between Asia and globalization, in fact, Peter Katzenstein distinguishes time and space transcending globalization from internationalization, which "reaffirm nation-states as the basic actors in the international system" (Katzenstein 2005). He further argues that the Asian region has repeated the process of globalization and internationalization mostly in relation to the "American imperium" (Katzenstein 2005). Borrowing Katzenstein's view, the current Japanese government's global promotion policy of the Content industry can be construed as a result of the process of Japanese popular culture's globalization, countered by a process of internationalization of politics.

This process may have instigated Japan, and perhaps other Asian countries also, to schematize state polices to support and promote their industries that are centered within their territorial nation-states. Japan appears as moving quickly toward an internationalization of state policies through the support of the Content industry. Strengthening Japan's identity upon a globalized product such as anime may be an indication how the Japanese government's attempt to play the role of a global actor may in fact be restricted through the local mindset of internationalization policies. Nevertheless, the emphasis on nation-state through Japan's Content industry support is believed to be directly linked to the notion of soft power, where the identity of the nation-state cannot be separated from the quest for power in the global image politics.

Notes

1 The crossover production of anime and video games is considered to be a "bundle content," also referred to as "synergy" by the Japanese government. Bundle content are given a high priority as is evident in current government promotions, which has mostly been focusing on promoting anime, manga, and video games together.
2 At the March 2008 Tokyo Anime Fair, there were various symposiums analyzing the decline of anime DVD sales in the United States.
3 Anime produced during the 1960s were mainly targeted at children (Kanayama and Kanayama 2005: 153).
4 Astro Boy, or Tetsuwan Atom, was imported by NBC in the US in 1964, and was aired throughout the country via 28 local NBC network stations (Kusanagi 2003: 5).
5 However, the approach by METI towards the anime industry does fall under Throsby's notion of how art and culture become elevated into an industry and pushes for policy changes.
6 The Korean Culture Industry Promotion Law, Law No. 5927, was promulgated on February 8, 1999, under the new government.
7 Even though the live-action film industry is part of Japan's Content industry, the lack of attention by the Japanese government towards the film industry has perplexed Japan film scholars, who question the effectiveness of the Content Industry Promotion Law. However, in my interviews with government officials, they stated that concentration on anime and video games is viewed as the most viable option since, they believe, Japanese live-actions films cannot be as successful as Hollywood films.
8 In 1999, the South Korean government set a goal to provide approximately 500 billion won (US$500 million) to their digital media industry, which was increased to 800 billion won (US$800 million) in 2001 (Foreign Content Industry Policy Report, May 2003).
9 Science fiction anime that features robots, also known as mecha, has dominated the industry from the 1960s to the 1990s. Popular titles include Astro Boy, Gigantor, Gundam, and Neon Genesis Evangelion. Many western anime scholars focus on this genre; examples can be found in the anime journal *Mechademia*, published by the University of Minnesota Press.
10 The former President George W. Bush appeared on the National Geographic Channel documentary "George W. Bush: The 9/11 Interview" aired on August 28, 2011. In this documentary, Bush talks about his experience following the September 11, 2001 attacks on the World Trade Center and states that September 11 will be marked on calendars like Pearl Habor Day.
11 However, there is still much room left for anime policy studies in relation to broadcasting.

References

Allison, A. (2006) *Millennial Monsters: Japanese Toys and the Global Imagination*, California: University of California Press.

Anderson, M. (2009) *Japan and the Specter of Imperialism*, New York: Palgrave Macmillan.

Appadurai, A. (1996) *Modernity at Large: Cultural Dimensions of Globalization*, Minneapolis: University of Minnesota Press.

Befu, H. (2003) "Globalization Theory from the Bottom Up: Japan's Contribution," *Japanese Studies*, 23: 3–22.

Bosche, M. (1996) "Signes D'orient dans la Vie Quotidienne: L'Invisible Colonisation Japonaise," *Le Monde Diplomatique*, November. Online. Available at: http://www.monde-diplomatique.fr/1996/11/BOSCHE/7416.

Buckingham, D. (2005) "A Special Audience? Children and Television," in J. Wasko (ed.) *A Companion to Television*, Oxford: Blackwell.

Ching, L. (2000) "Globalizing the Regional, Regionalizing the Global: Mass Culture and Asianism in the Age of Late Capital," *Public Culture*, 12: 233–257.

Ching, L. (2001) *Becoming Japanese: Colonial Taiwan and the Politics of Identity Formation*, California: University of California Press.

Choo, K. (2009) "Korean Female Comic Book Artists' Resistance and Empowerment: In Relation to Japanese Girls' Comic Book Culture," in T. Tanigawa and H. Haguchi (eds) *Border-Crossing Popular Culture: From Li Xianglan to Tackey*, Tokyo: Seikyusha Library Series.

Daliot-Bul, M. (2009) "Japan Brand Strategy: The Taming of Cool Japan and the Challenges of Cultural Planning in a Postmodern Age," *Social Science Japan Journal*, 12: 247–266.

Hannerz, U. (1996) *Transnational Connections: Culture, People, Places*, London: Routledge.

Hein, L.E. (1991) "Contemporary Images of Japan: My Students as Texts, My Students as Readers," *The Pacific Historical Review*, 60: 361–383.

Hines, C. (2000) *Localization: A Global Manifesto*. London & Sterling: Earthscan Publications Ltd.

Iwabuchi, K. (2002) *Recentering Globalization: Japanese Culture and Transnationalism*, Durham, NC: Duke University Press.

Kanayama, T. and Kanayama, T. (2005) "Japan," in A. Cooper-Chen (ed.) *Global Entertainment Media: Content, Audiences, Issues*, New Jersey: Lawrence Erlbaum Associates.

Katzenstein, P.J. (2005) *A World of Regions: Asia and Europe in the American Imperium*. New York: Cornell University Press.

Kellner, D. (2003) *Media Spectacle*, New York: Routledge.

Kelts, R. (2007) *Japanimerica: How Japanese Pop Culture has Invaded the US*, New York: Palgrave Macmillan.

Kusanagi, S. (2003) *How Japan Anime Has Been Viewed in America*, Tokyo: Tokuma Shinsho.

Lam, P.E. (2007) "Japan's Quest for Soft Power: Attraction and Limitation," *East Asia*, 24: 349–363.

McGray, D. (2002) "Japan's Gross National Cool," *Foreign Policy*, 130: 44–54.

Ministry of Economy, Trade and Industry (2001) *White Paper*, July.

Ministry of Economy, Trade and Industry (2003) *Effects on the Content Industry Global Distribution Report*, April.

Ministry of Economy, Trade and Industry (2003) *Foreign Content Industry Policy Report*, May.

Ministry of Economy, Trade and Industry (2004) *Japan's Video Game Industry Report*, May.

Ministry of Economy, Trade and Industry (2004) *Strategies for Creating New Industries Report*, May.

Ministry of Economy, Trade and Industry (2010) *Content Industry Development Research Group Report*, May.

Ministry of Education, Culture, Sports, Science and Technology (2000) *White Paper*, November.

Nakamura, I. and Onouchi, M. (2006) *Japan's Pop Power*, Tokyo: Nihon Keizai Shinbunsha.

Napier, S.J. (2005) *Anime from Akira to Howl's Moving Castle: Experiencing Contemporary Japanese Animation*, New York: Palgrave Macmillan.

Nye, J. (2004) *Soft Power: The Means to Success in World Politics*, New York: Public Affairs.

Otmazgin, N.K. (2005) "Cultural Commodities and Regionalization in East Asia," *Contemporary Southeast Asia*, 27: 499–523.

Otmazgin, N.K. (2008) "Japanese Popular Culture in East and Southeast Asia: Time for a Regional Paradigm?" *Japan Focus*. Online. Available at: http://www.japanfocus.org/-Nissim_Kadosh-Otmazgin/2660.

Schatz, T. (1997) "The Return of the Hollywood Studio System," in E. Barnouw (ed.) *Conglomerates and the Media*, New York: The New Press.

Straubhaar, J.D. (1991) "Beyond Media Imperialism: Asymmetrical Interdependence and Cultural Proximity," *Critical Studies in Mass Communication*, 8: 39–59.

Straubhaar, J.D. (2007) *World Television: From Global to Local*, Los Angeles, CA: Sage Publications.

Tada, M. (2002) *This is Anime Business*, Tokyo: Kosaido.

Thomas, A.O. (2006) *Transnational Media and Contoured Markets: Redefining Asian Television and Advertising*, New Delhi: Sage Publications.

Throsby, D. (2001) *Economics and Culture*, Cambridge: Cambridge University Press.

Woods, N. (2001) "International Political Economy in an Age of Globalization," in J. Baylis and S. Smith (eds) *The Globalization of World Politics: An Introduction to International Relations*, New York: Oxford University Press.

Woods, N. (2010) "International Political Economy in an Age of Globalization," in J. Baylis, S. Smith and P. Owens (eds) The Globalization of World Politics: An Introduction to International Relations, New York: Oxford University Press.

Yano, C.R. (2006) "Monstering the Japanese Cute: Pink Globalization and its Critics Abroad," in W. Tsutsui and M. Ito (eds) *In Godzilla's Footsteps*, New York: Palgrave Macmillan.

Yoshino, K. (1999) *Consuming Ethnicity and Nationalism: Asian Experiences*, Hawaii: University of Hawaii Press.

Yudice, G. (2003) *The Expediency of Culture*, Durham, NC: Duke University Press.

PART IV

China as a rising market

Cultural antagonism and globalization

13

CHINA'S NEW CREATIVE STRATEGY
The utilization of cultural soft power and new markets

Michael Keane and Bonnie Rui Liu

Introduction

In many respects, the first decade of the new millennium was one of the most open periods in the history of modern China. While far from the heady enthusiasm of the pre-Communist era, particularly the New Culture Movement (from around 1915 to 1930), during which foreign ideas were introduced to and integrated with indigenous ideas, the cultural scene in China was once again reinvigorated by international influences. Driven by the realization that culture can be converted into capital, the current ruling regime is endeavouring to position China as both an innovative and a creative nation (Keane 2007). Moreover, the regime has sensed that the recent fascination with Korean popular culture (often referred to as "hanliu," or the "Korean wave"), has lost some of its potency; in turn, cultural policy makers are hoping that the next cultural wave will be one from China—one that will regain China's status as the cultural core of Asia.

In this chapter, we will argue that Chinese media producers are beginning to come to terms with the need for innovation and evolution through incorporating lessons from international companies. The emergence of an independent sphere of production, the clustering of businesses in creative parks, and an increased desire to engage in co-productions are visible signs of a maturing industry. This image differs from the mainstream political economy of the media tradition. At the end of the 1990s, a "structures of domination" paradigm was indisputably the default setting in explaining how media conglomerates such as News Corporation and Time Warner were positioning themselves in order to consolidate their interests in China and form alliances with major domestic broadcasting institutions. Furthermore, these processes fundamentally weakened China's traditional culture and reinforced a western consumerist ethos.

Of course, this is an oversimplification of what is a mature research tradition. Many scholars of recent times, studying the political economy of media, have recognized the limitations of a rigid Marxist framework; it is one that, according to Mark Poster, "leads them to emphasise the control of all planetary media by capitalist corporations" (Poster 2008). This chapter hopes to emphasize that there has been a gradual transformation of the statist model to a much different kind of commercial model.[1] During the 1990s and particularly since 2004, the production landscape in China has changed. Large broadcasters have consolidated in major cities such as Shanghai and Beijing, but the international broadcasters have ultimately remained on the outside.

More significantly, it is evident that local independent companies have proliferated in film, television, documentary production, in post-production, as well as animation, advertising services, multimedia, and mobile content. Regional policies have been of assistance in supporting the emergence of innovative (small and medium) enterprises linking industries such as design, marketing, and distribution. In many instances, these enterprises are evolving with greater degrees of autonomy than has previously been allowed. A different kind of analysis is therefore needed, one that takes into account the role of independent production and the types of relationships that have been forged between independent companies and international corporations. In short, the connections that we will identify have more to do with internationals facilitating the professionalization of China's media industries, rather than exploiting or manipulating these industries.

We must begin, first, by identifying a landmark position—the admission on the part of China's senior cultural officials that China's media industries were underperforming in comparison with neighbouring countries and nations that were exporting to China. This so-called "cultural trade deficit crisis" provided the impetus for a series of new industry policies and initiatives to stimulate content production and to seek out regional and international markets. At the same time, however, a more positive outlook was emerging, one that contrasted with the suggested cultural crisis. An international study, the UNCTAD *Creative Economy Report* (2008), suggested that China was, in fact, a world leader in the export of cultural goods. We provide comparative data from this report as well as data compiled from the National Bureau of Statistics, the State Administration of Radio, Film and TV (SARFT), and independent market research. It is evident that conclusions regarding the vitality of China's media and cultural industries appear to be contradictory. What then, is the true story behind China's media and cultural industries?

In the second section of this chapter, we will look at the development of independent media in China over the past several years and, subsequently, identify the policy environment that has turned factories and free trade areas into creative clusters. Among the companies that now congregate in these clusters, we see a greater degree of international collaboration. We will pose the question, what are the benefits of such collaboration for Chinese media businesses? Finally, we provide examples of co-production and creative fusion in popular culture, specifically in television and animation.

Anticipating a more open China

In 1993 when China was advancing its claims to host the 2000 Olympic Games, the key slogan of the country was, "a more open China looks forward to the 2000 Olympics." However, this openness that the state talked of was merely a guise. Consequently, the rest of the world was not convinced by this talk and Sydney won the right to host the 2000 Olympic Games. China's "openness" was put on hold.

During the 1990s, China's television and publishing sectors began inching slowly towards commercialization. However, the focus on consolidating the domestic market, in particular the formation of media groups, and restrictions on co-productions constrained the development of innovative content. International sales of programs to foreign broadcasters were rare, apart from the occasional historical television drama, the most notable being *The Romance of the Three Kingdoms* in 1995 (Keane *et al.* 2008; Zhu 2009). As many authors have shown, most Chinese television exports found their way into video stores operated in overseas Chinese communities (Sinclair *et al.* 2000; Curtin 2007; Lee 2009). China's cultural scene was not particularly open either; in the 1990s, most international features regarding Chinese culture concerned the state's repressive measures to suppress the people's freedom of expression.

By the time the 2008 Olympic Games took place in Beijing, there were observable noteworthy liberalizations, culturally speaking. Visual artists were reinstalled as productive members of society; they were encouraged to contribute to wealth creation by selling their art in international markets and by attracting tourists into the many art zones that now exist in Chinese cities. The 798 Art District at Dashanzi in Beijing received a governmental makeover which subsequently refashioned it into a commercial art district—an officially managed and sanitized network of art galleries and coffee shops, depending on one's perspective on such post-industrial gentrification processes (Keane 2009a). The strategy of implementing creative clusters in Chinese cities once again reinforced the socialist dictum of collective endeavour. Meanwhile, design had become the driver of city renewal, epitomized by iconic symbols of modernity—in particular, the cityscapes of Beijing and Shanghai.

While culture has become a resource and even an industry for China, many gaps remain in the current blueprint for a more open and creative China. What is seen in China's audio–visual industries today (the main focus for this chapter) is a lack of reward for original content, along with the fear of failure among producers. This is compounded by a long legacy of state intervention in the audio–visual industries. Suffice to say, the challenging balancing act between satisfying propaganda officials and satisfying audiences, all the while creating profit, has done little to produce a creative management culture in China.

For media producers, the saying, "content is king," takes on a different meaning in China. Good content is not necessarily that which excites and stimulates audiences; good content must meet the requirements of state policy. Of course, as the Chinese media market matures, as competition increases between provincial

236 Michael Keane and Bonnie Rui Liu

and city broadcasters, and as more independents emerge to service the industry, the search for content that has the potential to become a commercial hit increases. Politically, however, producers and investors continue to play it safe. Compare this with the corporate culture of American television where, according to Caldwell management, "rarely strong arms uniformity upon executives, but rather exploits career contestation within the institution for organizational efficiency" (Caldwell 2008). By comparison, the American/Hollywood model is one where failure to be creative can lead to the "revolving door" for executives; in the USA, career volatility is expected.

In the following analysis of China's creative strategy, we seek to create an understanding of and engagement with the concept of production culture in Chinese audio-visual media. To Caldwell, production culture has a plural and generic meaning; it is a collective of discrete cultures and subcultures. Likewise, Caldwell argues that the term "industry," which is often used loosely by practitioners and academics alike, is heterogeneous. In China, the term industry is increasingly heterogeneous—it is comprised of subsectors, large and small state media organisations, independent companies, distributors, and dedicated outsourcing centres. Chinese industry is manned by contractors, casual workers, and copyists. Moreover, the national industry is increasingly typified by entrepreneurial businesses that work across media platforms, formats, and genres. In the sense that a production culture is emerging in China, the up and coming, dynamic, and independent production sectors, by linking up with international practices, constitute the beginning of a productive circuit of labour, investment, and ideas.

Soft power and cultural security

In order to explore the roots of an emerging production culture in China, we also need to take into account the nation's international ambitions. The 2008 Beijing Olympic Games, and especially its spectacular opening ceremony, are fondly remembered by many of China's leaders as a manifestation of "soft power" (Nye 1990). One of the key elements of Asian soft power is cultural influence. Rather than the traditional legacies of learning as exemplified by Confucius and his contemporaries, soft power is embedded in iconic modern forms that demonstrate "coolness" and economic value. Japan has expressed its modern youthful brand of soft power through Japanese popular culture; Japan's so-called "Gross National Cool" (McGray 2002) has put products such as Pokémon, Mario Brothers, and Hello Kitty onto the global markets. Less internationally known, but equally profitable, are Japanese "manga" (graphic novels) such as *Hana Yori Dango*, which was, in 2001, remade into a hit television drama entitled *Meteor Garden* in Taiwan (Deppman 2009). In response, the Diet (Japan's national parliament) formulated the "Japanese Cultural Industry Strategy," which aimed to "enhance the competitiveness of areas that represent the good traits and uniqueness of Japan ... and present them to the world" (Abe 2007). South Korea has also carefully managed the Korean Wave, which coincidentally emerged during the same time as the 2002 Football World Cup. Korean cultural influence is best illustrated by the success of its television dramas, films, and movies (Chua 2008; Black *et al.* 2010). While Korea's success is the result of increased self confidence within its creative sectors, its success has also been enabled and supported by government support agencies such as the Korean Culture and Content Authority, or KOCCA (Pease 2009).

In China, soft power has become a key issue in the reform of its cultural, media, and creative industries (Keane 2010). Many Chinese popular culture producers that we spoke to are currently sensing a change of direction in China, one that is challenging them to look externally, rather than just internally, toward the domestic market. Instead of reacting to international media with excessive regulatory barriers, the current Chinese administration is seeking to find ways to overcome some of the bureaucratic hurdles. The rise of the soft power rhetoric can therefore be linked to an national panic called "cultural security," or *wenhua anquan* in Mandarin. Academics, along with Ministry of Culture officials, entered this debate, expressing dire concern regarding the influence of Japanese and Korean culture on Chinese youth. Furthermore, the fear of western values embedded in cultural imports drove a reactionary cultural policy agenda. Cultural security echoed the strident anti-globalization rhetoric in the years leading up to China's accession to the World Trade Organisation (WTO) in 2001; a leading spokesperson is Huilin Hu from Shanghai Jiaotong University. In 2002, Hu maintained that China should have the ability to determine, legislate, and administer its national culture. He further argued that the Chinese state must forcefully protect China's "cultural ecology" to ensure that China's core cultural characteristics are protected. (Hu 2000, 2002; Knight 2006). In 2003, the National Philosophy and Social Science Foundation embarked on a project entitled "China National Cultural Security in the Opening Up Environment." In August of the same year, China's General Secretary, Hu Jintao, established the "Ensure National Cultural Security" initiative for the Political Bureau of the Central Committee. In the ensuing Fourth and Sixth Plenary Session of the Sixteenth Central Committee, cultural security joined political security, economic security, and information security as official national discourses.

Since then, the concept of cultural security has been quoted extensively. Academics have expressed the view that China's culture will decline if external cultures are allowed to further permeate and influence China; in short, it is a standard argument for protectionism dressed up as nationalism. By 2005, it had become obvious that cultural insecurity was the key issue concerning many of China's conservatives. For example, import–export numbers at that time were causing alarm in China. In the "normal" manufacturing economy China was exporting globally, its GDP was consistently in the double digits, and many of China's manufacturing companies were internationalizing, following the national plan to "go out" (*zou quchu*). In China's cultural sphere, however, the cultural security focus on growing domestic capacity and traditional culture had led to a neglect of outward looking opportunities. A sideways glance at the neighbouring countries of Korea and Japan indicated that the answer lay in the field of media content.

How, then, should China maintain its cultural security? One solution was to come up with a better soft power model. In early 2009, the theorization of soft power received more national support with the publication of Wuwei Li's book, *Creativity is Changing China*. A trained economist and director of the Research Centre for Creative Industries at the Shanghai Academy of Social Sciences, Li in his book states his case for the transformation of China's media and cultural industries. In the broader context of economic development, Li calls for a renovation of China's industrial structure—shift from infrastructure to human capital, from technology to content, and from "made in China" to "created in China" (Keane 2007). According to Li, cultural soft power will open up a more international sphere of activity in China.

However, what is the true meaning behind Li's words? Can China really "create" its way out of the economic crisis? Will the nation be able to export its media and culture? In contrast to Beijing's emphasis on assuring cultural security, Li, in his book, talks about "borderless industries" and "creative communities," the latter connecting with international expertise and investment.

In 2005, the release of two national government documents was the first indication that the Chinese government had reassessed the importance of China's cultural trade imbalance. The first document, entitled *Measures on Strengthening the Management on the Cultural Products Imports*, was issued on 28 April 2005 under the imprimatur of the Central Propaganda Department in concert with the Ministry of Culture, State Administration of Film, Radio and Television (SARFT), the Ministry of Commerce, the General Administration of Press and Publications (GAPP), and the General Administration of Customs. Appealing once again to the notion of cultural security, the document called for an improvement in the structural variety of imports while still maintaining control over the volume of imports. This was a comprehensive document that took into account publishing, audio-visual products, movies, television dramas, and animation. Moreover, the language of the document demonstrated strident and unfriendly cooperation models—the state would encourage but strictly control the supervision of co-produced movies, television dramas, and animated productions.

Within a short time, two other documents came to light that examined the outward flow of cultural products and services. In July 2005, the document, *Opinions on Strengthening and Improving the Export of Cultural Products and Services*, emerged from the General Office of the State Council. In 2006, the document, *Several Policies about Encouraging and Supporting the Export of Cultural Products and Services*, was issued from the General Office and subsequently endorsed by a consortium of eight ministries and institutions.[2] Interestingly, the Central Propaganda Department was not listed as endorsing this document.

In summary, in emphasizing four main principles, these "outward bound" documents drew public attention to the fact that the export of products was linked to the import of management skills and logistics. According to the documents, the working plan was to look outward while internally fixing the structural problems within media and cultural sectors. The national government pledged to provide more support for both state owned and private enterprises that were engaged in the export of cultural goods and services. These measures of support included, first, the simplification of outward bound administrative procedures. Second, a registry of outward bound cultural goods and services was established with the purpose of providing better data; overseas offices would be established and manned by professionals in order to foster sales of media programming and promote Chinese culture. Third, the relevant agencies would coordinate international trade shows and events to enhance China's international image in a positive manner. Fourth, "going out" foundations have been established at central and provincial levels; these foundations provide a range of assistance, including help with translating and subtitling of videos and film products. In addition, these foundations can subsidize the costs of international transportation of props and rental fees in overseas venues. To make this possible, the import–export Bank of China and the China Development Bank have been given the authority to provide loans related to the export of cultural products and services. Finally, businesses engaged in exports have been exempt from a range of business taxes.

These measures largely reflected the insecurities within the Ministry of Culture regarding cultural security. In April 2006, the official position was outlined for the first time to the general public by senior cultural officials. Wei Ding, the assistant Minister of Culture during that time, announced the nation's deficit in international cultural trade; Ding revealed that the ratio of imports to exports of cultural products stood at 10 to 1. Qizheng Zhao, a member of the Chinese People's Political Consultative Conference (CPPCC), was critical of China's performance, stating, "the country's weakness in culture should be blamed" (*China Daily*, 2006). The general manager of China's Arts and Entertainment Group, Yu Zhang, confessed: "China's foreign trade in culture is very weak." In the television industry, Xinjian Zhang, the deputy director of the cultural market department with the Ministry of Culture, painted a bleak picture: "most exported Chinese television dramas are old fashioned and poorly packaged by international standards, which doom them to failure" (*People's Daily Online*, 2006).

Yet, within two years, the national pessimism of the cultural trade deficit had subsided, and cultural insecurity turned to triumph. Somewhat unpredictably, it was the release of the United Nations' *Creative Economy Report 2008* compiled by UNCTAD and the United Nations Development Programme that brought China's hopes up. The findings from the United Nations pointed to China's status as "the leading player in the world market for creative goods" (UNCTAD 2008: 46). This re-evaluation was welcome news for officials in the Ministry of Culture. The *Creative Economy Report* was widely circulated and extensively cited in the media. From the title of apparent basket case in 2006 to world leader in 2008, China's export tide had quickly turned. While far from constituting a "wave," it was a substantial force made even more significant by volume.

However, this turnaround proved illusory. While purporting to capture the intangibility of the term "creative economy," the UNCTAD report did not attempt to capture the intellectual property components of audio-visual data.

240 Michael Keane and Bonnie Rui Liu

Instead, it relied on trade estimates: "the physical auditing of imports and exports of goods across national borders" (UNCTAD 2008: 94). The report stated, "what many regard as the core of creative activity—the creation of intellectual property [rights], is not directly measured for the simple reason that IPRs are increasingly disembedded from material products" (UNCTAD 2008: 91). Consequently, what the report properly considered is about material products, the number of items, and their stated trade value in customs audits. In addition, the study was based on longitudinal surveys of flows conducted by UNESCO (UNESCO 2005). The methodology employed meant that emerging categories of cultural goods and services, namely online forms of distribution, were not well accounted for.

By reading creative export in this manner, Italy was the leader among developed countries in 2005 with exports of 28 million USD, followed by the USA with 25.5 million USD and, after that, Germany with 24.76 million USD; these figures reflect Italy's strength in painting, design, and fashion. The idea of Italy as a creative hegemon, beating out the USA and the United Kingdom, would be a surprise to most observers. In audio–visuals and new media, however, Italy drops right out of the picture. Even though China is described as a developing country in this report, they beat out every developed country with cultural exports estimated at a massive 61.36 million USD. Additionally, Hong Kong ranked second with export numbers of 27.67 million USD; Hong Kong was also categorized as a developing nation (though how Hong Kong can be seen as a developing nation is another issue that should be explored). In audio–visual exports, Hong Kong ranked in the top ten exporters of developing countries, standing at 3 million USD. India is ranked first, followed by Mexico, then the Republic of Korea, Thailand, and, finally, Argentina. Both China and Taiwan are surprisingly beaten out of the top ten by Singapore. The data in this report that was supposed to offer welcoming news was weakened by category confusion. Goods and services that obviously should have been categorized as manufactured goods were included, goods such as handbags, belts, sunglasses, laser discs, and carpets. This diverse conglomeration of so-called creative products demonstrates the tendency to characterize developing nations (such as China) as "creative nations."

The other side of the ledger

How does one reconcile China's status as a successful exporter of creative products as illustrated in the UNCTAD report with the admission of cultural insecurity by state officials? Is China truly in danger of losing its culture? How then, does one accurately account for the value of cross-border trade? In order to gain a different perspective, we can look at data compiled by China's own industrial bean counters in the film and television industries, the sectors in which China is seriously seeking to counter the influence of Japanese and Korean soft power. By doing so, we find a different story, one that brings us back to the cultural trade deficit.

To begin, there has been growth in China's export sectors. Since 2003, China's success story undoubtedly lies in their cinema industry. In 1998, China produced 82 feature films, their lowest production number since 1979. By 2007, however, the number of feature films had jumped to 400. Out of these 400 films though, many were low budget films that received limited distribution and success. Nevertheless, the data shows that China's industry has been steadily gaining momentum. Moreover, prior to 2003, Chinese productions accounted for only 10 percent of the total box office revenue in the PRC, with Hollywood and Hong Kong films accounting for the other 90 percent. In 2003, the leading film in Chinese box office sales was Yimou Zhang's *Hero*, which also garnered the majority of earnings in that year's total exports of 80.6 million USD. In the following year, a surge of interest in Chinese films oversaw Zhang's *House of Flying Daggers* receive revenues of 12.5 million USD in the United States and 10 million USD in Japan. By 2008, China's film export revenues had jumped to 370.85 million USD (Xinhua 2007, Fan 2008). Since 2003, the bulk of box office revenues in China have gone to Chinese productions, most notably big budget films co-produced with Hong Kong.

While Chinese film has made significant improvements in recent years, China's television industry has been struggling to compete in overseas markets. Simply put, the content of China's television programs lacks compelling contemporary content. Over 50 percent of China's television exports find their way onto Taiwanese and Hong Kong channels. Other markets (roughly in the order of sales volume) include Singapore, Malaysia, Japan, Korea, the United States, Indonesia, and Thailand. The majority of sales and income come from television serials. Moreover, since the mid-1980s, China's television exports have been heavily reliant on one main genre, the historical costume drama (Zhu *et al.* 2008). Sales in Asian markets in the 1980s included *Tales of the Red Mansion* (*Honglou Meng*) and *The Water Margin* (*Shuihu Zhuan*). In the 1990s, *The Romance of the Three Kingdoms* (*Sanguo Yanyi*) and a remake of *The Water Margin* performed strongly, most notably in Taiwan and Hong Kong. The following decade, *Swordsmen* (*Xiaoao Jianghu*), *Kangxi Dynasty* (*Kangxi Wangchao*), *Yongzheng Dynasty* (*Yongzheng Wangchao*), and *Grand Mansion Gate* (*Dazhaimen*) recorded decent earnings in Taiwan (Keane 2008).

In 2003, China's revenues from serial drama exports to its core markets of Taiwan, Hong Kong, and other areas of Southeast Asia were hit hard by the popularity of South Korean dramas. As a result of the Korean wave, the proportion of serial dramas in total TV exports dropped from over 80 percent in 2002, to 50 percent in 2003, and 58.7 percent in 2004. These factors combined together meant that the price per episode decreased by almost 50 percent due to competition from Korean dramas. In effect, the TV drama market in Asian markets are clearly volatile and rely heavily on a few big hits. In 2005, the value of China's TV exports was 9.96 million USD (National Bureau of Statistics 2006). In 2006, it had surged back to 24.85 million USD, only to fall to 17.86 million USD the next year.

On the other hand, imports of television programs in 2007 accounted for 47.17 million USD (SARFT 2008). The value of the imports of television dramas, as well as broadcast hours, has declined in the past few years; for example, in 2005, the numbers stood at 401.6 million RMB (National Bureau of Statistics 2006, SARFT 2008). This had much to do with SARFT regulations in *Rules for* the *Administration of the Import and Broadcast of Foreign Television Programs*, Article 8, that limited the amount of foreign programs a television station is allowed to purchase. Allocations are decided at the beginning of each year and vary depending on locality and reports submitted by the stations. The stations with the most to gain from importing television dramas are the satellite TV channels with the most money, usually affiliated with a provincial media group; a prime example would be the Hunan Satellite Television channel. In cases where the purchase of a foreign TV serial drama exceeds the allocated quota, it is common practice for a station with much money such as Hunan to buy the rights off another station. Alternatively, as we will see, television stations enter in co-production arrangements with regional producers. In this way, the product counts as local, while still exhibiting a "foreign flavour."

Independent production and the changing media environment

As concerns over the cultural trade deficit grew, it became apparent that Chinese media producers were facing difficult challenges, notwithstanding the optimism of the UNCTAD report. The solution to China's malaise lay in structural reform, which has occurred gradually and incrementally through independent productions.

In order to understand the gradual emergence of an independent production culture in China, it is necessary to first understand changes in the regulatory climate. According to regulations for the management and production of radio and television programs, which came into effect in 2004 (SARFT 2004), all radio and TV production enterprises must apply for a license. The license applies to production and trade in programs and includes feature programs, columns programs, entertainment programs, animation, and TV and radio dramas. Similarly, film production enterprises have to apply for a license in order to legally engage in production.

Television and film independents that hold a license can only reapply for permits on a case-by-case basis. There are two types of licenses: the first type is valid for 180 days and the second type may last for up to two years. By the end of 2008, 3,343 independent production companies were plying their trade, most of them servicing the TV industry in one way or another (SARFT 2009). These independents are made up of five main categories—television drama, film, animation, documentary, and advertising. Undeniably, there has been a significant restructuring of operations; over 80 percent of television production companies are now classified as independents. The acceleration of the independent production sector was facilitated by SARFT policies that allocated licenses for independent production, particularly for television dramas in the late 1990s.[3]

Independent media production companies set up shop in developed, metropolitan areas; first, in Guangdong Province, far from the centre of politics, and then in Beijing, Zhejiang Province, and Shanghai. Many independents have located their companies in special zones and media clusters, which have been fast-tracked by municipal and provincial governments. This clustering effect is in response to the Five Year National Economic Development Plan, which determined that creative clusters will be the frontline development model for China's cultural and creative industries. An example is the Eleventh Five Year Plan for the Development of Beijing's Cultural and Creative Industries.[4] According to this plan, Beijing will prioritize cultural and creative industries; furthermore, building on the Olympic Games, China will deepen and strengthen capitalization. There will also be economic and political support for the chosen enterprises that promise to create renowned brands that will enhance the cultural soft power and influence of Beijing and, in doing so, will promote the "harmonious development" of the economy, culture, and society of Beijing.

Undeniably, independent companies have responded to these policies. However, many chose to operate outside the clusters. The business of media independents is first and foremost the production of TV dramas, followed by advertising, documentaries, and animation. In comparison to television stations that are solely state owned, there are more content restrictions for independent producers. Independent production companies cannot produce news programs without official news report authority, they cannot acquire rights for transmitting sport events, and they cannot import any programs from overseas without cooperation with TV stations. Consequently, the independent production sector focuses on entertainment programs, in particular TV dramas.

Due to a high demand for content, the television drama market was the first sector that was opened to independent production. By the end of 2008, there were 1,974 channels operating in China, and 1,764 of these broadcasted television dramas. TV dramas occupied 89 percent of the total broadcasting time (SARFT 2009). According to Xingguo Li of the Communication University of China, the vice president of Chinese Television Artists Association (Yingdan 2007), independent production occupies nearly 90 percent of China's total output of television dramas.

Asides from TV dramas, independent companies have directed their investments and skills into creating high-quality entertainment programs. Compared to the in-house production model (for example, where a program is produced and distributed by the broadcaster), independent companies prepared themselves for innovation and have searched for alternative distribution channels. According to the China Entertainment TV Program Report 2006–2007 (Shanghai TV Festival 2006), Enlight TV (*Guangxian Chuanmei*) produced 12 entertainment programs which were broadcast on 300 television stations and 600 channels; Joyful Cultural and Entertainment TV (*Huanle Chuanmei*) produced a total of 1,000 hours, broadcast on nearly 300 television stations and 700 channels.

Independents are branding channels by positioning programs; elsewhere, they aspire to professionalize channel operations, including the processes of packaging, marketing, and advertising. Independents are targeting satellite TV channels, as they have the capacity and ability to cover the whole nation, but are desperately lacking in quality content. In 2000, Yinhan Communication Co. Ltd (*Yinhan Chuanbo*) paid 80 million RMB to acquire year long operation rights for the

Beijing TV "Life Channel"; they subsequently professionalized the channel by adding lifestyle programs (Zhou 2006). Subsequently, more independents followed this model. Baoli and Huayi Media Group invested and controlled a 50 percent share of Hainan STV and transformed it into the "Travel Channel" in 2003; Shanghai Camera Media (*Kaimaila Chuanmei*) acquired 15-year operation rights for Neimenggu STV at a cost of 60 million RMB per year and turned this into an entertainment channel in 2004; Egasus and Taihe Entertainment International (*Paige Taihe*) acquired three-year rights for CETV-1 (Central Education TV) for 300 million RMB (Song 2007).

Currently, independent companies have three kinds of business relationships with television stations. The first is where the TV station or channel outsources production (or part of the production), including packaging, advertising content, content production, and management. Under this model, the independent company cannot possess copyright to the programs. *Lucky 52* (*Xinyun 52*), the longest-running Chinese game show, was produced by Qinxinran Media Organization; it was the first TV program localized from an international format. In 1998, Qixinran paid 4 million RMB annually for the original program format of *Go Bingo* from UK distributor ECM; after one year, however, they relinquished the license, claiming that it was not suitable for Chinese audiences. The subsequent move of Qixinran, which is not unusual for Chinese production companies, was to localize the game show for CCTV (Keane *et al.* 2008). This revised format became the top rated game show in China and was the leader in using product placements. Despite Qinxiran's claims to have recreated this format, 60 percent of the revenues went to CCTV, the broadcaster.[5]

From this example, it can be said that while independents have "arrived" in China, in many respects, the broadcasters still have direct control. Because of the difficulties of distribution in China, most independent television companies survive on the small amount of revenue generated from the outsourced business model.

Another common model is co-production, although this somewhat differs from the co-production model seen in film and animation where domestic companies often share resources and join forces with internationals. *Police Life* (*Jingcha Rensheng*) was "co-produced" by the Guanhua Centenary Media Company, Gold Shield Media, and Shanghai Oriental TV. Gold Shield Media, which is the film and television production unit of the Chinese Ministry of Public Security, provided the content (the human subjects) and interview rights while Guanhua produced the program and distributed to TV stations. The program, however, was commissioned by Shanghai Oriental TV, which offered a broadcasting platform and advertising time, but not a share of revenue from program sales. This investment strategy is reflected in the third model.

The international standard for TV independents is to produce programs and sell the product to the buyer (for example, the TV station or cable network) that offers the best price; however, in order to reduce their cash outlays, most TV stations in China allocate a few minutes of time in the program. The production company is then tasked with finding the sponsorship. The Enlight TV Production Co. Ltd has

China's new creative strategy **245**

produced several well-known entertainment programs, including the first of the genre, *Entertainment Live Report* (*Yule Baodao*).

Independent production comes with its own uncertainties. Often, when a program is successful, it is subsequently replaced if national TV stations decide to make their own version. This demonstrates the fragility of the concept of copyright in Chinese media industries. *Entertainment Live Report* suffered the fate of replacement; the program suddenly vanished from the Beijing TV market and was replaced by a similar program, *Daily Cultural Report*, which was produced by Beijing Television (BTV). In order to minimize such risks, independent production companies will engage in cross-media business or diversify in a range of program genres. Enlight Media began producing entertainment reporting programs, but has moved into producing television dramas. Qixinran Media began producing game shows, but has now transferred its attention to animation and film production.

In 2002, Qi Cartoon commenced as the animation branch of Qixinran. The co-founder of Qixinran Media, Yuan Mei, has previously stated that she believes that experiences learnt from overseas programs are valuable, but there is a need to focus on developing a distinctive production brand and character style. Though the company has produced animated content for international companies already, the company is looking to co-produce animation with these international enterprises and to absorb new knowledge and experiences from them.

In recent years, animation has shown signs of rapid growth and development. Companies engaged in original production have increased in number, as opposed to outsourcing these projects. In 2004, 52 organizations applied to SARFT for animation production projects; by 2005, this number was 105, and by 2008, grew to over 250 (SARFT 2006, 2009). In 2004, the central government announced that they would provide subsidies for animated programs broadcast by TV stations.[6] Among a variety of industry support measures was a stipulation stating that 60 percent of all animation produced had to be domestic productions. The subsidy had the desired effect of encouraging production companies to engage in animation. In effect, this meant that a fee was paid to the producing entity, usually by local government agencies, above and beyond the broadcast fee paid by broadcasters (see Keane 2009b). With this stimulus, along with the sense that animation was an industry of growth, annual production increased dramatically. In 2004, the annual output of original animation was 20,000 minutes; by 2008, it had reached 130,000 minutes (Report on China's Animation Industry 2004–2005; Report on China's Film and TV Animation Industry 2008). The emergence of animation in China coincided with competition for international contracts. Due to the lower costs of production in China, there is a great deal of outsourcing. Laikwan Pang writes that the development of animation in China is producing "another type of sweatshop" (Pang 2009). While it is true that low costs drive the development of the animation industry, the income earned by animators in China is significantly higher than the income earned in many other service industries. Our research has confirmed that many young people are attracted to animation, for the professional rewards, as well as the chance to participate in a new "creative industry" (Keane 2009c).

Moreover, while OEM dominates the Chinese animation industry, there have now been numerous instances of co-production with overseas companies that is leading to an increase in local capabilities. As the aforementioned policies indicate, there is a concentrated shift to encourage original production in China; this raises an interesting point in relation to the role of animation in the national mediasphere. In China, the animation sector has, to a large extent, been directed by regulatory authorities to produce content for children and youth; the result is that the overwhelming majority of animation features cute animals and magical spirits who "educate" children in the areas of morality and patriotism. Partnership with international companies provides an entry into a more sophisticated sphere of production, one that follows the Japanese model of anime.

A prime example demonstrating the benefits of working with an international company can be found in the Sandman Animation. Nelson Chu, vice-president of Sandman Animation, a company located in Suzhou Industrial Park, is optimistic of the future of Chinese animation. He believes that, "sooner or later, good content will get good payment. It's only a matter of time for the market to grow from a children's market to a more sophisticated market." As for the complex issue of outsourcing versus co-production, Chu believes that China will not move into an animation sweatshop economy but, rather, that both models will converge: "service and co-production are beneficial to animation industry in China in terms of growth of competence and knowledge/technique transfer."[7]

While international companies are often reluctant to release their core IP and market access, Chu states that this nevertheless provides valuable opportunities "to learn from their experience, quality standard, management methods, and help attract and maintain talents with a big revenue due to high price of overseas animation industry." He says, "from a development point of view, when the animation industry in China is very young in the beginning, companies do some service and production work as a start while learning through cooperation; then they gradually seek to shift the focus to creativity."[8]

Xu Shian, a developer working at another independent animation company in Suzhou, believes that core capability is extremely important but taking a long-term development approach is necessary in order to exchange experiences with international companies and to secure wider international possibilities.

Concluding remarks

In this chapter, we argued that Chinese media producers are beginning to come to terms with the creative economy by incorporating lessons from international companies. We have identified the emergence of a new production culture in the form of independent television and animation companies. While media companies in China operate within a constrained political field, often aggregating in clusters and monitored by officials, they nevertheless are open to new ways of operating— across platforms, across genres, and across markets.

Ultimately, China's capacity to become a major exporter of creative content remains unclear. Certainly, measures have been adopted to assist exporters, following the reverberations of cultural security debates at the turn of the millennium and its displacement by the more positive discourses of soft power and creative industries. Significantly, however, if a new kind of production culture is to flourish in China, propaganda officials will need to take a more arm's length approach to management. The clustering of businesses in parks and zones may not be the best recipe for success. Can you truly get out-of-the box creativity by putting people in boxes? The model of creative clusters is a model of collective endeavor inherited from the past.

Notes

1 The work if Zhao Yuezhi (2008) in particular is exemplary in making a distinction between political domination, capitalist expansion, and local emergence.
2 The Ministry of Finance, the Ministry of Commerce, the Ministry of Culture, The People's Bank, the General Administration of Customs, the State Administration of Taxation, the State Administration of RadioFilm and Television and the National Copyright Administration within the General Administration of Press and Publication.
3 Temporary Regulation for the Management of Production Organizations in 1995, Regulation for License of TV Drama Production in 1995, and Regulations for the Management of Radio and TV in 1997.
4 Beijing Municipal Commission of Development and Reform, available online at http://wenku.baidu.com/view/9c5e7d0fba1aa8114431d98a.html.
5 This fact was taken from a personal interview conducted with Liu in May 2009.
6 From 2002 to 2004, several consecutive policies were proclaimed by the central government, including Development Planning for Film and TV Animation during Tenth Five Year Plan and Notice for Strengthening the Management of Imports and Broadcasting Animation by SARFT, and Several Suggestions on Strengthening and Improving the Morality Construction for Minors by CPC Central Committee and the State Council and Several Suggestions on Development of Film and TV Animation.
7 From a personal interview with Michael Keane in October 2008.
8 From a personal interview with Michael Keane in October 2008.

Bibliography

Abe, S. (2007) Policy Speech at the 166th Session of the Diet in Tokyo, Japan. Online. Available at: http://www.kantei.go.jp/foreign/abespeech/2007/01/26speech_e.html.
Black, D., Epstein, S., and Tokita, A. (2010) *Complicated Currents: Media Production and Soft Power in East Asia*, Melbourne: Monash University Press.
Caldwell, J. (2008) *Production Culture: Industrial Reflexivity and Critical Practice in Film and Television*, Durham, NC: Duke University Press.
China Daily (2006) "Cultural Deficit Cause for Concern," March 10. Online. Available at: http://www.china.org.cn/english/culture/161006.htm.
Chua, B.H. (2008) *East Asian Pop Culture: Analysing the Korean Wave*, Hong Kong: Hong Kong University Press.
Curtin, M. (2007) *Playing to the World's Biggest Audience: The Globalization of Chinese Film and TV*, Berkeley: University of California Press.

Deppman, H.C. (2009) "Made in Taiwan: An Analysis of Meteor Garden as an East Asian Idol Drama," in Y. Zhu and C. Berry (eds) *TV China*, Bloomington: Indiana University Press.

Fan, C. (2008) "National Box Office Over 4.3 Billion, New Record in all the Statistics," Administration Centre of Digital Film Content, SARFT, 2008. Online. Available at: http://www.dmcc.gov.cn/index/asp/newstop/200911291129.asp.

Hu, H. (2000) "National Cultural Security – Strategies for the Development of Chinese Cultural Industries in the Globalization Environment," *Xinhua Digest*. Online. Available at: http://www.cqvip.com/qk/97001X/200002/index.html.

Hu, H. (2002) "While Positively Developing, Safeguard China's National Cultural Security" (*Zai jiji de fazhan zhong baozhang Zhongguo de guojia wenhua anquan*), *Wenyi Bao*, October 10, 2002.

Keane, M. (2007) *Created in China: The Great New Leap Forward*, London: Routledge.

Keane, M. (2008) "From National Preoccupation to Overseas Aspiration," in Y. Zhu, M. Keane, and R. Bai (eds) *TV Drama in China*, Hong Kong: Hong Kong University Press.

Keane, M. (2009a) "Great Adaptations: China's Creative Clusters and the New Social Contract," *Continuum*, 23: 221–230.

Keane, M. (2009b) "Between the Tangible and the Intangible: China's New Development Dilemma," *Chinese Journal of Communication*, 2: 77–91.

Keane, M. (2009c) "Understanding the Creative Economy: A Tale of Two Cities Clusters," *Creative Industries Journal*, 3: 211–226.

Keane, M. (2010) "Re-imagining China's Future: Soft Power, Cultural Presence and the East Asian Media Market," in D. Black, S. Epstein, and A. Tokita (eds) *Complicated Currents: Media Flows, Soft Power and East Asia*, Melbourne: Monash University Press.

Knight, N. (2006) "Reflecting on the Paradox of Globalisation: China's Search for Cultural Identity and Coherence," *China: An International Journal*, 4: 1–31.

Lee, A. (2009) "Hong Kong Television and the Making of New Diasporic Imaginaries," in Y. Zhu and C. Berry (eds) *TV China*, Bloomington: Indiana University Press.

Li, W. (2008) *Creative Industries are Changing China (Chuangyi Gaibian Zhongguo)*, Beijing: Xinhua Publishing.

McGray, D. (2002) "Japan's Gross National Cool," *Foreign Policy Journal*. Online. Available at: http://www.foreignpolicy.com/articles/2002/05/01/japans_gross_national_cool.

National Bureau of Statistics (2006) "Imports and Exports of TV Programs," Beijing, National Bureau of Statistics of China. Online. Available at: http://www.stats.gov.cn/tjsj/ndsj/shehui/2006/html/0422.htm.

Nye, J. (1990) *Bound to Lead: The Changing Nature of American Power*, New York: Basic Books.

Pang, L. (2009) "The Transgression of Sharing and Copying: Pirating Japanese Animation in China," in C. Berry, N. Liscutin, and J. Mackintosh (eds) *Cultural Studies and Cultural Industries in Northeast Asia*, Hong Kong: Hong Kong University Press.

Pease, R. (2009) "Korean Pop Music in China: Nationalism, Authenticity and Gender," in C. Berry, N. Liscutin, and J. Mackintosh (eds) *Cultural Studies and Cultural Industries in Northeast Asia*, Hong Kong: Hong Kong University Press.

People's Daily Online (2006) "China's Cultural Trade Deficit on the Rise," April 19. Online. Available at: hhttp://english.people.com.cn/200504/15/print20050415_181119.html.

Poster, M. (2008) "Global Media and Culture," Presentation to the LSE Information System and Innovation Groups ICT in the Contemporary World Seminar, London School of Economics, October 7. Available at http://www2.lse.ac.uk/management/documents/Poster-paper.pdf.

Report on China's Film and TV Animation Industry, 2008 (2009) *Report on Development of China's Radio, Film and Television*, Beijing: Social Sciences Academic Press.

SARFT (2004) Regulations issued by state administration of radio, film and television. Online. Available at: http://www.sarft.gov.cn/downstage/page_3.jsp

SARFT (2006) Speech, Annual Conference of National Film and TV Animation. Online. Available at: http://www.sarft.gov.cn/articles/2006/05/10/20070910200240370206.html.

SARFT (2008) *SARFT Statistics*. Online. Available at: http://gdtj.chinasarft.gov.cn.

SARFT (2009) The Notification for the Annual Production and Distribution of Animation in 2008. Online. Available at: http://www.sarft.gov.cn/articles/2009/02/04/20090204144951660452.html.

Shanghai TV Festival and CSM Media Research (2006) China Entertainment TV Program Report 2006–2007. Online. Available at: http://www.csm.com.cn/index.php/research/showReport/id/29.

Sinclair, J., Yue, A., Hawkins, G., Pookong, K., and Fox, J. (2000) "Chinese Cosmopolitanism and Media Use," in S. Cunningham and J. Sinclair (eds) *Floating Lives: The Media and Asian Diasporas*, Queensland: University of Queensland Press.

Song, L. (2007) "The Private TV Program Production Companies: From the Edge to the Centre," *Visual and Audio Industries Journal*. Online. Available at: http://media.people.com.cn/GB/5345566.html.

UNCTAD (2008) Creative Economy Report 2008. Berne: UNCTAD, UNDP.

UNESCO (2005) *International Flows of Selected Cultural Goods and Services, 1994–2003*. Montreal, Quebec: UNESCO Institute for Statistics.

Xinhua (2007) "Chinese Film Overseas Box Office Over 190 Million, Broke into Blockbuster Market," Online. Available at: http://news.xinhuanet.com/overseas/2007-01/08/content_5576566.htm.

Yingdan, X. (2007) "90% from the Private Production in China's TV Drama Market," *Xinhua Daily* (*Minying dianshi gongsi zhan dianshiju shichang jiucheng fenge*), 2007.5.28. Online. Available at: http://www.ccmedu.com/bbs33_45123.html.

Zhao, Y. (2008) *Communication in China: Political Economy, Power, and Conflict*, Lanham, MD: Rowman & Littlefield.

Zhou, J. (2006) "The Features and the Business of Private Program Production Companies," *Visual and Audio Industries Journal*. Online. Available at: http://media.people.com.cn/GB/22114/70684/70685/4795250.html.

Zhu, Y. (2009) "Transnational Circulation of Chinese TV dramas," in Y. Zhu and C. Berry (eds) *TV China*, Bloomington, IN: Indiana University Press.

Zhu, Y., Keane, M., and Bai, R. (2008) *TV Drama in China*, Hong Kong: Hong Kong University Press.

14

RENATIONALIZING HONG KONG CINEMA

The gathering force of the mainland market

Michael Curtin

It is common for media globalization to be characterized as the erosion of national cultural sovereignty under the onslaught of the world's largest media conglomerates. Such portrayals evoke the specter of a hydra-headed Hollywood juggernaut spreading its tentacles into every corner of the globe. This macro level analysis of media imperialism directs attention to a worldwide system of domination that favors capitalist interests, particularly those based in the United States (Guback 1969; Schiller 1969). Critics point to the ubiquity of media products such as Batman, *CSI*, and Lady Gaga, while also portraying the world's masses as susceptible, even gullible, participants in a transnational circuit of culture that feeds corporate conglomerates and impoverishes local modes of expression and public life (Miller *et al.* 2008). Many scholars and government policy makers argue that national governments are the best hope for stemming the tide of media imports, pointing to policies that aim to promote indigenous values and responsible citizenship by employing various strategies, ranging from local tax subsidies to public service media and from import quotas to outright censorship.

Global studies scholars acknowledge that cultural power is unequally distributed throughout the world, but this school of thought sees globalization not as a centralized structure of power but rather as an interactive dynamic that unfolds at a variety of levels. They say globalization has no uniform logic and no central command center but rather is a push and pull process with many unexpected outcomes (Tomlinson 1999). The interaction between global and local institutions is therefore radically contextual. Researchers point to examples of local media competing with dominant global counterparts in many parts of the globe, and they pay attention to the ways that popular culture appropriates, reconfigures, and reinterprets global hegemonic texts. Although conscious of systemic patterns of power, global studies scholars are especially alert to local contingencies, differences, and disjunctures (Appadurai 1996). For example, they argue that national governments are not necessarily the best antidote to globalization, since they too are characterized by unequal structures of power that advance the interests of elites through the fabrication of supposedly indigenous values and cultural artifacts. With respect to China, these researchers are quick to point out the many internal differences that belie the fiction of national unity as promoted by the Chinese Communist Party (Pan 2010). Global studies scholars therefore acknowledge that national political action can be a site for contesting cultural domination, but they also aim to uncover other important sites of cultural struggle and to explain them within the context of globalization.

Although they differ in their approaches to globalization, these two schools of analysis share a set of central questions with respect to modern media. They ask: What are the relations between global, national, and local institutions? How do these relations of power affect the creative workers and media users? How do they affect the political and socio-cultural fortunes of human communities? And where might we expect to find the thriving centers of cultural endeavor in an increasingly transnational media environment? Ultimately, these questions revolve around the constitution and contestation of spatial boundaries and relationships. These relationships have shifted throughout history; they have never been fixed or stable. They are rather the product of a complex interplay of political, economic, and social forces as well as migratory and cultural flows that give shape to our understanding of who and where we are in the world at any given time. In ancient and medieval times, imperial regimes exerted their influence across space by subduing local populations and building alliances at strategic cities and towns within their spheres of influence. This was superseded by the modern system of states that were predicated on the establishment of fixed political boundaries and the internal cultivation of national populations. Under both systems, political and cultural power often coincided, as centers of creative activity developed around the centers of political rule. But capitalism also endowed many cities around the world with resources that grew from industrial and commercial activity rather than political power and military conquest. Especially important in this regard were port cities—such as Mumbai, Lagos, Beirut, and Hong Kong—that functioned as centers of trade, finance, manufacturing, and culture.

Port cities often operated in between the grand empires or on the margins of powerful states. They were places where the exchange of goods, ideas, and cultural artifacts was the basis of metropolitan prosperity. The emergence of modern publications, movies, and sound recordings enhanced and expanded the circulation of popular culture. These cities were especially well situated to facilitate the circulation of transnational cultural goods and influences. They became centers of regional media economies that transcended national borders and served as launch pads for the circulation of cultural products even further afield—Indian movies to the Gulf States, West African music to the Americas, and Arab television to Europe. Such cultural flows accelerated in the latter part of the twentieth century with the emergence of satellite television, digital recordings, and internet communication. At first, these new technologies seemed to serve the interests of western media powerhouses based in Hollywood, New York, and London, but over time they facilitated counter-flows within and between regions, and from the margins to the centers. These circulations also enabled new ways of thinking about one's affinities with others and about one's place in the world. Some dreamed of life in Hollywood or America but many others looked to cities such as Mumbai for leadership in fashion, culture, and lifestyle (Mitra 2010). For those that were politically disempowered in their locality or nation, these cultural centers fed their imaginations with alternative ways of seeing the world.

National governments were uneasy with cultural competition from afar, whether it came from Hollywood or Mumbai, and they grew even more unsettled as it became easier to circulate music and screen media in the digital era. At the same time that cultural products were moving more fluidly across national borders, so too were capital, technology, and commercial goods circulating widely, eventually tying countries into an interdependent global economic system (Castells n.d.; Harvey n.d.). As states saw their cultural and economic sovereignty eroding, they found their decision making and administrative power increasingly being constrained by forces from afar. Many political leaders and cultural critics decried the fact that states were finding it difficult to develop policies that would allow them to manage the circulation of ideas and images within their national borders. They felt pressure from western powers to allow transnational media to flow freely and they felt exasperated by a rising enthusiasm among their citizens for cultural options from afar. If governments set import quotas on movies, consumers would turn to the lively black market in DVDs. If they banned satellite dishes, audiences would turn to the internet. Such developments helped to heighten tensions between global hegemons, national governments, and port cities.

The history of Chinese cinema provides an excellent case example of these shifting relationships. Hong Kong, a port city and cultural leader, has undergone dramatic changes since 1997, when the former British colony was handed back to the Chinese government. Once an unruly and relatively independent competitor for the affections of Chinese audiences worldwide, the Hong Kong movie industry has been brought to heel by the Chinese Communist Party through a set of government policies that have drawn movie companies into the mainland market and disciplined them to accept the primacy of favored state enterprises, such as China Film and China Central Television (CCTV). The government has also successfully exploited its relationships with western media companies by controlling the content and revenue streams from the limited number of movies it allows to be released each year.[1] The government has cagily manipulated both western and Hong Kong movie companies to serve its own ambitions, which are to build a movie infrastructure that will ultimately be popular with national audiences and competitive with Hollywood in global markets. It is able to do this largely because China is currently the most rapidly expanding movie market in the world with box office receipts of 2.7 billion USD in 2012, making it now the world's second largest movie market. The Chinese middle class is reputedly flocking to newly constructed movie theaters in major cities and industry experts estimate that the

Peoples' Republic of China (PRC) is currently on track to become the world's second largest theatrical market by 2015 (Coonan 2010).

Beijing's apparent success at controlling its domestic movie market runs counter to what many critics and researchers see as the unrelenting global expansion of western media conglomerates. It raises the prospect of a new center of cultural power based in Beijing under the watchful eye of the state, suggesting that under certain conditions, national regimes may indeed be able to assert their cultural influence on the global stage and may furthermore be able to tame the power of nearby media capitals in cities such as Hong Kong. After elaborating the particular histories of Hong Kong and PRC media, the final section of this chapter examines this proposition and suggests that the transnational reach of Beijing based media may be constrained by the political agenda that informs media policy. It contends that Beijing is unlikely to become a global media capital so long as it remains the seat of national government. This is because media capitals flourish at cultural crossroads, not at the centers of political power. Beijing may build a vast internal media infrastructure, but it will forever struggle to achieve cultural influence beyond its borders.

Beijing has succeeded nevertheless at taming the market power of foreign competitors within its national borders. It has exploited its relationship with Hollywood and it has tamed the influence of nearby Hong Kong. Indeed, the creative community in the latter city has suffered from a serious erosion of its movie-making capacity. Hit hard by piracy, speculation, and hyperproduction during the late 1990s, the quality of Hong Kong films spiraled downward, causing it to lose the affections of audiences in key overseas markets, such as Malaysia, Singapore, and Taiwan (Curtin 2007; Chan *et al.* 2010). Film companies were floundering just as the mainland market was opening up to partnerships with the Hollywood studios. Interestingly, the Chinese leadership established joint-ventures with American partners while turning a cold shoulder to the Hong Kong industry, whose films were treated as foreign imports for seven long and turbulent years after the city's return to Chinese sovereignty. The PRC government essentially starved the industry at a moment of crisis and only opened the door slowly when it was sure it had the upper hand in its relationship with "Hollywood East." Once an independent crossroads of cultural production, Hong Kong has been allowed into the national Chinese film market on conditions that were set by the Communist Party leadership (Pang n.d.). Although it remains somewhat autonomous and continues to make films that are targeted at audiences outside the mainland, the most lucrative projects are now blockbuster co-productions with movie companies in the PRC. This has not only affected the content of movies but also the ways in which they are conceived and executed. It has furthermore transformed the lives of the creative talent that once clustered in the former British colony but now spend much of their time working with partners in the mainland. Their stories provide one way of understanding the dramatic changes that have taken place since the early 1990s.

Peter Ho-Sun Chan is one of the most successful directors and producers in the Chinese film business but, unlike his counterparts in Hollywood or Mumbai,

254 Michael Curtin

he is still looking for a home. Chan was born in Hong Kong in 1962, lived in Thailand as a teenager, and attended the University of Southern California as an undergraduate student. He started working in the movie business during the 1980s, first in marketing then as an assistant director, apprenticed to some of the leading lights of Hong Kong's golden age, including Jackie Chan, Sammo Hung, and John Woo. When Peter got his first shot at directing in the 1990s, the director revealed a deft touch with urban melodramas. Chan, during this decade, churned out a string of highly successful movies for young adults such as *Alan and Eric, He's a Woman, She's a Man*, and *Comrades*. During the 1990s, the Hong Kong industry was booming, but its success was tinged with anxiety about the fact that Great Britain had agreed to relinquish sovereignty over the city to the People's Republic of China in 1997. The Chinese leadership in Beijing portrayed this as a glorious return to the motherland, but it was greeted with misgivings by many Hong Kong citizens who had grown accustomed to the prosperity and freedoms they enjoyed as a British colony. In the decade leading up to the transfer of sovereignty, Chan recalls, "people who could emigrate would do so. There was a feeling that you should make as much money as you could prior to the handover since everything after that would be a big question mark" (Chan 2009).

Chan, like many of his peers, began looking for other options and he has been on the move ever since. He took a shot at Hollywood during the late 1990s; in 1999, he directed *The Love Letter* for DreamWorks, starring Hollywood stars Kate Capshaw and Tom Selleck. By all reports, production went smoothly, but the film was released that year opposite *Star Wars: The Phantom Menace* and was therefore smothered at the box office. Chan nevertheless earned respect for his effort and was in line for more projects, but ultimately opted out of Hollywood, stating his discomfort working with the highly corporatized protocols of American film production. Chan then decided to start his own Asian film distribution company, Applause Pictures, and turned to churning out regional co-productions. Chan worked with filmmakers from Thailand, Japan, and Korea to craft titles aimed at mature audiences with a cosmopolitan sensibility. Many of these projects succeeded, due in part to the regional circulation of screen media and popular music via satellite, digital recordings, and the internet. These new technologies helped to fuel the emergence of an East Asian youth culture in major cities throughout the region (Chua and Iwabuchi 2008). For example, young people in Tokyo began having more in common with their counterparts in Singapore than they did with young villagers in rural Honshu. Audiences in Japan might share a national consciousness, but young urbanites in countries across the region were just as likely to feel affinities with those that shared their tastes in music, movies, and television dramas. Applause Pictures rode the crest of this trend, succeeding with a slate of movies in 2001 and 2002 that included a horror film entitled *The Eye*, a sex comedy, *Golden Chicken*, as well as a torrid tale of lust and vengeance, *Jan Dara*. These titles played well with niche segments in cities throughout East Asia, with the exception of People's Republic of China. Government regulations in the PRC required movies that were released to mainland theaters and television channels to be acceptable to general audiences, which included children, parents, and seniors. For many years, officials had resisted proposals to implement a movie rating system that would allow screening of films targeted at mature audiences. Portrayals of violence, sexual liaisons, and the supernatural remained off limits. Applause Pictures might succeed in Taipei, but they could not gain access to viewers in Shanghai through legitimate distribution channels. Since Applause executives were focused on other markets, this initially caused them little concern. However, during the first decade of the new century, China's GDP exploded, more than tripling in size, making China the world's second largest economy. Although China's per capita income continues to lag behind most countries in East Asia, its urban middle class is booming and the construction of new theater screens is proceeding at a ferocious pace. The country continues to add about 600 new film screens each year; most of them multiplexes in prosperous cities (Coonan 2010).

As the PRC market mushroomed, Peter Chan and his colleagues found it ever more difficult to ignore. When they were pitching new projects, investors would inevitably ask them if film treatments could be adapted so they might be made acceptable to mainland censors. Applause executives at first resisted because of two major reasons: it would not only entail changes to the style and content of their movies, but there were also other challenges associated with the film business in mainland China, which include cronyism, piracy, and a general lack of financial transparency (Yeh 2010; Yeh and Davis 2008; Davis 2010; Song 2010). However, Chan eventually relented, and directed *Perhaps Love*, a musical, in 2005, and *The Warlords*, a historical drama, in 2007; both films fared exceptionally well in PRC theatres. As a producer, Chan has likewise shifted his attention to projects with mainland appeal. Despite the many problems associated with doing business in the mainland, China today ultimately looms large in the calculations of directors and financiers in the East Asian movie business.

While the mainland film industry is booming, Hong Kong, which was once the capital of Chinese cinema, contrastingly, is littered with the corpses of film companies that have been unable or unwilling to adapt. As for Hong Kong's creative talent, many have fled the industry and those that remain must keep an eye on distant markets. In fact, Peter Chan claims that the shrewdest strategy for a Chinese director today is to pursue an artistic vision without any allegiance to a particular audience or locale (Chan 2009). That is certainly a big change from the late decades of the twentieth century when Hong Kong filmmakers shot most of their productions on the streets of the city and consciously fashioned their movies for local fans. Hong Kong's film culture was then renowned for midnight premiers, where the cast and crew would mingle among moviegoers, observing and listening to audience reactions, and sometimes even adapting the final cut accordingly (Bordwell forthcoming; Teo 1997). Movies were ultimately made for locals and their response was considered as a rough predictor of overseas success in markets such as Malaysia, Singapore, and Taiwan. The creative community made its home in this post-colonial and transnational city, among a population that had largely migrated from elsewhere and was in the process of developing a distinctly indigenous along with a cosmopolitan identity. Moviemaking was therefore a local business with a translocal sensibility (Zhang 2010). Aspiring Chinese talent moved to Hong Kong from many parts of Asia, even as far away as Europe and North America, because they saw the city as the most promising place to build a film career. Movie executives similarly saw it as the best place to raise financing, recruit labor, and launch projects (Curtin n.d.).

Today, however, Hong Kong is but one node in an increasingly dispersed circuit of deal-making and creative endeavor that is increasingly driven by the exigencies of the mainland market. Filmmakers must be attentive to Chinese government officials that explicitly make use of import policies, subsidies, and regulations to shape movie messages and to nurture the development of large national enterprises in hopes that someday they will be able to compete with their Hollywood counterparts. The mainland officials favor big movies with big stars, and tread with caution in regard to themes and dialogue. Nevertheless, China's production values are growing ever more competitive with global standards. Occasional blockbusters do indeed break out to regional and even global distribution, such as *Hero* in 2002, as well as 2008's *Red Cliff.* Most are historical dramas, which are safe with censors because they displace controversial issues into a distant past. These films are also popular with officials because they promote the image of China as a grand and united civilization with a long and distinguished history.

Audiences in East Asia seem to sense the caution and calculation behind these efforts, and many consequently opt for Hollywood products, which are arguably no less cautious or calculated. The difference is that Hollywood filmmaking is periodically rejuvenated by sleeper films and independent features and has a structural mechanism that allows innovative projects to break through the institutional inertia and insider dealings of the industry. In fact, studio executives grumble that the annual Academy Awards ceremony expends most of its attention on outliers such as 2008's *The Wrestler, Slumdog Millionaire,* and *The Hurt Locker.* As currently constituted, the Chinese movie industry has no such mechanism. Instead there is a yawning gap between state-sanctioned feature film extravaganzas and the sadly undernourished mid-range and independent movies (Chan *et al.* 2010; Song 2010; Zhang 2010). Chinese independent films are micro-budgeted projects that are either destined for the international film festival circuit or are opportunistic features that are largely produced for the satellite television market. The former are seen as unprofitable art cinema while the latter are categorized as "main melody" films, since most conform to ideological guidelines that favor uplifting characters and pro-social themes, as well as being subsidized by the state (Song 2010).

Similarly, television also suffers from various institutional constraints. In turn, mainland China, which has by far the world's largest national television audience, remains a net importer of programming. Low-cost genres such as talk, reality, and variety flourish, but few are innovative, and those that are innovative find themselves quickly besieged by imitative competitors (Keane *et al.* 2007). Drama and comedy, signature genres of the world's most successful television enterprises, flounder, largely because of the same caution and calculation that prevails in the movie business. Besides the constraints on content, mainland television enterprises also suffer from structural limitations. Shanghai and Guangzhou media have exploded in size and Hunan provincial television has proven itself to be a leading innovator, but most television companies are nevertheless run by provincial or municipal units of government that are eager to maintain the authority and status of ownership. This makes it difficult for companies to merge and makes it difficult to shake out the weakest performers (Diao 2008). Provincial and municipal television enterprises are hampered as well by regulations that favor the state-sanctioned national champion, China Central Television, which is also the organization that oversees national television ratings. Provincial and municipal telecasters are furthermore discouraged from building overseas distribution channels, a privilege that largely belongs to Beijing-based institutions that sit snugly under the wing of the state, where they are closely monitored for content and tone.

If today there is a geographic center to Chinese media, it is within the Chinese Communist Party offices in Beijing—not because the party micromanages the day-to-day operations of television and film companies, but rather because it systematically doles out favors and franchises to those that acknowledge its supremacy. The party leadership is quite successful at keeping a leash on domestic players and at exploiting joint-venture partners from overseas. News Corporation and Warner Bros. have both thrown in the towel after more than a decade of failed joint-ventures, and the general consensus these days among western executives is that India is better for investment.[2] The CCP's system of control is fairly obvious to viewers in the mainland who generally seek alternatives via the internet as well as the DVD black market. Young people rely especially on internet viewing, employing a host of strategies to circumvent the "Great Firewall" in order to acquire products that could never find their way into the Chinese cinema and airwaves.

As for the Hong Kong movie industry, it has undergone a systematic process of "resinicization" since the 1990s, as leaders of the PRC have deftly wielded the carrot and the stick in order to tame the industry and bring it into the fold of nationally sanctioned media institutions (Chan and Lee 1991). This has undermined Hong Kong's status as a transnational and relatively independent center of creative endeavor. Once known for its rambunctious, reflexive, and visceral cinema, the city's creative community has shriveled and those that remain have, such as Peter Chan, capitulated to a system that is built around the cautious, calculated blockbuster feature film that will appease state censors, party officials, and major financial backers. This is vastly different from the days when Hong Kong filmmakers pitched their products to local cinema circuits and overseas distributors. The movie business then operated outside the reach of national politics, sheltered by the benign neglect of the British colonial regime. Producers cobbled together movies in a freewheeling fashion and at a ferocious tempo, turning out popular products, occasional gems, and a good deal of rubbish. But the pace, scale, and diversity of production helped to foster a flexible ensemble of film companies that provided job opportunities to thousands of professionals as well as training for those that aspired to join the industry. Hong Kong became a magnet for talent from near

258 Michael Curtin

and far and became an incubator for creative experimentation (Curtin 2007). The Hong Kong film industry was home to prominent names such as Peter Chan, Maggie Cheung, Leonard Ho, Ann Hui, Hark Tsui, Michelle Yeoh, Peter Pau, Kar-Wai Wong, and Christopher Doyle.

In 1997, the PRC reclaimed Hong Kong after more than a century of British colonial rule. The terms of transfer provided a 50-year transition period in which the city would operate as a relatively autonomous Special Administrative Region, but it was clear from the beginning that Beijing intended to exert its authority; many believed it likely that government scrutiny of the media industries would increase significantly. This posed a problem for Hong Kong film and television companies that were accustomed to producing satirical and ribald comedies, in addition to fantasy, horror, and crime stories. The city's creative class grew nervous as the deadline for transition approached, as they believed the very genres that had proven most prosperous were likely to become targets of censors and propaganda officials. Consequently, many producers, directors, and actors began to explore job options abroad—even those that remained in place quietly began moving resources and families overseas in case of an official crackdown. Moreover, the industry entered into a cycle of hyperproduction, spewing out as many movies as possible in hopes of generating maximum revenues before the fateful moment of transition. This flooded the market with low-quality products that alienated loyal audiences both at home and abroad. Hong Kong's reputation and its cultural capital suffered tremendously as a result. No longer willing to risk the cost of a movie ticket or home video purchase, consumers bought pirated videos that sold for only a fraction of retail price. As audiences turned a cold shoulder to the industry, so too did media professionals in other parts of Asia. Distributors stopped buying, producers stopped collaborating, and directors declined to take Hong Kong talent onto their projects. In the decade following the handover, the industry's transnational network of audiences, distributors, and creative talent slowly dissolved (Curtin 2007; Chan et al. 2010; Bordwell forthcoming).

In retrospect, anxieties about the handover to Chinese sovereignty were somewhat exaggerated, but the effects on Hong Kong's reputation and its productive capacity were profound. Beijing leadership did not directly dip its hands into the messy domain of censorship but instead kept its distance and withheld any assistance during a time when the Hong Kong industry was under tremendous stress. In the years following the 1997 handover, movie companies started shutting down their operations, in addition to the disappearance of support services and dispersal of talent. To make matters worse, Chinese government policy regarding censorship remained cloudy. Therefore, many producers moved ahead with urgent caution with respect to content issues, fostering a culture of self-censorship that further alienated audiences—especially those in important export markets such as Taiwan, Singapore, and Malaysia. As the irreverent and innovative qualities of Hong Kong media products diminished, overseas revenues likewise declined and producers were confronted with two options: to either focus on the tiny domestic market of the SAR itself or to enter into projects, usually co-productions, with mainland media partners. The former would entail significant downsizing while the latter would require products that were fashioned for censors as much as they were for audiences. The Beijing government also sent signals that it would brook no challenges to the supremacy of state institutions such as China Film and CCTV. If Hong Kong firms were to participate in the rapidly growing mainland media economy, they would do so within parameters established by the Communist Party. State policy has gone through many twists and turns since 1997. At times Beijing has lightened its touch and has even adopted policies that exhibit concern about the dismal fortunes of Hong Kong film companies. Yet it does so within a broader context of consistent favoritism for national media institutions, providing them with a host of benefits that protect their market leadership (Davis 2010; Yeh 2010).

For many years Peter Chan tried to operate outside the gathering force field of the mainland market, testing the waters in Hollywood and fashioning features for pan-Asian audiences. However, Hollywood was not Chan's cup of tea and pan-Asian movies worked only until it became apparent that they too needed to incorporate the mainland market into the their aesthetic and financial calculations. Currently, Chan shuttles back and forth from Hong Kong to the mainland, hatching deals and making use of production facilities that have the most favorable rates. As best as Chan can, he remains a Hong Kong bred, western savvy, pan-Asian filmmaker that has ultimately also been forced to acknowledge the inexorable power of the mainland movie market and the Chinese state.

Despite the fact that the Beijing leadership has followed a consistent policy of promoting national champions under its wing, it is an unlikely location for a transnational media capital. Instead, Beijing remains a seat of national power where politics and favoritism mix uneasily with creative aspiration. In spite of all the institutional clout of the Chinese Communist leadership and all the travails of the Hong Kong industry, the latter remains a leading presence in the Chinese movie market. It is quite telling that the most successful Chinese movies released in the PRC each year are co-productions that are conceived and executed by a geographically mobile ensemble of film personnel led by Hong Kong producers. For example, three of the leading films of 2010 are historical dramas produced and directed by Hong Kong talent and its actors are Hong Kong's leading stars: Hark Tsui's *Detective Dee and the Mystery of the Phantom Flame*, John Woo's *Reign of the Assassins*, and Wilson Yip's *Ip Man Two*. Why does Hong Kong remain a formidable force and why does Beijing continue to find it difficult to assert regional and global cultural influence?

My recent research attempts to capture this spatial dynamic through the analysis of media capital, a concept that at once directs attention to the leading status of particular cities and to the transnational regimes of accumulation that promote the concentration of resources in specific locales (Curtin 2004, 2012). Media capitals are powerful geographic centers that tap human, creative, and financial resources within their spheres of circulation in order to fashion products that serve their audience's distinctive needs. The media capital's influence is dependent upon

260 Michael Curtin

their ability to monitor audience preferences, tap the popular imagination, and operationalize resources within their cultural domain. A media capital's success is therefore relational: its products flow outward while attracting the very best human and cultural resources within its sphere of circulation. Its preeminence is dynamic and contingent, for it is subject to competition from other cities that aspire to capital status. Dubai, for example, is self-consciously attempting to challenge the leadership of Beirut within the sphere of Arab satellite television and Miami has recently arisen as a transnational competitor to Mexico City. Thus, the concept of media capital encourages a spatial examination of the shifting contours of accumulation and dissemination, which both shape and are shaped by the imaginary worlds of audiences. Such research seeks to understand why some locales become centers of media activity and to discern their relations to other locales. Media capitals emerge out of a complex play of historical forces and are therefore contingently produced within a crucible of transnational competition. Cities as diverse as Hollywood, Mumbai, and Lagos operate as media capitals within their respective spheres of circulation. Although qualitatively different in many respects, cities that become media capitals exhibit a shared set of characteristics with respect to institutional structure, creative capacity, and regulatory policy.

Institutionally, media capitals tend to flourish where companies show a resolute fixation on the tastes and desires of audiences. In order to cater to such tastes, they adopt and adapt cultural influences from near and far, resulting in hybrid aesthetics. Such eclecticism and volatility is moderated by star and genre systems of production and promotion that help to make texts intelligible as well as attractive to diverse audiences. The bottom line for successful firms is always popularity and profitability. Although often criticized for pandering to the lowest common denominator, commercial film and television studios are relentlessly innovative, as they avidly pursue the shifting nuances of fashion and pleasure. In the early stages of development, a media capital may be characterized by small businesses with an opportunistic outlook; many of them chase the latest trend with abandon, churning out products on shoe-string budgets and releasing them into the market with little promotion or even strategic calculation. As media capitals mature, however, firms begin to formalize their institutional practices and, oftentimes, they integrate production, distribution, and exhibition within large corporations. Profitability is derived from structured creativity that feeds expansive and expanding distribution systems. Marketing considerations become woven into the conceptual stages of project development and financing. Media capitals therefore emerge where regimes of capital accumulation are purposefully articulated to the protean logics of popular taste. The mercantilist opportunism of the emerging filmmaking community gives way to industrialized modes of production and distribution.

Just as importantly, media capital tends to thrive in cities that foster creative endeavor, making them attractive destinations for aspiring talent. The research literature on industrial clustering shows that creative laborers tend to migrate to places where they can land jobs that allow them to learn from peers and mentors, and from training programs that are sponsored by resident craft organizations. Job mobility and intra-industry exchanges further facilitate the dissemination of skills, knowledge, and innovations. Thus, a culture of mutual learning becomes institutionalized, helping to foster the reproduction and enhancement of creative labor (Scott 2000). Workers are also inclined to gravitate to places that are renowned for cultural openness and diversity (Florida 2005). It is remarkable, for example, that the most successful media capitals are usually port cities with long histories of transnational cultural engagement. Also noteworthy is the fact that national political capitals rarely emerge as media capitals, largely because modern governments seem incapable of resisting the temptation to tamper with media institutions.[3] Consequently, media capitals tend to flourish away from centers of state power, favoring cities such as Los Angeles, Hong Kong, and Mumbai, which are usually disdained by political and cultural elites. Successful media enterprises tend to resist censorship and clientelism, and are moreover suspicious of the state's tendency to promote an official and usually ossified version of culture. Instead, commercial media enterprises absorb and refashion indigenous and traditional cultural resources while also incorporating foreign innovations that may offer advantages in the market, even though such appropriations tend to invite criticism from state officials and high-culture critics. The resulting mélange is emblematic of the contradictory pressures engendered by global modernity, at once dynamic, seemingly capricious, and yet also shrewdly strategic. Their choice of location is no less calculated: media capitals tend to accumulate in cities that are relatively stable, quite simply because entrepreneurs will only invest in studio construction and distribution infrastructure where they can operate without interference over extended periods of time.

The characteristics of media capitals outlined above, when applied to Hong Kong at the zenith of its success, helps to explain why its influence has waned as its screen media industries have increasingly fallen under the sway of the mainland market. Rather than an industry vitally in tune with its audiences, Hong Kong producers and directors today find it difficult to secure investors unless their films target viewers in ways that are sanctioned by the PRC leadership. They are pressured to observe content standards that are fashioned for what the party leaders see as a general audience of patriotic moviegoers. Sexuality and violence must be treated cautiously, rebels and malefactors subdued by the forces of order, and supernatural themes kept out of sight. Contemporary political satire is taboo and public issues can be handled only obliquely. The commercial logics of the Hong Kong industry have now been skewed towards objectives that satisfy the state. Its blockbuster co-productions perform well in the mainland, while overseas markets have declined. Once a transnational media capital, Hong Kong is increasingly becoming a service center of a national Chinese cinema.

One might map Hong Kong's transition and China's rise by comparing the characteristics of national, imperial, and global media. Table 14.1 delineates the tendencies of each and the distinctions between them; it aims to provoke reflection on such distinctions rather than to establish ironclad categories. It further shows that the characteristics of global and national media are quite different and suggests why it might be difficult for a national media enterprise to achieve

262   Michael Curtin

TABLE 14.1 Spatial typologies of media

Type	Sphere	Center	Characteristics	Mechanisms
Global	Expansive	Media capital	Mobile	Commercial
Imperial	Expansive	Imperial capital	Hegemonic	Strategic
National	Retentive	State capital	Integrative	Administrative

global leadership and vice versa. Finally, the chart helps in explaining the recent trajectories of development in Chinese cinema and suggests why Beijing will prove an unlikely successor to Hong Kong as the media capital of transnational Chinese cinema.

As suggested in Table 14.1, national media are intimately connected to the production and maintenance of the modern state. They observe boundaries set by political leaders and they play an important role in producing the national imagery, helping to create a meaningful history of the nation and a palpable image of a united people. National media integrate and educate populations, and are administrative in the sense that they render otherwise disparate individuals as a productive populous. National media may also be used as direct tools by the political leadership or they may be manipulated remotely via institutions of civil society. In either case, they serve the interests of the state and are commonly headquartered in the national capital.

By comparison, imperial media throughout history has been tied to the geographically expansive aspirations of ruling groups. In the modern era, imperial exertions of power have been organized by nation-states that have seen media as crucial to their transnational objectives. Telecommunication networks, news agencies, and broadcasting institutions have all been strategically deployed by states to achieve imperial aims. In some respects, cinema has been a less significant medium of imperial rule, largely because of Hollywood's prolonged dominance over the international film trade. Movies have, however, returned to prominence in light of China's soft power ambitions. The Communist Party leadership has explicitly proclaimed its desire to generate films that would compete globally with Hollywood. It is no coincidence that the ceremonies at the 2008 Beijing Olympics were choreographed by one of the state's favored filmmakers, Zhang Yimou, director of blockbusters such as *Hero, House of Flying Daggers,* and *Curse of the Golden Flower.*[4]

As for global media, they are transnational in orientation as well, but are distinguished by the structuring logic of capital accumulation rather than by the logic of the nation-state or imperial regime. Less interested in political assertions of power, global media panders and plays to far-flung audiences, resolutely shaping their content to the popular tastes of audiences and seeking to transform those tastes in hopes of solidifying their popularity in each territory they enter. Global media is also expansive, flexible, and mobile, searching for market opportunities regardless of political boundaries; they constantly probe for new openings and shift their infrastructures accordingly. Global media fundamentally aims to insert themselves into distant cultures and build up their commercial presence over time.

Such a comparison aims to delineate different tendencies among media, not to suggest that such categories are impermeable boundaries of difference. So, for example, national media may serve the domestic interests of the state but they may also be operationalized for imperial ambitions. The history of the British Broadcasting Corporation (BBC) is as a good example. At certain moments of its history, the BBC served the British Empire as much as it served its national audience. Today, however, BBC's emphasis is clearly on domestic viewers and listeners. Its international service allows domestic entertainment content to circulate overseas, providing an ancillary revenue stream to support domestic operations. While still an implicit projector of soft power, especially via its news operations, BBC's imperial pretensions have nevertheless waned along with the British empire; it would therefore be categorized as a national, somewhat global, rather than imperial medium.

Hollywood provides another example of such complexity. At its inception, Hollywood movies aimed to serve an expansive and diverse national audience through the calculated production of popular texts. Although resolutely commercial since the 1910s, it was periodically reined in by the state through censorship and even occasionally collaborated with the government, particularly during military mobilizations. Despite these national inflections, Hollywood nevertheless has been an enduring example of global media. Driven largely by commercial imperatives, it has relentlessly probed for new markets worldwide for more than one hundred years. The recent full flowering of neo-liberalism has allowed it to expand its presence even further afield, so that industry executives now perceive overseas markets as the most important part of their business (Schuker 2010).

With respect to Chinese cinema, the commercial movie industry was, during its prime, a good example of an expansive and mobile global medium. It was born in Shanghai and Hong Kong in the 1920s, and then expanded to export markets in Southeast Asia during the 1930s. As the mainland movie market was buffeted by war and revolution, the center of Chinese commercial film shifted south to Singapore, only to be buffeted yet again by waves of nationalist fervor on the Malay Peninsula during the 1950s. The center of the industry then relocated to Hong Kong, where it matured and flourished, serving local audiences but also fashioning products with an eye to crucial export markets in various parts of East Asia as conditions permitted. The Chinese commercial movie business pursued opportunities wherever they arose and even if its products were not ubiquitous worldwide, it was undeniably global in orientation. The Chinese film industry during this time was anchored by a resident creative community that tapped talent and resources from near and far, making Hong Kong the central node in transnational circuits of Chinese popular culture.

Mainland cinema during this period became an instrument of the state—a bridge between the Communist Party and the people. It was thoroughly national in every respect, acting as an integrative force in the service of a communist regime. Since the 1980s, the CCP has reorganized the national economy in a free market manner. Media institutions now operate in a more decentralized fashion and they pursue audiences as they might pursue media consumers, but their guiding principles remain those of the party and ownership remains in the hands of the state. A state's desire to project soft power overseas is part of an imperial state policy, but a policy that is likely to fail, as audiences can choose from other commercial and popular fare. Mainland programming has therefore proven to be of little interest to audiences in Hong Kong, Taipei, or Singapore, and it is even less interesting to audiences in Tokyo or Bangkok.

The nationalization of Hong Kong media helps to explain why its status as a media capital is eroding. It furthermore helps to explain the limitations on Chinese state media, despite their stated desire to increase their cultural influence abroad. One therefore wonders where the center of gravity will emerge for the Chinese film industry? Will it be a primarily national industry situated in Beijing or might a global Chinese film industry reemerge in one of the port cities of China?

Notes

1 Twenty foreign commercial imports are released through China Film on a revenue sharing basis each year ("The Big 20"), allowing the government enterprise to retain hundreds of millions of dollars in distribution fees. Foreign movies have helped to draw audiences to theaters and the government has used the box office revenues to help fund the expansion of its domestic industry.
2 Most prominently in this regard is News Corporation's decision to sell its ownership stake in Star TV, which generated a flurry of press coverage (Young 2010).
3 London is an exception, largely because of the residual advantages of an empire that made it such an important maritime and financial center. Its importance as a center of media activity has been perpetuated largely because it has exploited its access to the wealthy global Anglophone market and because the state has exercised restraint in its oversight of creative institutions.
4 For critiques of Zhang's work, see Zhao (2010) and Wang (2009).

Bibliography

Appadurai, A. (1996) *Modernity At Large: Cultural Dimensions of Globalization*, Minneapolis: University of Minnesota Press.

Bordwell, D. (forthcoming) *Planet Hong Kong: Popular Cinema and the Art of Entertainment*, 2nd edition, Cambridge, MA: Harvard University Press.

Chan, J.M. and Lee, C.C. (1991) *Mass Media and Political Transition*, New York: Guilford Press.

Chan, J.M., Fung Y.H., and Ng, C.H. (2010) *Policies for the Sustainable Development of the Hong Kong Film Industry*, Hong Kong: The Chinese University of Hong Kong Press.

Chan, P. (2009) *A Discussion with Producer/Director Peter Ho-Sun Chan on Global Trends in Chinese-Language Movie Production*, Taiwan Cinema Website: Government Information Office. Online. Available at: http://www.taiwancinema.com/ct.asp?xItem=58252&ct Node=124&mp=2.

Chua, B. and Iwabuchi, K. (2008) *East Asian Pop Culture: Analyzing the Korean Wave*, Hong Kong: Hong Kong University Press.

Coonan, C. (2010) "Chinese Box Office Totals $1.14 Billion," *Variety*. Online. Available at: http://www.variety.com/article/VR1118025904.html?categoryid=1278&cs=1&query=china+box+office.

Curtin, M. (2004) "Media Capitals: Cultural Geographies of Global TV," in J. Olsson and L. Spigel (eds) *Television after TV: Essays on a Medium in Transition*, Durham, NC: Duke University Press.

Curtin, M. (2007) *Playing to the World's Biggest Audience: The Globalization of Chinese Film and TV*, Berkeley: University of California Press.

Curtin (2012) "Global Media Capital and Local Media Policy," in J. Wasko, G. Murdock, and H. Sousa (eds) *Handbook of Political Economy of Communication*, Malden: Blackwell.

Curtin (in progress) *Media Capital: The Cultural Geography of Globalization*, pp. 541–557.

Davis, D.W. (2010) "Market and Marketization in the China Film Business," *Cinema Journal*, 49: 121–125.

Diao, M.M. (2008) *Research into Chinese Television Development: Television Industrialisation in China*, dissertation, Sydney: Macquarie University.

Florida, R. (2005) *Cities and the Creative Class*, New York: Routledge.

Guback, T.H. (1969) *The International Film Industry: Western Europe and America since 1945*, Bloomington: Indiana University Press.

Keane, M. (2010) "Keeping Up With the Neighbors: China's Soft Power Ambitions," *Cinema Journal*, 49: 130–135.

Keane, M., Fung, A.Y.H., and Moran, A. (2007) *New Television, Globalisation, and the East Asian Cultural Imagination*, Hong Kong: Hong Kong University Press.

Miller, T., Govil, N., McMurria, J., Wang, T., and Maxwell, R. (2008) *Global Hollywood: No. 2*, London: BFI.

Mitra, S. (2010) "Localizing the Global: Bombay's Sojourn from the Cosmopolitan Urbane to Aamchi Mumbai," in M. Curtin and H. Shah (eds) *Reorienting Global Communication: Indian and Chinese Media Beyond Borders*, Urbana, IL: University of Illinois Press.

Pan, Z. (2010) "Enacting the Family-Nation on a Global Stage: An Analysis of CCTV's Spring Gala," in M. Curtin and H. Shah (eds) *Reorienting Global Communication: Indian and Chinese Media Beyond Borders*, Urbana, IL: University of Illinois Press.

Schiller, H.I. (1969) *Mass Communication and American Empire*, 2nd edition, Colorado: Westview.

Schuker, L.A.E. (2010) "Plot Change: Global Forces Transform Hollywood Films," *The Wall Street Journal Asia*, August 2.

Scott, A.J. (2000) *The Cultural Economy of Cities*, Thousand Oaks, CA: Sage Publications.

Song, T. (2010) "Independent Cinema in the Chinese Film Industry," dissertation, Queensland: Queensland University of Technology.

Teo, S. (1997) *Hong Kong Cinema: The Extra Dimensions*, London: BFI.

Tomlinson, J. (1999) *Globalization and Culture*, Chicago, IL: University of Chicago Press.

Wang, T. (2009) "Understanding Local Reception of Globalized Cultural Products in the Context of the International Cultural Economy: A Case Study on the Reception of Hero and Daggers in China," *International Journal of Cultural Studies*, 12: 299–318.

Yeh, E.Y. (2010) "The Deferral of Pan-Asian: Critical Appraisal of Film Marketization in China," in M. Curtin and H. Shah (eds) *Reorienting Global Communication: Indian and Chinese Media Beyond Borders*, Urbana: University of Illinois Press.

Yeh, E.Y. and Davis, D.W. (2008) "Re-Nationalizing China's Film Industry: Case Study on the China Film Group and Film Marketization," *Journal of Chinese Cinemas*, 2: 37–51.

Young, D. (2010) "News Corp Sells Controlling Stake in China TV Channels," *Reuters*. Online. Available at: http://www.reuters.com/article/idUSTRE67810L20100809.

Zhang, Y. (2010) "Transnationalism and Translocality in Chinese Cinema," *Cinema Journal*, 49: 135–139.

Zhao, Y. (2010) "Whose Hero? The Spirit and Structure of a Transnationally Integrated Chinese Blockbuster," in M. Curtin and H. Shah (eds) *Reorienting Global Communication: Indian and Chinese Media Beyond Borders*, Urbana: University of Illinois Press.

INDEX

Note: page numbers followed by "n" refer to notes, and followed by "t" refer to tables.

addictive capitalism 204
Althusser, L. 180
Americanization 61, 72, 155–6, 215
Analog Girl 123, 126–7, 128
animations, Chinese 245–6
anime, Japanese: elevated to culture in Japan 218, 223; globalization 220–3; government support and promotion 213, 218–20, 223–4, 225; marketing Japan's national image through 224; *mukokuseki* aspect of early 214–15, 220, 221, 223; production 225, 226; and role in television programming 220–2; sales 213, 217, 219, 220 *see also* Pokémon
anonymization 215
Appadurai, A. 62, 114, 140, 179, 180, 184, 223, 250
Applause Pictures 254, 255
"Asianized western" 127, 129, 159
authenticity 10, 49, 123, 127, 131, 135, 145, 151

Barrett, L.E. 140, 141, 142, 151
Barthes, R. 207
Befu, H. 214, 215, 216, 219
Berger, P. 5, 76
Big Mountain 142, 145
Big O 125, 131, 132
Bourdieu, P. 124, 177
British Broadcasting Corporation (BBC) 263
Bunjob, J. 148–50, 150–1

cable television 156, 182
Caldwell, J. 236
Cantopop and Mandopop 116, 118, 121, 128, 130
capitalism: addictive 204; commodity 104; economy of signs and symbols 77; global 76, 89, 90, 94, 96, 120, 122, 210; Pokémon mimicking of 197, 208–9, 210, 216
Chan, P. 253–5, 257, 259
Cheah, P. 132
Chen 87, 88
Children's Fun Publishing 60, 63, 64, 67, 68, 69, 71
China: accession to World Trade Organization 21; animation industry 245–6; Children's Fun Publishing 60, 63, 64, 67, 68, 69, 71; children's literature debate in 25–7; children's publishing, foreign products in 21–2; consumption lifestyle 6, 30–4, 64, 92, 255; cross-generational differences 24, 32–4; cultural values 79, 80; Disney comics *see* Disney comics in China; Disney films 60, 69; Disney history in 59–60; Disneyland advertisements 50; Disneyland visitors from 45, 49–51, 55; Disney's youth entertainment, controversy over 63; economic boom 255; economic nationalism 70–1; elitism 35, 36, 37; "exploiting the global" 80, 89–90, 90–2; globalization process 15, 21, 24, 27, 31, 180–1, 184; intellectual property rights 26; literary renaissance

268 Index

26; McDonald's 56; media joint ventures 60–1, 63, 67; middle-class 6, 30–4, 64, 92, 255; middle-class culture, youths' partial identification with 23–4, 34–7; modernity 56, 76, 78; Olympic Games 2008 235, 236, 243, 262; one child policy 31; online gaming market 159, 161, 164, 166, 168; parental pressure on youth 33; per capita income in Shanghai 23; political conflict with Japan 70–1; Pop Culture China 127, 129, 159; Pottermania in 25–7; regulation of foreign media companies 48, 60, 80, 180; sexuality issues in media 86, 88, 89; taste culture 34; transborder visuality flows 77, 81, 90–1, 91–2 *see also* China's film industry; China's media industries, new strategy for; Disney comics in China; *Harry Potter* franchise study; magazine covers, study of Chinese

China's film industry: and analysis of media capitals 259–61; censorship 254–5, 256, 258, 261; exports 241; growth in 240–1; historical dramas 256, 259; imports 59, 60, 61, 241; independent films 256; international co-productions 244, 253; move from global to national media 263–4; movie market 252–3, 255; Peter Chan operating in 253–5, 257, 259; state control of 16, 252, 253

China's media industries, new strategy for 15, 233–49; animations 245–6; anticipating more openness 235–6; Beijing an unlikely media capital 253, 259; Beijing CCP geographic center to 257; clustering 235, 242–3; co-productions 15, 60, 233, 244–5, 246, 253, 257; content 235–6, 241; copyright in 244, 245; cultural exports deficit crisis 234, 237, 239–40, 240–1; and cultural security panic 237–9, 240–1; defining "industry" 236; film industry *see* China's film industry; independent media production companies in changing environment 242–6; licenses for production enterprises 242; reconciling cultural insecurity with success of cultural exports 240–2; relationship between independent production and television stations 244; soft power 236–7, 238, 262, 264; television channel branding 243–4; television corporate culture compared to that of US 235–6; television Disney co-productions 60; television exports 235, 239, 241; television imports 241–2, 256; television suffering from state constraints 256–7

Chinese diasporas 127, 166
Chinese wuxia games 162–3, 166
Ching, L. 31, 214, 216, 217
Chow, C. 117, 122, 129, 131
Chow, R. 127, 130
Chua, T. 118, 121, 128
Chungmuro 173, 176, 178, 182, 183
Cold War 8, 61, 63
commodity capitalism 104
communication, political economy of 44–5
Concave Scream 125, 126
Conde Nast Publications 97, 98
Connell, R.W. 96, 107
The Consequences of Modernity 43
consumerism 62, 72; in China 6, 30–4, 64, 92, 255; in Japan 52, 199, 204; masculinities and concept of global 94, 95–7; visuality a prime motivator 77
Content Industry Promotion Bill 2004 213, 218
Cosmopolitan 80, 82–3, 85–6
Creative Economy Report 2008 234, 239–40
Creativity is Changing China 238
cultural capital 22, 37, 91, 177, 181, 187
cultural flows: from Asia to West 3, 12–13, 216, 218; Chinese disruption of 16, 92; new technology speeding up 152, 167, 223, 251
cultural globalization 2, 3, 15, 42, 61–3, 76, 90, 140, 155–6
cultural homogenization 42, 62, 72, 116
cultural hybridization 4, 5, 11, 114, 156, 180, 186, 223
cultural imperialism 61, 62, 113, 180, 215
cultural-linguistic markets 158–9, 164
cultural power 63, 250, 251, 253
cultural proximity, notion of 158–9, 216–17, 222
Culture Industry Promotion Law 1999 224–5
"culturization of economy" 218, 220
cute games 160, 161, 162–3, 165, 168
cuteness 204–5, 206–8, 216

Davis, D. 21, 23, 30, 31
Davis, S.G. 44, 45
diasporas: Chinese 127, 166; Jamaican 142
Disney: controversy in China over youth entertainment products 63; films in China 60, 69; Global Disney Audience Project 62; history in China 59–60; in international markets 60
Disney comics in China 7–8, 59–75; appeal of family and moral values 69; criticism of capitalist ideology 68–9; Donald Duck 61, 67, 68–9; Duck family 65, 68, 69, 72;

educational element 67–8; European joint-ventures 60–1, 63, 65, 67; *Four Colors Comics* 65; launches 64, 66; localization strategies 67–71; *Lustiges Taschenbuch* 65, 69; Mickey Mouse 49, 59, 65, 67, 68, 69, 72; *Mickey Mouse Magazine* 64, 65, 66, 69, 70, 71; *Topolino* 65; *Ultimate Fans of Mickey Mouse* 61, 63, 64–5, 66, 68, 69, 70, 71; *W.i.t.c.h.* 64, 66, 70–1, 72
Disney English School 68
Disney Worldwide Publishing 60
"Disneyfication" 7, 8, 60, 61–3
Disneyland: advertisements for 50; expanding into Chinese market 48; expense of a trip to 44–5; global expansion strategy 45; maximising profits in 44–5; as part of modernity project 43–4; political economic perspective on 44–5 *see also* Hong Kong Disneyland; Tokyo Disneyland
DoCoMo 205
Donald Duck 61, 67, 68–9
Dorfman, A. 62

East Hope Group 26
Egmont 60, 63, 64, 65, 69
Eisner, M. 59–75
Electrico 115, 122–3, 124, 128
Esquire 80, 84–5, 94, 96
"exploiting the global" 80, 89–90, 90–2

Factory Girl 46–7
Fanon, F. 129
fantasy games 160–1, 161–2, 165
FHM 86–9
Fighters of the Enchanted Sword 163
films: content distribution 175; market sizes 175; Pokémon 204, 206; regionalization of market 159; in Singapore 132, 133 *see also* China's film industry; Hong Kong film industry; Korean film industry
Four Colors Comics 65
Friedman, J. 62, 157, 180
Frith, S. 140, 151
Fung, A.H. 15, 49, 50, 107, 180–1, 184

Game Boy 200, 201, 204, 209
gay civil rights movement, Taiwan 96
General Agreements on Tariffs and Trade (GATT) 179, 181
Germany 65, 66, 175, 240
Giddens, A. 43, 54, 76, 78, 104, 140, 141, 150, 151, 157
Giroux, H.A. 62, 67, 68, 199
global capitalism 76, 89, 90, 94, 96, 120, 122, 210

Global Disney Audience Project 62
global local nexus 106–8, 180
global media 262–3, 262t
globalization: of anime 220–3; Asia and relationship with 226–7; challenge for Japan 225–6; China and process of 15, 21, 24, 27, 31, 180–1, 184; cultural 2, 3, 15, 42, 61–3, 76, 90, 140, 155–6; of cultural economy imposed on Korean film market 181–4; cultural-linguistic markets diverging from 158–9, 164; defining 187; Disneyfication of global culture 7, 8, 60, 61–3; economic 3, 179–80, 184, 252; Fung's model of glocalization and 180–1, 184; Japanese popular culture a new site of 14, 214, 216–17, 219, 225–7; Korean outbound and inbound 11–12, 184–7; "many globalizations" 5; media 155–6, 166, 180–1, 250–2; modernity in 157–8; of move from mainstream to alternative music scene 116, 123, 125; "nation-less" products of early Japanese 13–14, 214–15, 221, 222, 223; nation-states and challenge of 184–5; pink 216; of reggae 150–2; regionalism a constituent of 216–17, 222–3; reverse 12, 226; two-tiered system 156; weakness of many theories of 158; "West–rest" model 155, 157, 158
glocalization 79–80, 90, 91, 157; Fung's model of globalization and 180–1, 184
GMM Grammy 149
GQ 94, 99
GQ Taiwan 9, 97–108; association with American brands 101; black and hispanic cover models 99; challenges for parent company 97; changing gender representations 103–4, 103t, 107; cover stories 104–6; distancing from gay readership 104; ethnicities and countries of origin of cover models 98–100, 99t; formation of 96–7; global local nexus 106–8; Hollywood stars as cover models 100–1, 100t; localization 101–2, 103–4, 104–6, 108; masculinities 9, 98, 104, 105–6, 107, 108; methodology 97–8; pressures to use local models 101–2; repositioning 9, 102, 103; target readership 101, 104; use of Chinese models 102
Great Britain 25, 95, 175; governing of Hong Kong 46; indie music scene 121–2, 125, 130, 135; relinquishing sovereignty over Hong Kong 254, 258
Grossberg, L. 199
The Guitar Magazine 139

270 Index

Hafez, K. 158
Hai, F. 22, 26, 27
Hall, S. 151, 155
Hannerz, U. 62, 217, 222
Hardt, M. 210
Harry Potter franchise study 6–7, 21–41;
book publication in China 21, 22;
consumption lifestyle 6, 30–4; counter
projection through characters 28–30;
cross-generational differences 24, 32–4;
cultural agency 22, 37; elitism 35, 36, 37;
global interfaces 6–7, 24, 27; intellectual
property rights 26; intercultural
comparisons 29, 30; methodology 22–3,
38–9n; middle-class culture, youths'
partial identification with 23–4, 34–7;
Pottermania 25–7
Harvey, D. 179, 180
Hearst 80–2, 83, 85
Hein, L. 225, 226
Hello Kitty 205, 216
Hesmondhalgh 118, 121, 122
Hines, C. 226
Ho, C. 118, 127, 129, 133
Hollywood: Academy Awards 256; Chan
working in 254; influence on Korean
film industry 178–9, 180, 181, 186;
innovative projects in 256; joint
partnerships with China 253; as a
national and global media power 263;
opening up of Korean market to 172,
178–9, 186; stars on cover of *GQ Taiwan*
100–1, 100t; television and decline of
221
homosexuality, visual codes of 83–4
Hong Kong: aspiring to be Asia's world city
48, 55; as a British colony 46; Chinese
identity 47, 55; creative exports 240;
Factory Girl 46–7; McDonald's in 56;
modernity in 7, 45–7, 54–6; Star Ferry
Riot 46 *see also* Hong Kong Disneyland;
Hong Kong film industry
Hong Kong Disneyland 7, 47–51;
advertisements in China 50; attempts
to impose American behavior in 55;
Chinese mainland visitors consumption
of 45, 49–51, 55; and comparisons with
Tokyo Disneyland 54–6; dress of visitors
51; joint venture with government 47–8;
lack of interest in spending money at
50; languages within 49; localization
efforts 49; low visitor numbers 45,
48; maintaining difference between
mainland and Hong Kong Chinese 47,
55; problem of lack of familiarity with
Disney 49–50

Hong Kong film industry 15–16, 250–67;
alienation of audiences 253, 258; and
analysis of media capitals 259–61; anxiety
over British relinquishing sovereignty 254,
258; in boom times prior to 1997 255–6,
257–8, 263; co-productions in PRC 253,
259; loss of creative talent 255–6, 257,
258; making films for local audiences
255–6; Peter Chan 253–5, 257, 259;
"resinicization" of 16, 257; state control
of 16, 252, 253, 257; transition from
media capital to service center 16, 261
Huang Yi Online 164
Humpback Oak 133
Huntington, S. 5, 158

imperial media 262, 262t
India 128, 159, 175, 240
indie music scene: British 121–2, 125, 130,
135; deterritorialized nature of 114, 123,
131; in Indonesia 123; and world music
129–30
indie music scene in Singapore 9–10,
113–38; aesthetic dissidence 124–7;
airtime 128; authenticity issues 10, 123,
127, 131, 135, 145; against backdrop
of a "cultural orphanage" 114, 116; *Big
O* magazine 125, 131, 132; in context
of mainstream music culture 117–19;
criticized for selling out to market 122;
as a "defined against" genre 118–19;
defining term "indie" 117, 119; English
as language of 114, 115, 119, 120–1,
127, 128, 135; and heavy metal 132;
incomplete localization of 10, 114,
116, 123, 129–30, 131; influence on
independent film making 132, 133;
influence on society 131–4; inspired
by British scene 125; labelling a wide
range of music as indie 129; lack of
acknowledgement by West 116, 130; live
performances by Western acts 129–30;
lyrical content 126–7; marginalization
of 128–9; musical style 115, 127; as
a political symbol 132–3; *Prey* 126;
reverse stereotyping 123–4; social media
and evolution of 134; a subculture
of discontent 120–1; susceptibility to
cultural imperialism 113; *Unity Song*
134–5; *What Do You See?* 115
Indonesia 123, 167
internationalization 226–7
internet: in China 252, 257; and cultural
proximity 158; and development of
Asian game culture 167, 168; and
emergence of an East Asian youth

culture 254; file sharing 134; illegal downloading 220; speeding up cultural flows 152, 167, 223, 251
Italy 175, 221; creative exports 240; Disney comic publishing 60, 65, 66
Iwabuchi, K. 51, 52, 56, 62, 63, 71, 94, 127, 129, 157, 158, 162, 214–15, 219, 221, 222, 254

Jamaica: growth in popularity of reggae 141–2; Rastafarians 141; rock steady genre 141; ska and reggae genres in 140–1
Jamaican diasporas 142
Jameson, F, 204
Japan 13–14, 213–29; advertisements 52; as an alternative to western culture for other Asian countries 215, 216–17, 219; anime *see* anime, Japanese appropriation of western products 52; Asian learning about modernity from 56, 157–8, 222–3; bursting of bubble economy 198; challenge of globalization for 225–6; Chinese film imports 241; consumerism 52, 199, 204; Content Industry Promotion Bill 2004 213, 218; Cool Japan 213, 214, 218, 220; cultural industry building 223–5; cultural products in South Korea 221–2; culturalization of commodities 217–20; cuteness 204–5, 206–8, 216; DoCoMo 205; drama exports 157–8; economy 198, 199; expressive strength of creators 205; fears over 217; food culture 52, 215, 220; in global youth culture market 198, 200, 205, 210; government support for content industry 14, 213–14, 216, 217–20; "gross national cool" (GNC) 200, 213, 236; Hello Kitty 205, 216; Intellectual Property Rights scheme 2002 213; Japan National Railway (JNR) advertising campaign 52; manga 66, 70, 205, 213, 218, 236; men's fashion magazines 94, 97; METI 214, 217, 218, 219, 223, 224; MEXT 218, 223, 224; modernity 7, 51–2, 54–6; moral panics over youth in 199; nation-less popular culture of 13–14, 214–15, 221, 222, 223; national image revamp 214, 218, 220, 223, 224; new strategic industries 218t; political conflict with China 70–1; popular culture a new site of globalization 14, 214, 216–17, 219, 225–7; profits from Content industries 217; sales of video games and anime to US 213, 217, 219, 220; soccer match

incident with South Korea 222, 223; soft power 198, 210, 213, 214, 224, 227; South Korean influences on 224–5; study of American students' views of 225–6; study of South Korean students' attitudes to 224; video games 162, 163, 213, 219, 220, 225 *see also* Pokémon; Western negative images of 225–6; youth in 198–9, 202, 203 *see also* Pokémon; Tokyo Disneyland
Japan International Contents Festival (CoFesta) 220
Jin, J. 86
Jin Yong Online 164
Jung, J.Y. 180

Katzenstein, P. 226
Keane, M. 233, 235, 237, 238, 241, 244, 245
Kellner, D. 215
Kim, B. 182
Korean film industry 11–12, 172–93; American film distribution in 172, 178–9, 186; changes in production from 1990s 173–4; Chungmuro 173, 176, 178, 182, 183; concerns over new system 183–4; content distribution 175; corporate investment in 182–3; cultural hybridization 180; films exhibited at theaters by year 191–2t; globalization of cultural economy imposed on 181–4; government support for 185, 225; Hollywood influence on 178–9, 180, 181, 186; imported films by nationality 190t; market share of exhibited films by country 188–9t; new generation of local filmmakers 12, 176–8; outbound and inbound globalization 11–12, 184–7; overview of current situation 174–7; "packaged cinema" 182; prejudiced division between imported and domestic films 12, 173–4; screen quota system 181, 182, 183, 184; *Shiri* 172, 181; size of market 2002-07 175; state control of 173; theater system 182; theoretical issues 178–81; viewership 12, 175–6 *see also* South Korea
Kuo, P.K. 114

Lash, S. 77
Latin America 44, 61, 159
Lee, K.Y. 113
Lee, M. 45, 46, 48, 49, 50
Li, J. 35
Li, W. 238
Life and Death of the Hollywood Kid 180

272 Index

Lim, C.T. 131
Lineage 160, 161–2, 168
The Lion King 69
localization 4, 5, 62, 72; Disney comics
in China 67–71; of Disneyland 49, 53,
54, 55–6; of *GQ Taiwan* 101–2, 103–4,
104–6, 108; of McDonald's 63; of online
games 165–6, 167–8; of products by
transnational fashion corporations 102,
104, 107; of Trends Group magazines
80–2 *see also* Thailand, localized
production of Jamaican music
Lustiges Taschenbuch 65, 69
Luvaas, B. 123
luxury goods market 32, 36, 52, 102

Ma, E. 76, 78, 83, 107
Magazine Business Association of Taipei
(MBAT) 95
magazine covers, study of Chinese 8–9,
76–93; from collaboration to localization
80–2; competition among lifestyle
magazines 82; *Cosmopolitan* 80, 82–3,
85–6; criticisms from overseas head
offices 83, 85, 90; early glocalization
79–80; *Esquire* 80, 84–5; "exploiting the
global" 80, 89–90, 90–2; *FHM* 86–9;
homosexuality, visual codes of 83–4;
international standards of visual styles
81; issues of sexuality 86, 88, 89; *Men's
Health* 83–4; selecting celebrities and
artists for 82–3; shortage of Chinese
celebrities for 82 *see also GQ Taiwan*
male bodies, objectification of 107–8
Mandopop and Cantopop 116, 118, 121,
128, 130
manga 66, 70, 205, 213, 218, 236
Maple Story 163, 168
Marley, B. 142, 145, 146, 147, 151; covers
145, 146, 148
masculinities: "commodity capitalism" and
104; global consumerism and concept
of 94, 95–7; in *GQ Taiwan* 9, 98, 104,
105–6, 107, 108; hegemonic 105, 107;
"situated" 98, 107
Mattelart, A. 62
McDonald's 56, 215, 216; localization of 63
media capitals 253, 259, 259–61
media globalization 155–6, 166, 180–1, 250–2
media typologies 261–3, 262t
mediascapes 180, 223
medieval games 160, 161, 165
Men's Club 94
men's fashion and lifestyle magazines:
emergence in Taiwan 95, 96–7; *Esquire*
80, 84–5, 94, 96; *FHM* 86–9; gay

readership 96, 104; global rise of 94–5,
96; *GQ* 94, 99; in Japan 94, 97; *Men's
Health* 83–4; *Men's Style* 101; *Men's Uno*
95, 101, 102, 104 *see also GQ Taiwan*;
magazine covers, study of Chinese
Men's Health 83–4
Men's Style 101
Men's Uno 95, 101, 102, 104
metrosexuality 96, 104, 106–7, 108
Mickey Mouse 49, 59, 65, 67, 68, 69, 72
Mickey Mouse Magazine 64, 65, 66, 69, 70,
71
Mitchell, T. 77, 124
Mitsuhiro, Y. 52, 53
modernity 43–4; Asian 158, 164, 167,
168; Asians learning from Japanese 56,
157–8, 222–3; Chinese 56, 76, 78;
comparing Hong Kong and Japanese
54–6; Disneyland as part of project 43–4;
factory symbolic of 78; in globalization
157–8; in Hong Kong 7, 45–7, 54–6;
in Japan 7, 51–2, 54–6; late 78; multiple
modernities 76, 158; time and space 43,
46, 167, 226
modernization theory 157
Mondadori 60, 65
Mosco, V. 44
Musical Youth 142, 145–6
Muzer Records 146, 147

nation-states 184–5, 226, 250, 251
National Bureau of Statistics (NBS) 35, 234,
241
national media 262, 262t, 263
Negri, A. 210
neoliberalism 199
new man culture 9, 95, 108
Ngan, I. 46
Nintendo 197, 200, 201, 202, 210, 219
Nite Spot Production 144, 145, 146
Nobunaga's Ambition 168
Nye, J. Jr. 213, 236

The Observatory 130
Oddfellows 125, 134–5
OK Mocca 139
online gaming in Taiwan 10–11, 154–71;
Chinese topic games 166; Chinese
wuxia games 162–3, 166; current state
of market 154–5; cute games 160, 161,
162–3, 165; fantasy games 160–1, 161–2,
165; *Fighters of the Enchanted Sword* 163;
Huang Yi Online 164; *Jin Yong Online*
164; levels of relationships 164–5; *Lineage*
160, 161–2, 168; localization of products
167–8; *Maple Story* 163, 168; market

structures 166, 168, 169; medieval games 160, 161, 165; *Perfect World* 168; periods of gameplay 161; popular games 159–62; *Ragnarok Online* 162–3, 168; *Sango Online* 160; US games in 160–1, 165–6, 167; *World of Warcraft* 160–1, 162, 166, 169

online gaming market (OLG): Chinese 159, 161, 164, 166, 168; Japanese 168; localization 165–6, 167–8; new technologies 164, 167; popularity in Asia 164–5; regionalism in 165, 166, 167, 169; Taiwanese *see* online gaming in Taiwan

Oriental Land Company 53

Otmazgin, N. 222–3

Pai Reggae Festival 149

Paquet, D. 174, 176

Perfect World 168

Phillips, M. 60, 61, 62

Pikachu 205–6, 207, 209

Pokémon 13, 197–212; across a variety of medias 201, 204; cartoons 204, 205–6, 206–8, 208–9; commodity fetishism 204; culture and capitalist ideology 197, 208–9, 210, 216; cuteness 204–5, 206–8; interactivity and communication 202–4; invasion of West 200–2, 204–5, 209–11; METI White Paper examining success of 219; mimicking of contemporary times 200; motivations of designer 201–2; Pikachu 205–6, 207, 209; relation of usefulness and intimacy 206–8; sales of 197, 200; *South Park* parody 226; trading cards 209–10

political economy of communication 44–5

Pop Culture China 127, 129, 159

port cities 251, 261

postcolonialism 119

postmodernism 114, 119, 167, 205, 215

Prey 126

Ragnarok Online 162–3, 168

Rangsipammanakul, P. 143–5, 150

Rastafarians 141, 149–50

reggae: globalization of 150–2; international 145; Jamaican 140–1, 141–2; origins 140–1; rasta 145, 148, 150, 151 *see also* Thailand, localized production of Jamaican music

regionalization: a constituent of globalization 216–17, 222–3; geo-cultural proximity and 158–9; in online gaming market 165, 166, 167, 169

"rising Asia thesis" 5

Robertson, R. 62, 76, 79, 129, 140, 155, 157

rock steady genre 141

Sailor Moon 70

Sandman Animation 246

Sango Online 160

satellite television 158, 182, 242, 243, 251, 254, 256

Saxophone Pub 146, 147

Shiri 172, 181

Singapore: bilingual education policies 113; creative exports 240; films 132, 133; history 114–15; Mandopop and Cantopop 116, 118, 121, 128, 130; mother tongue languages 119–20, 127; People's Action Party (PAP) 119; resistance through popular music 120; state-led modernization 120; use of English in 114, 115, 119–20, 120–1, 127, 128, 135; Western mainstream music culture 117–18 *see also* indie music scene in Singapore

Singapore International Film Festival 132

ska genre 139–41, 147

Ska Variety 139

soft power: of China 236–7, 238, 262, 264; of Japan 198, 210, 213, 214, 224, 227

South Korea: Culture Industry Promotion Law 1999 224–5; cute games 162–3, 165; fantasy games 161–2, 165; games content as compared to US content 165; influence on Japan 224–5; Japanese cultural products 221–2; Japanese television programmes 158; Korean wave 183, 185, 186, 187, 225, 233, 236–7; localization of games for different markets 165–6; soccer match incident with Japan 222, 223; study of students' attitudes to Japan 224; Taiwanese market for online games 154 *see also* Korean film industry

South Park 226

State Administration of Radio, Film and TV (SARFT) 234, 238, 241–2, 245

Straubhaar, J. 156, 159, 216, 222

T-Bone 145–8, 150, 152; international success for 147–8

Taiwan: constructions of masculinity in 107; creative exports 240; emergence of men's fashion magazines 95, 96–7; gay civil rights movement 96; Japanese television drama 158; LBGT groups and pink economy 96; localization of luxury brand advertising 102 *see also GQ Taiwan*; online gaming in Taiwan

Tajiri S 200, 201, 202, 203

Tang, R. 26, 27

Teerapenum, N. 145, 148

274 Index

television: advent in US 220–1; Chinese channels, branding of 243–4; Chinese exports 235, 239, 241; Chinese imports 241–2, 256; Chinese independent production companies 242–6; Chinese suffering of state constraints 256–7; corporate culture of American *vs.* Chinese 236; Disney co-productions 60; independent Chinese companies and relationships with television stations 244; Japanese anime and role in programming 220–2; Japanese exports 157–8, 220; regionalization of market 158, 159

Thailand, localized production of Jamaican music 10, 139–53; GMM Grammy 149; Job Bunjob 148–50, 150–1; Muzer Records 146, 147; Nite Spot Production 144, 145, 146; popular music 140, 144, 145, 147, 148, 149, 150, 151; production of localized reggae in 10, 139, 143–50, 151–2; Rangsipammanakul 143–5, 150; record companies 143, 144, 145, 146, 147, 148, 149, 152; reggae and ska music festivals 139, 149; Reiley Beach 148–9; ska genre in 139–40, 147; T-Bone 145–8, 150, 152; tourism 143, 146, 148

Tham, J. 121

Third World 142, 145

Throsby, D. 223, 224

time and space 43, 46, 167, 226

Tokyo Disneyland: built on an imaginary America 7, 53–4; and comparisons with Hong Kong Disneyland 54–6; high levels of spending at 54, 56; languages within 53; localization efforts 53, 54, 55–6

Tokyo Love Story 157

Topolino 65

transborder visuality 8–9, 76–7, 90–1; flows in China 77, 81, 90–1, 91–2; Trends Group modes of 77, 81, 90–1

transnational corporations 2, 3, 4, 12–13, 15; localization of products 102, 104, 107

trend, meanings of 79

Trends 8–9, 79–80

Trends Gentlemen 80

Trends Group: autonomy 80, 90, 92; from collaboration to localization 80–2; creating new urban identities 78; criticisms from overseas head offices 83, 85, 90; ethos of a trendy lifestyle 79; formation of 79; state restrictions on 80, 90; transborder visual exchanges 77, 81, 90–1; Trends Tower 77–8, 91 *see also* magazine covers, study of Chinese

Turner, M. 46

UB40 142

Ultimate Fans of Mickey Mouse 61, 63, 64–5, 66, 68, 69, 70, 71

UNCTAD *Creative Economy Report 2008* 234, 239–40

United International Pictures (UIP) 172, 178, 186

United States of America: advent of television 220–1; Americanization 61, 72, 155–6, 215; bias against Japan 226; Chinese film imports 241; content distribution 175; corporate culture in television compared to that of China 235–6; online games 160–1, 165–6, 167; Pokémon in 197, 201, 204, 209–10; reasons for success of cultural products in global markets 156; sales of Japanese video games and anime 213, 217, 219, 220; study of students' views of Japan 225–6; universalism 156

Unity Song 134–5

Urry, J. 77

video games, Japanese 162, 163, 213, 219, 220, 225 *see also* Pokémon

Vietnam 167

visual culture 89, 90

Wang, F. 83, 84–5

Wang, J. 21, 30, 31, 37

Wang, Y. 70, 71

Wasko, J. 44, 61, 62

Watson, J.L. 54, 56, 63

Wee, W.L. 120

Wei, M. 25

What Do You See? 115

W.i.t.c.h. 64, 66, 70–1, 72

women's magazines 94–5, 108

Wong, E. 116, 131

Wong, M. 128, 130

world music 10, 130, 142, 152

World of Warcraft 160–1, 162, 166, 169

World Trade Organization (WTO) 21, 179, 181

Yano, C. 216

Yoshimi, S. 53, 54, 56

youth culture: categorization of 211n; Disney 8, 63, 72; emergence of East Asian 4, 63, 255; Japanese goods in global market of 198, 200, 205, 210

Yudice, G. 218

Zhang, S. 85–6

Zhang, X. 76, 78

Zhang, Yimon 241, 262

Zhang, Yu 239